Ruin & Recovery

D0912247

Ruin & Recovery

Michigan's Rise as a Conservation Leader

Dave Dempsey

Foreword by William G. Milliken

Ann Arbor
THE UNIVERSITY OF MICHIGAN PRESS

Foreword

$\mathcal{M}$ichigan has a long and proud history of conservation. The country's second national park was established in Michigan. We were leaders in banning PCBs and DDT. We took the lead in protecting the future of our tremendous Great Lakes resources.

The people of Michigan adopted bond proposals to increase recreational opportunity and spent their hard-earned dollars to clean up the state's waters and lands in 1968 and 1988. The people of Michigan also amended the state's constitution to protect the heritage of the Natural Resources Trust Fund in 1984 and adopted the "bottle bill" in 1976.

Michigan citizens have always held natural resources and outdoor recreation among their highest priorities. And they are willing to make—and indeed insist on making—sacrifices to improve and protect their environment.

We must be concerned about what our landscape will look like in the future and the opportunities it will provide to future generations of our citizens. That means *all* our citizens—whether they live on farms, in rural areas, or in our cities.

One of my great regrets is that despite extraordinary efforts by organizations like the Michigan United Conservation Clubs and the Farm Bureau, by Attorney General Frank Kelley, and by members of my own administration, we were never able to achieve legislative adoption of laws to give proper incentives and tools to allow local units of government to properly manage growth.

While there have been exemplary initiatives at the local level—like the remarkable achievement on Old Mission Peninsula in Grand Traverse County to preserve the character of that area—state government simply has not done enough.

Recently, I have been reading a good deal on the subject of land use and more specifically about the trends here in Michigan. I ran across one absolutely stunning statistic. A report by the Michigan Society of Planning Officials predicts that if things do not change here in Michigan, in less than 25 years we will increase our state's population by a little over one million people. But the land area that will be converted for residential and commercial use to serve those one million new citizens will be equal to the amount of land that *nine* million people lived on when I was governor in 1978.

Persons who gave generously of their time to meet or speak at length with me and ransacked their files, attics, and minds for helpful memories include Jack Bails, the former deputy director of the Department of Natural Resources; Merrill "Pete" Petoskey, the former DNR wildlife chief; Verna Courtemanche, who battled the Berlin and Farro waste site across the street from her home; Don Wilson, who championed the protection of the Bridgman sand dunes; William G. Milliken, the former governor of Michigan and the only acclaimed environmental leader to hold that job; and Andrew Hogarth, the assistant division chief of the Department of Environmental Quality's Environmental Response Division, who took special pains to assure the accuracy of the text on chemical contamination. I also want to thank Patrick Diehl, my colleague at the Michigan Environmental Council, for his patient proofreading of early drafts of the manuscript; no one cares more about getting it right than Pat.

Thanks also to the friends who have supported, tolerated, and encouraged me in my environmental work and in life: Derwin Rushing, Tom Vance, Joe VanderMeulen, Kathleen Aterno, Libby Harris, Carol Misseldine, Leslie Brogan, and Margaret Schulte. My mother Barbara and my brothers, Thomas and Jack, have also loyally supported me in the face of logic to the contrary. My apologies to the many unnamed others who contributed to this book in large and small ways. I will thank you personally all the rest of my life.

Of course, I cannot overlook the important role in my personal and writing life of two dear people—Pam Omer and her son, Taylor. They have personally endured my own ruin—and what I hope is a recovery; they accepted and supported me when they had little reason to do so. I owe them an immeasurably great debt. I respect and cherish these two, who have the fierce hearts of wolves, the discerning intelligence of owls, and the playful humor of river otters. Their love of the natural world and its animal inhabitants has deepened mine.

Contents

Prologue   1

1   A Delightful Prospect   11

2   Exploiting Inexhaustible Resources   19

3   The Dawn of Michigan Conservation:
    Sportsmen Lead the Way   37

4   Renewing the Forests   49

5   The Public Health Roots of
    Environmental Protection   65

6   The Crusade to Free Conservation
    from Politics   74

7   The Lady of the Parks   91

8   The Builders   108

9   Forced to Be First: Banning the
    "Hard Pesticides"   124

10   Reclaiming the Tainted Wonderland   139

11   The Age of Action   162

12   Saving Places   194

13   Chemical Wastelands   220

14   The Heart of an Ecosystem   245

15   The Third Wave   263

Epilogue   283

Notes   305

Index   329

Illustrations following pages 116 and 244

Prologue

To a young man raised among the usually clear-flowing streams of Kansas, the sight of Portage Creek in southwest Michigan during the middle 1960s was startling. It looked like a blueberry milkshake, John Hesse thought as he performed stream work as a research assistant during his master's studies at Michigan State University. "It was that color, but not quite the thickness of a shake," he remembered years later.

For decades the paper industry had used the creek, a major tributary of the Kalamazoo River cutting through the Kalamazoo community, as its sewer. Coupling with the city's poorly treated sewage, untreated wastes from the recycling and de-inking of paper extinguished almost all aquatic life for miles downstream in the River. It was almost impossible to find fish. Sludge worms, considered highly "pollution tolerant," were almost the only aquatic life to survive. Counting the number of sludge worms in a square foot sample of mud along the riverbank was one of Hesse's more unpleasant jobs. About the diameter of a 12-pound-test fishing line, the worms numbered in the thousands, and it was difficult to know where one worm ended and the next began.

But 10 miles north and west of the city, Hesse made a discovery. In a curve of the river where waves splashed against the shore, the water's movement created enough oxygen to enable a minnow-sized forage fish, a nine-spined stickleback, to survive—but only in that small zone. The spot was in Plainwell, just down the bank from Dean's Ice Cream Shop, Hesse remembered. "I'd never thought about a fish being able to adapt like that," he said.

In the same area of the river another tough organism thrived, the rat-tailed maggot. Part of the Diptera family of insects, the maggot was able to draw oxygen from the surface of the river with a long breathing tube. The sludge worms manufactured their own oxygen by waving back and forth in the river current from the banks.

Fish were not the only sufferers. Hesse and the other researchers washed themselves with germicidal soap after any contact with the river to prevent the possibility of infection from the poorly treated human wastes dumped into the water. Hesse broke the rules at least once. On a steamy day, he jumped from a boat and swam across Allegan Lake. He was hospitalized with skin infections. Examining the staggeringly high *E. coli* bacteria counts in the river later, he was astonished.

James Bedford remembered a different color than blueberry when describing the Kalamazoo River in the mid-1960s. Later an organic chemist with the state, Bedford also visited the river as an MSU graduate student. "By the time you got below Kalamazoo, the river was very white with paper waste," he said. "Not much could survive in a river that badly degraded. There might have been a few places where there were carp."

The insult to the river delivered by paper companies on Portage Creek and the river, and by the city of Kalamazoo's wastewater treatment plant on the main stream, was compounded by more paper waste added at Otsego and Plainwell. A half dozen mills contributed their effluent.

Asked to remember his early work in the Water Quality Division of the Department of Natural Resources in 1972, Andrew Hogarth also volunteered the Kalamazoo River as a special case. His job was to assist in a water quality study of the river. Hogarth remembers that by the Bryant Millpond, a site just downstream from Allied Paper Company, the river was grayish white with paper waste: "I thought, what good is it to do fisheries work in this river when the water quality is so bad?"

While to each of these young men the condition of the Kalamazoo and its tributaries was stunning, it was nothing new. The Kalamazoo River had come a long way since the first Europeans encountered the waters known as the Kikalamazoo, translated by some as "the mirage" or "reflecting river." One early local bard wrote the following lines.

Toward Michigan's waters so broad and so blue
Flows the bright bubbling River—the Kalamazoo.

But not in the mid–twentieth century. All up and down the Kalamazoo, cities and industries dumped their wastes with little or no treatment. In 1929, at one of its first meetings, the state Stream Pollution Control Commission issued an order against upstream sources of Kalamazoo River pollution. Citing wastes dumped by the city of Albion, the Kelsey-Hayes Wheel Corporation, and the Union Steel Products Company, the commission said that "such discharge aforesaid so pollutes the water of said Kalamazoo River, being one of the streams of this State, so as to destroy fish life and be injurious to public health."

Cleanup did not follow.

In 1937 the *Kalamazoo Gazette* described the river as "grossly polluted." In September 1947 and again in 1948, companies upriver from Kalamazoo released cyanide to the river, killing 20,000 fish the first time and 200,000 the second.

In an installment of a series entitled "Save Michigan's Streams" that ran in the *Detroit Free Press* during 1947 and 1948, conservation writer Jack Van Coevering said, "The Kalamazoo River used to be one of the outstanding small-mouth bass streams in the United States. Anglers came from everywhere to fish its winding waters. Today, fishermen come no more. The Kalamazoo River ranks among the worst-polluted rivers in Michigan."

Van Coevering said some of the problems noted as early as 1927 at Albion persisted: "The Union Steel Products Company there has an 'on and off' rating for pollution. Company wastes are believed to cause fish killings occasionally."

But the river, he wrote, "gets its worst slug at Kalamazoo." Noting that the city of Kalamazoo had ignored warnings from the state health commissioner to treat its sewage since 1922, he said the city had acquired a site for a sewage plant in 1931 but never built it. The worst pollution of the stream, though, came from eight paper mills.

"After leaving Kalamazoo the river does not recover from the load of wastes which it is forced to carry until well below Allegan," a city 40 miles downstream, Van Coevering added. "Downstream cities, such as Plainwell and Otsego, insist that the river is so polluted when it reaches them that it is useless to clean up their own sewage. Therefore, they dump in more untreated sewage."

Dale Granger, then a young professional with the state Water Resources Commission, the successor to the Stream Control Commission, said that in the late 1940s and early 1950s the Kalamazoo River was "fouled clear from Kalamazoo to the river mouth [at Lake Michigan] with paper wastes." One paper mill at Plainwell, he said, discharged so much fiber to the river that the commission showed the company how it could make money by installing wastewater treatment and recapturing the previously lost material.

For the 1949 summer season, the Michigan Department of Health added large stretches of the Kalamazoo River to its list of condemned waters, along with areas of 36 other rivers and lakes. The department's table of the condemned waters, issued on July 13, 1949, had the following heading: "Pollution control inadequate for recreational swimming and allied purposes. Areas and waters condemned based on past inspections and water tests and subsequent known improvements." The department advised against swimming in the Kalamazoo River from Albion to Ceresco, a reach not far from the river's source; from Comstock to Allegan, including the entire Kalamazoo metropolitan area; and from Saugatuck to Lake Michigan.

Cleanup did not follow.

A quarter century later, the state of Michigan put matters a little more technically. In an evaluation of the Kalamazoo River watershed conducted in the summer of 1971, the department catalogued old and new assaults on the stream. Where the south branch of the river ran past a Marathon Oil Company oil well field in Jackson County, oil slowly seeped into the stream, retarded only by a straw baffle that intercepted the flow from marshes into which pollution had leaked. High densities of coliform bacteria, signaling the presence of sewage, polluted the river below Albion, in the Battle Creek area, and downstream of the Kalamazoo River sewage plant. State inspectors found sludge deposits with a white fungus just below the Battle Creek sewage plant.

men, served up nickel beers and whisky. Food was free if drinks were bought. Fights were common. Later, the pious would suggest that the village's fate was brought down upon it by the sins of some of its inhabitants.

October 15 did not immediately reveal that it would be a landmark day in Michigan history. Periodic fires had smoldered in the countryside, often arising in the slashings of past logging operations. Chips, bark, and brush heaps, all left behind by timber operations or farmers clearing their land, provided the fuel. Still, as resident Theresa Hardies, 7 years old at the time, remembered 70 years later, the day began bright, warm, and sunshiny. She attended school in Metz as usual. But at noon, alarm spread through the village about menacing clouds of smoke rolling up from the southwest. Soon the instructor dismissed school.

At about the same hour the Detroit and Mackinac Railroad station agent contacted the main office in Tawas, asking for help in moving people out of the village to escape the oncoming flames. An engine from Onaway was dispatched. At Metz, the crew of a freight train helped organize an evacuation train consisting of eight wooden cars and a steel gondola, in which many of the approximately 75 passengers later clustered. But it took precious time to round them up. The villagers were reluctant to leave their homes and belongings.

At home, Theresa Hardies found her mother packing. The railroad ran through her parents' farm, and Theresa, her mother, and three sisters climbed aboard. Sparks were cascading all around them, and the riders stamped them out.

The train rolled slowly southeast in an effort to outrun the fire. Dictating the speed was the intense fire, which crackled close to the track. Its heat was so fierce the engineer feared warping rails. In spots where the fire came particularly close to the track, the engineer backed the train and then accelerated quickly to push through the flames.

But two miles southeast of Metz at a place called Nowicki's Siding, logs were stacked on both sides of the tracks. The engineer prepared to back up, but the fire had closed behind the train. Opening the throttle, he tried to break through the roaring fire. But the engine stopped between the burning piles, arrested by twisted rails. The conductor, a man named Kinville, called to the passengers to climb out.

Jerry Annis, a passenger on the train, said, "I got my wife and baby out, but we could not do a thing to help the women and children in the first car. Some of them got out, but all of us were more or less burned. . . . Those who got out dashed into the ditch, and finally groped and crawled to a small open field filled with stumps. We dug away the top dirt and ashes with our hands and held our faces in the earth. The air was fearful; breathing was difficult and a man could not walk far and live."

A traveling cigar salesman who survived the train disaster, Frank Becker, told the *Detroit News*, "As I leaped from the car I could hear the wailing of little babies and the screams of women and children. My God! Those sounds are still ringing in my ears."

The escaping passengers remained in the field until three o'clock in the morning. Accompanied by Kinville, Annis started down the tracks for help in the village of Posen. Foster, the engineer, tried to follow, but because of severe burns was able to reach Posen only by crawling.

Theresa Hardies was one of those who had climbed out of the gondola and lain in the field to save herself. On the morning of October 16, her father, Edward, and her brother found her there. Edward Hardies ran to the side of the train, calling to his wife, "Emma, Emma." There was no answer.

It would later turn out that there were almost no remains of Emma Hardies, three of Theresa's sisters, and others among the 15 people who perished at Nowicki's Siding. Almost all was ashes. The *Saginaw Courier-Herald* reported, "All that remained of William Barrett, the brakeman, was gathered up on two spades."

It was reported that only the skulls and bones remained of those who had died in the steel gondola. Metal objects on their clothing and dental fillings were the only means of identification. A farmer presented Father John Kaplanowski, pastor of St. Dominic parish in Metz, with a cigar box containing the bones of his sister, who had died in the fire. Seeking refuge in the water tank, the train's fireman had been boiled to death.

The fire claimed other lives in the area. On the evening of October 15, as the fire raced east from Metz, increasingly dense smoke alarmed occupants of the Herman Erke Lumber Camp in the Trout Lakes area, a mile from Lake Huron. Three men, John Samp, John Grosinski, and Leo Buskowski, who had been cutting ties and posts, walked up the road about eight o'clock to gauge the seriousness of the approaching fire. Returning hurriedly, they told Mrs. Erke they would all have to dash for Lake Huron. Mrs. Erke's three children were roused from bed and rushed toward the lakeshore.

But the fire outran them. Said Grosinski, "We ran as fast as we could go, but the fire beat us. The smoke choked us. There was an awful puff of fire. I could see the others fall on their faces, but I kept on. I ran into a small clearing and fell down and stayed there until morning."

Treated for serious burns and other injuries after walking to a nearby quarry the next day, Grosinski was the only survivor from the camp. Fallen to the ground, John Samp was discovered holding a lantern in one hand, his other clasping the hand of Matilda Erke. Mrs. Erke was discovered holding her baby, Lorene, the child still grasping a china piggy bank with a few coins inside.

The downstate Michigan press carried the news of the catastrophe in banner headlines. "Rescue Train Trapped between High Walls of Flame," the *Detroit News* reported. "Whole Country Burning, Says Bishop Williams." "Relief Train Leaves Track and Is Burned; Fireman Seeks Safety in Water Tank and Is Boiled to Death; Whole Families Die," screamed the *Saginaw Courier-Herald*. The *Detroit Free Press* cried, "Forest Fires Sweep Northern Michigan; Many Lives Are Lost." A local newspaper was more restrained. "A Frightful Calamity," said the *Presque Isle County Advance*. "The Thriving Village of Metz Wiped from the Map by Fire."

CHAPTER I

A Delightful Prospect

To the traveller, the country presents an appearance eminently picturesque and delightful. In a considerable portion of the surveyed part, the surface of the ground is so even and free from underbrush, as to admit of carriages being driven through the uncultivated woodlands and plains, with the same facility as over the prairie or common road. The towering forest and grove, the luxuriant prairie, the crystal lake and limpid rivulet, are so frequently and happily blended together, especially in the southern section of the peninsula, as to confer additional charms to the high finishing of a landscape, whose beauty is probably unrivalled by any section of country.

—John T. Blois, *Gazetteer of the State of Michigan*, 1838

*T*he conservation impulse did not accompany nineteenth-century European settlers into Michigan. The imperative of the pioneers was to subdue and tame the land, not to protect it. Yet even in the earliest days of Michigan's official life as a territory and state, sometimes prosaic observers turned lyrical upon examining the landscape.

One of the best early-nineteenth-century descriptions of Michigan appears in Henry Rowe Schoolcraft's *Narrative Journal*, recounting an 1820 trip organized by territorial governor Lewis Cass to explore the southern shore of Lake Superior and the headwaters of the Mississippi River.[1] Schoolcraft rode up the St. Clair River by canoe, and he describes the adjacent lands as

rich, and handsomely exposed to the sun. . . . Indeed, the succession of interesting views, has afforded us a continued theme or admiration, and we can fully unite in the remark of Baron LaHontan, who passed this strait in 1688, "that it is difficult to imagine a more delightful prospect, than is presented by this strait, and the little Lake St. Clair."

Mackinac Island prompted Schoolcraft to rhapsodize.

There is no previous elevation of coast to prepare us for encountering the view of an island elevated more than three hundred feet above the water, and towering into broken peaks which would even present attractions to the eye of the solitary traveller, among the romantic and sublime scenes of the wilderness of Arkansaw.[2]

over 40 feet high, the mound contained "an immense number of skeletons," according to Bela Hubbard, who participated in the early government land surveys and later became a noted naturalist and writer.[10] He ascribed the remains to the Hurons and other Algonquin tribes. Like most other such features, it was stripped and looted over the years and even by the 1830s was barely half of its original height. It no longer exists.

One of the most significant yet least noted Native American influences on the natural resources of the state was the use of fire as a management tool. Parklike oak lands covered much of the southern three tiers of Michigan counties. Early settlers found them tempting because unlike thickly wooded lands, which required considerable effort to clear, the oak openings could be quickly put under the plow, yielding good crops almost immediately. In many cases, the settlers may have been enjoying the results of Native American land practices. Indians used fire to maintain trails and forest openings, clear fields for domesticated crops, herd animals toward a harvesting zone, and fertilize cropped land and encourage wild food plants.[11] In addition to creating the oak openings, fire may well have maintained the jack pine plains of central lower Michigan. Native American agricultural practices are also thought to have converted beech-maple forests in the northernmost extremity of the Lower Peninsula to pine oak by the time of European settlement.

First contact between Europeans and Native Americans had also significantly altered the face of Michigan by the early nineteenth century. The fur trade, conducted principally by French and English firms for approximately 200 years in the Great Lakes region, had significantly depleted the beaver population of Michigan. This, in turn, altered the region's hydrology.

According to the naturalist Hubbard, great beaver trapping grounds extended from Lake Erie to Saginaw. The beaver laboriously dammed the streams of the region, creating large impoundments on the generally flat lands, "so that very extensive surfaces became thus covered permanently with the flood." In time these backwaters were colonized by grasses and exotic plants, then filled with muck or peat. Although his estimate is questioned by today's ecologists, Hubbard suggested that 20,000 acres lying within a 12-mile semicircle around Detroit consisted of marshy tracts or wet prairies created by the beaver.

The fur industry set the pattern for resource exploitation that would later consume forests, rivers, the air, and groundwater. Over 50,000 beaver skins were shipped through Michilimackinac in 1767, although not all of these were harvested in Michigan. Other fur trading posts at Niles, Detroit, Grand Rapids, and Sault Ste. Marie handled tens of thousands of additional skins during the peak years. But beaver populations plummeted throughout the 1800s, forcing a closure of all trapping in 1920.

"But for the avarice of the fur traders, the beaver might still supply an article of export and of wealth to extensive tracts of unimproved lands in Michigan," Hubbard wrote. "In this neighborhood the traces of their former being are not only exceedingly numerous, but have an intimate relationship to the topography of the country" (362).

As Michigan became a territory, several other native wildlife species were either long departed or close to it. The giant beaver, American mastodon, Scott's moose, and flat-headed peccary disappeared somewhere between 4,300 and 11,400 years ago. A casualty of early European settlement was the bison. Standing over five feet tall and weighing up to a ton, Michigan's bison roamed prairies and oak openings in what are now the southern two tiers of counties in the Lower Peninsula until about 1800. A few may also have wandered into the western end of the Upper Peninsula.[12]

At the dawn of the nineteenth century, about 4,800 whites resided in all of Michigan Territory, and more than 14,000 Native Americans resided in the Lower Peninsula.[13] More extensive Native American populations may have inhabited the territory as recently as a century earlier, but conflict stimulated by the fur trade apparently disrupted native settlement patterns, and disease epidemics such as smallpox and typhoid imported by Europeans took a significant and tragic toll.

Historians make much of the fact that Michigan's settlement by Europeans proceeded at a much slower pace than that of states to the south. Some of the same surveyors whose notes have enabled the Michigan Natural Features Inventory[14] to construct a valuable picture of the state as it appeared 200 years ago have also been blamed for the reluctance of easterners to settle in Michigan. The alleged culprit is a resource now known as wetlands.

In *Michigan: A History of the Wolverine State,* Willis Dunbar notes that the surveyor general of the United States, Edward Tiffin, sent men into southeastern Michigan in the fall of 1815. They examined land in Jackson County during a wet season, and "Tiffin, in turn, reported to President Madison early in 1816 that Michigan apparently consisted of swamps, lakes and poor, sandy soil not worth the cost of surveying. He declared that in his opinion not more than one acre in a hundred, or perhaps one in a thousand, could be cultivated."[15]

While the surveyor's findings may not have made good copy for travel brochures, Dunbar disputes that they were widely publicized. Instead, Michigan's poor reputation may have resulted from fatal outbreaks of malaria—also associated by Americans of the time with swamps and bogs. "Don't go to Michigan, that land of ills; the word means ague, fever and chills," went a warning rhyme in the East.

But the most likely obstacle to early settlement was geography. Since it was not on the direct western land route of settlement, Michigan could not be populated until water transportation was improved. One historian points out that the "whole Great Lakes region was settled tardily."[16] The great cities of the lakes, including Buffalo, Cleveland, Detroit, and Chicago, all lagged behind cities with convenient access to markets via water, including Cincinnati. Wetlands may also have played a physical part in deterring travel. Reaching Detroit from Ohio by land required a trip through the nearly impenetrable Black Swamp that swung from west of present-day Sandusky almost to Monroe. This natural obstacle deterred migration.

When European settlement began in earnest in the 1830s, the chief route was water navigation from Buffalo to Detroit. Steam navigation had come to the Great Lakes in 1818; in 1825, New York State completed the Erie Canal, throwing open a new water route west. Americans in search of land soon responded. By 1836, the year before official statehood for Michigan, Maryland speculator Gordon reported "a torrent of population . . . which is rapidly covering the whole state." Between 1830 and 1840 Michigan's population grew more than sixfold, jumping from 31,639 to 212,267.[17]

This, then, was when Europeans dramatically altered the face of the state. What did Michigan's native landscape look like on the eve of its great change?

Extensive lake plain prairies covered the southeastern corner of the state, the Saginaw Bay region, and southwestern lower Michigan.[18] The bed of ancient glacial lakes, these plains presented an attractive appearance to the early French settlers. Cadillac, the French commandant of Detroit, wrote in 1701 that the banks of the Detroit River

> *are so many vast meadows where the freshness of these beautiful streams keep the grass always green. These same meadows are fringed with long and broad avenues of fruit trees which have never felt the careful hand of the watchful gardener; and fruit trees, young and old, droop under the weight and multitude of their fruit, and bend their branches towards the fertile soil which has produced them.*[19]

Today Michigan's most endangered landscape, with only tiny, isolated pockets remaining, these generally flat lands extended from the Ohio border at Toledo northeast through the Detroit area and around the tip of the Thumb to the base of Saginaw Bay. Closed-canopy forest characterized the clay lake plain, while oak savannas thrived on upland sand lake plain, and wet prairies or marshes occupied the lowest lands.

These habitats are largely extinct today for several reasons. When ditched and drained, they became highly productive for agriculture. They also lay in the path of early and continuous population growth and expansion, particularly in what is now the Detroit metropolitan area.

Another largely vanished landscape reached roughly from what is now Battle Creek west to Kalamazoo and south to the Indiana border. Savannas marked by only a few trees per acre spread across much of the area. The state's most extensive tallgrass prairies occupied a portion of this region, including one at Schoolcraft that occupied nearly 20 square miles. Almost 50 prairies dotted the district. Attractive to early farmers, most of the former prairies remain under cultivation today.

Human influence may well have played a significant role in maintaining both the savannas and the prairies. Fire, triggered by lightning strikes or set by Native Americans, likely cleared and kept an open understory among oak-dominated forests as well.

The oak openings that spanned much of this southern district pleased Bela Hubbard, who likened them to

a majestic orchard of oaks and hickories, varied by small prairies, grassy lawns, and clear lakes. They resemble those exquisite pictures of park scenery, where the vision roams among groups of lofty oaks and over open glades gemmed with flowers; while the distant woodland bounds the horizon, and the velvet-skirted lake reflects the light from the open prairie, or is faintly visible from the bosom of the glen.[20]

From the prairies, savannas, and oak openings of the southernmost counties, the land changed character as one moved north. South central Michigan was characterized by extensive, poorly drained lands, including a large wetland complex that occupied what is now the Lansing—East Lansing area. After ditching and tiling during the 1870s, the district became highly productive for agriculture, with the richest organic soils in what is now Clinton County supporting specialty crops like mint production today.

But the most dramatic and historically most important transition occurred roughly along a line from today's South Haven to Bay City. South of that line, forests were dominated by hardwoods, but to the north were majestic mixed and softwood forests featuring the future prize of the lumbering industry—the white pine. While the pattern of emigration and soils of the south lent themselves to rapid agriculture development in the 1830s and 1840s, the northern districts would remain largely idle until after the Civil War—and then the forests would be quickly mined, with lasting effects on Michigan's character.

The contrast between the utilitarian and aesthetic perspectives can be illustrated by comparing early views of the Upper Peninsula. After seeing the shoreline that includes the Pictured Rocks, naturalist Hubbard wrote the following description.

The lake coast presents a succession of bold and rocky cliffs, with leaping streams and dunes of sand, which give many strange and wild features to the scenery of that wonderful region; wonderful no less in these, than in its mineral riches. (6)

But after bringing poetry to the tongues of the earliest European visitors, the landscape of the Upper Peninsula chiefly inspired dreams of wealth. The central and western reaches of the peninsula were rich with ore and metals. Ancient peoples had mined copper deposited close to the surface with crude tools thousands of years ago. The Europeans would introduce new technologies to pull more copper, iron, and other precious commodities from the earth. John Harris Forster told the Pioneer Society of Michigan decades later:

The settlement of the Upper Peninsula of the so-called Lake Superior region was accomplished by men very different from [those who settled in the Lower Peninsula]; their motives were different; they had not the spirit of colonists, of founders of states, but were rather adventurers,—DeSotos—going in quest of silver, copper, and iron lands, despising, or viewing with indifference, the invit-

ing woodlands and rich savannahs, so attractive to the eye of the agriculturist. There was "speculation" in their eyes; the hope of making a speedy fortune in the newly discovered mineral region of the north was uppermost in their minds,—the absorbing and impelling interest.[21]

Even in the south, however, the eerie beauty of the land escaped the attention of all but a few visitors. It is a mark of how much Michigan has changed in the short span of generations that the Frenchman Alexis de Tocqueville wrote the following description of a trip on horseback from Detroit to Flint in 1831.

When at midday the sun darts its rays at the forest, one often hears in its depths as it were a long sigh, a plaintive cry prolonged into the distance. It's the last effort of the expiring wind; everything about you then enters into a silence so profound, a stillness so complete, that the soul feels penetrated by a sort of religious terror; the traveler stops, then he gazes about. Pressed against each other, their branches intertwined, the forest trees seem to form a single whole, an immense and indestructible edifice, under whose vaults reigns an eternal darkness.[22]

De Tocqueville's perspective as an outsider enabled him to describe what he called the "cold and passionate" race of pioneers with a single-minded determination to clear the forests and harvest prosperity. The Michiganians of his visit were part of "a people which, like all great peoples, has but one thought, and which is advancing toward the acquisition of riches, sole goal of its efforts, with a perseverance and a scorn for life that one might call heroic, if that name fitted other than virtuous beings."

He did not detect, perhaps he could not detect in such a short visit, the other point of view—a stunned admiration for the beauty of a state with endless coastlines, deep forests, scenic rivers, rippling grasslands, and craggy bluffs. But it was here. And while the consumptive view of nature would dominate the state for decades, it would gradually be overtaken by an alternative set of values. The aesthetic impulse would ripen first into a desire to conserve resources for future use, in later decades into a determination to *preserve* them. These two divergent views—one utilitarian and one that is animated by a belief in guarding nature's integrity—characterize debates in Michigan to the present day.

But as statehood dawned in 1837, there was a fortune to be made from nature's bounty for the lucky few.

CHAPTER 2

Exploiting Inexhaustible Resources

In the times of our fathers these same waters swarmed with the choicest varieties of fin life, contributing a no scanty support to many a pioneer and frontier home. Fish food constituted much of their living, and on that they placed great reliance and felt secure. . . . Now, why are not such or similar catches reported in the "tracts" and papers of to-day? Ignorance, improvidence, living out the proverb, "After us a famine"—fishing in season and out of season, but oftener out of season—not knowing the significance of close times nor caring—a waste by which the very air is become offensive—manuring lands with food fishes—emptying the vile refuse and poisonous filth of mill and manufactory into the once mirror-reflecting waters, alas! These are the answer.

—*Report of the State Commissioners and Superintendent on State Fisheries for 1873–74*

From the first, westward-rolling waves of settlers regarded Michigan's riches literally—not as scenic or ecological wealth but as natural capital to be exploited and cashed in. What often escapes notice is the distinguishing difference between the practices of farmers and those of other early Michigan industries. Making a commitment to the land they claimed as home for their own descendants, farmers understood that their prosperity depended on careful management of this private resource. But other early Michiganians viewed the common resources of fish, wildlife, and forests as a limitless bounty whose swift exploitation was necessary and virtuous.

Although the adjective *rich* ornaments the prose of cultivator and exploiter alike, it is easy to perceive a difference in their attitudes. Writing of the days just before his family embarked from the state of New York to Dearbornville, John Nowlin remembered his father saying of the future Nowlin home:

the soil was as rich as a barnyard, as level as a house floor, and no stones in the way.[1]

By contrast, John Gordon, the Maryland speculator, noted that some lands of southwest Michigan were thinly timbered but added:

There are patches however covered with Burr Oak and very rich. Heavy timber can be had within a few miles on the Pawpaw. We could see from various parts of the road a large portion of this tract distinctly enough to form a good idea of its quality which as before stated we did not think highly of. . . . I am however, partial to heavy timbered Land and have a good deal before me to make selections from.[2]

The difference in the two descriptions underscores that the farmer's land would become a home as well as a source of prosperity. The task of the speculator, by contrast, was to spot land with the greatest commercial potential, snatch it up, and sell for a tidy profit.

Although timber was cleared from the southern Lower Peninsula to make way for agriculture early in Michigan's history as a state, little was known of the abundant resources of the north country. The northern interior was almost unpenetrated by settlement; most development occurred at river mouth harbors along the Lake Michigan and Huron shores. State geologist Douglass Houghton was first to make an official report of this region. Charged in the late 1830s with evaluating the state's natural resources by the earliest legislature, Houghton said of the north, "[T]he forest abounds promiscuously" with dozens of species.

It may be considered, then, as a question fully decided, that more than one-half of the State is heavily timbered, in that part lying above the northern railroad; that the sugar and pine are here the most common, as well as the most valuable timber; that the other kinds are found in situations equivalent to their occurrence further south, upon streams and bottom lands, or upon plains and openings. . . . The pine, if not wasted or wantonly destroyed by fire or otherwise, will furnish an abundant supply for a long time to come.[3]

Other natural sources of wealth caught the eye of investors. Geologist Houghton described a mineral district in the Upper Peninsula 135 miles long containing copper and iron in sufficient quantities to suggest potential for profit, although he added, "I would simply caution those persons who would engage in this business in the hope of accumulating wealth suddenly and without patient industry and capital, to look closely before the step is taken, which will most certainly end in disappointment and ruin." Although major mineral development did not occur until after 1860, the mining industry contributed both to boom and bust in a nineteenth-century state economy heavily dependent on natural resources.

The Bountiful Fishery

Of all the natural resources evident to the eye, Michigan's fisheries were the first to be ruinously exploited. Fish were so plentiful that they seemed limitless. In the 1870s, commercial fisherman George Clark remembered, "In the Detroit River, about a mile below Woodward Avenue, in the month of May 1829, and a number of years after, S. Gilliot caught and packed five hundred

barrels yearly of wall-eyed pickerel, besides what were used and sold fresh."
Clark also remembered that it was common to catch from 1,000 to 5,000
whitefish with a single sweep of a seine off Grosse Ile, in the lower Detroit
River. By the time of his elegy in 1874, Clark said, "And now there are but few
points, compared with former fishing, where White Fish can be caught at any
amount, and it requires the best of seines and fixtures to catch them."[4]

Commercial fishing was in place in Lake Superior by 1833 and began on
Lake Huron in 1835.[5] The tasty Great Lakes whitefish swiftly became the basis
for a profitable industry. Between 1830 and 1840, total commercial fish catch
in Michigan more than tripled to 7 million pounds.[6] On the eve of the Civil
War in 1860 the catch climbed to 17.5 million pounds. The industry employed
620 workers in the Lower Peninsula and accounted for $109,838 in value
added.

But size alone is not a good measure of the fishing industry's impact. The
treatment of a native species, the sturgeon, illustrates the single-mindedness of
the early exploiters.

Descended from an ancient stock thought to reach back 50 million years,
the sturgeon is also long lived as an individual, maturing at 15 to 25 years and
sometimes living well past a half century. But it is not an attractive fish. Its
primitive appearance and bony plates repelled early anglers. Even worse, it
was thought to consume spawn of other species, got in the way of catching
whitefish, and had few known commercial uses.

State fisheries officials a century later argued that "no single animal was
ever subjected to such deliberate wanton destruction as the lake sturgeon. By
the time it finally became recognized as a valuable fish, it had largely been
destroyed as a troublesome nuisance."[7] Sturgeon incidentally caught in nets
were destroyed. Sometimes they were stacked in rows, dried, and burned.
Some were used as fuel for boat boilers.

In the 1870s, the smoking of sturgeon brought the species into commercial
demand. The development of sturgeon caviar, the use of sturgeon hides for
leather, increased use of sturgeon oil, and the production of carriage glass
from a gelatin derived from the swim bladders of sturgeon increased appreciation for the fish. By 1888, a state agency observed, "The once despised sturgeon has become one of the most valuable, commercially, of the many fish
that are caught in the great lakes and deep rivers of this state. . . . Nearly every
part of it is utilized in some way."[8]

But the newly discovered commercial uses of the sturgeon only increased
its slaughter. From an 1880 catch of 4.3 million pounds, sturgeon harvests fell
in the next 20 years to 140,000 pounds. Over a century later, the species has
not recovered. Classified as endangered by the U.S. Department of Interior in
the 1970s and still declared a threatened species by the state in the 1990s, the
sturgeon was handicapped by its slow rate of breeding. It may also have been
a victim of long-lasting toxic chemicals, since its long lifetime permits it to
accumulate the poisons over decades.

Methods of fishing also jeopardized the sturgeon and other species.

Although the first state regulations on commercial fishing were legislated in the late 1850s, the taking of young fish was permitted into the twentieth century. The state Board of Fish Commissioners deplored the practice.

> Of my own personal knowledge, the catch of young sturgeon as small as two pounds in weight, is of frequent occurrence on the fishing grounds of the State. It should not be tolerated. The taking of immature fish of all kinds is the most destructive agency in depleting the commercial fisheries of the state, and should be abandoned by the fishermen, thereby preserving their own means of livelihood, and also for a greater reason than all else, the preservation of our commercial fisheries.[9]

Pollution was contributing to the alarming decline of the commercial fisheries. In his first report to the U.S. commissioner of fish and fisheries in 1874, James W. Milner commented that sawmills were dumping "immense quantities" of sawdust, slabs, and sidings into the Great Lakes. "The sawdust covers the feeding and spawning grounds of the fish, and is so obnoxious to them that in the vicinity of numerous mills, as at Muskegon, Michi., the fisheries become greatly reduced in numbers and success."[10]

Whitefish were suffering a fate similar to that of the sturgeon, although their more robust rates of reproduction made for a slower decline. Whitefish catch in Lakes Superior, Michigan, and Huron plummeted from 8.1 million pounds in 1885 to 5.3 million pounds in 1893, with an even more marked decline from 315 pounds per net to 127 pounds per net in the same period. Fishing effort was increasing at the same time catch was declining. In 1885, 58 steamers and 733 smaller boats trolled for whitefish; in 1891, 70 steamers and 1,423 boats crowded the lakes.[11]

Ignorance was only one factor in the decline of fisheries and other resources. Powerful political lobbies were another. In the late nineteenth century, commercial fishermen exerted considerable muscle in the Michigan legislature, thwarting regulatory efforts. In their first report on December 1, 1874, Michigan's fish commissioners observed that the catch of whitefish

> is very appreciably diminishing, to the evident alarm of the States that border on the lakes, and of the country at large. The causes of this decrease are too transparent for enumeration or designation. The simple mention of the naked fact opens a volume replete with bitter recollections and reproof. Avarice, human greed, regard neither the times nor the modes of capture, and ignorance is their stupid associate and ally. Decay and famine have ever followed, and ever will follow in the footsteps of such a copartnership.

Although the commissioners concentrated most of their early efforts on hatching whitefish to replenish the lakes, before long their reports called for stricter regulation as a method of assuring natural reproduction. But their call for legislation licensing commercial fishermen met fierce resistance. In 1895, the board blamed the commercial industry for killing its legislative proposal after a favorable report by a joint House-Senate committee on the bill.

In the late 1890s the frustration of the agency was evident. Noting that the legislature had found it worthwhile to enact strict laws to protect peach orchards from disease, the commissioners said that in contrast "[T]he great commercial fisheries of the State are constantly subjected to the most destructive methods of fishing, with the certain prospect that in a short time they will become absolutely extinct."

In 1897, newly elected governor Hazen Pingree sided with the fish commissioners early in his first term. He met with Herschel Whitaker, president of the board, and Casper Alpern, president of the Alpena Fish Company. After listening to both, Pingree lectured Alpern.

"Yes, it's all right for such men as you to talk about the passing of laws for the benefit of the fish people, isn't it?" replied the governor.

None of the millionaires that have been made by the lake fisheries contribute any money to replace the fish they have themselves taken from the lake. Now, you can go to work and do everything you want to protect the fish industry of Michigan, and I'll guarantee that no one will molest you. You look like a prosperous man . . . and I am sure I wish you all success and three square meals every day in the future. You deserve them, so does everybody else. But here you fellows have been using nets with meshes smaller than the law allows, and yet you are not punished. With your small meshed nets you go out and catch whitefish before they have a chance to spawn. My friend, the fisheries of Michigan would be worth many millions of dollars a year to the state if you men who are now kicking hadn't killed the goose that laid the golden egg.[12]

Pingree urged the legislature to pass a law requiring larger meshes, penalizing the taking of small fish, and closing fishing entirely during spawning periods. Going along with the governor, the legislature closed fishing from October 30 to December 15 in all Michigan waters except Lake Erie near Monroe. But the measure proved hugely unpopular. The affected fishermen complained they suffered financial hardship. Meanwhile, out-of-state fish firms dumped frozen fish on the Michigan market during the closed season, reaping significant profits.

The 1897 session of the legislature also debated the commissioners' proposals for regulations on the number of commercial fishermen and controls on the amount of gear or catch—and defeated them. Punishing the agency for its advocacy, the legislature also slashed the commission's budget by almost 50 percent. For many years the Board of Fish Commissioners and its successor agencies would stay away from the prickly political issue of Great Lakes fisheries regulation, and often from the lakes themselves, concentrating instead on stocking Michigan's streams with sport fish. Meanwhile, the fisheries of the open lakes would ultimately decline to critically low levels.

Nor were the inland fisheries safe from the scythe of humans. One of the most beautiful and sought-after sport fish, the grayling, began to decline early in the state's history.

A resident of cool water streams of northern lower Michigan and the Upper Peninsula, the grayling was dubbed the "aristocrat" of fish. Lumberman and pioneer conservationist William B. Mershon praised the grayling for its "graceful shape with lines trim and adapted to glide through the water with great ease. . . . My experience has taught me that ounce for ounce in weight, the grayling will try your tackle one-half more than the brook trout or any other Michigan fish, with the possible exception of the black bass. . . . It is delicious in flavor and suits my taste better than any other fish I have ever eaten."[13]

The same desirable qualities contributed to the grayling's doom. In the transactions of an early sportsman's association, L. D. Norris complained that two camps of "non-residents and strangers" killed 5,000 grayling in August 1877 on the Au Sable River. "Many were eaten, more were wasted. For two miles below their camps decaying fish whitened the stream, and the offal and fish entrails left unburied in camp tainted the air, as the dead fish poisoned the water."[14]

Slaughter alone did not menace the grayling. The spring spawning season for the fish coincided with the annual log run on streams in timber country. Sediments unleashed by the log drives probably buried grayling eggs. But an even bigger threat, sportsman George Alexander speculated, was the introduction by the state and sportsmen's groups of rainbow and brook trout to the Au Sable, the Manistee, and other northern rivers: "[I]t seems to be demonstrated that the actual cause of the disappearance of the grayling was due to the trout eating, first, the fry and then the small grayling, and that those persons who believe that the log driving was responsible for the disappearance of the grayling are mistaken."[15]

Whatever the precise cause, by the 1930s the Michigan Department of Conservation acknowledged "that our native grayling has followed the passenger pigeon and the heath hen into Limbo." Wrote Alexander: "[M]y old friend, the Michigan grayling: I shall never again see you or your equal" (173).

Game for the Taking

In 1701, the French commandant of Detroit, Monsieur De La Mothe, wrote the following description of the lands along the Detroit River.

> Under these vast avenues you may see assembling in hundreds the shy stag and the timid hind with the bounding roebuck, to pick up eagerly the apples and plums with which the ground is paved. It is there that the turkey hen calls back her numerous brood, and leads them to gather the grapes; it is there that the big cocks come to fill their broad and gluttonous crops. The golden pheasant, the quail, the partridge, the woodcock, the teeming turtle-dove, swarm in the woods and over the open country intersected and broken by groves of full-grown forest trees which form a charming prospect which of itself might sweeten the melancholy tedium of solitude. There the hand of the pitiless mower has never shorn the juicy grass on which bisons of enormous height and size fatten.[16]

It was a picture of a wildlife paradise whose aesthetic values would elude the nineteenth-century settlers fanning out across southern Michigan. The necessities of everyday survival and prosperity in a farming economy would spell the demise of some species, particularly the detested wolf and coyote. But market hunting was the greater menace. In the 1870s it accounted for the slaughter of tens of thousands of deer for export to eastern markets.

An early conservationist, Henry B. Roney of East Saginaw, took the trouble to estimate the number of deer killed in 1880. Piecing together newspaper accounts, interviews, letters, and railroad shipping receipts, Roney announced that 70,000 deer had been killed. He reported that a Roscommon County man claimed to have killed 81 deer that fall. The *Ogemaw Herald* reported that a party of five had killed 34 deer in a month, and the *East Saginaw Courier* attributed 2,468 deer kills to Chase Benjamin of Alpena in 29 years.[17]

Roney was equally outraged by the legendary slaughter of passenger pigeons at Petoskey in 1878, which he traveled north to witness. In the preceding two years, mammoth roostings of the pigeons had attracted market hunters to the Petoskey area. But in spring 1878, more pigeons appeared than ever before, and a slaughter in Michigan that year would play a decisive role in driving them to sudden extinction.

A bird of the eastern woodlands, the passenger pigeon has been called "probably the most gregarious bird in existence." Huge numbers of the migrating birds, which featured a long wing and narrow tail, filled skies for days. The beating of their wings in such masses was described as louder than thunder. Lighting on trees in massive numbers, the pigeons brought down large limbs. They were a coveted food.

The *Pentwater News* reported one of the cruder methods of taking passenger pigeons in an April 1876 edition. A writer described a trip to the countryside near Shelby to observe a netter in action. "The birds were fluttering in the net and imagine our surprise when we saw him hastily throw himself down on all fours and as fast as one could count dispatch the birds by breaking their necks by biting them in that portion of the body."

The 1878 season, farther north, awakened Roney's ire. The *Emmet County Democrat* observed on March 29, 1878, "Great flocks of pigeons are seen flying in all directions recently, and almost every man and boy is seen with musket marching towards the woods, and by the way, Will Smith, L.C. and O.N. Watkins went out one day last week on a pigeon hunt and succeeded in capturing about 400 of these beauties." Once the word got out about the sheer number of birds, sportsmen and market hunters from around the Great Lakes region hastened to the area to get their share.[18] Roney estimated that of the 5,000 "men who pursue pigeons year after year as a business" in the United States, 400 to 500 had rushed to the Petoskey area.[19] The passenger pigeon was bringing an unimagined economic boom to the area.

Local folk could find gainful employment hauling pigeons from the nesting area in their wagons, wringing the heads off the birds, and packing the pigeons in barrels. Local entrepreneurs had their hands full supplying the eager hunters with the barrels, providing the ice to keep pigeons fresh, and sending the meat to its destination. In early April 1878, an average of 40 barrels of pigeons a day, or about 18,000 birds, shipped out from Petoskey.

The sheer density of the passenger pigeons made their killing efficient. A favorite technique was netting. Netters occupied spaces miles from the nesting grounds, where birds flew to find food away from their young. Covering a bed with corn or wheat and sprinkling it with salt or sulfur, the netters then stretched the net out, attaching the forward side to bent saplings. A man lying in wait would release a trigger arrangement when the birds roosted, covering perhaps hundreds of the birds. Netters farther from the nesting grounds sometimes used stool pigeons to lure the wild birds into landing.

In the spring of 1878, however, there were even easier ways to harvest the passenger pigeon. Hunters and netters flocked to the nesting grounds themselves in search of adults and the squabs, their young.

> *Sportsmen were engaged in the unsportsmanlike activity of firing guns into groups of birds and killing a dozen at one shot. Other men moved long poles in the air, knocking down the birds in their flight. Most, however, were concentrating on the young birds—squabs that had hatched only recently. Those with poles knocked the nests to the ground; others climbed to the trees and pushed the wingless birds to waiting accomplices. Some were slashing down the trees and seizing the birds as they fluttered from their nests. . . . After the birds were in hand, it was but a short time until they were off to market. The heads were wrung from the bodies and the wings torn apart at the first joint. The bodies were then thrown into wagons and hauled to Petoskey.[20]*

In his expose, Roney called the market hunters "a reckless, hard set of men" and warned that the passenger pigeon "is threatened with extinction." Estimates of the number of passenger pigeons killed at Petoskey in 1878 ranged from 1.5 million, by the market hunter E. T. Martin, to a billion by the outraged Roney. Responding to Roney's charges, Martin wrote in the January 25, 1879, edition of *American Field* that the "hunt" was a boon to the local economy and prevented the pigeons from stripping bare the fields of local farmers. He added, "The pigeon never will be exterminated so long as forests large enough for their nestings and mast enough for their food remain. . . . [T]he pigeons are as much an article of commerce as wheat, corn, hogs, beeves or sheep. . . . The pigeon is migratory, it can care for itself."

But in 1879 far fewer pigeons returned to the area. Still, the *Emmet County Democrat* announced in late August, "Next spring we confidently expect to see millions of the birds in the vicinity, as the beech trees are loaded with nuts, their favorite food. Hope springs eternal."

But they were never to return in abundance, and before long sightings of passenger pigeons were so rare they excited considerable talk. Sportsman William B. Mershon collected scattered reports in his 1907 book about the passenger pigeon, including a flock of about 60 in Kent County in 1890, one male and two females in Washtenaw County in 1893, and two near Saginaw Bay in 1905, although these may have been Carolina doves. By 1914, they were extinct everywhere, likely a victim of the destruction of their habitat by lumbering as well as their killing by greedy market hunters.

The Timber Quest

On land, the abundant forests soon became a magnet for economic expansion. Government policies fostered the industry and made many rich. In the 1830s and 1840s, the generosity of Congress reduced the standard government price for land in undeveloped regions to $1.25 an acre. These included enormous grants of "swamp lands." Michigan was one of 15 states that benefited from an 1850 federal act that directed the secretary of the interior to compile lists and plats of swamplands and send them to governors of the participating states. If the majority of a section was swampland, the state received it. But much of the land classified as swampland from imperfect maps turned out to be productive pineland.

Michigan's state government was equally lavish. The state transferred 750,000 acres of land received from the federal government to the Sault Ste. Marie Canal Company in exchange for the construction of locks. Another act gave liberal land grants to railroad companies as an incentive to extend their lines to undeveloped areas.

Although a large area of Michigan contained marketable stands of pine and other species such as oak, maple, beech, cherry, elm, hemlock, cedar, and balsam, the early speculators and lumbermen had eyes chiefly for the so-called cork pine. Often found on ridges and uplands, these choice trees were the kings of the forest, anywhere from 100 to 300 years old and between 120 and 170 feet tall. Trunks were as big as 5 feet in diameter. Lightweight and featuring "creamy-white" wood, these trees were of the greatest commercial value.

Although largely untouched into the 1850s, the north woods became the fodder for amazing industrial growth in the next decade. The number of lumber firms in the Lower Peninsula rose from 926 to 1,641 between 1860 and 1870. Employment in the industry jumped from 6,394 workers to 20,575. And the value added to the economy by lumber rose from $1,820,971 to $11,390,940.

Comparing Michigan to the other leading lumber states of Maine, New York, Pennsylvania, Ohio, and Indiana, Barbara Benson noted that during the 1860s "the growth was the greatest for Michigan, where investment in sawmills more than tripled and output, as measured by value of product, more than quadrupled. Within a brief period, Michigan had become the premier lumber-manufacturing center in the United States, a position it retained until 1900."[21]

By the early 1870s the industry was large enough to support its own journal, the *Michigan Lumberman*. Boasting that Michigan's "annual tribute" of the pine was greater than that of any other lumber producing section in the world, the publication told its readership:

> *You are the sole contributors to the sustenance of over one and a-half millions of human beings, and you will find this point no exaggeration if you trace each million feet of your product to its final resting place. The benevolent spirit engaged thus in supplying the necessities of his fellow men, must feel this phase of the picture the acme of hope to be thus unconsciously raised to a pedestal for future fame to herald as a benefactor of his race.[22]*

Before the industry could achieve such majesty, prime land had to be spotted and secured for its new owners. Forestland was literally first come, first served as the north country opened up. "Land lookers" able to survey and stake claims to the undeveloped land of the north were rewarded—or their employers were—with rights to its development. Ambition and drive were the primary tools for success in this field, as the story of David Ward attests.

Born in New York in 1822, Ward moved to Michigan with his family in 1836. He remembered bitterly the treatment his father received at the hands of an unscrupulous businessman for whose family he surveyed and selected prime Michigan land for purchase; the man cheated Ward's father out of the one-quarter land allotment to which he was entitled, David Ward claimed. Coupled with friction among his own relatives and townspeople in Michigan, this disappointment seared Ward and taught him to enter only into formal, witnessed contracts during his own career as a land looker. In each land looking contract he stipulated that he would receive one-quarter of the lands selected.

After repeated illnesses during his early years teaching in Michigan, Ward enrolled in the University of Michigan Medical School in 1850. His classmate and roommate, Robert C. Kedzie, who played a significant role in Michigan's conservation history, remembered Ward thus: "At that time David Ward was poor and felt keenly the fact that the 'Detroit Wards' looked down upon him for his want of money: 'but I'll show 'em! I'll show 'em. I'll be as rich as any of 'em before I die.' Prophecy literally fulfilled."[23] Kedzie said he was struck by Ward's "grim determination" to succeed both as a student and as a man of business.

After receiving his medical diploma in early 1851, Ward journeyed to the north to resume a land surveying business at which he had dabbled previously. He examined and marked lands in the central Lower Peninsula, in the general region surrounding what is now Mount Pleasant. He also described an unsuccessful trip to the Upper Peninsula and one to the White River watershed in western Lower Michigan. But the most memorable surveying trip was the one he made to an area near the headwaters of the Au Sable and Manistee Rivers in March 1854.

Taking a tip from a friend that there was good cork pine to be found in the area west of Otsego and Bradford Lakes and also southeast of the future site of Frederic, Ward engaged three men to assist him. He learned that the Sault Ste. Marie Canal Company was also aware of the potential for high-grade pine in the region and was sending out its own land lookers in the spring. Swift action was essential.

Ward wrote that

> [t]he man whom I chose to remain and explore the land with me when on the ground, was double-fisted, stout, hardy, willing, determined, and well-drilled by prior expeditions, John Bailey by name. He carried his hundred pound pack with a rifle and ax in his hand from Saginaw to Bradford Lake without lessening the weight of his pack and without a murmur through the whole distance of one hundred and sixty-five miles.[24]

Moving up the ice of the Tittabawassee River, through the forest, and then across the ice of Houghton Lake, Ward and his companion trudged through snow 3 1/2 feet deep and through temperatures he estimated as cold as 30 degrees below zero. Each night the party camped well to the side of the trail, not cutting or breaking anything to avoid raising suspicion from their "Soo" rivals. Ward made haste to select pinelands in the area of Otsego and Bradford Lakes, including "a tract of some nine miles of cork pine along the west side of [Otsego] lake and beyond [that] was the finest and most extended that I ever saw."

For three weeks Ward and Bailey fought the cold and deep snow to select 16,000 acres of the most promising pinelands. Then it was time to head south and make a legal claim to the land. The two men threw away all provisions but those they would need for the return. On the first day out they crossed the tracks of the Soo company's explorers.

This "quickened our steps," Ward wrote. They fast-marched southeast, crossing the pine plains until spotting on the southeast shore of Higgins Lake two men Ward suspected of being provisioners for their rivals. Pretending they were simple travelers heading from Grand Traverse Bay to Saginaw, Ward and Bailey asked for directions. They were not only shown the way to their destination on a pocket map but also told that an overturned canoe with provisions was parked at the mouth of the Tobacco River, where it enters the Tittabawassee. Three days later they found the canoe and helped themselves to it as well as the food it was protecting. "Yes, you would have more than laughed to have heard us scream and yell our Indian war whoops of joy!" Ward said.

The canoe and Bailey's strong arms helped them reach Saginaw that night—a distance of 50 miles in 7 hours. A 33-mile ride in a livery rig that night got them to Flint early the next morning. Ward wired William A. Howard, the investor backing the survey, that he would need a horse and buggy, land warrants, and money ready when he arrived in Detroit. Riding fresh horses to Pontiac, Ward and Bailey spent what must have been a restless night there before jumping aboard a train to Detroit the next day. Ward left Bailey there and met Howard, who gave him the necessary supplies, including lunch. Traveling out from Detroit on a new plank road, Ward's horse kept a "fair trotting gait" for most of the next 18 hours, enabling the land looker to reach Lansing at 6 A.M. He jumped aboard a stage at 8 A.M. and reached Ionia just after 5:30 P.M. on April 27.

"I immediately repaired to the United States Land Office, found the Land Office Receiver, Frederick Hall, at the office, gave him my selected pine land list of descriptions, with land warrants and money to purchase the same, which he locked up in the Land Office safe overnight," Ward said. After a night of deep sleep he worked with Hall all the next day to perfect his certificates of purchase. About 20 minutes after Ward finished, the Soo Canal purchasing agent rode up with a "horse reeking with sweat." Twenty minutes was the margin by which Ward had won rights to 16,000 acres of forestlands, including 4,000 of his own.

At about the time Ward was making his claims to lands in the interior of the northern Lower Peninsula, the Saginaw Valley was becoming the first region of the state to go into lumber production in a big way. Endowed with an estimated 3 million acres of high-quality white pine, the valley was served by a system of rivers that made it easy to float logs to sawmills. Approximately 864 miles of waterways, including the Cass, Chippewa, Tittabawassee, Bad, and Shiawassee Rivers, fed into the Saginaw Valley. In 1854 these streams fueled 39 Saginaw Valley sawmills, with the capacity to turn out 100 million board feet of lumber per year.[25] The mills and the logging operations that supplied them moved up both the east and west coasts of the Lower Peninsula between the 1850s and 1880s. By 1860, sawmills occupied most river mouths along Lake Michigan north of Muskegon.

And so the glory days of Michigan's timber industry, the wave of cutting and milling and shipping and selling that cleared the primeval forest, got under way. The source of considerable folklore, particularly the saga of the lumbermen and their camps, Michigan's nineteenth-century logging industry also tells a dramatic story of resource consumption.

The romance of the camps probably eluded many of those working in them. "A logging camp in the Michigan woods was no place for weaklings or for the ladies," wrote Rolland Maybee in *Michigan History*.[26] "At best it was a temporary camp for the sheltering and feeding of men and teams during the late fall and winter months in almost complete isolation. The men were hired to work from dawn to sundown, six days a week, in almost all kinds of weather and conditions."

C. A. Harper, an intelligent young man who worked in a Clare County camp in 1882, described the life thus.

> On all sides are woods in all the wilderness of nature undisturbed. There is grandeur in this forest where no mark of man is yet found, but the life and the work we lead here is far removed from an ideal existence. I have been here ten days at work helping put up a telephone line, connecting the headquarters with the camps.

The work of getting out logs has not yet commenced, but we are at work making roads and log-ways and putting up buildings for the winter. I get $26 a month and board.

Select society is a little hard to find in the back woods. All association is with men, rough, drinking, swearing fellows who work hard without complaint.

For the most part they are good-hearted fellows, not given in any marked degree to virtue. Whenever possible they will get drunk, but a man is discharged if he brings liquor into camp.[27]

Harper commended the "well cooked" food supplied to meet the hearty appetites of the loggers but complained about the sleeping arrangements. There were no pillows, and "one's bedfellows are not always desirable. One night a fellow bunked with me who had just come in from a big drunk." About 60 men slept in the log building Harper occupied. Lights went out at nine o'clock.

Most camps were small during the early years of the logging era. With business largely restricted to the winter months, when snow cover enabled horse teams to drag the cut to nearby riverbanks, camps cut 1.5 million to 3 million board feet in a season. In the 1870s camps began to grow and were vastly expanded when logging railroads penetrated deep into the interior of the Lower Peninsula late in the decade. Production totals doubled and tripled.

The loggers went to bed early and slept soundly because they arose early and worked hard. A lumberjack's working capacity was about 20 logs a day, and food joined ample sleep as a necessity. Cooks and teamsters arose at three-thirty, the cooks to prepare the five o'clock breakfast. After eating, the crew dispersed to the day of work. Small groups of men called choppers and sawyers specialized in cutting or felling the timber and cutting tree trunks into logs, usually in 16-foot lengths. Using 7-foot saws developed in the 1870s, choppers began to trim and top the fallen tree, while sawyers cut the butt end into logs. Swampers and skidders took charge of the sawed logs, using a horse team and chains to drag them out onto the nearest logging trail. Decking platforms along the trail held cross piles of the logs and were loading places for sleighs that would haul the cut to the banking ground along a river or creek. Scalers assured that a log's board feet were recorded, and stampers oversaw the use of heavy stamping irons to indicate the ownership of each log.

Getting the timber to the water was not the end of the work. When spring thawed thousands of logs out of the mixture of snow and ice that had encased them during the winter, the drives began. The goal was to get the logs to mills.

River driving was demanding, sometimes punishing work. It was critical to get the logs downstream during warm weather, enabling lumber firms and their owners to recoup their investments. Jam crews had the task of breaking logjams, working throughout the daylight, whether the 12 hours of March or the 16 hours of June. Suffering through the cold rain, snow, and wind of northern Michigan springs, the drivers helped hasten millions of logs to the mills. There, sorting and rafting crews divided the logs according to their ownership marks. This could be a complicated task. In 1878, about 1,100 different log marks were noted on the Tittabawassee.

The lumberjack worked in a dangerous occupation. The pressure to get the wood out caused significant injury and loss of life. In the 1884–85 season it is estimated that there were at least 60 fatal accidents in Michigan. A typical issue of the *Northwestern Lumberman* included a section entitled simply "Casualties."[28] An Alpena logger had his leg broken by a falling tree. Adam McLaren, near Lakeview, "had his right arm caught between a tree and a load of logs, by which it was mangled and split open from the wrist to the elbow." A young man named John Larock working in the Saginaw district died from injuries growing out of a cut in the hand sustained while chopping.

With the coming of the logging railroads in the late 1870s the pace of harvest accelerated quickly. A Michigan log jobber named Winfield Scott Gerrish, visiting the Centennial Exhibition at Philadelphia in 1876, saw a small locomotive and was inspired to build a steam railroad to connect holdings in the Lake George area with the Muskegon River, six miles away.[29] In 1877, while others struggled to get logs to rivers in poor sleighing conditions, the new Lake George Railroad was able to get its logs into the Muskegon River. Quick to see the benefits of rail over the vagaries of uncertain snow conditions, logging firms constructed 32 narrow-gauge railroads by 1882 and 89 by 1889.

At the same time, standard railroads also spread across the northern Lower Peninsula and Upper Peninsula. The Pere Marquette reached from Saginaw to Ludington in 1874. The Michigan Central Railroad developed from Detroit to Bay City and along the Lake Huron shore all the way to Mackinaw City. It also ranged from Jackson through Lansing to Saginaw and through West Branch, Grayling, and Gaylord to the Straits of Mackinac in 1882. The Pennsylvania Railroad ran from Grand Rapids through Cadillac to the straits the same year.

The combination of more efficient transportation and cutting methods boosted harvests dramatically, with "firms formerly cutting three to five million feet a season . . . now cutting thirty to fifty million during a full season." Markets were hungry for Michigan pine as well as other lumber. In the 1870s, over 100 mills ran full tilt, around the clock, on the Saginaw River between Saginaw and the river mouth below Bay City.[30] The west shore counties of the Lower Peninsula and Menominee County in the Upper Peninsula sent enormous amounts of wood to Chicago, which in turn passed the lumber on "to inhabitants in a broad fan-shaped swath of land reaching to the Great Plains and beyond."[31] Residents of Nebraska, Kansas, and even Colorado and Wyoming bought wood from the Chicago market to construct houses and other buildings. In 1867, the west shore of Lower Michigan produced for these markets 492 million feet of lumber, 84.4 million laths, and 26.8 million shingles, with a total value of $7.9 million.[32]

Eastern markets also consumed Michigan wood. Eastern Canada, Philadelphia, Baltimore, and Albany all received sizable quantities of the timber. "Probably more than half the houses built in the Northern States in the last year used the growth of Michigan forests in their construction," one periodical estimated.[33] Michigan lumber vessels even headed for foreign ports, including London, Glasgow, Hamburg, and Calais.

The river runs seriously damaged habitat. A hundred years later, in an assessment of the Manistee River, the Fisheries Division of the state Department of Natural Resources observed:

> The major problem in managing the Manistee River system is the presence of a tremendous amount of sediment. . . . The origin of this bedload is perturbations of the uplands surrounding the river during the logging era. The loggers not only removed many log jams and large woody debris from the stream channel, they rolled logs down the banks and drove them to market in the spring. . . . Huge amounts of sediment were transported to the river. . . . The fish within the stream channel lose valuable habitat for feeding, resting, and spawning.

The report indicated that extensive stream bank stabilization work and removal of the sand would be critical to restoring a high-quality fishery in some stretches of the river.[34]

A few voices began to sound an alarm that the massive cut was impossible to sustain. In 1868, the *North American Review* discussed Michigan's future at length.[35] While praising the abundance and quality of Michigan's natural resource base, the magazine dismissed claims that the white pine would last forever.

> It is common to speak of the pine lands of Michigan as "inexhaustible." We hear of the supply that may be expected for "ages to come" from this prolific source. Men think of the lumber forests of the Peninsula as they do of the coalbeds of Pennsylvania and Ohio, and laugh at the predictions of the alarmists. Yet these predictions are not hasty, but are based on exact calculations. . . . The most sanguine calculation cannot carry the lumber business beyond the present century.

The magazine made two other interesting observations. First, it indicated that there was no likelihood that owners of the timberlands would practice conservation, as they "will use their opportunity, and will let the future take care of itself. They would not be American, if they should voluntarily curtail a profitable business, in view of spreading it over a longer period of years."

Second, it forecast a bitter future: "But the lament will come from the next generation: the people of this will only boast the swift change of the wood and the wilderness to fertile field, and exult in the lines of towns and cities which spring up along its watercourses and along its lakes."

The decline in Michigan forest productivity came sooner than most believed possible. In its February 7, 1880, edition, the *Northwestern Lumberman* published an analysis of the "decadence of the quality of the timber supply of Michigan" under the heading "Depleted Forests."[36]

The industry journal pointed out that while absolute numbers of board feet reaped from Michigan forests were still climbing, it took more logs to produce the same amount of timber. Between 1870 and 1879, the average log run down the Tittabawassee River fell from 229 feet to 143 feet. Grand Rapids logs shrank to less than 204 feet. The article noted that in the previous decade, "clean cutting"—the practice of taking only the high-grade timber and leaving other trees standing—had been succeeded by the practice of taking everything off the land that could produce saw logs. The *Lumberman* commented, "It stands the lumbermen in hand at this time to hew to the line, and save all their chips, for the time of their harvest in Michigan is drawing to a close and there will soon be but stumps in the field to show where great bodies of valuable pine have been gathered into the storehouse of a nation's need."

After claiming the best pine, the logging industry briefly found wealth in the state's hardwoods, including birch, beech, maple, cedar, and hemlock. The Upper Peninsula, last to be exploited, saluted the end of the white pine era in 1906 but looked forward to a "very big timber cut" regardless. The *Houghton-Calumet Sunday Mining Gazette* reported in October 1906:

> For a region in which the white pine is no longer king, and which not so many years ago led all districts as a source of lumber supply, the cut of timber in the upper peninsula of Michigan will foot up a very considerable total during the season now opening, but it will be much less than were the supply of labor adequate to meet demands. . . . [A] far greater number of operators are devoting their attention to hemlock, cedar, mining timber, cordwood, and pulpwood.[37]

But the move to hardwoods only postponed the inevitable decline. Before long, absolute timber volume began to fall. In 1870, Michigan ranked first among the states in production of lumber, turning out an amazing 2.25 billion board feet. The state maintained its lead in 1880 and in 1890, hitting a peak of 4.25 billion board feet in the latter year. Then production shrank. In 1899, Michigan fell back to second behind Wisconsin, producing 3.01 billion board feet. In the next five years production shrank to just over 2 billion board feet, putting the state fourth. By 1920 Michigan was sixteenth in timber production among states, turning out just less than 750 million board feet.[38] The lumber barons who had reaped profit from the forest harvest in many cases moved on to new fields of plenty, including the still largely unexploited forests of the Deep South and Pacific Northwest. The lumberjacks either followed them or stayed behind and lamented the loss of the good old days. In April 1927, a Marquette newspaper published a colorful obituary of one of those who stayed behind, the six-foot-tall 66-year-old "Roarin' Jimmie" Gleason.

> Wherever there are men to whom the song of saws, the sound of axes, the cry of "Timber-r-r!" and the scream and crash of falling trees is as remembered music, the story of "Roarin' Jimmie" makes good reading. Gleason belonged to the good old days of the pine, when men were men, whiskey was whiskey and work was work, and all of them as violent as forked lightning. Gleason won his name by the volume to which his voice attained upon the consumption of the fourth drink. . . . Time passed and before his disbelieving eyes the world

changed. The cream of the timber was cut off, the saloons, scenes of his victories, dwindled and passed out of existence. He could still do a day's work, he could still roar, but old age was creeping upon him and he could find no place in the changed world into which he could fit. So last Friday night, in his sleep, he passed on.[39]

The attitude of most lumber barons themselves was as hardhearted at the end of the white pine era as it had been while the profits were there for the taking. Wellington Burt, who began his career as a common Saginaw Valley lumberer in the late 1850s, through a combination of luck and shrewd investments in timber and ore amassed a fortune estimated at $90 million by the time of his death in 1919. In a perhaps apocryphal story, Burt visited one of his lumber camps, run by a man named Bill Callam. When Burt saw horses used to haul sleigh loads of logs down to a river, he is said to have snorted, "Mr. Callam, the horses are too fat. Trim them down, sir, and when the logs are out, dispose of them." Callam supposedly replied, "Mr. Burt, you can get someone else to run your camp if it's your idea to starve horses to save money."[40]

Although Burt served as mayor of East Saginaw in 1867 and later lavished some of his wealth on civic improvements, he decided in the 1890s that it was time to make his money elsewhere. "Mr. Burt, in the belief that Saginaw was on a downward course and would never recover from the depression following the decline of lumber and salt manufacture, had determined to close out all his business interests here," reported a Saginaw County historian.[41] "[L]ittle may be said of him in a complimentary way concerning his disposition and policy toward industrial or commercial projects." Burt is remembered today chiefly because after a bitter fight with city of Saginaw officials and his own family late in his life, he rewrote his will to eliminate most bequests to the community and to prevent his immediate heirs from receiving his fortune.

The timber industry's collapse punished Michigan all the more because the timber crop on northern Michigan lands was not succeeded by another crop. If any thought had been given to the future of the pinelands, it was based on an assumption that farms would replace the forests, just as they had done in the southern part of the state. But sandy soils spelled failure for many of those trying to reclaim the cutover lands, often described as "pine plains." In 1889, W. J. Beal, the botanist for the Michigan Agricultural College (later Michigan State University) Experiment Station, observed that "if the poor homesteader has to depend for his living from the start on what he can dig out of the soil and has no other business to help him, the plains are no place for him."

As farms failed on the northern lands, families abandoned them, and hundreds of thousands of acres in the north country reverted to state ownership due to nonpayment of taxes. Essentially neglected by the state, which until the early 1900s sought to sell them off to private owners once again, these vast reaches were scourged by forest fires that often burst from the slash of earlier logging operations.

A 1929 U.S. Department of Agriculture bulletin summarized the scale of Michigan's forest devastation. The emphasis in the department's numbers was on staggering waste. In the Au Sable watershed, for example, it estimated that fire consumed 20 billion feet of pine but loggers took just 14 billion feet.

From a statewide base of 380 billion board feet of saw timber, the department estimated, 35 billion feet were cut and burned in clearing land, 73 billion feet were burned and wasted, 204 billion feet were cut for lumber, and 40 billion feet were cut for other products, including railroad ties, shingles, and ship timbers. By 1926, over 92 percent of the original timber stand in the state was gone.[42]

Exploitation of the forests had yielded vast wealth for some. These federal researchers estimated in 1929 that the value of all the sawed lumber reaped from Michigan was $2.5 billion—and $3 billion if other timber products such as logs, poles, posts, and shingles were added. This sum, they said, was twice the value of all the gold produced in California. They observed that "many individuals amassed fortunes; but for everyone who succeeded hundreds made only a bare living or lost what they had."[43]

Almost none of the timberland had been replanted during the boom period. After less than a half century of intense logging, much of northern Michigan was a waste.

> All about stood stumps, big stumps, close together, rotted by time and blackened by fire, ugly and desolate, but marking the places where within the generation mighty pine had reared their ragged plumes in dignified congregation. The same black that was on the stumps was on living trees, too; whole halves had been eaten from the butts of oak by creeping flames; smaller oaks, fire-killed, stood black and dead, while a clump of fresh brush rose from the living roots. . . . In places were lonely Norway pines, watchers over this devastation, and occasionally the blackened corpses of mighty trees still reared themselves high, without limb or branch, straight, slim and tall, like great exclamation points set there to emphasize the ruin that was where a forest had been.[44]

Exhausted, depleted, the remains of Michigan's northern forests were a monument to exploitation. Some wildlife and fish species had become extinct, and others were dramatically reduced in number. What would the new century make of this waste?

CHAPTER 3

The Dawn of Michigan Conservation: Sportsmen Lead the Way

The pine forests no longer stretch from here to the straits of Mackinaw. They are gone. The countless flocks of pigeons that you all remember in the early days, that darkened our skies are no more. Michigan at one time teemed with elk; and yet the memory of the oldest inhabitants can hardly go back to the date when the last one was slaughtered. . . . The Michigan Association, of which I am the President, stands for the betterment of life out doors; for the protection of wild things, the increase in wild life, and the doing of that which will enable everyone to get his full benefit from a life out of doors.

—William B. Mershon, September 1910

*I*n the early decades of the American republic, protection of natural resources was rarely an issue. The go-get-'em impulse to stake out and develop the frontier trumped most other considerations. In a new nation that distrusted government limitations on personal freedom, and that seemed to be endowed with limitless natural wealth, Americans saw little reason to set aside resources either for their own sake or for use by future generations. Yet a few Americans saw disturbing empirical evidence of a threat to the future, and others, including the New England transcendentalists, proposed a new vision of humankind's place in nature as a piece of a greater whole rather than a conqueror.

In 1849 the U.S. commissioner of patents warned of the wanton waste of timber and slaughter of buffalo. In 1851, an iconoclast named Henry David Thoreau told his Concord, Massachusetts, neighbors that "in Wildness is the preservation of the World." In the 1840s and 1850s paintings, drawings, and publicity about the picturesque landscapes of the Hudson River and of the western frontier signaled a new appreciation for the nation's scenic beauty.

But scholars of the U.S. conservation movement generally trace its origins to the 1864 book *Man and Nature* by George P. Marsh, a three-term U.S. congressman from Vermont who also served for more than 20 years as ambassador to Italy. While largely unheralded at the time, the book has since come to be seen, in Lewis Mumford's words, as "the fountainhead of the conservation movement." Marsh argued that humans were altering the land and had an obligation to restore it. The first expression to a general U.S. audience of a new vision of the relationship between humans and the natural world, the book is credited with inspiring the generation of conservationists who would launch the country's first forestry and parks programs.

"Man has too long forgotten that the earth was given to him for usufruct alone, not for consumption, still less for profligate waste," Marsh wrote. He added that man "is to become a co-worker with nature in the reconstruction of the damaged fabric which the negligence or wantonness of former lodgers has rendered untenantable."

Marsh's work actually followed the first official recognition in Michigan that explosive development was consuming unprotected natural resources. Five years before Marsh's monumental book, the Michigan legislature had already enacted the state's first meaningful conservation law. In a petition, "A. Sheeley, John Hull and 31 others" asked Senator Henry Barns to enact a law regulating fisheries in Michigan. Facing concern about already dwindling fish and game resources, lawmakers hurried to catch up with surrounding states and with Canada, who had acted to limit the killing of game and capture of fish. Technically the forerunner of the twentieth century's comprehensive game and fish regulations, these early measures were fostered chiefly by concern about damage to the state's economy. Just a little more than two decades after Michigan's 1837 attainment of statehood, some of its fish and game were already noticeably declining.

The first attempt at fisheries law in 1859 would have prohibited the use of standing nets near the connecting channels of the Great Lakes. In the late 1850s, commercial fishermen had strung gill nets at the mouth of the Detroit River and racked up enormous catches. The state's attorney general had threatened to seek an injunction stopping the practice under common law. Although this provision of the bill was not enacted, it touched off a debate about the proper role of Michigan's commercial fishery that would continue for a century. The legislature did approve, however, a ban on the netting of fish on inland waters in 12 southern Michigan counties.

Noting that nearly all the states along the Atlantic coast and in the Great Lakes region had provided by law for fisheries protection, the Committee on State Affairs reported:

> Modern art and the gradually diminishing supply, and the increasing price of fish, have stimulated the most extraordinary means to take them. Stationary nets of over a mile and a half in length are set across the usual courses of these shoals of fish, and either all are taken or driven back in their course. . . . The penalties in this law are deemed just, but the amount is immaterial so that they are sufficient to effect the object, and thus protect a business scarcely second to any other of natural wealth and of interest to the commerce of the State.[1]

Senator Barns, who had first recommended control of commercial fishing, also sponsored a successful measure in 1859 to set the first closed seasons for deer, turkey, mallard, and otter, among other species. Hunting of deer, for example, was banned from January 1 to August 1. Barns also argued in defense of this bill that it was necessary to keep pace with other states and Canada, since their citizens "have made incursions into our State" and hunted at inappropriate times. The result, he said, was that "several species of birds and animals have become so scarce as to indicate their almost entire annihilation unless some law is interposed to protect them from destruction during incubation and to full growth, and thus protect the interest of the State in a commerce of very considerable importance."[2]

The major limitation of the 1859 game law was that it was difficult to enforce. The $5 fines it authorized for each out-of-season taking of deer or other game were an ample sum at the time, but only county prosecutors could bring actions. In the middle of the nineteenth century and for 100 years afterward, however, prosecutors often turned a blind eye to poachers, responding to community sympathy for peers who were regarded in many cases as simply trying to feed their families.

The next significant step to address depletion of the state's resources was the creation in 1873 of the state Board of Fish Commissioners. The three-member panel was to appoint a superintendent of fisheries, and the mission of the team was to select a location for a state fish hatchery to propagate the commercially valuable whitefish, as well as to supervise fishery management generally and to promote enforcement of fishing laws. While deploring the decline of the fisheries and the greed that contributed to it, the commissioners embarked on their new task with high confidence. Commissioners noted that the domestication of wild rice fed "a tenth part of the world" and predicted a similar bounty from the artificial propagation of whitefish and other species. In the spring of 1873, the commissioners oversaw the planting of 40,000 salmon fry in lakes and rivers from Oakland to Cass County and in the Au Sable River.

Fisheries superintendent George H. Jerome, who took the position in 1874, oversaw the operation of the first state hatchery at Pokagon. During his tenure the state introduced Atlantic and Chinook salmon, without success, as well as shad. A second hatchery at Detroit contributed to increasing stocking of whitefish in Michigan's waters. "He was a pioneer in fish culture," a later report of the fish commissioners noted, "and the new enterprise was full of discouragements and disappointments, but like all pioneers he possessed that sturdy and strong individuality which makes its possessor conspicuous amongst his fellows." Jerome set the tone for a bold, vigorous Michigan fisheries program that would reach its zenith with the successful introduction of salmon to the Great Lakes in the 1960s. But his best efforts could not curb the growing consumption of Michigan's whitefish by commercial netters.

By and large, legislators did not initiate the early laws. Citizens petitioned for them and for new statutes that followed in the 1860s and early 1870s. Nationally, sentiment for conservation was barely awakening; in the 1870s, "scattered clubs of hunters and fishermen began to ponder the depletion of their quarry."[3] Sportsmen in Michigan were doing more. The state's game and fish conservation efforts assumed new momentum and significance when citizens united in 1875. Ten clubs from the southern part of the state, including representatives from Allegan County, Battle Creek, Kent County, and the Lake St. Clair Fishing and Shooting Club, met in Detroit on April 28 to form the Michigan Sportsmen's Association.

The purpose of the new group was expressly political, although not partisan:

securing the enactment of judicious and effective laws for the protection, at proper time, of wild game of fur, fin and feather, whose flesh affords nutritious food, and the pursuit of which furnishes a healthful recreation, and also all birds that assist the agriculturist and horticulturist in the production of their crops, by the destruction of noxious animals and insects, and the enforcement of all laws for such purposes.[4]

The association consisted largely of professional men, including physicians, academics, and successful businessmen with leisure time for outdoor activities, in contrast to sportsmen's organizations of the next century, which would encompass a broadening middle and working class with a desire for hunting and fishing as recreation activities. The association's membership apparently prompted charges that it was elitist. In an address at the fourth annual meeting of the group in 1879, Dr. E. S. Holmes said:

It has been asserted that sportsmen's associations are purely selfish—that the object of game protection is to prevent the general public from enjoyment and the health and recreation of taking, and the nourishment of partaking of wild game. Without pretending that sportsmen are possessed of more disinterested benevolence than the rest of mankind . . . it is an unquestioned fact that the accomplishment of the objectives for which game protection and sportsmen's associations are organized will promote the welfare of all classes of the community.

Holmes added that the philosophy of the association was to treat the state's game "as a wise husbandmen would treat his domestic animals, so as to continue and increase the supply, that as population increases there may be an occasional full meal for all."

The association sought to educate both legislators and the public about the need for conservation measures. Distributing 1,000 copies of its proceedings in 1876 and 2,500 in 1881 to the legislature, other sportsmen's clubs, and the press, the association hoped to soften resistance to restrictions on the taking of game and fish. But there is evidence that the association recognized early that it had an uphill battle to win favorable conservation laws.

An example is the association's 1879 debate over a resolution to ban the use of trap nets or pound nets in fishing. The pound net was notorious at the time for the dramatic leap forward it made in angling efficiency. The pound net consisted of a lead net and a trap, or pot. Fish striking the lead followed it into the pound, which they were unable to escape. The small mesh of the pound net captured fish of all sizes, in contrast to gill nets, which only caught fish of a chosen size.[5] Measures to ban the trap nets were repeatedly introduced and defeated in the legislature.

At the 1879 association meeting, one member recognized political realities. He "explained the magnitude of the fishing interests" in the state and added that if the motion to ban the nets passed "it would bring to bear upon the Association, in opposition to it, an influence that would be strongly felt, not only in this, but in other matters; that the probability of its passage by the Legislature was very small, and he thought it inexpedient to attempt it." Heeding his advice, the association amended the motion before its passage to limit the ban to the Detroit River, Lake St. Clair, and the St. Clair River.

The frustration was only beginning for these concerned sportsmen. An 1880 association resolution called on members to use their influence to secure the election of candidates to public office "who are known to be in favor of the passage and enforcement" of game and fish protection laws. But, responding either to resource-dependent commercial lobbies or their own reluctance to break new legal ground, officeholders often found reasons to delay or deny the association's requests.

Market hunting was an early target of the association. Seeking to stop the massacre of deer and other game for out-of-state commercial markets, the sportsmen drafted a measure in 1877 banning the transport of most Michigan game across state lines. They modeled the proposed law after statutes enacted in several other states, including Illinois. To win its passage, the association retained an attorney, John L. Burleigh—in less genteel terms, a lobbyist. The state Senate deadlocked on the measure, defeating it on a tie vote. In 1879, the bill cleared the legislature but was vetoed by Governor Charles M. Croswell on the grounds that it ran afoul of the interstate commerce clause of the U.S. Constitution.

One argument against the unsuccessful bill was the lack of information about the extent and effect of market hunting. The association had largely relied on anecdotal information and the invective of such members as Secretary H. B. Roney, who scalded not only the market hunters but also others who killed wildlife for pleasure, citing them for "piggishness."

To answer the call for hard proof, Roney conducted surveys of the 1880 kill, emphasizing the toll on deer. Based largely on information supplied by railroads, he estimated that 850,000 pounds of venison had been shipped out of state in 1880. He also charged that many deer were killed simply for their hides, which sold for $1 to $3 apiece. He estimated that market hunters had slaughtered 10,000 deer solely for this purpose. Armed with these numbers, the association renewed its drive to pass a ban on the export of game. Showing the necessary persistence that would characterize conservation lobbies of later generations, the association won passage of the bill on its third try in 1881.[6]

The law prohibited the killing of deer, ruffed grouse, quail, or wild turkey for any reason other than their consumption as food within the state and provided for a $50 fine and 30-day imprisonment for violations. In a national precedent, the law also banned the killing of deer while in the water—considered an unsportsmanlike activity—and outlawed the possession of deer in the red or spotted coat, coveted by the hide traders.

Passing a law was one thing; enforcing it was another. The traditional reluctance of local officials to bring actions against violators of game and fish laws demanded a new response. Illustrating the conventional attitude of citizens toward the game laws is an incident reported by Augustus H. Mershon at the 1881 meeting of the association.

On the morning of June 10, 1881, Mershon observed two men in the town of Harrison with a dead deer as well as a boat, a gun, and a reflecting lantern in their wagon. To Mershon the case was open and shut: the men had killed the deer out of season and done so through "shining," then and now considered an unsportsmanlike practice. Mershon rounded up witnesses, and although the local prosecutor refused to act, Mershon's East Saginaw Protection Club brought a complaint in the district court at Clare. The club quickly established the facts of its case. After a brief deliberation, the jury returned a not guilty verdict. According to Mershon, jury members explained that the deer might have been tame, since no one had proven it was wild.

Mershon was bitter. "I am satisfied that no jury can be impaneled in the ordinary way, by the officers now in charge, that will convict any of the violators of the Game Law, no matter how direct the evidence and positive the testimony." Adding his own judgment to his father's, association secretary William B. Mershon said, "Please remember, gentlemen, these violations are not made by the settler and the homesteader, but by a lawless set of idle, whisky-drinking bums."[7]

The association turned to high-minded but ultimately futile efforts to address the need for enforcement by organizing new game protection clubs and rallying support from farmers and businessmen. In March 1882, the association appointed and paid a "protective agent," Cyrus W. Higby, to travel around the state. Despite organizing 20 new protection clubs, including one in Harrison, Higby concluded that the work could not succeed without the appointment of a responsible state official.

Out of this experience came the association's next major crusade: passage of a law creating a state game and fish warden. Its long struggle and ultimate success set the pattern for legislative conservation battles that would continue for the next 120 years.

The game and fish warden bill did not win immediate approval. After its defeat in 1883, William B. Mershon suggested sarcastically in a letter to the editor of *Forest and Stream* magazine that association members should come to the next meeting in Jackson and "bring along your member of the legislature and let [him] hear what a fine thing [he] . . . did by defeating our 'Game Warden Bill.'"

The association did not quit. Embellishing upon the original proposal, association president E. S. Holmes suggested in 1885 that the warden should be independent of politics. If appointed by the state Board of Fish Commissioners as he proposed, the warden would be immune from pressures from the governor. Nearly 50 years later, the same idea would prevail with legislation removing the appointment of the state Department of Conservation director from the governor's control and vesting it in an independent commission. But the legislature of the 1880s was not ready for such a bold step. In its fourth incarnation, a bill establishing the office of state game warden won legislative approval and took effect March 15, 1887. The governor was given power to appoint the warden for a 4-year term at a salary of $1,200 per year, plus expenses. Although not everything the association had wished, the law still made Michigan the first state in the nation to establish a paid state game warden. By the end of the twentieth century the state would field more than 200 conservation officers, direct descendants of the 1887 game warden, more necessary than ever to fish and wildlife protection. A direct result of citizen organizing, the warden was a national landmark and a monument to the power of persistence.

Michigan sportsmen were soon frustrated by implementation of the new act. Even though the law called for gubernatorial appointment of the warden, they clung to a hope that the office would be divorced from politics. Instead, Governor Cyrus Luce appointed William Alden Smith of Grand Rapids to the job. A lawyer and a member of the state central committee of the Republican Party, Smith had no other obvious credentials for the job. One sportsman said he doubted Smith could tell a "ruffed grouse from a blue jay."

Smith, however, briskly set up shop. In a March 26, 1887, letter to Governor Luce, Smith described the situation:

> I am just beginning to fully realize the importance of my new position. Letters and telegrams come pouring in upon me from every quarter of the state. It seems to me all the parties interested in the matter of state wardens have been waiting to swoop down upon and overwhelm the appointee. Still I am determined to enter upon the discharge of my duties systematically, energetically, and discreetly.[8]

A few weeks later he wrote Luce that he intended to appoint "men who stand high in their communities" to the deputy warden positions created by the new law. This, he said, "will do much towards creating and maintaining a public sentiment in favor of these laws, which I think will be of more efficacy than a system of prosecutions at this time."[9] At the end of two years Smith had appointed 151 deputies covering most of the state.

He did not neglect enforcement either. In his first monthly report, filed at the end of April 1887, Smith reported 35 arrests and said several trials and convictions had occurred before the end of the same month. The state's new emphasis on prosecuting violators created new challenges for the warden, he said:

> [I]t is needless to add that prior to the passage of the game warden act, but little attention was paid to the game and fish laws and they were generally dis-

regarded. The sentiment of people soon changed when it became generally known they were to be enforced, and in the place of open and flagrant violations the department had to deal with offenders who covered their violations as far as possible.

Michigan sportsmen were pleased with the work of the new warden. Reporting on the annual meeting of the Kalamazoo County Fish and Game Protective Association in January 1888, the *Kalamazoo Gazette* noted that the group found "everything indicates a grand improvement in the observance of game and fish laws throughout the state," which was attributed to the warden. "The results are so encouraging that all sportsmen hope each succeeding year will eclipse its predecessor and convince all lovers of legitimate sport that the game of the state, which was rapidly becoming exterminated, will soon replenish itself under the strict enforcement of the laws."[10]

Although thwarted in some counties by the refusal of boards of supervisors to pay his deputy wardens, Warden Smith boasted that in the first 21 months of his office, he and his subordinates had made 482 arrests for violations of fish and game laws and obtained 398 convictions, with total fines and costs collected of $5,632.11.[11] He also reported distributing virtually all 10,000 copies of his compilation of game and fish laws and said that "ignorance of these laws can rarely be claimed in excuse for the violation."

By 1895, Smith's successor, Charles Hampton, reported that "Michigan leads in fish and game protection." He cited 324 convictions and $3,320 in fines in the preceding year and credited in part amendments to the game law enacted in 1893 that expanded the search and seizure powers of the warden and deputies and strengthened regulations regarding possession, use, sale, and transportation of fish and game. He said the Michigan system was more effective in assuring enforcement than that of other states, including those that spent far more on warden salaries.

While Hampton praised the growing public sentiment for enforcement of the game laws, there were pockets of resistance. Sportsman William B. Mershon wrote Governor John Rich in 1894 to point out that many county boards of supervisors still refused to pay the deputy wardens. "In Clare County, they have been killing brook trout with dynamite, not only destroying the larger fish but also the small fry," Mershon said, asking Rich to support higher pay for local wardens. He added, "Hampton is a splendid State Game Warden but can't be everywhere & the local warden can often get evidence that would convict that the State Warden could not get."[12]

Asked in 1893 by Governor Rich to investigate charges against Prosecuting Attorney H. R. Wickham of Harrison—where Augustus Mershon had spotted the deer poachers 12 years before—Hampton reported that "for a number of years in Clare County the fish and game laws have been flagrantly violated and among the violators have been many of the prominent citizens of the county, and often-times the officers themselves." Hampton concluded that Wickham was interfering with the warden's powers in the county by insisting that a local judge issue no more warrants for violators of the game laws without his concurrence.

> In doing so he entirely usurped his authority and interfered with something which the law expressly places in the power of the warden and his deputies. He could not have been ignorant of this fact and I therefore conclude that he took such action for the sole purpose of preventing the punishment of men who have been violating the game and fish laws.[13]

Hampton concluded that "a warning such as you have undoubtedly already conveyed to Mr. Wickham will be sufficient to make him more careful in the future."

The warden also clashed with the governor and staff. Appointed to a four-year term in 1891 by Democrat Edwin Winans, Hampton was serving under the Republican Rich when he wrote in October 1894 to complain about "lying republican newspapers" who claimed Hampton was making Democratic stump speeches. "Please don't let it be known," he wrote Rich's secretary, A. P. Loomis, "that I have done more work for the State this month, have personally made more complaints, seizures and arrests, have conducted more prosecutions and convicted more violators than my republican predecessor did in any three months of his whole four years. I sincerely hope the good work of the republican editors may go on until the republican party will lose so many votes, that you will lose your job and I will hold mine." He signed the note "truthfully yours." Rich won reelection that November, and Hampton was replaced.[14]

Hampton's successor was a man who would later serve as governor himself. Chase S. Osborn, an active sportsman and Sault Ste. Marie newspaper publisher, expressly sought the warden's job as a political plum, once again smudging the line the Michigan Sportsman's Association had hoped to draw. Perry Powers, president of the Michigan Press Association, had asked all Republican journalists in the state to support Osborn's appointment, enclosing a card containing a standard endorsement. Over 60 editors signed a petition supporting Osborn, and U.S. senator John Patten also spoke out for his appointment.[15] The typical argument used for his appointment was that it would be a suitable recognition of the importance of the Republican press. In Osborn's mind, however, the appointment was a stepping-stone in a new political career. It "proved an excellent avenue by which to enter politics," one biographer wrote.[16]

While Hampton contended that he kept politics out of the appointment of deputy wardens, Osborn "could, and in fact did, use [the appointments] to enhance his political standing."[17] He appointed at least two newspapermen as wardens. In addition, he used the office to a greater degree than his predecessors as a platform for publicity. In July 1895, in a story entitled "State Game and Fish Protector Hot after Law Breakers," the Detroit Journal reported that Osborn and deputies had arrested 59 violators and achieved 47 convictions in the previous month, collecting $867.50.

The article also disclosed that Osborn was emphasizing enforcement of laws governing commercial fishing in the Great Lakes and noted approvingly, "These laws have not been enforced in the past, and fishermen had come to regard them as a dead letter. However, they are very much in evidence at present, and it is proposed to keep them in that condition."[18]

Osborn's use of the office for political advancement did no lasting damage. As the legislature continued to enact and refine game and fish laws, the services of the warden became increasingly critical. In 1895, for example, the legislature enacted the first deer hunting license law, limiting the deer taken by any one person in the season to five and charging nonresidents a $25 license fee, residents 50¢. Half the revenues would remain with the county in which the license was issued; half would go to the state. Michigan thus became the first state to require a hunting license for all participants in a sport. Osborn reported that the law "resulted in a great saving to game but will not materially enhance the exchequer, for the reason that very few non-residents participated in the chase this year in Michigan," and because county clerks often kept all the money from the resident licenses. He added, "As a class the non-resident hunters who have previously come to Michigan were not desirable, and the undesirable ones particularly were driven elsewhere."[19]

Although public attitudes had changed considerably since the 1870s, when the Michigan Sportsmen's Association first agitated for conservation laws, wardens continued to run afoul of local sentiment. Warden Charles Pierce complained in 1908 that three men caught dynamiting fish in the north branch of the Au Sable River had received a mere $25 fine, "about the heaviest we can expect up in that country." Sportsmen's clubs continued to press for stricter enforcement of game laws, but the wardens were still seen in many rural quarters as an intrusion on local customs in which game and fish were ready food sources, no matter the season.

The sportsmen themselves were not always in agreement on wise conservation policy. They had waged a battle over the spring shooting of migratory birds, a practice that took a harsh toll on some species. In an 1889 petition to Governor Luce opposing a bill introduced in the state House of Representatives, the Grand Rapids Gun Club argued that "any Spring shooting is detrimental to the interests of true sportsmen because it disturbs the birds about mating time, and it must be borne in mind that the death of each female bird in the Spring, means at least one brood less in the fall."[20] But other sportsmen favored a spring season, arguing among other points that Michigan should not restrict shooting unless other states did so. In 1899, against the advice of Osborn in his final report, the legislature provided a season for waterfowl hunting from September 1 to May 1.

Its most ambitious aims realized with the enactment of the 1887 warden law, the Michigan Sportsmen's Association entered a steep decline and ceased to be an important factor in state legislation. But one of its most active members, William B. Mershon, continued to monitor the condition of fish and game and in the first decade of the 1900s, organized a new lobby, the

Michigan Association for the Protection and Propagation of Fish and Game. Mershon and the group initiated a new sportsman's fight for a conservation system free of partisan politics.

Mershon is little remembered today, except as the namesake of a chapter of the state's Trout Unlimited organization, but his name is sprinkled throughout the official and unofficial records of Michigan's most significant early conservation fights. Born in 1856 and called "the last of the real Saginaw timber titans" upon his death in 1943, Mershon in his 87 years played a number of roles, including service as mayor of Saginaw in 1894–95. He was the grandson of E. J. Mershon, who built the first planing mill in the Saginaw Valley and started the family fortune that would derive from lumbering. Ironically, Mershon later blasted the state's mismanagement of the forests and joined the fight to institute a new forest policy. The author of two books, including one on his years as an ardent hunter and fisherman who ranged the continent for recreation, Mershon remembered fondly his first childhood kill, a wild pigeon taken not far from his Saginaw home with a 16-gauge double barrel gun. The virtual extermination of the passenger pigeon in the Saginaw region by 1880 may have contributed to his conservation conscience.

"Future generations should have hunting and fishing," he wrote in one of his books. "These incentives to the life out of doors should be perpetuated. It is late, very late—but not altogether too late to make the start. . . . The State should own, or purchase now if it does not own, large areas and set them aside forever for the people to enjoy the grand, health-giving, mind-purifying sport with rod and gun."

Mershon used his personal wealth to bankroll many legislative and educational conservation campaigns. His 1910 idea to strengthen conservation took the form of a proposed game and fish commission with power to manage wildlife and fish, going beyond the warden's powers merely to enforce game laws. In 1911, when the association called for the creation of an "honorary," nonpartisan commission of five members appointed by the governor, duties for fish and game management were divided between the 38-year-old Board of Fish Commissioners and the Game Warden Department, housed in the new Public Domain Commission.

In February 1911, state senator L. W. Watkins, chair of the Game and Fish Committee, introduced the commission measure. With support of the Michigan Audubon Society and the Conservation Committee of the State Federation of Women's Clubs as well as Mershon's Association, the bill passed the Senate, but its ultimate fate might have been forecast by Watkins himself, who said at the September 1910 meeting of the Association for the Protection and Propagation of Fish and Game in Owosso:

> But the trouble with legislation for game and fish is this: The men who come to this Association meeting are men who really wish game and fish protected; and they send a little delegation down to Lansing of earnest representatives of this Association. But after this public hearing, the men that come down to Lansing do not see the men that come down there and want this game and fish

protected simply that they can shoot them. It is not the man who wants the game and fish protected ultimately, even though he has to hang up the gun forever, who does the most work down there, but it is the man with selfishness in his soul, who wants to get out a little earlier in the morning in the open season and get the biggest buck or the biggest bag of game and has no thought of conserving the game interests of the state.[21]

Although he worked feverishly for passage of the bill, Mershon was ultimately frustrated. On April 18, the commission bill, already reported to the House floor by the fisheries committee, was referred to the game panel, thus killing it.

Embittered by the defeat, Mershon expressed disgust with the legislature. He had written the following remarks a few years earlier to Forestry Commission chair Charles Garfield.

I hope that the people of Michigan will awake to the necessity of turning the rascals out, and giving our state a fair business administration by honest men without political taint or ambition. If we could have more of these departments managed by commissions that would not look for personal gain any more than our fish commission and our forestry commission, or some of the other commissions we have in the state, we would be better off.

Despite his outrage at political interference with conservation, Mershon remained active in efforts to promote reforms in the capital. Along with other citizen conservation pioneers, he could already take pride in over 35 years of gradual progress in the enactment of laws to conserve fish and wildlife—and more important, an expanding awareness on the part of the public that Michigan's natural resources had been carelessly wasted and deserved protection. This sentiment would ultimately propel Michigan into lasting national leadership.

CHAPTER 4

Renewing the Forests

The interests to be subserved, and the evils to be avoided by our action on this subject, have reference not alone to this year or the next score of years, but generations yet unborn, will bless or curse our memory according as we preserve for them what the munificent past has so richly bestowed upon us, or as we lend our influence to continue and accelerate the wasteful destruction everywhere at work in our beautiful state.

—Report of special House committee on
preservation of forest trees, 1867

*E*ven as loggers exhausted the timber resources of the Northeast and stepped up their harvest of Michigan trees in the 1860s and 1870s, the first calls came for forest preservation both nationally and in the state. Sometimes high-minded and sometimes alarmist, advocates of trees and forests cited "scientific" concerns that have a quaint air today. Others mourned the prospect of coming economic devastation of Michigan's forest regions. Only a few put forest preservation in purely emotional terms. Well into the 1900s, the economic value of logs far outstripped the ecological value of forest habitats, let alone the spiritual value of the north woods. But the fight to reverse the destruction of the native forest was a passionate one nevertheless.

Nationally, the first major statement of concern about the disappearance of the U.S. forests appeared in an 1865 official document of the U.S. Department of Agriculture.[1] Frederick Starr Jr., warned of "an impending national danger," estimating that 100 million acres of forested land would be cleared in the 1860s and each succeeding decade for farming alone. The settlement of the largely treeless Great Plains, he noted, had sharply increased demand for wood products from the lakes states. He warned of a largely economic danger. Starr feared that shrinking supplies of timber would continue to drive up wood prices, threatening economic prosperity and the ability of citizens to own homes.

Officials first expressed significant interest in the fate of Michigan trees in 1867. Acting on a petition from T. T. Lyon and Sanford Howard of the Michigan State Board of Agriculture, the legislature appointed a special committee "relative to the preservation of forest trees."

The petition is an interesting artifact of its time, mingling sentiment with fact and supposed fact. In the same sentence in which they deplored the "most reckless, improvident, and . . . injurious warfare" waged against Michigan forests, the petitioners charged that the disappearance of trees was modifying the state's climate, lowering temperatures and increasing drought. This was a frequent refrain of the earliest forest conservationists, who argued that forests stimulated rainfall and their cutting led to desertification even in temperate regions.

Chaired by Representative Robert C. Kedzie, who had witnessed the celebration of tree-felling on his family's pioneer homestead in Lenawee County 40 years before, the panel conducted what it called a "thoughtful and conscientious investigation" of the matter, analyzing precipitation and temperature records collected at Michigan Agricultural College (now Michigan State University). It noted that "our winters have greatly increased in severity within the last 40 years, and this increased severity seems to move along even-paced with the destruction of our forests." The panel found that "abundant and well distributed rain is associated with large forest growths, and if these forest growths are extensively removed, the rains diminish, or become capricious, droughts and floods alternating, while in regions destitute of all vegetable growth, rain is unknown."[2]

A scholar of wide-ranging interests, Kedzie may have been one of the few Michigan citizens to have read George P. Marsh's seminal 1864 conservation work, *Man and Nature,* for he quotes from it approvingly in the committee report: "I greatly doubt," Marsh had written, "whether any one of the American States, except, perhaps, Oregon, has at this moment more woodland than it ought to preserve, though no doubt a different distribution of the forest in all of them might be highly advantageous."

The legislative report noted that government buildings at Nashville and Chattanooga were built with Saginaw pine and that Chicago's emergence as a wood marketer depended on Michigan forests. It suggested "our people should ponder, and ask themselves whether they are not 'killing the goose that lays the golden egg.'"

Given the committee's scale of concern, its recommendations were relatively modest. It called for legislation permitting the exclusion of cattle and swine from roadways in order to promote the planting of shade trees and for another measure permitting roadside property owners to plant trees in the edge of public highways or to pay a percentage of their highway tax by planting trees. The legislature responded by enacting a law sanctioning shade tree planting along roads and penalizing the removal or destruction of such trees by humans, "horse or other beast."

Kedzie continued to be a missionary for the cause of tree planting. In an address to the Livingston County Agricultural Society in October 1867, he elaborated on his concern. Citing the American conviction "that in the long run everything will come out right, and that no care or forethought is necessary for the future," Kedzie said he was perturbed by the loss of Michigan's forests.

> *The fact that almost the entire surface of our State was originally covered with forests, is worth your thoughtful consideration. . . . The fact that these forests have cost us no labor or care to obtain them, and that we had more than we wanted, so that we regarded them as a troublesome encumbrance, is no reason why there should be no limit to their destruction. . . . What other States and countries can only secure by planting and rearing with patient toil and long waiting, we have found ready to our hand; and all we need to make our State the most beautiful and lovely land the sun shines upon, is to stop our useless and thoughtless destruction of one of the most beautiful of God's gifts to man.*[3]

After this expression of feeling, the professor cited four practical reasons for sparing Michigan forests designed to persuade his audience of farmers. They control extreme fluctuations in rainfall and protect crops like winter wheat from harsh winds, he said. They also protect farms from the sweep of southwest winds from Texas, New Mexico, Utah, and Colorado, he said, implying that without sheltering trees the state's climate would suffer from the dry air of that far-off region. Finally, he said, roadside trees stop sand and snow from blowing over agricultural lands.

Kedzie mixed concern for belts of roadside trees—something that was apparently practical to approach politically—with worry about the loss of whole forests. For the latter he proposed no official remedy, only public soul-searching. Despite Kedzie's concern and the approval by the legislature of his panel's limited recommendations, the destruction of the northern forests continued largely unchecked.

Meanwhile, observers and commentators became increasingly anxious about the nation's timber loss. *Scientific American* editorialized in 1876, under the headline "Timber Waste a National Suicide," that "a period, so near as to be practically tomorrow, is at hand when our existence as a nation will end."[4] Theories abounded that the deserts of the Southwest had once been heavily forested and that the shaving of trees in Italy and Turkey had brought about drought and famine. Such concerns helped prompt the introduction of the first forest preserve bill in the U.S. Congress in 1876 and the appropriation by the Congress the same year of $2,000 for "some man of approved attainments" to report on forestry matters. The funds would seed what ultimately became the U.S. Forest Service.

Five years later, in 1881, a Grand Rapids man who would play a critical role in the slowly emerging Michigan forestry movement took a seat in the state House of Representatives. Charles W. Garfield, born in Wisconsin in 1848, first came to revere trees as a child, the story goes, on the trip that brought his family to reside in Michigan. Encountering a monumental roadside tree near Martin, on the coach road between Kalamazoo and Grand Rapids, the stage stopped, and its occupants gaped. Reputed to be 10 feet in diameter, the champion walnut reportedly prompted Garfield's father to urge, "Take off your hat, Charlie, to that noble tree."[5]

An 1870 graduate of Michigan Agricultural College, Garfield became a nurseryman and horticulturist, then secretary of the state horticultural society in 1876. As a new member of the state House in 1881, Garfield introduced a modest bill reminiscent of Kedzie's work a decade and a half before. It required the planting of shade trees along both sides of public highways 100 feet apart and within 8 feet of the highway edge, protected existing shade trees on roadsides, and credited roadside property owners for a portion of their highway tax if they planted trees. Grander ideas were not likely to succeed at a time when the industry was still cutting away in the north woods and when a large number of legislators had ties to the state's resource industries. In 1871, a majority of senators had ties to the lumber or mining industry or had other business affiliations; even in 1881, 18 of the 132 members in the legislature had past or present ties to the lumber industry.

Although these early measures made little headway in checking forest destruction, they set the stage for later actions. Coming at a time of growing alarm about the future of the state's forest economy, the forest and tree protection proposals marked the first reverse swing of the policy pendulum away from a largely laissez-faire approach to the state's timber. Trees and forests, Garfield and others were saying with increasing force, were not simply private property but a source of public wealth and critical to the public welfare.

Six years after Garfield's single term in the House, the legislature created the Independent Forestry Commission "to institute an inquiry into the extent to which the forests of Michigan are being destroyed by fires, used by wasteful cutting for consumption or for the purpose of clearing lands for tillage or pasturage. . . . Also as to the protection of denuded regions, stump and swamp lands."[6] The wording of the law suggests that advocates of a state forestry policy were in part skillfully capitalizing on public concern about the hugely destructive forest fires of 1871 and 1881. The October 1871 fire, occurring at the same time as the historic Chicago inferno, reached from Manistee and Holland on the western shore of the Lower Peninsula to the Au Sable region and Thumb on the east. It burned an estimated 2 million acres, killed an estimated 200, and rendered 15,000 Michiganians homeless. Driven by fierce winds, the September 1881 fire drove farmers into the Cass River to save themselves, outran fleeing horses and people, and roasted crops not directly consumed by the fire. It raged through the Thumb region, leveling whole villages, killing 282, burning over a million acres, and causing $2.5 million in losses.

Although causes of the fires were never pinpointed, a combination of drought conditions and careless forest practices certainly contributed to the blazes. It was a common practice for lumbering operations to abandon their wood wastes. Several accounts blame these slashings, "and with their heaps of limbs and tree-tops, knots, etc., the result of lumber camps, they were regular tinder boxes ready for the flame."[7]

Despite the catastrophes, there was an almost careless attitude toward forest fire. No state or local official was charged with putting out such fires, and citizens generally disregarded them until they became an actual menace. Like the autumn burning of leaves in a later era, the fires seem to have been tolerated, if not welcomed, as a sign of the season and of progress. Even as late as 1907, University of Michigan professor Leigh Young said, "[W]henever the wind got in the north in the fall the smoke was so thick in Ann Arbor that you could see it blowing by the street lights at night, you could smell it first thing in the morning. You couldn't travel from Ann Arbor to the Straits of Mackinac at any time during the summer without seeing the smoke of several fires along the way."[8]

The 1887 Independent Forestry Commission included Garfield of Grand Rapids among its members and as one of its directors, Dr. W. J. Beal of the Agricultural College serving as the other director. The commission organized a forestry convention at Grand Rapids in January 1888. The agenda of the convention included talks on nut-bearing trees, the amount of remaining valuable timber in the state, the planting of trees in "barren and waste places" on agricultural lands, the need for preventive forest fire legislation, and the relationship between forests and climate, presented by Kedzie.

Of importance was that the convention also discussed a proposal for a state forestry reserve made by the Michigan Sportsmen's Association. The association phrased its request as a "state park [that] would prove a great public benefit in the protection of game, our forests, and the source of our streams." An area close to the headwaters of major northern Michigan rivers was suggested. A spokesperson for the association explained to the convention that such a preserve would serve as protection for "fin, fur, and feather, as a sanitary influence for the whole state, and as a preserver of the Manistee, Muskegon, and Au Sable." Supporters at the convention cited precedents: the creation of Yellowstone National Park in 1872 and the reservation by Wisconsin of 21 townships earlier in the 1880s.

"Since the organization of the commission," Garfield said, "I have felt that if it could crystallize but just one thing, and that, to set aside and preserve from vandalism an area of native forest, it would have justified its existence."[9] He explained that such a preserve would assure "perpetual reservoirs" because trees hold water in place; would provide for the scientific study of native flora and fauna; and would enable the state to experiment with tree culture. Six townships in the area of Houghton and Higgins Lakes, he said, would make an excellent reserve: "There are a few settlers, but they would be glad to leave, if paid a nominal price for their claims." The convention approved the Sportsmen's Association's resolution.

W. J. Beal of the Agricultural College, in a presentation entitled "Cutting and Removing Logs for Lumber," decried the wasteful practices of the industry, saying, "Desolation follows the track of the lumberman. All of the beauty and most of the value is removed from the land where the timber has been removed. Stumps, rubbish, the poor trees, the small young trees are burned or charred and the ground left to grow up to briers, pin-cherries, poplars, birches, willows, scrub oaks and other worthless trees and plants."[10] Speaking on the problem of forest fires, he added, "There is no denying the fact that a new country, where cutting logs, manufacturing lumber and shingles is the leading business, abounds in rough characters who do not hesitate to do most any mean thing when there seems to be any excuse for it."

The reaction of the local press to the convention proceedings was favorable but cautious. The *Grand Rapids Daily Eagle* termed it "a success." The *Daily Democrat* was more restrained. It disputed the idea that river flow was any greater because of the destruction of moisture-absorbing trees and observed that when Michigan was largely covered by forest, diseases such as "fever and ague" were more abundant than they were now with a vastly larger population: "Wherefore we may conclude that a small amount of forest is greatly to be desired, but that large tracts are not blessings without alloy. In Michigan, as in other states, the overabundance has caused wanton destruction. Any effort which will repair the waste should be heartily welcomed."[11]

The more forceful sentiments of the convention—and the call for the forest preserve—apparently reached beyond established public opinion. One delegate complained that the convention had failed to make any worthwhile economic argument for forest conservation, arguing that "money is what we are farming for. There is too much sentiment."

The act establishing the commission required it to survey townships across the state on the extent and nature of forestland within their borders. Although frustrated by the lack of cooperation from many township supervisors, the commission received 722 responses. Few reported useful statistics on forest cover. But an overwhelming majority opposed new forestry legislation. About 488 saw no need for it, while 128 favored it and 105 took no position.

Perhaps for this reason, succeeding legislatures first took away the commission's appropriation, then in 1891 abolished it outright. The frontispiece of the commission's first report, showing a photograph of forest waste with the caption "The Lumberman Has Taken What He Wanted," likely did not endear the agency to the industry. And with timber harvest still near its peak, legislators and opinion leaders were not yet persuaded of future devastation.

The Rise of the Michigan Forestry Movement

The elimination of this first state commission on the forestry question was only a temporary setback. The decline of the state's forest stands was undeniable. At the 1888 Grand Rapids forestry convention, Beal cited a story in a lumber industry journal that argued, "At best the vast [pine] forests of Michigan have melted away until the most optimistic view can but acknowledge that its end is in sight." The coming decade would prove the accuracy of this assessment.

After peaking in the early 1890s, Michigan's timber production soon began its precipitous decline. Public esteem for the lumber industry, the source of state pride for the previous several decades, tumbled in tandem with declining harvest. By the late 1890s, the state's forestry pioneers, including Garfield and Beal, were joined in their laments by Michigan's governor. At an 1897 observance of Arbor Day at the Agricultural College in East Lansing, Governor John T. Rich decried the increase in windstorms and blamed a four-foot fall in Great Lakes water levels on forest clearing. But returning to the themes of Kedzie's committee 30 years before, Rich added that shade trees along highways "add much to the beauty of the country and to the pleasure of riding or bicycling."

Kedzie drew a careful line in his remarks at the same event, probably reflecting popular opinion. Harvesting the pine had done much good, he said, sheltering the wounded in Civil War hospitals on Lookout Mountain and helping meet the needs of states to the west. But the consumption of hardwood after the pine were gone threatened the state's future, Kedzie added: "When a man safely passes some critical point, we say he is 'out of the woods,' but when Michigan is 'out of the woods,' the critical point will only be reached."

A. A. Crozier described the grim scene in Michigan's north. Reporting on the landscapes he encountered while traveling to farmers' institutes in the region the past two winters, he said, "I think some of you will be as surprised as I was when I say that in traveling nearly two thousand miles through some forty counties in the lumber regions of the State, I cannot now recall having seen in any one place as much as a single standing acre of white pine in good condition." Riding from Manistee on the Lake Michigan shore to Saginaw, he added, he had seen an almost continuous succession of "abandoned lumber fields, miles upon miles of stumps as far as the eye can see."[12]

Such scenes, and the swift abandonment of the north by the lumber industry, fostered a new political consensus that the state had been exploited and cheated. The rage deepened as a series of attempts to convert the wastelands to farms failed. Just a decade after wiping out the state's first forestry commission, the legislature created a "permanent" commission in 1899. Charles Garfield was named president of the three-man panel.[13] Although the commission's work, like that of the earlier panel, was limited largely to collecting information and launching public education efforts, the legislature also gave it tentative permission to move ahead with the experiment that Garfield and the Sportsmen's Association had proposed in the 1880s—the first step toward the creation of a state forest preserve. The law authorized the commission to withdraw from sale up to 200,000 acres of state swamplands and tax-reverted lands for this purpose. Working with the state land office, the commission set aside from homestead sales over 100,000 acres in Roscommon and Crawford Counties later that year and early in 1900. In May 1901, at the next session of the legislature, lawmakers approved a reserve of approximately 35,000 acres—the genesis of the modern state forest system.[14]

The establishment of the forest reserves was also an early acknowledgment of the failure of the state's policies toward the sandy lands of the north after the stripping of their trees. In 1869, the legislature had provided for the forfeiture to the state of lands in tax delinquency. By the 1880s, this spurred the sale of lands by owners wishing to reduce their tax liability, often to speculators or dreamers convinced they could convert the cutover north into productive agriculture. Many of the buyers were immigrants or poorer residents of Chicago and other cities, persuaded to take a chance on the self-reliant life of the country. Too often their dreams died in the sands where the pines had once grown or in inferior soils that had supported hardwoods.

Rural communities of the north continued to believe their destiny lay in agriculture. "Booster booklets spewed from printing presses: extensive newspaper advertising campaigns were launched, traveling and permanent exhibits of farm products were maintained: 'A Farmer for Every Forty' was the significant slogan adopted by one group when thousands of forties within its area were not producing even a good stand of bracken."[15] But farm after farm failed; villages dwindled away. Ruins were often the only monument to these failed dreams.

In the depression that swept the nation in 1893, the legislature persisted in the policy of trying to resettle the barren lands with a "tax homestead" act. For only 10¢ an acre and residence on the property for five years, anyone could buy a chunk of tax-reverted land. But by 1896, buyers had acquired only about 40,000 acres this way of the millions available in Michigan. And many of these were scavengers, taking isolated parcels on which marketable timber remained, making a profit, and then forfeiting the land through tax delinquency.

The legislature's 1899 and 1901 acts authorizing the forest reserves, then, were only a grudging admission that the state could lose nothing by trying forestry on the barren lands. The Forestry Commission sought to portray the reserves as good business for the state. Also echoing the rhetoric of the emerging national forestry movement, which touted the economic benefits of sustained yield forest practices, the Michigan commission said in its first report that it had "not approached the question of forestry from its sentimental side, but rather from its business side."[16] Saying that it had no intention of interfering with lumbering then under way, it added, "The new State forestry must begin where the old forestry ends. Methods of reforestation and the scientific study of forestry must be carried on upon lands from which the virgin forest has been removed."

While this statement may have been intended to quell any opposition from the lumber lobby in Lansing, the commission—through its president Garfield—was more outspoken in an educational bulletin entitled *A Little Talk about Michigan Forestry,* of which 5,000 copies were made and distributed around the state in 1900. Garfield attacked the "thoughtlessness in the great waste of our forestry heritage" and challenged the lumber barons to help in the reforestation of "large areas of land that they have rendered barren." Garfield envisioned

great areas of trees all up and down this beautiful state, protecting head waters of our rivers, making use of our unfertile sands, giving variety and beauty to our gentle hills and refreshing the weary, whether human or otherwise, with nature's quiet cathedrals. Some time it may be, our state shall be so ruled by men of vision and men of taste—sometime, it may be fondly hoped, our legislature shall have the leisure from the petty politics and the strident voice of the lobbyist and the crank to turn its attention to the State of Michigan—to renew its waste places with forest life—to make this peninsula, which is bound to shelter 10,000,000 of people, as beautiful as God intended it to be.[17]

Not all of those observing the forest reserves in their backyards were impressed. In a refrain that would echo through the twentieth century, residents of northern Michigan resented policies made by downstate legislators and state officials, arguing that immediate development by private interests was more beneficial than long-range public lands management. In July 1902 the commission and guests traveled to Roscommon to tour the new reserves. "Flags were at half-mast on the flagpoles in the village," reported a local newspaper:

and the reception they received from the people, although civil and without any hostile demonstration, was speakingly that their presence was not wanted. They were told in unmistakable terms that their forestry scheme cannot and will not be tolerated in the county. . . . I shall not dwell upon the absurd claim which the state put forth on these lands; this will be left to the courts to decide. The people of Roscommon are unanimously against forestry being established in the county and will never allow it. The future will decide. Our motto is "Down with forestry."[18]

At about the same time newspapers were talking up the purchase of 65,000 acres in the area by a Chicago investment company, deriding the state for its failure to recolonize the area. The *Detroit Tribune* observed that the land would support a farming population of 3,000 and that "the methods of the corporation should be watched and imitated." The *Roscommon News* urged readers to "go down to Lansing, and tell them of the number of acres under cultivation" and described the forestry proposals as "an evil that menaces us." The newspaper complained that "so far, those interested in the [forestry] scheme, or at least those nonresidents, have had it all their own way. . . . [The governor], like the majority of our southern neighbors, know[s] nothing of the possibilities of these lands, and look[s] upon them in the light presented by those interested in ridding themselves of vast tracts of land which they have stripped of their personal value."[19]

The commission's only significant allusion to the local sentiment was its statement in a report on its activities in 1903 and 1904 that misunderstanding had aroused opposition in the vicinity of the preserves. But it had quelled such concern, the commission reported.

Men who were quite strong in the feeling that we were going to convert large areas of land into a wilderness understand now that a crop of forest products is as important to grow as anything we can develop from the soil in Michigan; that in the interest of the future of our State, and of every part of it, the growing of

timber in order that we may furnish raw material for manufacturers and cor-
porations which utilize timber products, we are carrying on a business that is
coordinate with agriculture, and in truth, a part of it.[20]

Suspicious locals were not the only audience the commission had to woo
to the advantages of a forestry practice that would restrict logging in order to
assure a continuous supply of lumber. The lumbermen were skeptical as well.
In the commission's 1902 report, John Hubbell of Manistee said the opposition was logical, considering that while the lumber business as a whole might
benefit, individuals would suffer, unable to pay off their loans or afford the
greater expense from maintaining logging camps and roads over time and
investing in forest fire prevention. Besides, he said:

The representations made that by this plan the business becomes perpetual, fur-
nishing a supply of timber forever does not appeal to the average lumberman as
very desirable. Lumbering is a hard, rough business. He does not care to be
everlastingly at it, and is very much in doubt whether his children will thank
him for such an inheritance. He prefers to do as large a business as he can, rush
it through while about it, cut clean, finish it up, and quit.[21]

A new, more rational age was coming to the forestlands, at least as the
forestry proponents saw it. Replacing the colorful, impulsive, and rapacious
lumbering industry of the 1800s, modern forestry would provide for scientific
management of public forests over decades. A new voice, belonging to a man
later remembered as one of the 10 most influential people in U.S. forestry,
would sound this refrain in Michigan for a quarter century. The name of this
Michigan forestry champion was Filibert Roth.

The vaguely Teutonic overtones of Roth's philosophy of scientific forest
management were no coincidence. Born in 1858 in a region of Germany where
forestry had been widely practiced, Roth emigrated to the United States in
1870, settling in Wisconsin with his family. At the age of 16 he moved to Fort
Worth, Texas, to join his father, who was murdered when Roth was 18. For
the next seven years he lived in the West, driving cattle, hunting buffalo, and
working on farms and in the woods. "He not only saw but participated in the
exploitation of previously untouched resources in soil, forage, and timber
which was the order of the day."[22]

Migrating eastward, first to Wisconsin again and then to Michigan, Roth
enrolled at the University of Michigan in the fall of 1885 and received his
bachelor of science degree in 1890. Studies in the structure of woods followed,
and in 1893 Roth moved to Washington, DC, to become a special agent and
expert in timber physics with the federal government. There he came under
the influence of one of the great early names in U.S. forestry, Dr. B. E. Fernow,
chief of the Division of Forestry in the U.S. Department of Agriculture. In
1898, Roth followed Fernow to Cornell University's College of Forestry in
New York to become assistant professor of forestry. But in 1900 he returned
to the nation's capital and became chief of the new Forestry Division of the
U.S. Department of Interior's General Land Office in 1901, taking charge of

the nation's fledgling system of forest reserves. His impatience with what he perceived as bureaucracy and incompetence there led him back to the Department of Agriculture and in 1903 to the University of Michigan, which offered him the post of professor of forestry.

The job existed because Charles W. Garfield, the Forestry Commission president, and Professor Volney Spalding of the university's Department of Botany had successfully lobbied the university's board of regents to establish a forestry program in June 1901. Roth became its second faculty member— and soon the state forest warden under Garfield's commission. Garfield and Roth maintained a close friendship throughout the rest of their lives.

Roth sought to impart a sound methodology to the management of the new state forest preserves. He had somber news to report about the quality of the timber on the state lands, whose second growth had been repeatedly burned over.

> [T]he seedlings are all killed and the sprouts killed or injured sufficiently so that in a few years all growth is gone, and nature must begin her work anew. There are hundreds of acres of land in the reserve in this condition, and it is in this manner that the repeated fires have prevented millions of acres from producing any timber or revenue for many years past.[23]

Roth argued the state must protect and care for the lands, reforest and improve them, and survey and classify them. In the spring of 1904, he saw to the planting of 51,000 trees in the Crawford County reserve, including 30,000 white pine. On a four-acre parcel, Roth established seedbeds and a nursery. He organized a survey of 14 sections of the reserves and established head-quarters on lands next to the forest nursery. The year's expenses for the work totaled $4,775.83.

Switching hats to become forestry professor, Roth reminded readers that 25.7 percent of Germany's land area was in forest, half of it tended by state, cities, and villages, demonstrating the possibilities of public forest management. He criticized Michigan's northern land resettlement policies, arguing that "it is not good policy to colonize the poor man on the poor acre. . . . [M]uch colonization tends to pauperism and is a public injury." Noting that 6 million acres of northern lands were now either delinquent for taxes or forfeited to the state for nonpayment, Roth argued for the vast expansion of the reserves.

> But why should the State do these things now? Why not wait and let things develop? . . . According to the best estimates we use each year more than two thousand million feet of lumber and timber in our state. . . . But it takes 150 years to make white pine such as we have used in the past and it takes 50 years to make even fair pole timber fit for ordinary market. It is hardly a matter in which it is wise "to hold on and go slow and see how things turn out." . . . Millions of acres of private lands await the right care which can and will come, but can come only when the State goes ahead and establishes a proper and efficient system of protection and develops a just method of taxation for these

lands. . . . The possibilities are great and it is doubtful if our State will have such an opportunity again.[24]

But it would take more than the good example of the forest reserves to stimulate the legislature to act. Three other developments provided the impulse for a new state policy toward the tax lands, as they were called.

One was the continuing growth of the national conservation movement, of which forestry was a principal strand. Under President Theodore Roosevelt, the nation's system of forest reserves vastly expanded. The prime architect of Roosevelt's conservation and forestry policies, Gifford Pinchot, an acquaintance of Roth, successfully championed the idea of sustained yield forestry. And in the final year of Roosevelt's second term as president, Pinchot organized a historic White House conservation summit featuring 44 of the nation's governors, members of Congress, and members of the U.S. Supreme Court. Roosevelt presided over much of the proceedings. Although largely symbolic, the conference put conservation on the front pages of the nation's newspapers and prompted even politicians not noted for their attention to natural resources to issue statements appealing to growing public sentiment for better management of the nation's legacy.

Michigan's governor, Fred Warner, appended a statement to the conference proceedings noting that the state's citizens

have seen its vast forests practically exhausted, and its mines invaded to an extent that threatens their depletion. . . . Having in mind the lesson thus learned at so great a cost, the people of Michigan welcome any movement which seeks to insure only a wise use of these great gifts of nature and their preservation for the needs of future generations.[25]

The conference recommended a national resource inventory and the creation of a national conservation commission to help undertake it. A second conference in December 1908 recommended that states establish similar commissions—another impetus for pulling together Michigan's scattered land management programs. By the middle of 1909, more than 40 states had created such commissions.[26]

A second impulse behind a new state lands policy in Michigan was the uncovering of apparent graft in the policy of reselling the tax-reverted lands. A "commission of inquiry" appointed by Governor Warner in 1907 and a subsequent legislative study revealed that the state was losing huge amounts of money on the sales. The commission found that specific land sales it investigated had resulted in $31,777 in revenue on land valued at $250,526, a loss of $10.20 per acre. The commission's estimate of the state's losses between 1902 and 1908 was almost $9 million. Speculators in the lands and staff of the state's land office may have collaborated in the cheap sales, the commission reported: "We come to this conclusion because we find that certain dealers have sold State lands from days to months before they had acquired title from the State, and unless they felt sure of their ability to get what they wanted, when they wanted it, it is reasonable to suppose that they would not have made these sales."[27] Lumber and land companies were soaking up valuable parcels of land at bargain prices, cleaning off their resources, and in some cases dumping the lands back on the market or failing to pay taxes.

More sensitive to the legislature was a suggestion that a newspaper owned by a lawmaker was reaping great profits by publishing the state-paid tax land advertisements. Over a 30-year period, the *Gladwin County Record* was paid over $20,000 for the purpose. State senator Eugene Foster was one of two brothers who owned the paper, "and Senator Foster is about the most industrious plugger against any reforms in the present system," the *Detroit News* reported.[28]

While losses to the public treasury captured headlines, the commission of inquiry said the state's policy had resulted in devastating effects on the north country: "It is the general lack of adequate State protection and State care and interest in these north counties and in the State lands generally, that has made the State lands 'commons' in the eyes of the people, to be dealt with as any one desires."[29] The commission urged the state to embark on a program to rehabilitate lands far beyond those that had reverted to it, marking the most ambitious vision yet of the state forests.

The legislative panel appointed to review the commission's report made sweeping recommendations. It urged a moratorium on the sale of state tax lands until they were appraised for timber and other values. It called for the setting aside of all public lands for forestry "as are needed for this purpose" after the appraisal was conducted. It further recommended that "public lands be entirely removed from the influence of politics and placed under the control of a public domain commission." The committee's final recommendation was that "the present Legislature do not adjourn until it has passed all the needed legislation necessary to save forever to the State the remaining 1,000,000 acres of State lands, and put same beyond the reach of speculators who now infest the State Capitol."

A final reason for the legislature's change in policy toward public lands was the steep decline of communities of the north. In the first decade of the twentieth century one-third of townships in northern lower Michigan and one-fifth of those in the Upper Peninsula declined in population, a trend that would worsen in the following decade. "The many small towns that sprang up all over northern lower Michigan thrived as long as the timber in their vicinity lasted, but most of them fell into decadence with the exhaustion of the timber," stated a later federal report.[30] As loggers moved on, those remaining behind sometimes fell into poverty.

The previous fall's ruinous fires also contributed to the picture of a north that was paying the price for misguided policies toward the forests. The same season's blazes that had burned the village of Metz to the ground and killed the fleeing inhabitants on the train scorched over 2 million acres in both the Lower and Upper Peninsulas. Reelected just weeks after the catastrophe, Governor Warner was under pressure to show some change in policy toward the state's forestlands. In his January 1909 State of the State message to the legislature, he directed its attention "to the desirability of taking active measures to lessen the fire waste of general property which is steadily increasing and which, during the past five years in this country, has aggregated a billion and a quarter of dollars." Warner was lobbied for a more expansive statement. After an April 14 meeting with the governor that included other timberland owners, Frederick W. Newton of Saginaw reminded Warner of his visit to the fire-stricken regions the previous fall and of the suffering settlers. "Inaction on the part of this legislature means shutting the door of hope in their faces," Newton wrote, "and they might as well do what some talked of in their desperation last fall—pull out and abandon everything. Adequate fire protection is not demanded by lumbermen alone, but is urgently needed by the poor back-woods farmer."[31]

On April 22, with just weeks remaining in the 1909 session of the legislature, Warner sent a special message to lawmakers. In it he said that the session should not "come to a close without the enactment of some law that shall have for its object a plan by which those who come after us may have a share of Michigan's great timber endowment . . . some measure which will place our state in line with the progressive policy regarding forestry that prevails throughout the United States."[32] Schmidt of Saginaw wrote the following approving response: "I think your action will make the Republican Party well nigh impregnable at the next election. A tremendous feeling was being developed in the state and the previous democratic candidate was making a strong play by coming out definitely in favor of forestry legislation."[33]

But resistance in the legislature was not easily overcome. Immediately after the Metz fire, Charles Garfield, the president of the Forestry Commission, had sent out programs of the November 1908 forestry convention to likely members of the 1909 legislature and urged them to attend to "equip themselves for helping to solve the most serious problem before the state." He wrote William B. Mershon, who for more than 30 years had been active in rallying Michigan sportsmen and was by now serving on the Forestry Commission with Garfield, that all but one of the would-be lawmakers spoke out "frankly and flatfooted in the interests of forestry and in the proper handling of state lands. They admit they have been mismanaged."[34]

Mershon made frequent trips to Lansing in the spring of 1909 to assure the passage of two measures he, Garfield, and Filibert Roth believed were critical to a new forest policy. One, known as the Flowers bill for its sponsor, would transfer management of tax-reverted lands from the land office to a new public domain commission; the other, known as the Sterling bill, would require owners of cutover lands to pile and burn slash to prevent wildfires.

The Sterling bill stalled due to resistance from the Hardwood Lumbermen's Association, whom Mershon scored in a letter to J. H. Bissell, president of the Michigan Forestry Association. "It is truly stated, I think, that selfishness predominates the lumber fraternity. Lumbermen have destroyed the forests, they got them for nothing, and now are standing in the way of protecting them."[35]

Garfield wrote Mershon on May 1 that he had organized a drop of about 200 letters from Kent County on the legislature favoring the Flowers bill. Nonetheless, it was also defeated. On May 12, the House voted it down 45–37, provoking bitterness and despair from the forestry advocates and some newspapers. Under the headline "Public Domain Sacrificed to Politics and Greed," the *Detroit News* editorialized that "henchmen" of Governor Warner had privately lobbied against the bill. Game, Fish, and Forestry Warden Charles Pierce, blasted by Roth at the forestry convention the preceding fall for failing to stop the ruinous fires, was thought to oppose the measure because it would place his office under control of the new commission.[36] The *News* fumed that the defeat of the bill was "equivalent to denying the people of the state the protection that they have a right to expect of their state departments."[37]

Meanwhile, Garfield fretted in a letter to Mershon:

> If we are checkmated in the present Legislature, after all that has been done, there will be a hopelessness in the task before us, which has never been so strongly in evidence before. It seemed as if after the holocaust of last year and with that splendid work of the commission of inquiry in evidence, that if ever there was an opportunity to get rational laws enacted now was the time.[38]

But at nearly the last minute a new public domain commission bill appeared, at least partly in response to the negative publicity about the defeat of the first one and to public revulsion after the release of the report of the legislative committee detailing losses on sale of public lands. The new Aitkin bill awakened the suspicion of the forestry advocates. Garfield wrote that he had no faith in the measure because it was "prepared by the enemy." He and Charles B. Blair of the Forestry Commission wrote members of the state House that it should be killed because, with the defeat of the forest fire protection bill, expansion of the state's forest reserves would only increase "opportunity for public plunder." Despite this opposition from unexpected quarters, the bill cleared the legislature just before its adjournment. In its story on Senate passage of the bill, the *Detroit News* dubbed the measure the "public domain bill of a sort." The Senate bill, the *News* noted, would put Game Warden Pierce on the new commission. The House removed this provision and restored much of the original language of the Flowers bill.[39] The new public domain commission would have "power and jurisdiction" over all public lands and forest reserves and interests including stream protection and control, forest fire protection, and other matters previously under the autonomous commissioner of the land office; auditor general; and game, fish, and forestry warden. The commission was charged with appraising tax-reverted lands prior to sale. It could take actions to prevent forest fires and to "cause such lands as are unfit for agricultural purposes to be used for forestry reserve purposes," with a *minimum* reserve of 200,000 acres.

Garfield and Mershon were unsure of the new measure's worth and prepared to resign their positions on the Forestry Commission in protest.[40]

Mershon wrote angrily to an ally, Senator J. B. Shields, that Governor Warner and Warden Pierce and a machine benefiting from the sale of tax lands had killed useful legislation, adding, "Well, I am done now working for the dear public."

In a draft prepared but apparently never sent to Governor Warner, Garfield, who had argued for forest preserves for more than a quarter century, lamented that even

> the terrible conflagration of last year, with its unparalleled loss in soil fertility and young growing forests, did not make sufficient impression upon our law-making body to secure for us a more efficient system of fire protection or an adequate organization for coping with the great forest fire problem. . . . [W]e cannot but interpret the situation in any other way than as practically an expression of an entire lack of confidence in our ability to render service to the State in the matters referred to us for investigation and the care of the property of the State left in our keeping.[41]

But friends in the legislature took a more favorable, if not unequivocal, view. "I do not suppose that you are any better pleased with the Public Domain Bill than I am but it was the best thing and the only thing that we could get passed, and is a starter toward right conditions," Rep. Lewis Sterling of Iron Mountain wrote Mershon. The *Detroit News,* which had condemned the defeat of the Flowers bill, now sang praises for the version amended by the House, calling it "genuine land and reforestation reform."[42]

In the end Garfield and Mershon did not resign. They turned over the files of the Forestry Commission to the new Public Domain Commission later that year and hoped for the best. Through a combination of skillful appeals, public criticism of shortsighted officials, and fortunate timing, they had overcome decades of indifference and neglect by the legislature. Although Garfield and Mershon did not believe it at the time, their work on the Forestry Commission and their lobbying of the legislature had produced a major shift in management of northern lands that would provide the base for a rebirth of the forests.

CHAPTER 5

The Public Health Roots of Environmental Protection

Detroit adopted a sewer system by which the sewage of the whole city was poured into the Detroit River. When anything was said about the contamination of the river-water, and that this water would become unfit for use by those living on the banks of the river below the city, the reply was ready that it was not possible to pollute such a mass of water by any amount of sewage. But the country above Detroit is becoming thickly settled. . . . Just now there is no little excitement in the City of the Straits concerning contaminated water, and the fear is expressed that when the population along the river above Detroit becomes greatly increased, the water of the Detroit River will be unfit for domestic and potable use.

—Robert C. Kedzie, president's address,
Michigan State Board of Health, 1878

*M*ichigan's first environmental protection law took effect before statehood, although its drafters did not think of it that way. An 1831 territorial act prohibited the slaughtering or cleaning of animals within 80 rods of the Detroit River and the depositing or emptying of "offal or entrails" of any animal into the river. The same act also required those dressing or cleaning fish on the banks of the river to bury the entrails. The penalty for violations was capped at $50.

Although enough was known by then about the offensive odors and other nuisances that animal carcasses caused, for much of the nineteenth century public understanding of the link between basic sanitation and human health was rudimentary at best. Scientific knowledge of the connection was relatively recent and imperfect. Only in 1842 did Englishman Edwin Chadwick author his historic paper on the link between infectious disease and child mortality on one hand and polluted water supplies and poor sanitary practices on the other. In 1854 London physician John Snow traced an outbreak of cholera to a contaminated drinking water pump. After the Civil War, reformers in the United States took note of these and other developments and sought to educate and protect the public.

In 1869 Massachusetts became the first state in the country to establish a public board of health. Michigan was fourth to create such a board, in 1873, largely through the work of four pioneer sanitarians, Doctors Henry B. Baker, Ira H. Bartholomew, Homer O. Hitchcock, and Robert C. Kedzie.[1] Elected to the Michigan House of Representatives in 1872, Bartholomew introduced the bill to establish the state board, and Baker enthusiastically lobbied for it with newspaper articles and talks. Kedzie "did his utmost by lecture and demonstration in the legislative halls to convince the law-makers of the existing dangers arising from the use of poisonous wall paper, water contaminated with the causative agent of typhoid fever, and dangerous illuminating oils."[2] Kedzie was one of the first appointees to the board, and Baker was its secretary for decades.

Kedzie, the advocate of tree planting in his 1867 legislative service, predated a latter-day consumer protection movement with his exposé of the dangers caused by arsenic in wallpaper and paints, publishing a book entitled *Shadows from the Walls of Death*. Commercial interests attempted to remove him from the board but were unsuccessful.

Almost a century before controversy over the agricultural use of pesticides brought nationwide attention to Michigan, Kedzie inquired into the dangers of the leading insect poisons of the time, which also contained arsenic. He worried that "in the use of such destructive agents, not only the immediate benefits should be considered, but also the remote and contingent consequences." He enunciated a set of rules he thought should govern a "safe" pesticide, among which was "It must not injure the person who applies the poison to the crop." On this count he found most substances in use lacking. Focusing on paris green, a mixture of arsenic and copper as well as inert ingredients, Kedzie warned of a "deadly poison" that could produce dangerous effects through inhalation of dust or contact with sores, raw surfaces, or perspiration. He said cases of poisoning of farmers were "not infrequent."[3]

Kedzie's interests were wide ranging. Born in New York State in 1823 just before his family emigrated to its southeast Michigan pioneer cabin, Kedzie entered the new University of Michigan medical school after the death of his wife in 1848, apparently at least in part because he faulted the lack of adequate medical care for his loss. Graduating first in his class of seven in 1851, he began his practice of medicine in Kalamazoo. But while still a student, he investigated an outbreak of cholera in that city that claimed 15 lives and sickened a total of 25. Determined to be Asiatic cholera, which kills its victims through dehydration, loss of minerals, and kidney failure, the outbreak was probably related to contaminated water or food. But at the time this was not known.

Kedzie practiced in Kalamazoo and Vermontville until joining the U.S. army as an assistant surgeon in the Twelfth Michigan Infantry in 1862. He was wounded that year and returned to Michigan in the fall, joining the faculty of the Michigan Agricultural College, where he remained until his retirement in 1902.

Perhaps inspired by his investigation of the Kalamazoo cholera outbreak and other clinical observations, Kedzie became a forceful advocate for proper management of wastes. At a time when general knowledge of the connection between wastewater and health was limited, Kedzie performed a valuable service.

The early annual reports of the state Board of Health are filled with tales of disease and suffering caused by consumption of polluted drinking water. Examining an outbreak of "cerebro-spinal meningitis" in Lenawee County in 1874, Kedzie found two boys with dilated pupils, retraction of the head, dark spots, and discoloration of the skin over the sciatic nerve. He noted that the spring used for drinking water by one of the boys was 7 paces from the opening of two sewers and 6 paces from a privy in the opposite direction. A cemetery only 15 paces away, on ground higher than the spring, contained a fresh grave.[4] In the 1880 report of the state board, Kedzie noted that an outbreak of typhoid fever in Grand Rapids might have been associated with contamination spreading from the Fulton Street Cemetery, which sloped down toward drinking water wells used by several families. "These poor families appear to have been drinking a cold infusion of death!" Kedzie cried.

During the 1880s awareness of the need to protect drinking water supplies began to grow, but sanitary conditions still left much to be desired. Garbage piles, dead horses, manure, and streams of waste characterized most city streets. But drinking water supply was where expert and public attention focused. In an 1888 paper reprinted by the Michigan Board of Health, a committee on pollution of water supplies of the American Public Health Association observed:

> Many of our public water-supplies contain sewage, and its harmfulness in a general way is unquestioned even by those who have a financial interest in them. Yet there appears to be a hesitancy to acknowledge the real, the specific, danger. Typhoid fever is present in all our cities, giving annual death-rates of from 15 to 100 and over in every 100,000 of the population; but in the enumeration of its causes its prevalence is ascribed to many insanitary conditions before mention is made of the public water-supply. . . . [But] we cannot shut our eyes to the relation that exists between sewage in our streams and typhoid fever in the cities that are supplied by them.[5]

In 1887 the *Detroit Free Press* noted health concerns in large cities where "water supplies are rivers fed by little streams that carry off the filth and drainage from houses" and observed that in every town where well water was used, sewage wastes were probably percolating into drinking water supplies.[6] Armed with such information, the public began to support improved sanitation methods.

Kedzie commented, with admirable foresight, about a problem that would plague Michigan's environment and human health for a century, the disposal of raw sewage. Observing that night buckets containing the excrement of nearly 1,000 men at Jackson Prison were emptied into a sewer that quickly reached the Grand River, Kedzie argued against this pollution. He suggested that the waste could be sold to farmers for fertilizer.

"Other proofs that a systematic pollution of our rivers has already begun in our State might be brought forward, but they are not necessary," said Kedzie, "for any one can easily see that these evils will come in with an increase in our population, unless they are excluded by timely precaution on the part of the public authorities. The evil can be successfully resisted or averted only by combined opposition."[7] Kedzie called for development of sewer systems designed to prevent stream pollution, arguing that it would become too expensive to refit systems after cities grew.

His call was unheeded. As the state's population, particularly in southern counties, increased dramatically, other state officials also began to note the problem. In 1901, state game and fish warden Grant Morse devoted a paragraph to the "pollution of public waters" in his biennial report. Pollution of both inland waters and the Great Lakes, he wrote, was caused by sawdust, chemicals, and other refuse. While noting the effects that sawdust dumping had on the breeding and feeding grounds of fish under his control, Morse suggested a greater concern: "[T]he waters are rendered unfit for consumption and prove a serious menace to the healthfulness of the human family as well as our wild life." The "marked progress" of manufacturing industries such as pulp mills, beet sugar plants, and paper mills, all of which used chemicals and dumped refuse with little or no treatment, Morse said, warranted a closer look at the state's entirely inadequate control laws.

The legislature did not act immediately, and when it did move, it did so only haltingly. In the meantime, the only remedy for gross pollution was the common law of nuisance. Usually requiring a demonstration of serious harm, successful court nuisance actions could win injunctions to stop the condition, but damages for injury to human health or the environment were barred.

The first landmark in the battle to stop harmful dumping of sewage into the state's streams was a lawsuit brought against the city of Grand Rapids by the state attorney general in 1909. The city, whose population had climbed above 110,000, discharged all of its untreated wastes from sewer pipes into the Grand River and also collected 150 to 180 barrels of "night soil" from outlying houses not served by sewers. This was poured into the Prescott Street sewer and quickly reached the river. Downstream, the township of Wyoming and village of Grandville received the results. Grandville complained that the deposited sewage, stranded in a 20-acre pond at the village edge after floods, created such a stench that it constituted a public nuisance. Arguing on behalf of Grandville and Wyoming, the attorney general demanded that Grand Rapids install sewage systems that would provide some treatment of the wastes and dilute the odor problems.

In its defense, Grand Rapids argued that its wastes could not possibly have caused the downstream nuisance because of the dilution provided by the river. Privies located around the malodorous pond in Grandville probably contributed more to the problem, the city argued.

In its 1913 decision, the state supreme court noted the uniform testimony of witnesses from Grandville that the "stench and odors at Grandville arising from the river, and especially from the territory overflowed after the water receded, had been so nauseating as to be almost intolerable. Cellars were filled in many instances, and it appeared that after the water receded there was a sediment over not only the ground, but in the cellars, or a sticky, slimy manure; that there had been general complaint of this odor."[8]

A key witness for the state was Dr. Henry Baker, one of the founders of the state Board of Health and its secretary from 1873 to 1905. Rebutting the arguments made by Grand Rapids, he said that privies in Grandville could not have caused the extent of the odor problems noted in the village, and he added that he recommended against using wells in the area where the river flooding regularly occurred, because of the risk of waterborne disease. The sewage of Grand Rapids would not purify itself in the seven miles it took to reach Grandville, Baker said, and he added that "all streams of Michigan are more or less polluted." A civil engineer who testified for the plaintiffs said Grand Rapids could build a sewage disposal plant that would settle out the worst wastes for approximately $300,000.

In an early use of laboratory analysis in an environmental case, Dr. J. D. Brook of Grandville presented results from two samples he collected from the river, one upstream of the Grand Rapids discharge and one from the river reach at Grandville. While the upstream sample contained 10,500 bacteria per cubic centimeter at room temperature, the downstream sample contained 38,000. Inoculated with the upstream sample, an animal recovered in 48 hours, while inoculation with the downstream sample resulted in death in 24 hours.

Perhaps the most important legal issue argued by the plaintiffs was that a municipality had no more right to pollute public waters and create a nuisance than any private person. In a state with rapidly growing population, the question was far from academic; the attorney general argued that granting cities a right to dump wastes into rivers would harm downstream communities in a way that other parties could not legally do. The court agreed, saying that the city "is subject to the same rules as would be a private individual. . . . [I]t is interfering not only with the property and personal rights of the persons affected, but in a large degree with the rights of a large community of people by inflicting irreparable injury."[9] The supreme court issued an injunction restraining the city from continuing to dump its sewage into the river until the waste was "deodorized and purified" through a treatment system, giving it a year to comply.

Despite the cost to the city, local opinion supported the ruling. The *Grand Rapids News* noted that Grand Rapids itself had objected to upstream communities placing sewage into the Grand River but had resorted to the dumping of its wastes into the river to save money. "This city cannot continue to teach health measures to its own people, and at the same time disregard the pollution it causes to be scattered among those who live to the west of us. We must be consistent. There is nothing now to do but take the medicine."[10]

In the same year as the historic state supreme court ruling—which also firmly established the precedent that the attorney general could bring actions on behalf of the public health and other public interests—the legislature enacted a law requiring cities designing sewage systems to obtain approval from the state Board of Health. But it deferred action on stronger measures that would outlaw harmful pollution.

Government was often more responsive to the conscience of women who organized the national municipal housekeeping movement, which sought to address the ugliness and unhealthy conditions of U.S. cities in the late 1800s and early 1900s. Caroline Bartlett Crane of Kalamazoo was nationally noted for her efforts to clean up the cities of the United States, including their streets and skies.

"Municipal housekeepers were the environmentalists, consumer advocates, social workers, and community activists of their time," said O'Ryan Rickard in *A Just Verdict*.[11] "They worked for clean cities with clean air, disease-free food with labels that told the truth, and improved standards of living for children and the poor." A century later, the work of Crane's successors would be regarded as a cornerstone of the environmental justice movement.

Born in Wisconsin in 1858, Crane was devoted to her father, who influenced her to develop her mind and critical faculties rather than prepare for a domestic life. She graduated from Carthage College determined to pursue a career at a time when most women were confined by expectations to the home. She ultimately became a Unitarian minister and lived in Kalamazoo with her husband, a physician.

Crane's leadership in the housekeeping movement arose from her church activities. When she could find no expert to speak to her women's church study group about meat inspections, she organized a tour of slaughterhouses selling meat to Kalamazoo markets and discovered appalling conditions. Grease, hair, and blood covered the interiors of the slaughterhouses, and diseased animals were slaughtered along with the healthy. Spurred to action, Crane drafted a state meat inspection bill that passed in 1903 and a model local ordinance for Kalamazoo.

Crane's work soon broadened to include a host of problems plaguing Kalamazoo and other cities. She promoted improved street-cleaning methods, getting the cleaners to wear white uniforms and persuading merchants to clean sidewalks and streets around their businesses. Soon she was in national demand, performing audits of cities and recommending housekeeping improvements.

Environmental conditions did not escape her attention. Problems with garbage, sewage, and "smoke," or air pollution, troubled Crane. In a speech at Baltimore, she chided the city for its weak smoke abatement ordinance.

[T]he day has passed when any person sitting upon the City Council should say that the amount of smoke arising from a city is an index of prosperity. Dr.

Justus Ohage, Health Commissioner of St. Paul, dared to tell his people that it is, rather, an emblem of a city's stupidity. . . . It is perfectly possible for plants to be so equipped and so fired as to prevent the emission of dense smoke.[12]

In the same talk, Crane called for the construction and connection of sewers as "a public sanitary necessity" and improved treatment of drinking water to render it potable. After an inspection of Erie, Pennsylvania, Crane had urged cleanup of that city's water supply. The city did not follow through, and a January 1911 outbreak of typhoid fever cost 103 lives.

Crane's work was pioneering even if confined by the social limitations on women's activism in that age. Municipal housekeeping was not threatening to most men because it was viewed as a logical extension of women's accepted role as caretaker of the home. Crane, in fact, repeatedly urged the public to regard the city "as the larger home." Although other female urban reformers of her time, such as Jane Addams, are more often remembered, Crane was famous in her day. Her work foreshadowed the energetic and sometimes outraged activism of women in the 1970s and 1980s who would rebel against pollution that threatened the health of their families and neighborhoods.

The sewage problem and its toll on public health were serious enough to warrant an investigation by the International Joint Commission (IJC), a U.S.-Canada body established by the Boundary Waters Treaty of 1909. In 1912, the two governments asked the commission to analyze "to what extent and by what causes" pollution was rendering unfit the boundary waters. In a study that was not completed and submitted until 1918, the commission reviewed conditions from the Rainy River in the west to the St. Lawrence River in the east. The commission analyzed conditions along the boundary in all of the Great Lakes, although Lake Michigan was not within its purview.

The results were appalling. Below Port Huron and Sarnia, the waters of the St. Clair River were unfit for drinking for about 34 miles. Samples taken above the intake for the Detroit water supply in the Detroit River showed it to be unsafe without treatment, while the water intakes of Windsor and Walkerville on the Canadian side were "located in dangerous situations" because sewage was discharged directly above them and could be diverted, under certain weather conditions, into points where it would reach the intakes. Gross pollution extended downriver for miles from downtown Detroit to the mouth of the river at Lake Erie, making it "totally unfit" as a water supply source.

> *It is our opinion that such raw water would impose an unreasonable responsibility on any known method of purification, even with the most careful supervision. Unfortunately, Wyandotte, Trenton and Amherstburg are taking their water supplies from this part of the river.*[13]

In its study, the commission used *B. coli* as the indicator of fecal contamination from sewage pollution. A count of 5 *B. coli* at the head of the Detroit River signaled relatively clean water, while in a lower stretch of the river the count reached a staggering 10,592. The dumping of the untreated sewage of cities was not the only source of the problem, the report noted. Vessels were pouring their sewage waste and polluted ballast into the water.

The commission concluded that "the grossly polluted condition of boundary waters is doubtless the cause of the abnormal prevalence of typhoid fever throughout the territory bordering thereon." Typhoid death rates per 100,000 population in Michigan's boundary waters communities ranged as high as 163 at Trenton in 1907 and 123 at Wyandotte in 1908, far above normal levels. While the study itself had stimulated some communities to step up protection of water supplies through the use of chlorine and bleaching powder, the commission found the situation unsatisfactory. Violent outbreaks of typhoid continued and would persist given the extent of the pollution and the inefficient operation of water purification plants. The commission recommended that communities build collecting and treatment works to remove bacteria and other suspended materials, while vessels should disinfect their wastes before dumping them. It also called for a ban on the dumping of other problematic wastes, including garbage, sawdust, and other mill wastes and industrial wastes "causing appreciable injury."

The IJC also recommended a new treaty to remedy the pollution of the boundary waters—something that would not happen for more than half a century. The proposed pact, submitted in 1920 but set aside by both the Canadian and U.S. governments, would have given the commission the authority to initiate pollution investigations rather than being forced to wait for references from the two governments and would have assumed that pollution impaired water use unless it was otherwise demonstrated. The treaty would have "represented an astonishing advance in international law and organization," in the views of later observers.[14] Perhaps for that reason, it went nowhere.

One of the obstacles to cleanup was a belief among city engineers that chlorination of drinking water supplies was an adequate solution to the problem of raw sewage in rivers and lakes. Rather than construct expensive waste treatment systems that cities could ill afford, municipal officials favored treatment of the raw drinking water itself. This approach would dominate the response to bacteriological pollution for decades, until other conditions and an indignant public insisted on cleanup.

Despite the commission's report, pollution continued generally unabated. Michigan's food processing and growing manufacturing industries joined cities in using rivers as waste receptacles. By 1917, the Grand River pollution that Kedzie had noted 40 years before had appreciably worsened.

During its passage through the corporate limits [of the city of Jackson] it receives the sewage of about 33,000 people as well as some industrial waste, ashes, garbage and rubbish which render it exceedingly foul and turbid. The burden of sewage imposed on the stream is more than the water can carry and sludge beds are formed with consequent nuisances during the warm weather.[15]

In the first biennial report of the new Michigan Department of Conservation for 1921–22, the agency noted problems statewide with milk plants; sugar companies; paper mills; a tannery; and raw sewage from Pontiac, Owosso, and Flint. The state health department went farther, noting the following conditions.

The Raisin River in the vicinity of Adrian is in a filthy condition due to city sewage and industrial wastes entering the stream. . . . In the fall of 1920 fish were dying in great numbers in the Raisin River at points below Blissfield. . . . [W]astes from the sugar plant at Blissfield were responsible for the trouble.

In the fall of 1920 death of fish occurred in the Shiawassee river. Chemical tests were also made of the water in this river and revealed low dissolved oxygen content. The smallest amount of dissolved oxygen was found at Goss Bridge, about four miles below the Owosso sugar plant.

The effect of pollution on water supplies in regard to tastes in waters was shown at Marquette, Michigan this year. This city takes its water supply from Lake Superior. Wastes from the Cleveland Cliffs Iron Co. are discharged into this lake and investigation showed that the tastes complained of by citizens were due to these waste liquors which are produced in the manufacture of charcoal, wood-alcohol, and many by-products.[16]

Water pollution was seen as unacceptable by an ever-growing constituency. "If the State of Michigan is to continue to be 'The Playground of the Nation,' then its polluted streams and lakes must be cleaned up," wrote Dr. Walter G. Kinyon, a district officer of the Izaak Walton League in 1927. Urging Traverse City voters to back a $240,000 bond issue for a sewage plant, he added:

If the Grand Traverse Region is to retain its enviable reputation as "The Heart of Nature's Playground," then the Boardman river must be cleaned of its human sewage and become once again the habitat of the brook trout, the German Brown and the Rainbow Trout as it was some fifteen years ago. Our beautiful Grand Traverse Bay, instead of being an open cess pool, must be cleaned of its sewerage refuse and once again become the mecca of the perch and Mackinaw trout fishermen.[17]

But it would be decades before public tolerance of gross water pollution would end. Before long, the Great Depression would empty the purses of most municipal governments who dumped their wastes into rivers. And other battles over natural resources preoccupied the public mind.

CHAPTER 6

The Crusade to Free
Conservation from Politics

While there has been a lot of talk about conservation of forests and so on down at Lansing the talk is all rot, and when it is analyzed to the bottom the suggested action proves itself to be of the same unintelligent kind that has allowed the destruction of the natural resources in this state. Nothing can ever be done in the mighty work of up-building our forests and wildlife until the house at Lansing is utterly cleaned out.

—James Oliver Curwood, December 14, 1922

$\mathcal{E}$ arly in the twentieth century a new wind began to sweep the nation. Sportsmen, mostly well-to-do businessmen and members of the professional class, had championed the protection of fish and game from the Civil War on. Now a new group of Americans was clamoring for protection of natural resources. Joining forces with the outdoorsmen and proponents of sound resource management were civic organizations, women's clubs, and municipal reformers. They often had common aims, but their concerns arose from entirely different sources, including a belief that commercialism had gone too far and that the nation should save resources from development.[1]

Rallied to the cause by President Theodore Roosevelt and his informal conservation minister, Gifford Pinchot, who believed in "wise use" of forests and other resources, this new breed of ally sometimes perplexed its champions. In fact, Pinchot often competed with another friend of Roosevelt, Sierra Club founder John Muir, for the president's heart. Muir opposed the treatment of forests solely as sources of wood products for a growing society and found spiritual meaning in wild places, many of which he fought to keep from being developed. Pinchot, by contrast, opposed the setting aside of forests or other places for scenic values; he fought the provision in the New York state constitution that declared the Adirondack Park off limits to logging and called for the Park to remain "forever wild." Pinchot shouldered Muir aside in vying for Roosevelt's attentions, excluding him from the 1908 White House conservation conference. While the conference considered how to better harness the nation's resources for current and future generations and avoid waste, the Sierra Club's written conference statement spoke to other needs: "The moral and physical welfare of a nation is not dependent alone upon bread and water. Comprehending these primary necessities is the deeper need for recreation and that which satisfies also the esthetic sense."[2]

A key figure in the transition from traditional game protection to wildlife appreciation was adopted Michiganian George Shiras III. The son of a U.S. Supreme Court justice, Shiras was born in Allegheny, Pennsylvania in 1859, but paid his first visit to the Marquette area when he was 11 years old. His father, a trout fisherman, introduced Shiras to the still-wild Upper Peninsula, and its forests, waters, and wildlife won his loyalty. The young Shiras spent 65 summers and the last 4 years of his life in the Upper Peninsula. While following in his father's footsteps to become a lawyer, Shiras soon found more reward in his avocation as a naturalist, once explaining that in the Pittsburgh area

> I lived during most of my early years beneath a sun often obscured by clouds of smoke. At night that part of the Ohio Valley resembled an inferno from the glare of blast furnaces, coke ovens, and many standpipes shooting lurid flames far overhead in wasteful consumption of the natural gas from adjoining gas fields. . . . The contrast between such surroundings and those of my vacation period beneath azure skies in a lovely forest retreat sufficiently accounts, I believe, for the overpowering desire that finally caused me to give up the exactions of a profession life that I might be free to interpret the laws of nature rather than those of man.

An active hunter, Shiras served a single term in the U.S. Congress, representing a Pittsburgh-area constituency, in 1904 and 1905. Just before leaving office, he introduced the first federal legislation to protect migratory birds. It finally became law in 1913, and when it was challenged in the courts, Shiras filed a brief as part of the successful bid to support its constitutionality. Shiras also proposed a 1925 Michigan law that forbade the carrying of a gun in hunting areas outside the hunting season, significantly easing the enforcement of game restrictions.

But Shiras made his greatest contribution as "the father" of wildlife photography.[3] In 1889 he unsuccessfully tried to capture a deer on film on his beloved Whitefish Lake, east of Marquette. He persisted, however, and was the first to photograph wildlife in daylight from a blind or canoe and in 1891 the first to use an automatic flash and camera setup that animals triggered themselves, making night pictures possible. Displayed at a Paris exposition in 1900 and later published in the National Geographic, Shiras's pictures of moose, beaver, and deer caused a sensation. They gave thousands of hunters and nonhunters alike a glimpse of a world never before seen and now quickly receding. The striking images helped build public awareness of the beauty and mystery of wildlife. A few years before he died in 1942, Shiras published his work in a memoir, Hunting Wild Life with Camera and Flashlight. The title aptly described a new relationship with wildlife that did not require shooting—although Shiras remained a hunter.

The first Michigan organization devoted to the protection of what had previously been considered simply a "resource" was the Michigan Audubon Society. Part of a national Audubon movement inspired largely by the love of birds, the Michigan Society took flight in February 1904. Its initial roster of officers and supporters included some of the state's most prominent citizens— President James B. Angell of the University of Michigan; Chase Osborn, the former fish and game warden who would become governor in 1910; and the longtime conservationist William B. Mershon of Saginaw. But its engine was Jefferson Butler, secretary and treasurer and later its president. After Butler's death in 1914, Mershon wrote the following praise of Butler to a Grand Rapids newspaper editor.

> [H]e was about the whole thing. It is to his unselfish efforts that we owe the existence of an Audubon Society here in Michigan. Whenever there was work to do, he did it, and I am sorry to say with very little assistance from outside.

The Michigan Audubon movement, like the national Society, arose in part over anxiety about dwindling bird populations. Butler reports in his early history of Michigan Audubon that William T. Hornaday, director of New York City's Zoologic Park, estimated that bird life in Michigan decreased 23 percent from 1885 to 1898 and declined 40 percent in the nation at large.

The result of greedy, careless, or malicious destruction, these shrinking numbers alarmed the Michigan Audubon members enough to appeal to state authorities for enforcement in 1904. But state game and fish warden Charles Chapman refused to give out names of his deputies, which the Society had requested so that its members could work in unison with them. Chapman said the deputies "could do better work if they were not known" and defended his office by blaming lack of legislative appropriations. Inquiring of lawmakers about the reasons for the inadequate funding, Audubon members found suspicion of political favoritism by the warden: "Several members of both the House of Representatives and Senate expressed the opinion to the writer [Butler] that the game warden office was forced into politics, and that it would not be advisable to donate money for scientific and humane work along this line." The Society approved a proposal, later advanced by Mershon on behalf of sportsmen, that a three-member commission replace the game warden as an effort to rid the program of political favoritism.[4]

In another instance, Audubon Society member Clara Dyar of Grosse Pointe asked for the game warden's help to stop the shooting of game birds out of season as well as songbirds. Contacting the deputy warden in Wayne County, Audubon members received no action, and so they wrote to Warden Chapman in Sault Ste. Marie. He never replied to the specific complaint, and the Society "thereupon gave up all hope of assistance from the game warden or his office." The Society next asked the Wayne County prosecutor to enforce the law, which a 1903 amendment to the game law empowered him to do. But there was no reply.

As the first complaint died from lack of response, another arose. Butler was informed that a colony of great blue heron near Clarkston, northwest of Detroit, was under attack.

> The secretary visited the colony and found that the old birds were being shot during the nesting season, simply because the boys and young men found them easy to hit. . . . [T]his colony of great blue herons was being destroyed simply for the "fun" of destroying, as they are useless for food, commit no damage and are useful as scavengers.[5]

The Society's plea to the local game warden this time drew the response that Butler could prosecute the killers himself under the game law; the deputy had neither money nor time to do so. Although Butler was also unable to accept the burden of prosecution, he visited the colony again and heard shooting. He encountered two young men with guns, one of whom was carrying a heron's wings and explained that his mother wanted them for dusters. While Butler watched, one of the men shot a heron that had just left a nest of young. Butler threatened, somewhat ineffectually, to prosecute. While visiting neighboring farmers, Butler found little sentiment for the protection of the heron. A few in the area said the slaughter was shameful, but the majority opinion seemed to be that the shooting was just "a little sport" for young men.

The Society decided to concentrate on educating the public in order to change its indifference or even hostility to birds. Launching a campaign that emphasized the teaching of schoolchildren, Michigan Audubon distributed 20,000 educational leaflets during its first three years and posted the game laws in communities where bird destruction had been the worst. Butler argued that the "promiscuous killing" of birds in childhood deadened the consciences of boys and led to other bad habits and perhaps even to prison.

But another audience needed to hear the Society's message.

> [S]carlet tanagers, goldfinches, indigo buntings, Baltimore orioles, and many other kinds of our most beautifully gorgeous birds were commonly killed and sold to the millinery interests for their plumage. Three hundred hummingbird skins were sent from one community one season. This proved that the women of the state also needed educating.[6]

When appealing to a general audience, Michigan's organized bird lovers tended to rely on economic rather than aesthetic arguments, much as environmentalists of a later time would speak of pollution control as a way of reducing public health expenditures and increasing tourism. Rebutting the idea that their work was based on sentimentalism, Audubon members argued that they were only against killing of birds when it served no useful purpose. They said the taking of birds by "scientific men for scientific purposes" was acceptable because the resulting studies helped enlighten the public and strengthened the case for bird protection.

In a society that still liked to think of itself as agrarian despite the explosive growth of population in the cities, the Society preached the value of birds in controlling pests that interfered with crop production. Citing bulletins of the U.S. Biological Survey in the Department of Agriculture quantifying the number of harmful insects found in the stomachs of birds, Butler said, "The birds work for man and it is only fair that we should protect them. The odd thing is that man, the greatest [beneficiary] of the birds, should be their worst enemy." Butler suggested that sympathetic citizens feed birds during the winter, protect nests from boys and collectors, and protect birds from excess take by hunters.

Whatever the public arguments, it is clear that humane impulses were the primary source of Audubon energy. While some of Michigan's pioneer sportsmen had been sickened by the slaughter of animals and expressed affection for some wildlife, the new Audubon movement was primarily concerned with the survival, not the management for game recreation, of birds and other animals. The state had passed a law in 1897 offering a bounty for the killing of English sparrows, considered a nuisance because they ate grain. Butler said he could find no evidence of this and added, "Who can look at this bird with the temperature about the zero mark, hopping through the snow and chirping as happily as though it were a day in June, and say they despise it? They give cheer to many and brighten the lives of the disheartened and the ill, and afford amusement and inspiration to countless children."[7]

Study and protection of birds became increasingly respectable. The Society very early gained one of its most well-known benefactors, Henry Ford, who was on his way to becoming an automobile manufacturing legend. Ford provided the Society with enough money to distribute bird literature to 300 schools and permitted Butler to study birds on his farm. Also contributing to the educational effort was sportsman and Audubon board member Mershon, who sponsored "Mershon's Medals for School Kids." The contest rewarded students for essays and personal experiences in feeding, housing, protecting, and photographing birds.

In 1908 a future leader of the Michigan Society took her first aggressive action to protect birds. Edith Munger of Hart offered a resolution at the annual meeting of the state Federation of Women's Clubs asking members to pledge to wear no more bird plumage except ostrich plumes and feathers of domestic fowls. She reported that "there was much heated discussion on the resolution," but the federation approved it.

Munger became president of the Michigan Society upon Butler's death. She was a vital force for bird conservation, serving as the president for 21 years. Born in 1865 "in a small lumbering town on the edge of the woods," she traced her interest in the outdoors, like so many others who would make it their life's work as well as their passion, to childhood. "I was always keenly interested," she wrote, "in fact infatuated with all outdoor life, especially birds, wild flowers, and butterflies."[8] Graduating from Whitehall High School in 1881, she became a schoolteacher and tried to awaken her pupils to the natural world. After marrying, she moved to Hart in 1895, found the local boys shooting birds, and gave the first of many talks on the value of birds.[9]

Helen Augur Gilliland, a young girl at the time, vividly remembered Munger's presentations to her Hart area school more than 80 years later. "Her manner was such that instantly younger people respected her, and we admired what she was doing, and wished we could do these things."[10]

Her talks to older audiences were also well received. A newsletter reported on one such presentation.

One of the best lectures ever given in Romeo was that on "Bird Life," by Mrs. Edith C. Munger of Hart, under the auspices of the Monday Club at the Palace Theater on Monday evening last. Mrs. Munger has made a life study of birds and is thoroughly conversant with her subject. With her it is a labor of love, and with a pleasant voice and charming personality, she is eminently fitted for the instruction of others, and her choice collection of lantern slides is most interesting and helpful.

The magazine of a Detroit woman's club said Munger was "so full of her subject that the sight of different slides called forth snatches of verse, which well-known poets had written of this bird or that" and said she held her audience's undivided attention.

One local account of her life notes that she "must have clashed" with her husband, a well-liked physician and hunter. Louis Munger used a third floor tower room in the house they shared as a trophy room, displaying moose, deer, wolf, fox, and other wildlife he had bagged: "[O]ne wonders whether Edith, who felt so strongly about animal rights she was a vegetarian, didn't wince a little at the sight of the black bearskin rug in the second floor sitting room, or the pair of moose heads that greeted visitors in the entrance foyer."[11]

Munger and the Society also sparred with some sportsmen in the legislature. In 1909 the Auduboners pressed for a law banning spring shooting of birds. It was adulterated before passing the Michigan House of Representatives and died in the Senate. The Society had to content itself with measures protecting the bobwhite and outlawing the hunting of the prairie chicken, which was to become extinct in Michigan nevertheless.

Perhaps the most quixotic effort of the Society under Munger's presidency was a longtime effort to enact a cat license law. Believing that free-roaming cats were a major source of bird predation, Munger argued from at least 1914 on for such a law. "An enterprising boy with a dozen traps can destroy more rats and mice than the best house cat in existence," Munger wrote an official at the U.S. Biological Survey. "There was probably never a cat which could resist the temptation to catch a young robin or young bird just out of the nest and unable to fly."

Still at it in 1929, Munger awakened the skepticism even of such conservation writers as Albert Stoll Jr., who had served on the state Conservation Commission and was a longtime outdoor writer for the *Detroit News*. "A cat license stands about as much chance of passing the Legislature as does a bill calling for all members of the Legislature to stop tucking their napkins in their necks," Stoll wrote. "In 1919 a bill of this nature was introduced and every one except its sponsor thought it was a joke."[12]

Munger and the Society were outraged by the legislature's passage in 1917 of a law providing a bounty for the killing of all hawks and owls, which was designed to protect chickens and other birds. Once again, the helpful role of the raptors in consuming rodents and small mammals, rather than their beauty, was the chief argument for repealing the bounty. In sympathy with Audubon's objectives was Chief Clerk Charles Hoyt of the state's Game, Fish, and Forest Fire Department, who wrote the following comments to Munger.

> *I think [the law] was a mistake, as many of the hawks and owls are of much benefit, in fact more benefit to the farmer than a detriment, but you know the ordinary farmer or legislative committees do not usually take the time or trouble to post themselves in connection with such matters.*[13]

For years to come the Audubon Society's most effective efforts would remain largely educational. In the 1920s, Munger made regular radio broadcasts on station WWJ in Detroit, reaching thousands of listeners. Munger's most spectacular public and legislative success was a contest she launched to name a state bird. To honor the twenty-fifth anniversary of the Michigan Society in 1929, Munger worked with outdoor writers and the state departments of education and conservation to promote the contest. Somewhat to her surprise, 190,000 votes poured in, with the robin edging the chickadee by a vote of 45,541 to 37,155. Munger observed, "Thus thousands of men and women as well as school boys and girls were studying about birds, who had never before given their feathered neighbors a second thought."[14]

One of Munger's contributions was the expansion of a singular state park close to her home. Winning resolutions of support from the Oceana County Board of Supervisors and the local federated women's club, she convinced the local congressman that community sentiment favored the transfer of federal land to the state along the Lake Michigan shoreline south of Pentwater. After 12 years of work, she was successful in the mid-1920s in adding the shoreline lands to today's Silver Lake State Park, which features 1,500 acres of dunes.

Munger's career illustrates the growing role of women in conservation during the early part of the century. Women's clubs began taking on the issue as a priority during the administration of Theodore Roosevelt. Primarily from the middle and upper class, members of these clubs educated themselves through presentations by experts like Munger and agitated for protective legislation at both the national and state levels. Michigan forestry advocates credited clubs in the state with helping advance their cause, but their primary work was in educating members and the general public about the importance of protecting birds and other wildlife. Said the conservation chairman of the Detroit Federation of Women's Clubs in 1913: "[N]o one can study [conservation] without finding that it touches life and life conditions through a thousand avenues; and no matter how diverse and varied the interests of women are, there is no one who will not be deeply appealed to by this subject in some phase or other."[15]

Munger was so well known and regarded that she broke some of the gender barriers of her time. Of more than two dozen conservation advocates invited to meet with governor-elect Fred Green in late 1926, she was the only female. At the meeting in Green's Ionia home, she sat close to an even better-known figure whom she described as "alive and alert . . . so full of the joy of living." His name was James Oliver Curwood.

While Munger and the women's clubs generally relied on persistent, low-key persuasion, Curwood used other methods. By the time of the new governor's conservation conference, he had spent the better part of the decade condemning with bitter invective the mismanagement of the state's natural resources in public speeches and writings. But long before Curwood's crusade to cleanse the state's conservation agency, he had earned international fame as a writer of adventure novels. And by the end of his life, he would speak of conservation in a voice new to Michigan, a haunting spiritual identification with nature that mystified friends as much as it presaged the sentiments of a later generation of environmentalists.

Born in 1878 in Owosso, Curwood spent seven years of his childhood in Ohio but made Shiawassee County the base for most of his adult life. He displayed an early interest in the outdoors, spending hours playing along the Shiawassee River and hunting small game after receiving a gun from his father at the age of 8. He would remember these experiences wistfully during his adult life, as he observed shrinking wildlife populations and increasingly polluted rivers. By the time he turned 11 he was churning out convoluted stories on sheets of wrapping paper. After graduating from Owosso High School, Curwood completed two years at the University of Michigan but quit to write for the *Detroit News Tribune*. In 1908 Curwood began to make his mark as a professional writer, turning out the first of many best-sellers that inevitably featured muscular outdoorsmen as protagonists, pure and innocent heroines, and almost comically evil villains. *The Courage of Captain Plum* and *The Wolf Hunters* freed him to write fiction full-time.

Curwood began spending time in the wilds of northern Canada in the government's employ, writing about the beauties of the country to attract tourists and trade. Roaming from Hudson Bay to the mountains of British Columbia, he collected material invaluable in many of his 33 books. One writer estimated that Curwood spent at least nine months of each year in the woods from 1908 to 1926. These experiences helped him perfect the fictional formula that made him rich. In the 1920s, it was said, he was the first writer to make a million dollars from his craft, and he traveled to Europe in 1925 to be toasted for his accomplishments in fiction.

Curwood, to put it mildly, was a colorful and paradoxical character. A teetotaler, he warmed up with long minutes of stretching every morning before walking to the miniature feudal castle he built on the banks of the Shiawassee

River to work on his novels and stories. He boasted that he would live to be a hundred. Fearless in the wilds, he had a phobia of snakes. He was known for his malicious pranks as a child—including the manufacture of a "blood purifier" actually containing a powerful laxative that he sold to strangers in small towns—but ultimately renounced hunting as cruelty and waste.

For many years Curwood's northern journeys claimed large numbers of big game. He was known for his bravery in facing the grizzly bears of the mountainous northwest of Canada and said he had killed four of them in just two hours on one outing. But a life-changing event occurred on a trip to British Columbia in 1914. He later fictionalized it in *The Grizzly King*. Langdon, the hero, is thunderstruck as he realizes that he is trapped on a mountain ledge by Thor, a grizzly he has wounded.

> Had Langdon moved then he would have died. But Thor was not, like man, a murderer. For another half-minute he waited for a hurt, for some sign of menace. Neither came, and he was puzzled. His nose swept the ground, and Langdon saw the dust rise where the grizzly's hot breath stirred it. And after that, for another long and terrible thirty seconds, the bear and the man looked at each other.
>
> Then very slowly—and doubtfully—Thor half turned. He growled. His lips drew partly back. Yet he saw no reason to fight, for that shrinking, white-faced pigmy crouching on the rock made no movement to offer him battle. . . . Thor disappeared slowly in the direction he had come, his great head hung low, his long claws click, click, clicking like ivory castanets as he went.
>
> . . . "You great big god of a bear!" [Langdon] whispered, and every fibre in him was trembling in a wonderful excitement as he found voice for the first time. "You—you monster with a heart bigger than man!" And then he added, under his breath, as if not conscious that he was speaking: "If I'd cornered you like that I'd have killed you! And you! You cornered me, and let me live!"
>
> . . . [T]he day and the hour had brought its meaning in a way that he would not forget so long as he lived, and he knew that hereafter and for all time he would not again hunt the life of Thor, or the lives of any of his kind.

Curwood's epiphany was akin to a religious conversion. His transformational experience in the Canadian wilds set him loose on a new path of preaching conservation to the public. While recognizing the inevitability of hunting and fishing as recreation, he said, "I have ceased to be a destroyer, as I once destroyed, and my ruling passion is to help wild things to live, from flowers and trees and birds and beasts to man himself, rather than to indulge further in the dominant sport of my species—extermination."[16]

But it may be too simple to credit Thor alone with Curwood's change of heart and his later crusade. He was heartsick already about the degradation of the state and of the community where he had grown up and lived. In his autobiography he lamented, "Such was the Shiawassee of my boyhood—my river—clean and refreshing as it flowed along on all the pride of its ancient lineage. Would to God the greed and selfishness of modern commerce had refrained from polluting it! Verily, nothing is sacred to the overlords of business!" Curwood donated generous funds to clean up the banks of the river in Owosso and bankrolled the stocking of streams with fish and of preserves with game animals. He wrote a letter to one supporter stating that "Michigan is being cheated out of the birthright of her natural resources because Lansing plays first the game of politics, leaving the welfare of the State and its people a secondary matter."

Curwood's active role in Michigan conservation began early in the 1920s. His target: the new Michigan Department of Conservation. Seeking to improve the efficiency of state government, the state's governor, Alex Groesbeck, called in his first message to the legislature for the consolidation of the state's Public Domain Commission; game, fish, and forest fire commissioner; the Board of Fish Commissioners; the Board of Geological Survey; and the state Park Commission in the new agency. The legislature responded early in the 1921 session, passing a law empowering the department to "protect and conserve the natural resources of the state of Michigan."[17] Headed by a director appointed by the governor with the advice and consent of the state Senate, the department would be administered by a seven-member commission also named by the governor. Legislation establishing the Public Domain Commission in 1909 had named specific state officers to the panel, but now the governor would have a free hand to appoint commissioners, limited only by the mandate to make "special reference to their training and experience along the line of one or more of the activities vested in the department of conservation and their ability and fitness to deal therewith."

The initial appointments to the new Conservation Commission included two of the biggest names in the state's natural resource fields—*Detroit News* outdoor writer Albert Stoll and Filibert Roth, the early advocate of reforestation in Michigan, now a much-beloved forestry professor at the University of Michigan known as "Daddy Roth" to his students and graduates. But Curwood was suspicious of the commission's ability to manage conservation. The new director of the department it oversaw, John Baird, had ample credentials for the job, having served as the state's game, fish, and forest fire commissioner. But he was also a former state legislator, active in the Republican Party, and a supporter of the governor. Curwood believed that political patronage was interfering with effective enforcement of the state's game and fish laws.

By the fall of 1921 Curwood's anger was growing. In a letter to Stoll, he expressed outrage.

> *For six weeks I investigated simply how the wardens throughout the state, and particularly in the northern part,* DID NOT *do their duty. The average warden is picked out not for efficiency, but largely according to his popularity as a vote-getter in his particular section. . . . I can put my hand on wardens in this state who have hunted and fished out of season.*[18]

Not yet ready to launch his attack, Curwood managed to obtain a commission as a special unpaid deputy game and fish warden from Baird and

toured the north woods of Michigan in November 1921, making "a very intimate investigation" of fish and game enforcement. In a letter to Baird,
Curwood said he had found blatant poachers in the remote regions of the
Upper Peninsula, naming eight who he said kill deer "all the year round." He
estimated the communities of Skanee and Aura in Baraga County accounted
for 1,000 illegal deer kills each year. Curwood charged that the local game
warden had not only failed to stop the slaughter but had encouraged others
to break the law. He suggested that Baird should take action.

But while the tone of the letter indicates a desire to help the department,
Curwood had already made up his mind about Baird. After a September meeting of the Conservation Commission, Curwood concluded that it "can only
do what he [Baird] wants it to do or allows it to do. Before we can create big
results we must get rid of such men as John Baird and the Governor."

Organizing a mass meeting of 800 sportsmen and politicians at the Elks
Temple in Flint on December 9, 1921, Curwood laid out the results of his
investigation. He accused Baird and the department of spoiling the state's
conservation efforts through the appointment of favored political friends, lax
enforcement of laws, and unwillingness to restore the state's forests and clean
up its streams. He released a letter from a Kent County state representative
who alleged that two or three deputy game warden appointments there "had
been made solely for political purposes," rewarding the local manager of the
Groesbeck gubernatorial campaign and a "political henchman." Curwood
called for the formation of a Michigan conservation league to serve as a cat-
alyst for public education and organizing and also called for the election of
a governor and selection of a conservation commission on a "conservation
platform."

In that speech and interviews the same month Curwood blasted the state's
forest fire protection efforts, saying that there had been 1,422 forest fires in
1919 and 1920 with losses of $100 million, while few wardens patrolled the
woods. He attacked Baird for failure to punish a garbage facility on the
Huron River for killing "tons and tons of fish." He lamented the increasing
dependence of Michigan on other states for wood products and said the state
was not doing enough to reforest the north. Meanwhile, Curwood said, the
department was putting out publicity saying wildlife populations were
rebounding and the natural resource picture was brightening.

The charges of the world-famous novelist generated front-page headlines
across the state and approving editorial comment. The *Flint Daily Journal* ran
a front page headline, "Curwood Blames Politics for Conservation Evils," and
reported: "Charges made by James Oliver Curwood of Owosso that the
Michigan department of conservation is being diverted from its original purpose into a political machine which has for its aim the spending of moneys
where they will do the most good—for the politicians—put a new issue up to
Governor Groesbeck. Not alone the sportsmen, but the whole class of
Michigan taxpayers in general, will be interested in what the governor has to
say on the subject."[19]

Baird did not take Curwood's offensive lying down. Disputing the charges of rampant deer poaching in the Upper Peninsula, he launched a counterattack, suggesting Curwood had political ambitions. In December he demanded Curwood's deputy game and fish warden commission back in light of "recent utterances by you." Curwood replied sarcastically, "I congratulate you on your broadness of mind in re-calling my Deputy Game Warden Commission. You have undoubtedly noticed that the entire state press is almost solidly condemning you for the pettiness of such an act on your part. However, I am returning the commission cheerfully."[20]

Curwood was not universally acclaimed. Even some sportsmen had their doubts. In the February 1922 *Michigan Sportsman,* Edward Weeks asked teasingly, "Did James Oliver Curwood have hard luck in his hunting trip last fall? Did the loss of his fine bird dog leave him in a mental state that made him think all the game birds and game fish had been slaughtered when his dog was killed?" Weeks accused Curwood of mistaking natural fluctuations in wildlife and fish populations, some caused by the previous year's hot summer, for the results of state neglect and mismanagement. He said that Baird and the conservation department "are back of us fellows fighting, and working for our sports."[21] But a growing number of sportsmen agreed with Curwood.

Sometimes implicit and sometimes explicit in Curwood's commentary, and that of others who preceded and followed him, was the argument that conservation could only succeed if it was implemented and maintained for the long term. Politicians, geared to their survival in the next election, were too prone to abandon or corrupt the cause for short-term benefits. Michigan's politicians had stood by while the forests were stripped from the land and had done too little to check advancing pollution. Only a system that buffered the conservation department and program from politics could restore what had been lost.

Curwood had to defend himself against a newspaper report that he had said half of the Upper Peninsula's population hunted year-round without regard to hunting seasons, an exaggeration that northern sportsmen said undercut support for his proposed reforms. He corrected the error—claiming it was a misquote—but enthusiastically prepared for more attacks: "I must have some red-hot NEW stuff," he wrote to a friendly journalist. "One or two more shots and we will have them on the jump." He asked for information on conditions in the Saginaw River, which ran through Baird's home turf, and inquired about rumors that Baird had bought a poached deer. The campaign became deeply personal.

Curwood was not alone in his impatience with the policies of Baird and Groesbeck. Filibert Roth, in a passionate six-page letter written to Curwood after the two had met, urged the writer on, saying:

> [F]orestry needs you very much. . . . The going of the forest has called for effort to use the land otherwise; it has stimulated the pernicious land barter; has created land-development societies, and will do very much more in this direction. Our North Counties, once filled with poor settlers, ruled by pauper farming,

will be as barren of animal wildlife as of trees. . . . We need real appropriations,
we need real leaders.

After Curwood's Flint talk, Roth praised him for kindling a "counter-
fire," saying that the Michigan forestry movement of the first years of the century had fallen short of its goals because it was not a people's movement.
Curwood, he said, was raising conservation issues to the general consciousness for the first time. "As to our commission," he wrote, "it is doing nothing
beyond the routine of its component parts. . . . The great task of telling the
people the exact truth, the entire seriousness of the situation, the wretched-
ness of our bankrupt northern half of the State, the tremendous task, the
necessity for this task in view of our increasing dependence on lumber and
timber in the far West, all this work is not even planned, and the trained personnel [are] not even secured."[22]

Roth himself quit the Conservation Commission at the end of 1922, at
least partly out of frustration that the department was not doing enough to
promote reforestation. When Roth retired from the faculty at the
University of Michigan, Curwood wrote the president of the university to
call Roth "a great man . . . who is not only a teacher but a man who is the
guiding-star for the state at large; a man whose ideas must pass beyond the
classroom and be present before hundreds of thousands instead of hundreds." In a private note to Roth's colleague, Professor Russell Watson,
Curwood urged the two men to "come out broadcast in the press at the present time, giving the true conditions which brought about Professor Roth's
resignation from the Conservation Commission. . . . [T]he entire state
knows that Professor Roth is the best man in Michigan we could possibly
have on the Commission."

The war between Curwood and Baird—and the governor—continued for
five years. In late 1922 Curwood, dubbed "a publicity-hawg" by outdoor
writer Harold Titus, again landed in the newspaper headlines, calling the
Groesbeck team "political bunglers" and demanding the resignations of Baird
and Albert Stoll of the Conservation Commission. Curwood said an order by
Baird pulling game wardens off their regular duties to trap predators was the
last straw. "I believe in the absolute divorce of the conservation department
of Michigan from politics," he wrote.[23]

Much to Curwood's dismay, Groesbeck was reelected in both 1922 and
1924, and Baird continued to serve as director of the conservation department.
But there were signs that the Curwood campaign was winning support. In
early 1923 a sportsman from Vassar wrote in support of more Curwood
charges. "Things need cleaning up," the sportsman wrote. "Conservation has
entirely lost its meaning in the vocabulary of words, as pertaining to the protection of our game." Another wrote Curwood to complain that Baird had
suppressed news of an illegal elk killing in northern Michigan "because of the
social and political standing of the offenders." A third charged that the deputy

warden in Hillsdale County had been fired, despite an exemplary record, because he arrested a man furnishing fish to well-connected men in Hillsdale. The warden's replacement was the defeated Republican primary candidate for sheriff, the man wrote.

Curwood's chance to separate politics from conservation came, ironically, in the form of a successful politician. Turning back fellow Republican Groesbeck's bid for a fourth term in 1926, Fred Green rolled to an easy victory over his Democratic opponent that fall. Cultivating cordial relations with Green, Curwood said he was not interested in serving as director of the conservation department as some sportsmen's organizations suggested, but he happily accepted the governor's appointment to the Conservation Commission in January 1927. Newspaper reaction was mostly positive, with the hometown *Owosso Argus Press* reminding readers that Curwood had "fired the first bombardment in what was designed to be one of the biggest wars fought for the preservation of the state's natural resources." But memories of Curwood's attacks on Upper Peninsula hunters had not faded. The *Escanaba Daily Press* accused him of launching vicious attacks on Baird, adding that "among genuine conservationists, he is known as a theorist and more of a conversationalist than a conservationist."[24]

Once appointed to the commission, the tireless Curwood did not wait a beat. Three days after his appointment, he requested a half-hour meeting with Green and the new director of the conservation department, University of Michigan professor Leigh Young, to "outline constructive work which is not only logical and feasible, but with which I feel you will be in full accord."

Curwood's determination to right what he perceived as great wrongs done to the state's natural resources left little room for compromise or delay. He began to annoy fellow members of the commission, five of them appointed by Green, with his restless desire to push ahead. But the content of his program also staggered some of them. He wanted to close down or sharply limit seasons on several game species in order to restore what he regarded as troublingly low populations. He surveyed sportsmen about closing the partridge season for three to five years, setting off a controversy that the governor suggested he calm by proposing a closure one year at a time. Curwood told sportsmen in Roscommon and Crawford Counties that they should petition to close the deer season there because the deer "are worth tremendously more to you people alive than dead."[25] He also proposed that hunting only of antlered bucks be permitted during deer season, that all feeder streams be permanently closed to fishing, and that trout sanctuaries be established on every trout stream. Curwood's conversion had been so fundamental that he regarded many sportsmen as a low priority. "Today conservation thinks of our forests and wild life first, and of the man with the gun last," he told Green. An outdoor writer later observed, "Small wonder that many sportsmen came to vigorously oppose Curwood, who once would have been regarded as 'the sportsman's sportsman.'"[26]

Neither the governor nor Curwood's fellow commissioners were ready for the revolutionary reforms he proposed. By the summer of 1927, after just six months on the commission, he was complaining that he was tired of resistance to his constant and somewhat futile efforts. "I am growing tired—tired of fighting against the archaic ideas of the institution which calls itself a Conservation Department but which is in reality a butcher-shop," he wrote fellow commissioner Lee Smits.[27] At the August meeting of the commission, a majority tabled Curwood's motion to ban the hunting of "spikehorn" deer, which he said legitimized the slaughter of does. It was his last reform bid. Already sickened with a fever at the meeting, he retired to his bed shortly afterward and died August 13, 1927, of a streptococcus infection.

But Curwood had left two legacies, one immediate and one far reaching. One of his last projects on the commission and one of his last meetings had concerned the rescue of a superb stand of virgin white pine. In July, he had pushed through the commission a resolution supporting the acquisition by the state of the "Grayling Pine"—described by Curwood as the last remaining stand of high-grade virgin white and Norway pine in the entire state.[28] The Salling-Hanson Company had offered to sell the 78-acre forest island, and another 8,300 acres of cutover land, for $83,500. Although Curwood was unable to complete negotiations on the sale before his death, Karen B. Hartwick, daughter of one of the original partners in the company, bought the land and gave it to the state in the fall of 1927. She asked that a memorial building at the park be named after her late husband, Major Edward Hartwick, who died in military service during World War I. Today Hartwick Pines State Park, northeast of Grayling, preserves a 47-acre untouched remnant of Michigan's natural white pine heritage.

An equally significant Curwood legacy was his fierce advocacy of shutting partisan politics out of conservation. His half decade of public crusading for a "conservation commission on a conservation platform" aroused statewide attention and brought to the masses, for the first time, the importance of locking in place conservation policies whose benefits would transcend generations. Born of his outrage about the decline in the quantity of wildlife in Michigan and the quality of his own cherished Shiawassee River, Curwood's fight pushed the public debate farther in the direction of conservation than a more mild approach could have, even as it alienated him from many potential supporters.

In his last magazine article, published several months after his death, Curwood also spoke of the healing powers and spiritual value of the outdoors in terms Michigan had rarely heard prior to that time. He described a friend who had gone numb to life after his wife died. Curwood took him out into a wood and sat with the man, hearing "the musical ripple of a creek," watching a squirrel gnawing on a nut, enjoying a warbler's song, and noting the ambling of a woodchuck. The friend, Curwood said, had awakened again through this and other nature experiences: "He has brought himself down out of the clouds of man's egoism, and is learning and taking strength from nature, which he now worships as the great 'I am.'"

Curwood described his own attitude toward nature in similar terms and said it was "almost Indian," which he said might be due to the fact his great-grandmother was a Mohawk. "If I did not believe a tree had a soul I could not believe in a God. If someone convinced me that the life in a flower or the heart in a bird were not as important as these same things in my own body I would no longer have faith in a hereafter. . . . Nature speaks to every heart in the same language."

He predicted that conservation would within "the next few years . . . be recognized as the most vital problem in our existence, for so overwhelming has man's power become, so easy is it for him to exterminate entire species and forms of life, and so terribly has he already upset nature's balance that, unless he halts immediately, ruin and desolation lie ahead of him." Women, Curwood said, were a prime source of hope for conservation because of their "powerful influence." He said that Michigan's legislature and all legislatures would be compelled to act for the greater good. "But the voice of the multitudes must be heard before this can happen."

The great change in humanity's relationship with the environment would come more slowly than Curwood predicted, and yet some reforms that he championed followed closely upon the end of his life. In 1929, the legislature amended the act creating the department of conservation to create staggered terms for members—thus limiting the authority of any one governor to appoint his cronies in a single term. And it gave the commission, not the governor, the power to appoint the director of the department. This would become the rallying point—the untouchable pillar of the state's natural resources recovery—for Michigan's conservationists during the next 60 years.

Politicians quickly tested the strength of the pillar. After the Democratic sweep of the 1932 elections, the long-out-of-power party sought opportunities for patronage that it had not been able to enjoy for years. State senator George Cutler of Luther introduced a bill early in the 1933 session abolishing the Conservation Commission and restoring the direct appointment of the agency head to the governor. But a vigilant outdoor press opposed the move. In the April 23 editions of the Booth newspaper chain, outdoor editor Ben East reproduced a letter Cutler had sent to a constituent, thanking the man for speaking up in favor of Stephen Weaver's candidacy to become the conservation officer in Mason County. Cutler also favored Weaver's appointment, but conservation department director George Hogarth had told the senator that the appointment was made by a competitive civil service exam.

"I think in a short time we can get at Mr. Hogarth in such a way that he will make this appointment and am sure that will go a long way in clearing up the situation here in Mason County," Cutler wrote.

East asked rhetorically in his article, "Does the fact that [Cutler] failed in his attempt to 'muscle in' on the conservation department and obtain the appointment of Weaver through political pressure account for his introduction of a bill that would put the conservation department back under the political spoils system, with no commission and a director named by the governor with the approval of the senate?"[29] The front-page publicity had its effect. Within days Democrats as well as Republicans were condemning the proposal. Cutler backed down and the bill went nowhere.

But every few years, a new governor or new legislators would become impatient with their inability directly to influence the department's operations. In addition to wishing to influence staff appointments, they sought to spur the department to relax hunting and fishing restrictions or make resources available to favored constituents.

A bill to give the governor the power to appoint the conservation department director shocked sportsmen into action in 1937 after it passed the state House of Representatives. The Kent County Conservation League, with the help of outdoor editor East, appealed by telegram to 19 persons and clubs for help. The temporary coalition born from the meeting of this group defeated the legislation in the state Senate. Leaders of the coalition agreed that a more permanent organization was needed to help keep politics out of conservation for good. On November 9, 1937, representatives of 35 clubs met to draft and approve a constitution to create a new organization, the Michigan United Conservation Clubs (MUCC). Representing an estimated 6,000 club members in 1937, the new MUCC would speak for more than 100,000 by the end of the century. Whenever politicians sought to abolish the Conservation Commission or give the governor direct appointment power for the department director, MUCC would organize a fierce counterattack.

And during each of those fights it would be remembered that the organizing meeting of MUCC in November 1937 took place at the Owosso clubhouse of the Shiawassee Conservation Club—a building paid for and donated to the club by the late James Oliver Curwood.

CHAPTER 7

The Lady of the Parks

In the sixty years that I have been on the scene I've seen outdoors recreation grow from a few people in double buggies to multitudes of people in millions and millions of cars. I'm satisfied it won't stop when we do.

—Genevieve Gillette

*T*he message of Michigan's conservation pioneers did not always receive a warm welcome. Challenging the prevailing wisdom of their age, they were often regarded as impractical dreamers or even as crackpots. Their personalities also contributed to the reception they were given. Few of the biggest names in Michigan's march toward national conservation leadership were cuddly or cloying.

Sportsman William B. Mershon regularly threw up his hands in disgust at the failures of the legislature and the foolishness of his opponents and threatened to retire from the fray. James Oliver Curwood brushed aside objections, ridiculed critics, and relished personal attacks on his enemies. And Emma Genevieve Gillette, whose life was devoted to the expansion of Michigan's parks, offended some with her penchant for the spotlight, her earthy and sometimes caustic words, and her doggedness in the face of constant resistance. But like the other pioneers, she was successful because she was single-minded in the pursuit of her cause.

Also like the others, she had developed her affection for the outdoors in childhood. Born in 1898, she moved with her parents in 1901 to a farm on the Grand River near Dimondale, just southwest of Lansing. Gillette fondly remembered the landscape, which included a scenic beech-maple woods and a brook that tumbled down into it from a stony pasture. "No one around us in the country in those days had a telephone, so we were surprised all the first summer by the arrival of strangers in double buggies or hay wagons all in a gala mood. They would come to the door and ask if they could use our river bank that day for their picnic. Of course we never refused."[1] In fact, as soon as she was old enough, Gillette became the tour guide for the visitors, showing them to the water pump or providing a cake of ice from the family's icehouse. Gillette's mother said that the family should share the beauty of the land with those who did not have it, a lesson that made a deep impression on her daughter.

The young girl adored her father, David Gillette, the general manager of an agricultural implement company before the family's move to the farm. One day in the second grade her teacher grew angry at Gillette's lack of mathematics ability and threatened to lock her in the schoolhouse overnight. The next day she walked as far as the brook but stayed there while her classmates continued to school. "Finally here I was along the brook on a nice sunny day having the best time you could imagine, I had found a nice bed of pretty white flowers that were in bloom by the brook and I was picking some of them when along comes my father. . . . [W]e played by the brook for quite a long while" before her father coaxed her to go to school, Gillette remembered. By the same brook, she said, "my father would kneel down beside me and he would say, 'Bunny, can you hear what it says? The brook is talking to us. The brook is singing to us. It's a happy brook.'"[2] Surrounded by large trees, mostly elms, the brook attracted kingfishers and an occasional heron.

Two blows fell hard on this idyllic childhood. First, Consumers Power Company, the region's electric utility, proposed to build a dam and create an impoundment that would consume the family's beloved woods. David Gillette was reluctant to sell his land for the impoundment but ultimately did so after retaining timber rights because adjacent landowners had agreed to the plan. The trees were logged. "Nobody ever came after that to have a picnic in the place and it . . . has looked like a no-man's land ever since, just growing up to second growth and being a very poor asset and the worst of it is the impoundment never went in," Genevieve Gillette remembered. The loss of this treasured natural haven persisted in her memory.

The second and greater loss was the death of her father when Genevieve was 15. Half a century later she remembered accompanying his casket to Lansing's Mount Hope Cemetery in a snowstorm. "To me the end of everything had come. I idolized my father."

Yet she and her mother carried on. A year after David Gillette's death, Genevieve graduated from high school and enrolled in Michigan Agricultural College (MAC). But she was not sure what to study. She initially decided to take a class nicknamed "dumb sci," which she thought meant Latin. Gillette was disgusted to realize upon arrival at the college that she was taking a course in domestic science—sewing. "And I came home so, just so impossibly disillusioned about college completely and stamped my foot and said I was not going to take what those girls were taking." She met with the president of the college, Frank Kedzie, whom her father had known. Kedzie invited her to sit in on a chemistry class, which promptly led to an interest in plant pathology. That, in turn, led a professor to suggest that Gillette take landscape architecture. It was a fortuitous discovery; she took to this field of study with enthusiasm.

The first female graduate in the program when she finished at MAC in 1920, Gillette faced her next challenge—where to get a job. After sending out dozens of applications, she had only one offer. Jens Jensen of Chicago, a renowned landscape architect and designer of parks and natural gardens, needed an assistant. The work was not what she had sought—she chiefly provided office support—but under the guidance of the 60-year-old Jensen the young woman found her true calling.

On her first visit to his office, Gillette strolled up to his easel and asked Jensen about the plan covering it. He said, "That's a state park for the state of Illinois." Gillette had never heard of a state park, but Jensen opened her eyes to the term and to much else. A proponent of native landscapes, including the prairies of Illinois, Jensen incubated a passion in his young assistant not only for the establishment of recreation grounds but also for the preservation of natural areas for scientific and educational purposes. The two remained friends until Jensen's death in 1951.

After working with Jensen until 1924, Gillette left his employ with the mandate "to go home and make parks."[3] She moved to Detroit to work for Harry Breitmeyer and Sons, a family of florists and nurserymen. There she was able to make a comfortable living during business hours while devoting much of her spare time to the development of Michigan's parks. For nearly a half century she would continue this pattern, earning her living as a landscape architect while contributing hundreds of hours per year, tens of thousands of volunteered hours over her lifetime.[4] She and the state parks system would come of age together.

Even while still in the employ of Jensen, Gillette had joined the Michigan parks movement. Around 1922, she attended a meeting near Ludington of a group calling itself Friends of the Native Landscape. Composed in large part of Chicago and Michigan professionals who summered on Lake Michigan, the group took on, as one of its projects, the creation and expansion of Ludington State Park.

Michigan's park system was still in its infancy. Congress had authorized a new agency, the National Park Service, in 1916. Its first director, Stephen Mather, prodded states to establish their own park systems for areas of scenic, scientific, or recreational value that were not quite up to national standards. In the waning years of the state Public Domain Commission, Michigan's legislature had authorized the body to accept gifts and grants of property as parks. In 1917 the legislature appropriated funds for the purchase of a 200-acre scrap of virgin white pine at Interlochen as the state's first independently established park.[5] Two years later, the legislature created the state Park Commission and empowered it to create a system of state parks. The parks and their administration were consolidated in the new Department of Conservation in 1921.

While the first state park advocates in the 1880s had suggested a giant reserve in northern lower Michigan to provide a refuge for game animals and to protect the headwaters of major rivers, the parks created early in the new century had more to do with providing recreation for the public. The relatively new form of transportation known as the automobile provided unprecedented mobility to tens of thousands, and the explosion of population in Michigan's southeast corner created a constituency for parks. While the "wastelands" of the north were emptying out after the collapse of lumbering and the failure of the lands to support agriculture, the Detroit area was growing rapidly as it became the hub of the auto industry. Providing convenient places for factory workers and their families to enjoy the outdoors was an important impulse behind the expansion of the state parks system.

After only two years, the state owned 22 small parks with a total of around 1,500 acres.[6] The potential of the parks to boost tourism, as well as educate the public about the outdoors, was already exciting businesses and journalists alike. In an article entitled "Michigan: The Ideal Summers Resort for Tourists," the *Detroit News* noted that tourists had spent $67 million the previous year in Wisconsin and quoted the secretary of the private Michigan State Good Roads Association as saying, "Michigan's resorts are far superior to those of Wisconsin." The article touted the scenery and facilities at such units as Grand Haven, Orchard Beach (near Manistee), and Traverse City State Parks. The Lake Michigan parks were especially valuable, said Secretary Bert Wickham of the state Park Commission, because the lake "presents an effectual barrier against the hot prairie and plain winds that sweep in from the south and west, absorbing the heat they bear and storing it for release during the winter months." And the northern part of the state itself cast a special spell, said Wickham in language reminiscent of a tourist brochure: "The charm is not only in the cool and constant lake breeze, not alone in the variety of scenery, in the white sands of the lake, the continuous stretches of virgin forest, the many tumbling trout streams, but in an intangible something which breathes of vacation, rest and recreation."[7]

The 1922 meeting that Gillette attended near Ludington was apparently designed, at least in part, to discuss how scenic lands just north of the city might be protected. Gillette said that native landscape lovers from Michigan as well as Chicago flocked to the home of a physicist with a home in the dunes. There, she remembered, they put on a play dramatizing the threats to the area. A woodland fawn was menaced by lumberers and then by developers. When a builder began to strip the fawn's beloved groves, the animal sadly retired from the land. But Friends of the Native Landscape rallied the fawn, assuring it that they would work to protect its home.[8] Shortly afterward, the state received a gift of 300 acres to begin Ludington State Park. Within a decade local supporters had raised $25,000 to supplement state money and create a park of over 3,000 acres by the time of its official opening in 1934. Gillette believed the 1922 Friends meeting had whetted the enthusiasm of the community for the park.

Gillette's ally in this and many other parks efforts for the next three decades was P. J. Hoffmaster, the first superintendent of the state parks and an acquaintance from her days at MAC. After military service in World War I, Hoffmaster set out to create one of the best state parks systems in the country, dedicated to providing access for all citizens to the outdoors. In his first annual report as the parks chief of the Department of Conservation, Hoffmaster made the following statements: "What Michigan has done in this respect in the past few years is but prophetic of what she will accomplish in the years to come. . . . It should be borne in mind that the park sites established by the State of Michigan are the pleasure grounds of everyone. There is no class distinction. There is no clannish discrimination. They are established and maintained by the people of the State for the enjoyment of their friends and themselves."[9]

But for a while Hoffmaster had to content himself with a slapdash system thrown together without plans and with inadequate funding. Most of the early parks were gift lands—and not all would have qualified for a state park system on their natural merits. On a shoestring appropriation of $150,000 for 1920 and 1921, the Park Commission accepted the first two dozen park sites and made improvements at 17, such as roads, bathrooms, and drinking water wells. It asked for $139,500 for 1922 and $137,500 for 1923 before it was abolished and the parks program moved into the Department of Conservation. The move immediately reduced the parks staff and, as Hoffmaster acidly commented, resulted in less than 15 percent of the funding the old commission had sought.

This setback did not deter him from dreaming of better things. Hoffmaster and Department of Conservation director John Baird sought funding and authorization to continue rapid expansion of the system with worthy sites, including some in the Upper Peninsula.

Hoffmaster's vision also encompassed parks closer to population centers. In the 1920s Gillette arranged a meeting between the parks chief and Jens Jensen to discuss the need for Michigan recreation sites close to Detroit. Already endowed with a scattering of parks in Oakland, Monroe, and Livingston Counties by the automaking Dodge Company and four units contributed by Dodge attorney Howard Bloomer, the state system would never gain much ground in Wayne County, Detroit's home. But Hoffmaster and Gillette teamed up in the 1940s to scout out the potential of land that would become Kensington Metropark, a jewel in the necklace of Detroit-area regional parks established by a special governmental authority. Hoffmaster also convinced the legislature to purchase 46,000 acres of recreational lands 35 to 60 miles from the center of metropolitan Detroit: "We recognize, now, that where there are great concentrations of people there must be provided such facilities and opportunities for recreation as will help maintain health, both physical and mental."[10]

Gillette's close friendship with Hoffmaster worked in other ways. She was dispatched by the parks superintendent to examine potential state park sites on weekends, and she remembered sleeping on a bed of ferns at the lower falls of the Tahquamenon in the eastern Upper Peninsula about 1933, having taken four hours to drive the 21 miles from Paradise on a narrow trail. Along with outdoor writers who touted the area's many beauties, Gillette promoted acquisition of the falls as a park. It became one in 1947. Gillette was also helpful in bringing Hartwick Pines into the state's possession and protection; she is said to have spoken to a friend of Karen Hartwick and encouraged the transfer of the land that became Hartwick Pines State Park (see chap. 6) to the Department of Conservation. She arranged popular bird and wildflower exhibits, films and photographs by the Department of Conservation at the Detroit Flower Shows of the late 1920s and early 1930s, educating great numbers of urban Michiganians about the beauty and value of these natural resources.

Gillette was professionally active on many fronts. Through Jensen, who had designed the Dearborn Inn, Greenfield Village, and houses for the Henry Ford family, Gillette became familiar with the auto magnate and his wife, Clara, who became a good friend. The Fords supported Gillette's participation in Detroit mayor Frank Murphy's Thrift Garden program. Henry Ford arranged for his company's tractors to plow the gardens. An anonymous donor, who turned out to be U.S. senator Frank Couzens, provided thousands of dollars for the depression-era project. Gillette also drew up the master plan for the city center of Lakeland, Florida, in 1925 and became landscape architect for a federally funded housing project west of Pontiac, in Oakland County. An affordable housing project designed to meet the needs of families during the depression, Westacres provided commons for each family to raise vegetables, fruit, and chickens.[11] Gillette's successes won her additional commissions from Ferris State College in Big Rapids, the Starr Commonwealth school near Albion, and Albion College. Albion gave her an honorary doctorate upon her retirement.

By the mid-1930s Gillette was well enough known to be featured in a newspaper series on the opinions of leading Detroit-area citizens. In the sixteenth installment of the series, Gillette expounded on what she would do if she were the director of the state Department of Conservation.

> *I would take technically trained people of vision and ability and strive to build such an effective and efficient departmental organization that politics would find it hard to do any traveling in conservation circles. . . . Our State Park Department would not be in its present embarrassing position. Imagine having to play host to 9,000,000 tourists every summer and having to beg year after year for funds.*

She also said she would provide free admission to state parks and install a biology teacher in each park as a naturalist during the summer.[12]

Her concerns about the parks were well founded. After a sluggish start—only 220,000 people visited state parks in 1922—the popularity of the parks increased suddenly and dramatically. During most of the 1930s attendance ran at about 8 to 9 million visitors annually. But state funding for the parks did not keep pace. For the rest of her volunteer career, Gillette would cajole, plead with, and sometimes lecture state lawmakers to get better support of the park system.

She was able to do so in part because of her singular devotion to the cause. Gillette said she could never see herself tending to a baby and domestic chores, but undoubtedly her success in protecting the parks cost her considerable personal comfort and happiness. She never married and was adamant in her oral reminiscences that even a close alliance such as her partnership with Hoffmaster "never [had] any romance about it." It was "founded on a common interest in conservation achievements to be made."

Her friend would become the longest-serving director of the Department of Conservation in the century, running the agency from 1934 until 1951. One of Hoffmaster's greatest accomplishments—one that also reflects well on Governor Harry Kelly and an Ironwood businessman named Raymond Dick—was the acquisition of the land that would become Porcupine Mountains State Park.

The "largest unbroken tract of virgin hardwood timber in the U.S.," according to a Department of Conservation description, the Porcupine Mountains area encompassed 130,000 acres in Gogebic and Ontonagon Counties on the shores of Lake Superior in the western Upper Peninsula. Although not towering by Appalachian or Rocky Mountain standards, the Porcupines ranged as high as 1,420 feet above Lake Superior and provided countless scenic recesses. Hemlocks covered the lower altitudes, while sugar maples and oak spread over the ridges and upper valleys. Untouched white pines fringed rivers and streams. The Lake of the Clouds sat on a tableland high above the surrounding country, ridges on its flanks offering expansive views of Lake Superior and adjacent peaks. The mountains "are startling in their infinite variety of cool, dense forests; breath-taking heights; roaring and rumbling waterfalls; and awe inspiring vistas," said the department in its booklet describing its hopes to purchase a recreation area.[13] But there was a threat: "Logging companies are nibbling at the fringes and promise to invade the interior at an early date. The country they have left behind them is typical hardwood cut over land cleared of all standing timber except the defective trees. This should not happen to the Porcupine Mountains."

As early as 1925, Hoffmaster had proposed a state park in the area, his first recommendation calling for a minimum buy of 22,000 acres. He had written in a letter to Department of Conservation director John Baird that the area contained the highest point in the United States between the Alleghenies and the Black Hills, noting, "No other place in Michigan contains the extensive rock formations—bold cliffs and striking topography; no other portion typifies so well primitive Michigan with untouched forests."[14] But the legislature had never appropriated the money.

In 1943 the department was joined by conservationists. The legendary Aldo Leopold wrote in the May 1942 issue of *Outdoor America* that the remaining unlogged land in the Porcupines was "a symbol. It portrays a chapter in national history which we should not be allowed to forget. When we abolish the last sample of the Great Uncut, we are, in a sense, burning books. . . . To preserve a remnant of decent forest for public education is surely a proper function of government, regardless of one's view on the moot question of large-scale timber production." Michigan outdoor writer Ben East also decried the potential loss of the Porcupine forest, lamenting, "The mistakes made in the great pine harvest 50 to 75 years ago, mistakes Michigan still has ample cause to regret, are being repeated day by day in the hardwood country of the Porcupines."[15]

Raymond Dick, an Ironwood feed and grain businessman, was already on the case. "As one walks through these dimmed forest aisles with the rays of the sun slanting through the treetops, and the ground soft under foot and free from underbrush, one feels a sense of reverence and peace," he had written of the Porcupine Mountains.[16] In 1940 he had established the Save the Porcupine Mountains Association, an unusually effective lobbying instrument that eventually included in its membership Vice President Henry Wallace, the director of the National Park Service, former governor Chase Osborn, and Leopold. Dick invited Governor Kelly to visit the area. Kelly, who had lost a leg in World War I, was only able to get to the mouth of the Presque Isle River, but he committed himself to the project. In a special message to the legislature in early 1944, he asked the legislature for a $5 million appropriation to help buy land in the Porcupines as well as southeast Michigan parklands. He said that the area should be "purchased for preservation as a timber museum" to hold the land in trust for future generations. The legislature acted with unusual swiftness, appropriating the money before the end of February. But the Porcupines were not yet safe.

Debate in the legislature had revealed the problem. Rep. William G. Stenson had filibustered for 90 minutes against the bill, seeking an amendment to permit private interests to remove "dead timber" from the park area. Although defeated 63–2, the amendment signaled the interest of timber companies in getting at hardwoods in the Porcupines, whose value was inflated because of World War II needs. Lumberman Gordon Connor had asked the legislature to carve out 8,000 acres from the proposed 43,000-acre park but had been refused. Only 2,880 acres, or about one-third of the Connor holdings, were excluded. In response, he accelerated his timber cutting. In a letter to Hoffmaster, he made the following comment: "You perhaps do not realize we are the largest producer of lumber and lumber products in the Lake States." He renewed his request to exclude from the park timberlands owned by the company, this time asking for 2,500 acres, and enlisted the War Production Board in Washington, DC, in his bid.

Hoffmaster refused to back down. The company wanted to skin lands along the Presque Isle River, which his department said were among the most scenic in the park, and timber along the shoreline between the river mouth and the mountains. By then the company had laid track for a railroad across the Presque Isle River to cut through three-quarters of a mile of the park to get into land it owned outside the boundaries.[17] Conservation Commission chair Harry H. Whiteley said that if the railroad was built, "the Presque Isle River watershed would become a denuded waste and its beauty destroyed forever." He said the company was greedy and inflexible, adding, "I must say that in its larger aspects this case only represents the baronial concepts of the early lumber operators toward the natural resources which came within their grasp."[18]

Hoffmaster agreed to adjust the boundaries of the proposed park slightly, permitting cutting on 798 acres, but asked the Conservation Commission to initiate condemnation proceedings to take the remaining land. The commission did so in April, asking the attorney general to go to court to restrain Connor Company from cutting any of the lands now included in the park boundaries. Although the condemnation proceedings bounced around in courts for eight years, the state was able to secure the lands, and the company never touched the prime acreage.

The victory was an enormous one, celebrated nationally. "[I]t is no exaggeration to say it is being done in the nick of time," wrote Dorothea Kahn of the *Christian Science Monitor.* "The axes of lumbermen could be heard at the borders of the forest." *National Parks Magazine* editorialized, "It is little short of a miracle to have succeeded in this endeavor in the midst of a war. By so doing, Michigan has set an example to the whole nation. . . . Michigan conservationists, our hats are off to you!"

Hoffmaster's tenacity held the state firm in the face of unrelenting pressure from the company to appeal to war sentiment in order to get access to the virgin timber. It was an example of his steadiness in the job of building Michigan's conservation program. But his long service made him irreplaceable. Hoffmaster's death in 1951, Gillette said, left the department with a void of leadership. The Conservation Commission shelved plans for several parks he had hoped to develop, and the legislature further slighted the parks in annual budgeting.

By the mid-1950s, with post–World War II recreation demands peaking, the situation grew critical. It was bad enough that the Automobile Club of Michigan issued at its own expense a report entitled "The State of Our Parks." The condition of the 59 state parks and recreation areas was "not a very pretty picture," the club noted.

> [T]he luster of the jewel that is Michigan is dulled. The purpose of our parks threatens to become lost—lost not only to seven million Michiganians and millions of their fellow Americans, but to future generations as well. . . . California, for instance, spends about 45 dollars per acre per year on its parks. Michigan, on the other hand, spends only eight dollars per acre to operate and maintain its State Parks. . . . Obviously, state parks in other states are regarded as big business. The fact is that limited funds curtail services, and materially greater expenditures are needed to provide facilities and services of a quality to give credit to the state of Michigan.[19]

Attendance at the parks had climbed to 17 million in 1955, the club pointed out, arguing that there was no longer enough room for so many visitors. Camping spaces were at a premium; room to spread a towel on park beaches was scarce; sewage facilities were backing up; and some of the more popular parks were turning away visitors. Newspapers were calling the legislature penny-wise and pound-foolish for failing to invest in the system, sending tourists to other destinations. The club outlined several possible solutions for raising funds, including an admission sticker, a parking fee, admission fees, and a bond issue retired by park concession and oil and gas revenues. Or, the club suggested, the legislature could simply increase its annual appropriation to the parks and sustain it for a five-year period.

Winning approval in the capital of any of these ideas was no easy task. Politicians had regularly shortchanged the conservation department. Gillette once watched Hoffmaster's successor as director of conservation, Gerald Eddy, return to the agency from a trip to an appropriations committee. Eddy's shoulders slumped, his head hung, and he walked into his office and shut the door without speaking. "It couldn't have been any worse if it had been a funeral," Gillette said.[20]

Organizing and serving as president of the Michigan Parks Association, Gillette rounded up allies from a number of places, including the Michigan United Conservation Clubs and the United Automobile Workers. While her stubborn and persistent hectoring annoyed some who shared her goals, it was not a natural or easy thing for the now 62-year-old Gillette to work the legislature. She had spent little previous time lobbying. Yet her colleagues thought of her as indomitable. Herbert Wagner, a key figure in the Michigan Natural Areas Council, described her as "a mountain of knowledge and energy. She had a powerful, almost screaming, voice, and scared the bejesus out of the members of the State Legislature."[21]

Outwardly tough and persistent and self-described as "stout" all her life, Gillette presented a formidable appearance but was uncertain and insecure about her ability to change the minds of elected officials. She warmed up for the task by visiting her local legislator, Gilbert Bursley, taking along a book published by the U.S. Department of Interior that depicted prime shoreline park site opportunities in Michigan.

Despite the cordial reception she received from Bursley, the thought of going to Lansing was intimidating. Gillette pulled off the road three times on the way to the state capital, thinking she was silly to believe she could influence the politicians. On arriving at the capitol, she carried a heavy load of the Department of Interior books, drawing inquisitive looks from the sergeant at arms guarding the House chambers, who told her she might have been the first lobbyist for parks ever to appear there. Her first legislative target was Representative Hans Rasmussen, who chaired the Conservation Committee. Called out to speak with Gillette, he was skeptical of the parks. Gillette quoted him: "I've got a picnic table in my backyard and that does me. While we've got a nice park at Ludington, we don't go down there very often. If we have company, we have a picnic in our backyard, and that's easier and simpler." Although Gillette pointed out that many Michiganians were not fortunate enough to have such backyards, Rasmussen and some other legislators initially seemed unpersuaded. After another day of fruitless lobbying, Gillette walked out of the capitol feeling defeated. "I stood there and put my head against the door of the car and thought, 'Genevieve, you can't do this sort of thing. You've got to make more progress somehow.' I slammed the door of the car and took my stuff back into the Capitol and walked up to the door of the Senate."

Her work—and that of her allies in the Michigan Parks Association—paid off with passage in 1960 of legislation authorizing a $10 million parks improvement bond issue, the bonds to be paid off through park admission revenues. It was far less than Gillette had sought, but it was a recognition that the state needed to invest more in the parks.

Gillette did not let up with passage of the bond bill. At the request of the Parks Association, a special state legislative committee reviewed the condition of the state park system, reporting in 1963 that current funding was far from adequate to meet the needs of Michigan citizens for recreation. By 1966 the Department of Conservation estimated that $110 million was necessary to address the backlog of parks maintenance. Park supporters called for dramatic increases in state spending to meet the increasing demand for recreation. Their efforts were largely unrewarded until 1968. That year, as Governor George Romney prepared to present his annual State of the State message, Gillette spoke with an aide about his expected proposal for a large bond issue to be placed before voters that November. As Gillette remembered it, she instructed the aide to tell Romney that she and the Parks Association would not be satisfied with the $90 million bond he was thinking of proposing. The next day the aide called, saying, "Genevieve, Genevieve. [Romney] went up there and said it, $100 million . . . thanks to you."[22] When voters approved the bond in the fall election, Gillette reminisced about the long battle and the work of her many allies in her annual Christmas letter: "So much dedicated effort; ten years of thrills all the way. The best yet to come with the implementation just now beginning."

In the late 1950s Gillette received a letter from the head of the National Park Service's regional director that enlisted Gillette in one of the most important battles of her career. A small group of park supporters gathered with Park Service officials at the Michigan State University Union in East Lansing. The topic: a proposal to create a national seashore at Sleeping Bear Dunes in the northwest Lower Peninsula. The magnificent shoreline was one of the "opportunities" that had been identified in the Department of Interior's study of Great Lakes recreation sites. Gillette was initially guarded about the lakeshore proposal, doubting that sand dunes compared with the Rocky Mountains or other spectacular features of the national parks. Soon, however, she got into the spirit of things, challenging the regional director, Ronald Lee, to redraft the proposed park boundaries.

While the Park Service was concentrating on the 460-foot dunes and an adjacent recreational area around Glen Lake, popular with tourists and the wealthy as a summer resort, Gillette called Lee's attention to the mouth of the Platte River, 15 miles south of the dunes. Featuring old beach ridges that told the story of Michigan's natural history since the retreat of the last glaciers, the site reminded her of Jensen's teachings about native landscapes. She recognized that her proposal—which also included expansion of the park's boundaries to Good Harbor Bay and Pyramid Point east of the dunes—left some at the meeting aghast, but she thought Jensen, had he been alive, would have reproached her if she had not spoken up. Ultimately, the Park Service agreed with most of what Gillette proposed.

That turned out to be the easy part. Few national park proposals at the time had aroused such fierce opposition as Sleeping Bear Dunes. Introduced as legislation by U.S. senator Philip Hart of Michigan in 1960, the lakeshore idea was angrily attacked by residents of the area. The bill would have condemned the property of many who lived around Glen Lake for the park. A significant proportion of the local population also resisted the park as a federal "land grab" in an area that was doing quite well catering to tourists without the help of Uncle Sam.

The Park Service praised the region as nationally significant because of its scenic, scientific, and recreational values. The Park Service argued that the 77,000-acre park, including 45.5 miles of Lake Michigan shoreline, was urgently needed because of rapid vacation home development in the area. A growing and mobile population needed access to areas like Sleeping Bear Dunes. Beneath a photo of a deserted, sunny beach with the far-off profile of the Sleeping Bear itself, a Park Service publication contained the following questions: "The bounty of nature calls to be used and will be used but how and by whom? And in the using what will remain of the gift?"[23]

The opponents had a darker view. "This is a story of little people vs. big government," they said in a publication. "It happens to involve the people of Leelanau and Benzie Counties in northwestern Michigan. The important thing to remember as you read it is that IT COULD HAPPEN TO YOU!"[24] Some of the most vociferous opponents of the park were also among the wealthiest and best connected. U.S. representative Charlotte Reid of Illinois owned a cottage in the Glen Lake area and opposed the legislation.

Although not much troubled by a House bill introduced by U.S. representative John Dingell for a 26,000-acre lakeshore that would largely embrace land already in state or federal ownership, the Citizens Council of the Sleeping Bear Dunes Area sharply criticized the Hart bill, which included most of the areas Gillette had suggested. Council members accused Park Service officials of arrogance, of misleading area businesses about the benefits a national lakeshore would provide to tourism, and of exaggerating the scientific value of the area's geologic features.

The opponents relied on two chief arguments. First, they said, the state already had more than enough public land, with over 6.3 million acres in state and national forests alone. "Really, Senator Hart!" the council exclaimed in its publication. "Where do you draw the line on public ownership? Must Michigan be further nationalized?"

Second, the council said the lakeshore would take almost 1,600 homes, farms, and businesses. "If the power of condemnation is here granted to a federal bureau for so flimsy an excuse as recreation, no farm, home or business in America will ever be quite so safe again," the council warned. The lakeshore would "trample" property rights through a combination of outright condemnation and federal zoning of remaining private lands. The Platte Lakes Area Association termed the lakeshore proposal "just a political scheme that would run the nation right down the road to Socialism."

This was not the view of a small minority. At each congressional field hearing in the area during the early 1960s, crowds of angry park opponents overflowed the facilities. At a Traverse City hearing in November 1961, local U.S. representative Robert Griffin denounced the Hart bill: "Frankly, the citizens of this area are shocked that legislation of this nature would have been developed and introduced without first consulting with the people to be directly affected and without taking their views into account." Griffin said that the federal government was "broke" and could not afford new parks and said he could only support a much smaller park that did not intrude on private property rights.[25] Hart, who had been hung in effigy outside the site of the hearing by "a group of teen-agers and an elderly man" along with Sen. Patrick McNamara, cosponsor of his bill, and Secretary of the Interior Stewart Udall, hinted the next day that he might be open to compromise.

Termed "Phil's Folly" by the *Detroit Free Press,* the Sleeping Bear legislation died in the 1961–62 session of Congress, but Hart offered a new version in 1963. Still encompassing 77,000 acres, it relied more on rezoning of the private lands than outright acquisition. Griffin introduced his own bill, establishing a 17,000-acre park, mostly from lands already owned by the government. After a spring hearing in Washington, a U.S. Senate subcommittee came to Frankfort to hold a July 4 hearing on the new Hart proposal. Hart himself did not attend.

The fight over the lakeshore was drawing national attention. *U.S. News and World Report* observed that "feeling runs high as the battle continues. Drive through the area and you find bitterness among property owners. . . . A man whose family has owned property in the Sleeping Bear Region for more than a century [says]: 'My opinion is that if they do take over there is going to be some shooting going on.'"[26]

A crowd of 1,500 filled the Frankfort High School auditorium on July 4. When one of the senators asked supporters of the lakeshore bill to stand up, about 20 people did—including Genevieve Gillette. In testimony, Ove Jensen of the Citizens Council criticized Secretary of Interior Udall for not visiting the proposed lakeshore, in which Udall sought to include 92,000 acres, 15,000 more than the Hart bill. Private owners could better manage the area than the federal government, Jensen said.

> Promotion of this area for a proposed national park or recreation area has tacitly implied that this is a newly discovered area, whose features and beauty have been in some way overlooked or passed by—that something must be done immediately to "preserve" the area, to save it from imminent commercial exploitation and degradation. As a matter of fact, it is not new. It has been a

resort area for many, many years, and the reason it is largely unspoiled is not
an accident, but by design and determination of the people to keep it that way.[27]

Gillette had testified at the earlier hearing in Washington, making special
note of the Platte Plains area she had originally proposed for the lakeshore,
calling it "a tremendous find" for someone interested in natural history with
its sand and gravel terraces, bearberry and junipers, huckleberry and bracken
ferns, aspens, birches, pine, oak, beech, and maple. She was not enthusiastic
about challenging local sentiment and could have avoided the Frankfort hearing, but Park Service officials begged her to represent lakeshore supporters.
She began her testimony by suggesting that the auditorium audience was not
representative of the state's sentiment. Through the Michigan Parks
Association, of which she was president, and allied organizations, about
three-quarters of a million Michigan residents were on record as supporting
the lakeshore, she said.

Gillette alluded to a field trip made by the senators earlier that day to the
proposed lakeshore, saying that the areas they had inspected met the description of national parks made in 1918 by Interior Secretary Franklin Lane:
"national features extraordinary and unique—distinguished examples of
world architecture." She added:

> [National parks] provide us recreation in its fullest sense, pleasure as well as
> relaxation, development of spiritual qualities, and even for the everyday visitor
> an appreciation of and understanding of the natural phenomena and forces of
> nature. It has been said that every national park is an outdoor university where
> people can become acquainted with undisturbed plant and animal life—observe
> the wonders of the earth's formation even throughout its millions of years.
> Outstanding opportunities for this sort of thing you have seen today in the
> Sleeping Bear country.[28]

Reflecting her decades of frustration at inadequate state support for parks,
Gillette added that the area was also better off in a federal than a Michigan
park: "At the moment it has taken us 8 or 10 years to get two or three naturalists part time in our Michigan state parks."

Gillette scoffed at the arguments made by property owners that the park
would diminish the value of their holdings, pointing out that private property
adjacent to open space typically increased in value. She added, "On this 4th
of July here at this last hearing of this subcommittee, I must say that all this
talk about property rights has now worn pretty threadbare." This statement,
reported one local newspaper, "drew an unbelieving gasp from the audience."[29] Taking Gillette's comment out of context, another paper editorialized
a few days later: "With that statement Miss Gillette, an Ann Arbor resident,
who describes herself as an architect and a planner—dismissed one of the
basic tenets of American life—the right to hold property against arbitrary
seizure or limitations by government. . . . Fortunately, few of the others who
testified at Frankfort on July 4 in favor of a Sleeping Bear Dunes recreation
area were so ready to brush aside the question of property rights."[30]

Gillette was not pleased about becoming a symbol of government meddling in private lives. She said, "[W]hen I walked out of that school at noon when the meeting was over, I had good friends who lined up on either side of the sidewalk and turned their backs on me."

One of the few local residents willing to speak up for the lakeshore, Thomas House, said ruefully, "I am so well known that when I stood up for the bill—you asked for people to stand up for Mr. Hart's bill—I heard someone shout to me, 'House, the louse,' before they had heard exactly what I was going to say. It's nice to have such good friends."

The hearing did little good for the bill in the short run. "Boos Ring at Dunes Park Quiz," the *Detroit News* headlined its article. The paper observed that the ears of senators were ringing with outcries from opponents. "Boos and jeers interrupted the testimony of the supporters," the *News* added. The *Detroit Free Press* reported that Senator Milward Simpson of Wyoming received a standing ovation when he declared to the crowd his opposition to both the Hart and the Griffin bills. Although the subcommittee approved a compromise version of the bill in December 1963, containing 47,600 acres on the mainland and 32 miles of Lake Michigan shoreline, the measure died again.

The fight continued the next year. But the coalition supporting the lakeshore was growing, now encompassing the Michigan United Conservation Clubs and the United Automobile Workers, and resistance to the park slowly ebbed. Hart was undaunted, and so was Gillette. Muriel Ferris, an aide to Hart, asked Gillette to come to the nation's capital to push for the bill. Although surprised, she accepted the invitation to stay with Ferris and worked out of Hart's office, remembering "the example of having tried in the Legislature when I didn't know anything about it, and it had come off pretty well, so I thought maybe this would too." Spending more than two weeks in Washington, Gillette approached the offices of key legislators, winning a private meeting with powerful U.S. representative Wayne Aspinall, chair of the House Interior Committee. He told her he would support both the Sleeping Bear proposal and another to establish a Pictured Rocks National Lakeshore in the Upper Peninsula. The lobbying experience was mildly exhilarating. "Anyway, I began not to be frightened of those closed doors that I would have to open," Gillette said.

The fight was far from over. Still, by the late 1960s, most Michiganians favored some kind of national park at Sleeping Bear Dunes, and Gillette had strong allies in the new Mackinac chapter of the Sierra Club and the Michigan United Conservation Clubs. Formed in 1964 and officially incorporated in 1967, the Michigan chapter of the Sierra Club was particularly critical in organizing testimony and public letter writing in support of the lakeshore legislation. And the sudden invasion of the region by salmon-happy anglers and their families in 1967 and 1968 changed even local perceptions.

In a 1969 *Sierra Club Bulletin* article, state chapter chair Virginia Prentice said local residents had "staunchly clung to the belief that a horde of city-bred transients would invade the area only if the Park Service lured them in with carousels and cotton candy." But the fish had done it instead. She described the impact of heavy use of the Sleeping Bear area by the excited anglers. The mouth of the Platte River had gone from being "a lovely place for a picnic" to "a bulldozed boat-ramp and black-topped parking lot. . . . The beach area was littered with debris—the usual beer and motor oil cans, styrofoam and foil, stray items of clothing, and partially decomposed fish." She added, "Changes have been rapid and disruptive. Many indifferent observers, particularly area residents, became concerned individuals overnight."[31]

Although still challenged by many local property owners, legislation creating the Sleeping Bear Dunes National Lakeshore cleared Congress late in 1970, almost 10 years after the introduction of Hart's first proposal. It embraces a 35-mile stretch of Lake Michigan mainland shore, North and South Manitou Islands, and 56,993 federal acres. Most private lands around Glen Lake are excluded from the lakeshore, although several hundred private residences remain within its boundaries. Many owners of those residences were allowed by the 1970 legislation to remain on the land until they die, while others drew limited leases. Sleeping Bear Dunes National Lakeshore today is a natural monument of majestic, drifting sands and stunning blue waters. Gillette's friend Christopher Graham calls it "the work for which she is most remembered."

Graham came to know Gillette in the last of her active years on behalf of parks and natural areas. Serving as a member of the state's Wilderness and Natural Areas Advisory Board, she relied on the young landscape architecture student as a chauffeur. Graham also rented a room in her house after meeting her in 1974.

"I'd be sound asleep and then wake up at 7 o'clock and I'd hear her barking on the phone. She'd go to bed at 10, be up by 4:30 and start writing letters. Part of her success was she was so damned persistent," Graham said.

Although outspoken and often stubborn, Gillette was successful because she was also a good listener, Graham said. "She took a lot of time to learn, she'd ask people what was the right thing to do. Once she zeroed in on a course, she'd keep going until she attained her goal."[32]

Another ally who worked with her in later years was Ann Arbor attorney Clan Crawford, who welcomed her support in combating a proposal by the state Department of Natural Resources (DNR) to build a harbor of refuge for recreational boats at the mouth of the Platte River, near Gillette's beloved natural history display that became part of the national lakeshore. Crawford and Gillette both believed that the site should stay undeveloped. Fed in the summer by the clear waters of the Platte, the spot was perfect for family swimming. Thousands used it for that purpose on summer days. Crawford met her in Lansing to discuss the proposal with DNR officials. He said, "Genevieve had to be *handled*. She made a lot of noise. They ignored me. But they knew they had to try to win her over. She worked hard—she was incredibly persistent." The harbor-of-refuge proposal was ultimately put on the shelf.

In one sense, all of the 96 state parks that attracted more than 25 million visitors annually in the late 1990s are a testament to Gillette. But two features of Michigan's state park system serve as explicit memorials to Gillette, who died in 1986. One is the Genevieve Gillette Nature Center—appropriately housed in the state park named after her longtime ally, P. J. Hoffmaster, south of Muskegon. The other is a park whose purchase was leveraged by Gillette's life savings, which she dedicated to the protection of a special place. Thompson's Harbor State Park, on the northeast shore of Michigan's Lower Peninsula, is a rustic park with 7 1/2 miles of Lake Huron shoreline. It contains one of the largest populations of the state's threatened wildflower, the dwarf lake iris. On a chill fall day a park visitor can trudge the sandy shores and low dunes south of Rogers City, looking out over the brilliant blue of Lake Huron, and remember that this and many other peaceful parks were won by the warrior spirit of Genevieve Gillette.

CHAPTER 8

The Builders

A third of Michigan virtually is bankrupt, unable to pay its way with schools
and roads, getting poorer instead of richer from year to year, producing less and
less of value. This third of Michigan takes ten million acres or so, the most of it
being in the northern part of the Lower Peninsula, the rest in the Upper
Peninsula. . . . Whenever we get ready we can grow all the timber we want.
Growing timber is a simple affair. All you have to do is stick a little tree right
into the right sort of ground and wait.

—P. S. Lovejoy, *Detroit News,* May 24, 1920

The work of ripping down Michigan's natural resources had taken a few
scant decades. The short span from 1850 to 1900, a mere half century, was
all it took to consume the vast majority of the state's forests, wipe out several
abundant or exquisite fish and wildlife species such as the passenger pigeon
and the grayling, and forever alter the ecology of the Great Lakes. More
remarkable, it took only another half century—roughly the period from 1920
to 1970—for several generations to build a new kind of natural wealth in
Michigan. Hundreds of men and women, peopling the ranks of the state's
conservation agency and the state's major universities, were essential to the
job. Their professional and volunteer excellence won Michigan a national reputation for nonpolitical resource conservation and management. By the time
they were done, Michigan's forests were producing vast quantities of timber
again as well as rustic recreation; the state had become a hunter's paradise;
and tens of thousands of anglers were racing to get their boats in the Great
Lakes in what was fondly known as "coho madness."

The story begins with Michigan's forest builders. The barest beginnings of
the work of reforestation occurred when the legislature finally agreed to stop
dumping tax-reverted lands on the market and to accumulate a state forest
reserve in 1909. In fact, reforestation proceeded slowly for a time, far too
slowly for the likes of Professor Filibert Roth, the state's first forest warden
and an agitator for reform since 1903. He branded the new superintendent of
the state's forestry interests, the Public Domain Commission, an unworthy
steward. The first half decade of the commission's rule, Roth complained, was
the "dark ages" of Michigan forestry. The commission advanced cautiously,

not quite convinced even yet that the state's northern sand lands were unfit for agricultural development.

The legislature shared in this hesitation, amending the law creating the commission in 1911 to provide that it would also serve as an immigration commission "whose duty it is to collect and disseminate information concerning lands owned by the state . . . with a view of encouraging immigration into this state and settlement upon Michigan's undeveloped agricultural lands."[1] So while the commission set aside more than 230,000 acres in its first two years for the reserves, it enthusiastically moved to carry out the legislature's immigration mandate, vowing "to use its efforts to call the attention of the homeseeker and settler to the advantages to be derived from locating upon the good agricultural lands of this state" and to "induce the better class of immigrants from the rural districts of Europe to work as farm laborers in Michigan."

In an era when Michigan still lived in the immediate shadow of forest devastation, the commission sought to rebuild the state's appreciation of itself, said Augustus C. Carton, its secretary. "I think one of the first things the press will have to do is establish faith among Michigan's own people by advising them to look over Michigan and Michigan's opportunities before they seek other climes for investments."[2] Carton praised Michigan's potential for production of apples, beans, potatoes, sugar beets, and other farm products and lauded its railroads, shoreline, mines, and factories. Carton was especially anxious to check the stream of migration from rural areas to cities as Michigan industrialized.

By the last days of its existence in 1920, the commission was beginning to give up the dream of resettling the tax-reverted lands and was making a commitment to building a significant state forest system. It approved a plan to set aside at least 550,000 acres of state land for forestry and to plant 4,500 acres per year. Michigan's forest protection and management budget was now fourth among the states. But the menace of fire persisted; in 1919, nearly 420,000 acres of forestland burned. Clearly Michigan had much more to do in order to accumulate a forest legacy.

Enter the cantankerous, iconoclastic Parrish Storrs Lovejoy, known as P.S. A member of the University of Michigan forestry faculty from 1912 to 1921, Lovejoy was active in the Society of American Foresters and the Michigan Academy of Science. In both associations he was an early voice for scientific forest management. What distinguished him from technically likeminded foresters was his bristling impatience with politicians, sentimentalists, bureaucrats, and temporizers from all walks of life. He said the state's forestry problem was the result of "a long series of miserable fumblings, graspings, and limpings, with lack of understanding, lack of vision, lack of sense, and lack of courage so frequent as to be the rule."[3] Lovejoy annoyed and enraged land companies and northern communities with a 1920–21 series of articles in the magazine *Country Gentleman* exposing the duplicity of sales pitches to potential owners of the northern sand lands.

Lovejoy was also an effective educator of the general audience, precipitating a series of articles in the *Detroit News* entitled "Michigan's Millions of Idle Acres" in 1920. He authored the introductory column. In it, Lovejoy described the devastation of the northern pinelands to an urban audience, explaining how the economy of the entire state suffered from the lack of timber production. "If Iowa were to be forced to import corn from New York or if California sent to Florida for oranges, it would be no more preposterous than to have Michigan, with 10,000,000 acres of idle stump land, importing great quantities of forest products. We do that." But he offered hope that Michigan could replant the wastes and build a thriving forest economy. The *News* turned the series into a pamphlet and broadly distributed it across the state.

In 1923 Lovejoy assumed the role in which he would provide his greatest service to the state. Named head of the Department of Conservation's Land Economic Survey, he used his new office to supervise an inventory of the soils, minerals, climate, wildlife, recreational value, water power resources, and forest cover of northern Michigan, helping lay the groundwork for its reforestation and redevelopment. The survey sought to determine whether "every acre was doing that for which it was best fitted and to the best of its ability."[4] In its 12 years of existence, the survey covered 17 counties from Bay to Menominee and over 8.4 million acres of the state's 36 million.

Conceived by state geologist R. C. Allen in 1916, the project was initially dubbed a "soil and economic survey." Derailed by Governor Albert Sleeper during World War I and barely defeated in the legislature in 1921, the survey began to move forward in the early 1920s through the cooperation of both state and federal agricultural, conservation, and scientific institutions. "The Land-Economic Survey was an entirely new thing—a new departure from the stereotyped piecemeal surveys. Nothing like it has ever been attempted by any other state," wrote state geologist R. A. Smith in 1926. "[I]t is an inventory of all the physical resources which contribute or may contribute in an important way to the support and maintenance of community life."[5]

Lovejoy's aim was to build a state land policy out of the information the survey collected. The data his staff patiently collected "must come in such detail and volume as to be quite inescapable—overpowering. It must convince of the futility of any great 'agricultural development' in great areas and must make timber and game seem a whole lot better than the only other alternative—which is nothing at all."[6] Although the survey did not translate into the local initiatives Lovejoy had envisioned, its work heavily influenced land acquisition and management policies of the Department of Conservation. Lovejoy wrote a plan for the northern regions that would guide public land management into the next century. That policy returned to private ownership the relatively small amounts of land that were useful for such enterprise and maintained under the department's management parcels that would inevitably revert to the state anyway after failed agricultural exploitation.

Lovejoy was also one of the authors of an important tax reform in 1925. For years, northern landowners had complained of punitive property taxation rates that made it uneconomical to manage forests for long-term benefits. As taxes edged up annually, many found it in their interest to cut and run. The new Commercial Forest Reserve Act capped taxes on lands with productive potential at 5¢ an acre on softwood land and 10¢ an acre on hardwood. To recover some of the lost revenue, the state would assess a stumpage tax at the time logging occurred, when the landowner had revenue with which to pay it. The act proved a decisive factor in reforestation of the millions of acres of cutover northern Michigan lands still in private ownership.

Lovejoy's influence reached beyond Michigan's boundaries. After Lovejoy's death in 1942, Aldo Leopold wrote that Lovejoy "sired more ideas about men and land than any contemporary in the conservation field." Partly as a result of Lovejoy's persistent championing of the interests of the northern "cutover lands," Michigan's newspapers continued to educate and excite citizens about the great cause of reforestation. In 1929, the *Detroit News* once again attempted to rally public interest, announcing what it called "a plan for public participation in the reforestation of state-owned barren lands." The state now had 12 forest reserves embracing approximately 373,000 acres but enough money to plant only 15,000 acres a year.

The *News*'s solution was to enlist its readers as contributors. For $2.50 an acre, any individual or organization could plant 40 acres or more, covering the labor costs. The state made up the remainder of the $5.50 to $7.50 per acre cost. Outdoor editor Albert Stoll assured readers that donors would receive from the state a letter "stating that the reservation will forever be set aside as a forest reserve, subject only to administration by the proper forestry officials. . . . It becomes an enduring, permanent reservation and if in the future it becomes necessary or wise to harvest a timber crop, harvesting will be on a selective cutting basis, which will insure a sustained forest growth."[7] By now the ruin of the north country was so apparent to the readers of the *News* that the mention of cutting trees was made delicately. Although the *News* kicked off its program only a few weeks before the collapse of the stock market and the onset of the Great Depression, the project collected $20,000 within two months. It ultimately contributed to the planting of 15 million trees with contributions from more than 200,000 people.

An effective volunteer in Michigan's reforestation work was the writer Harold Titus of Traverse City, who served two stints on the state Conservation Commission totaling 20 years from 1927 to 1949. He made an early contribution to the cause with the writing, in 1922, of the novel *Timber*. Crediting Lovejoy with much of the book's technical detail, Titus set a romance against the backdrop of the ravaged north woods of Michigan. While John Taylor, son of the wealthy lumber baron Luke Taylor, woos the fiercely independent Helen Foraker, the young woman explains to John and readers a new way of managing forests that will produce sustained return over the long haul. "Foraker's Folly," the locals call the tract her father replanted, jeering at a crop that they believe will take 1,000 years to replace the primeval forest. But Helen sees more clearly.

She cries:

Oh, we were Prussians, we Americans! We were ruthless, heedless. All we saw was forest and a market for their products, so we butchered. We only saw the hour, only thought about personal gain. . . . Less than fifty years ago this land was stripped of its pine; today it is maturing another crop. The same could have been done with any other piece that grew good trees: Just keep the fire out and nature would have done much in time. . . . To exist as a nation, we must have forests; to have forests all we need to do for a beginning is to give this worthless land a chance. We can speed up its work by helping—by keeping out fire, by planting trees, by good forest practice.

Timber became a film and was shown in Lansing during the 1922 legislative session. Its climax, a raging forest fire that nearly destroys the Foraker plantation, may have helped persuade the lawmakers to make their "first decently generous" forest fire fighting appropriation, Titus said. The book was "the first novel of conservation anywhere," said the outdoor writer Ben East. "It appeared at a psychological time. Many thinking persons in Michigan and other sections of the country were feeling a growing discontent with the policies of letting cutover lands lie idle year after year, scourged by annual forest fires, or of trying to plant hopeless farm colonies on this poor land, fit only for the growing of timber crops. *Timber* crystallized that discomfort. It was hailed as the prophet of a new order." A Midland newspaper called the book "a stirring protest against the waste of Michigan's pride."

Appointed to the Conservation Commission by Governor Fred Green in 1927, Titus devoted much of his unpaid service on the panel to the job of building the state's Forest Fire Division. He joined the state's firefighters on the front lines, sometimes wearing a knapsack pumper and helping dig fire lines. He worked to increase state funding and to institutionalize an organized fire prevention program. By the 1930s, Michigan's Forest Fire Division enjoyed a national reputation for excellence.

When Titus left the commission in 1949, a newspaper called him "Michigan's grand old man" of conservation. Observers credited him with helping promote the recreation potential of the Upper Peninsula and building a popular constituency for conservation through his abundant writings.

The state forest system was about to expand even more dramatically. The Great Depression finally put an end to vain farm development plans in the north country. In the 1930s and early 1940s, more than 2.2 million acres of tax-reverted lands fell into the hands of the Department of Conservation, nearly doubling the agency's holdings. In a series of articles entitled "What Are We Going to Do . . . with 2,208,975 Added Acres?" Arthur Stace of the Booth newspaper chain answered his own question by pointing to the success of the last two decades of state land management.

[T]he Conservation department has been converting once-despised—but now valued—cut-overs into state forests, into state game areas, into state game refuges. It has been using them for trading purposes in acquiring additions to

state parks—Tahquamenon Falls, one of the state's choicest tourist attrac-
tions, was thus secured. It has been selling the better agricultural lands to set-
tlers and disposing of other lands that would best serve the public's interests
in private possession and on the tax rolls. It has been leasing oil, gas, and
other mineral rights on reverted lands thereby realizing millions of dollars for
the public treasury.[8]

But the most important value of the tax-reverted lands was as public forest, Stace concluded. In 1940, the department had 1.1 million acres of land in
state forests, up from 604,000 acres just 10 years before. National forestlands
had grown from 165,000 acres to more than 1.9 million acres in less than 20
years. Thanks to improved forest fire management, which enabled nature to
do much of the work of reforestation, and scientific forestry, Stace said,
"Michigan's state forests are already returning to their owners, the people
. . . opportunities for hunting, fishing, camping, touring, and other recreational pleasures." Although returns from timber harvest were as yet modest,
he added that they would pay bigger dividends in the future. While the time
it took to grow trees was too much to tempt "investments in young forests by
individuals impatient for financial returns," such time was not too much for
"the people of a long-lived state," Stace said.

Stace reflected a steadily building public consensus that Michigan's ownership of the northern lands was right and prudent. It was a consensus that
reflected well on one of the builders of the state's forest system, Marcus
Schaaf. Schaaf became Michigan's first state forester through appointment by
the Public Domain Commission in 1910. He had warmed up for the task by
studying at the Biltmore Forestry School in North Carolina, graduating in
1906, and then served as forester for the Cleveland-Cliffs Iron Company in the
Upper Peninsula. Termed "Teutonic" and "methodical" by a later state
forester, Schaaf might have worn the adjectives proudly, for his steady hand
steered the forest system ahead during turbulent times. He rarely permitted his
frustration to show at the slow growth of the forest system through the early
1920s and was unfazed by its explosive expansion afterward.

During Schaaf's career, the forest system expanded from 30,000 acres to
more than 3.6 million. In 1910, it took all day for a forest supervisor to travel
from the Higgins Lake headquarters of the forest system to the Houghton
Lake Reserve; by the time Schaaf retired in 1949, it was a trip of a half hour
by automobile. The forest fire lookout system in the early days consisted of
steps nailed to trunks of tall trees. Even the proper boundary lines of the
state's holdings were not definitively known.[9]

Under Schaaf's patient care, the state experimented with approximately 40
exotic species on the sandy soils of the cutover lands. The state attempted to
cultivate black locust, cottonwood, hickory, walnut, and various firs. Only
Scotch pine did well—and it not as well as the native pines. But the state's
emphasis gradually shifted from repopulating the plains with white pine to
planting aspen, maple, and other species that had become valuable for pulp.
The program's goals also broadened from merely replenishing the ravaged

lands to providing rustic recreation opportunities and stabilizing local economies.

Ironically, the Great Depression proved central to Michigan's reforestation efforts. Between 1933 and 1942 thousands of young men resided in Civilian Conservation Corps (CCC) camps scattered around northern Michigan. The CCC enrolled over 100,000 young Michigan men, planting 484 million trees; spending 140,000 days fighting forest fires; and constructing 7,000 miles of truck trails, 504 bridges, and 222 buildings. CCC members also revitalized the Michigan state park system, helping to establish Isle Royale National Park and improve campgrounds in Michigan's national forests.[10]

World War II ended the CCC program but also opened up the state forests to significant timber harvest for the first time. "[Y]ears of fire protection, coupled with little demand for the classes of old growth and second growth timber predominating on state forests, plus public sentiment against 'any more cutting,' had created a backlog of available material," the Department of Conservation said. Wartime demands knocked down all of these barriers, and by the end of the conflict, Michigan was open again to the idea of cutting in the northern forests, this time under carefully prescribed controls.

Schaaf's retirement in 1949 after 39 years with the Department of Conservation coincided with the resumption of forest plantings, which the war had suspended. A state forestry program that had employed 1 full-time forester in 1910 was now a 50-person operation. Although the program was to expand further in the decades following World War II, its modern outlines were now plainly visible. Schaaf left behind a legacy that would support the state's economy, its growing number of outdoor sports enthusiasts, and northern communities for more than a half century.

Citizen Watchdogs

The building of a professional conservation tradition in state government depended heavily on the vigilance of citizens fighting to keep politics from running the show. The founding of the Michigan United Conservation Clubs in 1937 began the modern era of public participation in decisions about the public's natural resources. For the first 21 years of MUCC's life, the watchdog's work belonged to its founder, sportsman Harry Gaines of Grand Rapids.

Born in 1891 in Cedar Springs, Gaines grew up in close touch with the outdoors. During much of his childhood he ran trap lines in the Rogue River, capturing rats, mink, and raccoon to sell their pelts.[11] "We learned much biology on those trips. And we learned how to catch brook trout in small streams—a real art," Gaines said. He had jobs shoveling gravel; in the superintendent's office of a furniture factory; and as a furniture salesman, buyer, shipping clerk, and credit manager until his call to conservation came. As president of the Kent County Conservation League in 1937, Gaines leaped to action when the legislature considered a bill to return to the governor the power to appoint the state's conservation director. "Harry unquestionably was the leader and the sparkplug," said MSU forestry professor Paul Herbert, who attended the first meetings organized to stop the bill. After killing the legislation with his "feverish" organizing efforts, Gaines was named president of the new MUCC, which would guard against future political power grabs. Gaines served without pay, expanding the coalition's membership to 83 clubs and working around his full-time job.

In 1940, MUCC president Herbert offered Gaines the job of MUCC secretary at a salary of $1,600 annually. The pay was low because club dues were capped at $10 a year. When the money did not materialize to pay Gaines, Herbert borrowed it from the conservationist president of the Motor Wheel manufacturing firm in Lansing. Gaines worked out of his Grand Rapids bedroom, depending on his wife and children for clerical help.

"The slight figure of Harry Gaines listening attentively at various meetings across the state was a common sight," *Michigan Out-of-Doors* noted in an account largely drawn from Herbert's reminiscences. Gaines estimated he attended 50 meetings a year. Described as "a small, wiry Irishman with red hair jutting wildly up from his scalp and rather long, drooping jowls," Gaines contributed to MUCC's rise with doggedness rather than charisma. Under his leadership, the organization successfully fought to protect from diversion by the legislature funds earmarked for wildlife management from the sale of hunting licenses and promoted the development by the state of public access sites for fishing. But Gaines was always proudest of defeating anticonservation bills, including repeated efforts to grant governors greater control over the Department of Conservation.

The growth of MUCC, ironically, helped lead to Gaines's demise. Refusing to relinquish control of the organization he had led to prominence, Gaines was moved aside in 1958 to make way for a new executive director, Jim Rouman. MUCC was building a staff of professional conservationists to cope with the increasing complexity of conservation issues and agencies. When visiting MUCC's Lansing headquarters one day, Gaines was appalled to find Rouman seated in a new chair and demanded that he return the furniture immediately. Gaines regarded the expenditure as a waste after his years of operating out of his house. "The furniture stayed, but Gaines never forgot about it," Herbert remembered. Gaines summarized his own career when he recorded in 1970 that MUCC "has always stood ready to stop scheming politicians or selfish persons who have not acted in the public interest."

MUCC's ranks included other conservation watchdogs of national significance. Herbert was one of them. The second president of MUCC after Gaines, Herbert attended a national wildlife conference called by President Franklin Roosevelt in 1935. The conference led to creation of the National Wildlife Federation, of which Herbert also became president. Chair of the Michigan State University Department of Forestry, Herbert was a recognized voice in matters of forestry and conservation.

Fred Brown was another distinguished MUCC president who combined a vocation as a Dow Chemical Company research and development scientist with his avocation. After moving to Michigan in the mid-1950s, Brown joined the Midland County Sportsman's Club, an MUCC affiliate. He moderated a weekly local radio show on conservation for eight years while monitoring state conservation policy. In the 1960s, he found himself testifying before the legislature against his employer on a proposed surplus water act. The bill would have permitted private interests to impound the headwaters of streams for their use, a breach of the public trust Brown vigorously opposed. The committee chair instructed Dow officials to negotiate with Brown and the MUCC to reach an agreement, which they ultimately did. But in one of the first disputes to arise under the act, a Montcalm County landowner whose farm was to be condemned for an impoundment turned to Brown for help. At his recommendation, MUCC joined forces with the man and won a historic ruling that the condemnation was an unconstitutional taking of private property for a private use.

His interest piqued by this exposure to water law, Brown soon became one of the state's leading citizen authorities on legal protection of water quantity and quality. Appointed to the state Water Resources Commission by Governor James Blanchard in the 1980s to fill the conservation seat, Brown sometimes exasperated Department of Natural Resources managers with his keen attention to every line of every proposed water pollution discharge permit. His unflinching demeanor and penetrating questions often resulted in changes tightening the conditions under which companies and local governments could dump wastewater into the state's rivers and lakes. Brown was particularly opposed to the department's practice of using the "assimilative capacity" of streams—in essence, dilution—as a method of helping industries to comply with water quality standards. In 1999, years after he left the commission, Brown was still requesting, and reading, each water pollution permit the Department of Environmental Quality proposed and made available for public comment.

His unusual perspectives as a former chemical industry employee, conservation coalition president, and citizen water commissioner fused into skepticism about assurances from government and business alike that water pollution was under control. He scoffed at claims by corporate officers that after decades of pollution regulation, voluntary initiatives and a new stewardship ethic in the private sector were more effective than government mandates. "Industry will do what it's required to do, when it's required to do it," Brown said in 1999. "They will do no more, nor will they do it any sooner. Whatever they do, they'll do it for their bottom line."[12] Of his own former company, Brown said, "They have violated every damn [water discharge] permit they've had, ever since the first one."

Brown's technical training and experience made him an indispensable force for water pollution cleanup in the 1970s and 1980s. Like many of his MUCC predecessors and successors, Brown was fierce in his commitment to defense of the state's natural resources from political exploitation. Without

Edith Munger, the longtime president of the Michigan Audubon Society, was one of the new voices of conservation in the first decades of the 1900s. Munger coordinated a contest resulting in the designation of the robin as Michigan's official bird and popularized bird conservation through a radio program and frequent speeches across the state. (Courtesy of Oceana County Historical and Genealogical Society.)

Log slides were the most efficient way to move logs to market along northern Michigan's rivers in the late 1800s, but one hundred years later in the 1990s, state Department of Natural Resources fisheries biologists said that sediment unleashed by the slides was still suppressing fish populations on such once-productive streams as the Manistee River. (Courtesy State Archives of Michigan.)

Forest fires ravaged the cutover lands of northern Michigan in the late 1800s and early 1900s, often erupting from the slash, or waste wood, left by loggers. The lethal Metz fire of 1908, which helped prompt the Michigan legislature to create the state's first conservation agency, is thought to have burst from such slash. (Courtesy State Archives of Michigan.)

The Lake of the Clouds is the cornerstone of Porcupine Mountains Wilderness State Park, which Governor Harry Kelly and Department of Conservation director P. J. Hoffmaster saved from imminent logging in 1945. The legislature approved a $1 million appropriation to allow the state to condemn the land for public use. (Courtesy State Archives of Michigan.)

Best-selling author and sportsman James Oliver Curwood made as many enemies as friends
with his 1920s crusade to rid the new Department of Conservation of political influence. But his
legacy endured for decades as the state's largest outdoors organization, the Michigan United
Conservation Clubs, fought to preserve an independent, nonpolitical commission system to oversee the conservation agency. (Courtesy State Archives of Michigan.)

Mounting public revulsion about water pollution resulted in a 1929 state law creating the Stream Control Commission, which used this mobile laboratory to do stream surveys. But the commission's enforcement powers were minimal. (Courtesy State Archives of Michigan.)

P. J. Hoffmaster, who served as Michigan Department of Conservation director from 1934 until his death in 1951, was a leader in the creation of the state park system. Hoffmaster and former college classmate E. Genevieve Gillette worked together to identify and seek funding for new park sites. (Courtesy State Archives of Michigan.)

Named head of the Michigan Department of Conservation in 1964, Ralph A. MacMullan soon waged a public crusade against the use of DDT, dieldrin, and other so-called hard pesticides. In 1969, Michigan became the first state to cancel most uses of DDT, three years before a federal ban took effect. (Courtesy State Archives of Michigan.)

What was known as smoke pollution in the first decades of the twentieth century stirred public fears as air pollution following a smog episode that killed residents of Donora, Pennsylvania, in the late 1940s. By the 1960s, the Great Lakes Steel Company's coke ovens and blast furnaces were regularly obscuring the downriver Detroit skyline. In 1965, the legislature passed the state's first air pollution control law in response to such scenes. (Courtesy Wayne County Department of Environment.)

their work, the state would not have moved ahead as far or as fast as it ultimately did in restoring degraded environments.

Hunting Renaissance

Modern Michigan wildlife management dates back to approximately 1913. Until then, the pursuit of game had been a business largely for an elite of the professional and wealthy, often on private preserves with more stringent regulations than set by law. But when Erasmus Hanson gave 4,000 acres near Grayling to the state for a game refuge, a new era of public wildlife lands dawned. One purpose of Hanson's refuge, and more than 600,000 other acres contributed to the state, was to give game species some breathing room after years of devastating market hunting.

The boom years of the 1920s transformed Michigan hunting. The expansion of the state highway system opened the gates for urban men and families to jump in their autos and head "up north" to pursue game. The number of small game hunters doubled during the decade, and sales of deer licenses jumped from 28,000 to over 75,000.[13]

Despite the thundering invective of James Oliver Curwood, at least one expert regarded the Michigan game program as a model during the 1920s. In a 1928 report prepared for the Sporting Arms and Ammunition Manufacturers' Institute, Aldo Leopold said that in spite of unsound organization, "the Department [of Conservation] contains a technical nucleus of extraordinary merit. The Land and Economic Survey, the State System of Forests, Game Refuges, and Public Hunting Grounds, and the Fire Control organization are expanding basic projects which score high even under the highest standards."[14] Leopold also had favorable words for the state's use of research to guide its game administration, observing, "I doubt if there are many states with like actual and potential resources in men and money, although the public is still unconscious of that fact." He praised the state's pheasant, deer, and bear management.

Michigan's leadership in game protection and restoration continued for decades. A high degree of professionalism characterized the Department of Conservation's programs; particularly after World War II under stern, long-serving wildlife chief Harry Ruhl, young game biologists such as Ralph MacMullan, the future agency director, developed reputations for research and management excellence. Ruhl was a tough boss but a respected wildlife manager. He was known for chiding and disciplining his subordinates and for standing up to critics who he felt were ignorant of good wildlife biology. On his retirement in 1967 after a 39-year career with the department, one observer wrote the following capsule description of Ruhl: "Taskmaster? YES! Ideal boss? NO! Graduates of his 'school' will agree to this, probably unanimously. But in their agreement will be a reflection of genuine respect. Among those graduates, incidentally, are a number of the nation's leaders in conservation."[15]

The career of Merrill L. Petoskey closely parallels the trajectory of the state's ever-growing wildlife management regime from the 1940s through the 1970s. A graduate of forestry at Michigan State University, Petoskey, known to friends as Pete, began work as a game ecologist with the state in 1947. Ruhl then assigned him to the Rose Lake Wildlife Experiment Station northeast of Lansing and required that he and his wife live in an old home on the state property with an outside toilet and an iron cooking stove fueled by chopped wood. It was a move typical of Ruhl's almost military management style, which caused chafing among his young employees but helped shape them for later greatness.

"The reason I had to move there was discipline," Petoskey said. "It was Ruhl's idea. He believed in discipline. There were no mustaches in the Division."[16]

Petoskey rose from doing habitat restoration on private farmland to district game supervisor, coordinator of the state's Pittman-Robertson federal aid program, waterfowl specialist, and supervisor of the state Conservation School at Higgins Lake. In the 1960s he became supervisor of education and training, coordinating a television show on conservation viewed by 12,000 students annually. In 1966 he became assistant regional manager. In October 1970, DNR director MacMullan called Petoskey away from a pheasant hunt to Lansing to become chief of the Game Division. Perhaps no other division chief was so well prepared for his job by wealth and diversity of experience.

Petoskey was a homespun Aldo Leopold, not just a game administrator. In a 1969 article in the department magazine, Petoskey described a ride home from the conservation school with his sixth-grade son, John. The younger Petoskey recited lessons he had learned to the approval of his father.

> The boy had a good understanding of the community relationship. He had begun to realize that he was only a small part of this wonderful world of nature. The idea of sharing it with other living things, with reason and understanding, was there. Nurtured, it could grow to help solve the frightening problems of our times—overpopulation, pollution, the mad clamor to make money in spite of what happens to the environment. But I wonder? Will there ever be enough people that really understand?[17]

Petoskey also argued that being outdoors was enough reward from a hunting experience: "Have you ever been on the edge of a cedar swamp that is glistening under a blanket of new fallen snow? Where no track has yet marked the coverlet and where the trees sparkle in the frosty morning sun like thousands of uncut Christmas trees whose lives will not end with the holiday? . . . [T]here's more to hunting than a chunk of meat. I'll argue that point with anybody." To emphasize his philosophy that the programs he administered were about more than producing more and better hunting, Petoskey initiated a name change from the Game to the Wildlife Division.

Despite his broad ecological view, Petoskey also knew that the bread and butter of his job was the state's deer program. From a high of approximately

1.5 million in the late 1940s, deer populations had plummeted to 400,000 in the late 1960s. Hunters grumbled bitterly about lost opportunities. No coward, Petoskey boldly promised 1 million deer by 1980. Calling it "one helluva tough assignment we've given ourselves," Petoskey challenged the prevailing hunter wisdom that doe hunting was the cause of the decline. A faction of hunters had at first opposed antlerless hunting and then emotionally demanded an end to it throughout the 1950s and 1960s. But Petoskey stuck to department-funded science that conclusively demonstrated that the taking of does had nothing to do with changes in the overall population.

It was not easy to defy the views of thousands of his own constituents, but Petoskey went one step farther. The real influence on deer, he argued, was clear-cutting of the early stages of forest succession. On land owned by the Mid-Forest Lodge in Roscommon County, deer numbers and take had climbed dramatically after the commencement of active tree cutting. Hunters on the private preserve had claimed 10 deer per square mile for the previous 10 years, while hunters in the rest of northern Lower Michigan had taken 3 to 4 per square mile.

"It's just plain, common sense range management," Petoskey said years later. "Producing deer food, plus habitat for a myriad of other species sharing the plant community, by clear-cutting aspen and jackpine and creating openings is the answer. Providing deer a full cupboard. The secret is to give deer good range with plenty of food. Well-fed deer the year around will give you back deer in numbers you can't believe!"

Petoskey proposed, and the legislature approved, the setting aside of $1.50 from each deer license to promote deer range improvement. The program budget jumped from $120,000 to $1 million in one year, and results were quick in coming. Deer populations and harvests jumped dramatically through the 1970s. Although Petoskey had moved on to the U.S. Forest Service by then, the state had more than 1 million deer in 1980.

He was typical of a breed of wildlife professionals unafraid to challenge both established doctrine and the beliefs of his paying constituency, the hunters. Proud of their training and knowledge, committed to letting biology rather than politics govern their decisions, Petoskey and peers won a national reputation for Michigan as a wildlife leader.

Coho Madness

MacMullan made another appointment that later stirred national waves. In 1964 he recruited Dr. Howard A. Tanner, who had grown up near Bellaire in northwest lower Michigan, to head the Fish Division. Tanner had his hands full.

The Great Lakes had become a near desert for fishing since the 1950s. Severely depressed by the invasion of the Atlantic sea lamprey, lake trout were no longer reproducing in Lake Michigan and were doing little better in Lake Huron. Another unwelcome guest, the almost-valueless alewife, had filled the

Lake Michigan niche opened by declines in native fish. Periodic die-offs of the alewives left heaps of dead fish on beaches and clogged drinking water intakes.

Catches of commercial species including lake trout, whitefish, perch, walleye, and herring sank from 12 million pounds in 1955 to 7 million pounds in 1965. Gross water pollution was no help, either, turning the waters of southern Lake Michigan and Lake Erie rancid. The number of fishing licenses sold in the state dwindled from approximately 1 million in the 1950s to 887,000 in 1965.

Tanner and his assistant and successor as fisheries chief, Dr. Wayne Tody, had two choices: either to attempt to recreate the commercial fishery or to strike out in a new direction. Tanner's only marching orders from MacMullan were to do something "spectacular" with the Fish Division's programs. Tanner and Tody chose to do something new with the Great Lakes fishery: they wanted to convert it to a sportsman's resource, serving hundreds of thousands of anglers eager to get recreation on the open lakes.

They had first to fend off the 100-year-old Great Lakes commercial fishery as well as the federal government. Jack Bails, a young fisheries biologist with the Department of Conservation, credited Tody with recognizing that the commercial fishery not only had less potential economic value to the state but was also physically interfering with sport fish. The Great Lakes commercial fishery set and lifted enough gill nets annually to stretch around the earth 2 1/2 times. "Wayne realized that neither salmon, lake trout or steelhead could survive to maturity with the heavy gill netting going on at the time," Bails said. "He pushed hard to control commercial fishing."

The federal Bureau of Commercial Fisheries had a scheme that also threatened to interfere with Michigan's sportfishing plans. It proposed to promote commercial take of the alewife, which comprised 85 percent of Lake Michigan's fish biomass, to make cat food. The bureau provided federal funds to encourage trawlers from the East Coast to come to Michigan to fish alewife. After a fierce dispute over whether the states or the federal government controlled the Great Lakes fishery, Michigan prevailed. The bureau was forced to back down.

Tanner and Tody put it bluntly in a 1966 prospectus.

These lakes should be a mecca for sport fishermen, but they are not. . . . Today Michigan probably has less than 100 full-time commercial fishermen. Their average wage is substandard. Through a program which combines the introduction of new sport fish, stream habitat development, extension of the spawning range by fishways, and an expanded program of fishery culture, we can be reasonably certain that populations of valuable anadromous sport fish can be increased many fold. . . . The impact of this fishery will be felt throughout central North America.[18]

"We decided it was most appropriate to manage the open lakes for sportfishing," Tanner said in 1999. But for which species? Because they do not

fight when hooked and would have high levels of DDT because of their extensive fat, Tanner said, "We couldn't create an exciting fishery with lake
trout."[19]

There was another idea—Pacific Northwest salmon. Introducing them to
an environment that consisted solely of freshwater was a gamble, but in a
sense Michigan had little to lose. "[W]hen you start at the bottom, there is
only one way to go," *Outdoor Life* magazine later observed. "The lake had
22,400 square miles of water. It also had a fantastic, teeming supply of forage
fish waiting for something to wade into them."[20] Additionally, coho salmon
were fast growing, were good fighters, and would have a ravenous appetite for
the alewives that dominated the food web of Lake Michigan.

Tanner and Tody's biologists reviewed the literature to find whether there
had ever been a successful introduction of salmon to freshwater. They found
scattered reports—one from New Zealand, one from a project in a Montana
lake. Pacific salmon had been introduced to Michigan waters in the early part
of the twentieth century but only as fry, not smolt. The spotty records of
returns did nothing to discourage the state. But there were many fisheries biologists in the Northwest who said the salmon simply would not survive in
freshwater.

Tanner and Tody decided to take the chance. Tanner had connections
with Oregon's resource agency from his prior job as fisheries chief in
Colorado, where he had also attempted to stock coho. At minimal cost to the
state, Tanner obtained 1 million coho eggs from Oregon, resulting in 850,000
one-ounce smolts after a year and a half of nurturing in the state's hatcheries.
The department released over 650,000 of the smolts into the Platte and
Manistee Rivers, tributaries of Lake Michigan, in the spring of 1966 and sat
back to see what would happen.

So barren had the Great Lakes become that the conservation department
had disinvested in them; the agency had no vessels that could monitor the
salmon in open waters. But there was soon no need. By late summer, the
quick-maturing "jack" salmon were showing up at the city of Chicago's water
intakes, and a healthy fishery had developed off city piers. By September the
jacks were returning to the Platte and Manistee. Bails barbecued several and
took them to members of the Natural Resources Commission. Anglers caught
more than 2,000 out of the two rivers that fall, a small taste of what was to
come.[21] Knowing that the jacks were merely a prelude, Bails made reservations a year in advance for a Manistee motel room during the fall of 1967.

By late summer of 1967, it was obvious that the coho experiment was a
success. Coho assembled in the lake off the Platte and Manistee rivers.
Feasting on alewives, they had grown in sixteen months from one ounce to as
much as 15 or 20 pounds and averaged over 10 pounds.

It was almost too much of a good thing. Anglers who had given up on
Lake Michigan as a source of sport suffered from a malady accurately
described as "coho madness." In *Michigan Conservation*, editor Russell
McKee catalogued the symptoms.

What event could be so unusual as to drive a tight-fisted penny pincher to a sudden and cheerful squandering of $2000 of hard-earned cash? What could cause dozens of peace-loving citizens to assault each other bodily with fists and poles, to the extent of considerable personal injury? What could cause scores of automobile owners to park illegally and then cheerfully accept the inevitable consequences of their actions—a plague of costly summons? . . . What could cause hundreds of men to go away on a treacherous sea—against all advice—in rubber rafts, bicycle boats, floating cars and trucks, canoes, and a host of other illogical craft? What could cause a man of usually normal habits to spend a night attempting to sleep on the boney frame of a boat trailer, wrapped in a single blanket? . . . The answer to all these questions, in case you have any lingering doubts, is quite simply the prospect many men have of catching many big fish.[22]

The return of the coho was an economic bonanza for businesses that typically suffered from a sharp decline in tourism after Labor Day. Hotels and motels, restaurants, service stations, and others reaped great profits from the rush to the spawning streams. The big money "comes in campers and station wagons, pulling boats on trailers," noted the *Detroit Free Press*. "It also comes in a silver and black Rolls Royce from Illinois and a Mercedes-Benz from Indiana." Waterfront property began to leap in value. In 11 coho counties, retail sales rose $11.9 million in 1967 and $26.8 million in 1968.[23] The mania had a tragic consequence, however. On September 23, 1967, 7 men drowned, 19 men went to the hospital, and 200 boats were wrecked on the big lake when a sudden squall interrupted their intent fishing.

Nothing, though, could interrupt the recovery of fishing on Lake Michigan and later on Lake Huron, when coho and chinook salmon were planted there. Persuaded by Michigan's success, Indiana, Illinois, and Wisconsin launched their own salmon programs. Adding chinook salmon and lake trout to the mix, Michigan wrote "one of the great conservation success stories of all time," said outdoor writer Ben East. Tanner won the 1968 Conservationist of the Year Award from the National Wildlife Federation. MacMullan won the *Outdoor Life* Conservation Award for the department's Lake Michigan sport fishery program as well his stand against hard pesticides.

It was ironic that at a later time, the introduction of the exotic salmon species might not have been possible. Although it did evaluate and reject several alternatives, such as the introduction of striped bass, Michigan prepared no environmental impact statement before dumping the smolt in the Manistee and Platte Rivers; the term *environmental impact statement* (EIS) did not exist in law in 1966. The DNR had not really known what exactly it was doing to the Lake Michigan food web.

But the DNR had known that the lake fishery was in dire shape and was an enormous waste of potential. The combination of Tanner and Tody proved remarkably effective. Tody was the inside person who organized the details, selected key staff, and assured that all things were in place to insure the success of the salmon program. Tanner was the visionary and outside person who promoted the introduction, arranged help from the West Coast states, and sold the program to the Conservation Commission and the legislature.

The success of the coho planting was no fluke. Trusting their intuitions as well as the best biology they knew, Michigan's professional conservationists hadn't hesitated to innovate. Free of political interference, and eager to rebuild the value of degraded natural resources, they had the room to try what some said couldn't be done. But they showed it could.

CHAPTER 9

Forced to Be First: Banning the "Hard Pesticides"

The effects of this storing-up of pesticides in animals from the smallest to largest is not completely known, but gaps are beginning to be filled in. Man, for the first time in his history, has chemicals at his disposal that can completely alter his own food chain. By wiping out certain insects or minute sea-creatures he removes link after link in the very delicately balanced chain of life on which he depends. . . . [T]here is enough evidence for us to be greatly concerned and to start bringing the unnecessary and widespread use of these persistent chemicals to a halt.

— Ralph A. MacMullan, *Michigan Natural Resources Magazine,* March–April 1969

*U*nited States agriculture's dependence on chemical pesticides reaches back into the nineteenth century. Terrified by insect plagues following the Civil War, first midwestern and then eastern farmers turned to the newly emerging profession of economic entomology for help. Sponsored in large part by federally funded agricultural experiment stations linked to land-grant colleges, these scientists first assisted farmers in attacking insects with substances like Paris green, an arsenic-containing pigment that worked wonders on the Colorado potato bug. The relief it provided to an apparent insect scourge was so welcome that most concerns about the possible harm to humans from eating the treated crop were brushed aside. This minor clash between agricultural and public health interests in the 1880s and 1890s foreshadowed more intense debates of the mid–twentieth century.

A. J. Cook, an entomologist from Michigan Agricultural College, sprayed fruit trees heavily with arsenical pesticides in 1880. After chemical analysis, he concluded that wind and rain removed nearly all of the applied arsenic from produce within three weeks. Cook's widely reported conclusion, that it was safe to eat as many treated apples as one desired as long as they had not been sprayed recently, promoted increased use of the compounds. What eluded scientists then as later, even in the face of suspected human poisonings, was the health risk of chronically consuming produce treated with pesticides at levels well below those that would cause immediate sickness or death.[1]

By the early 1900s, pesticide makers had begun to work almost in tandem with the land-grant colleges and state and federal agriculture agencies in a "war against insects." Memories of the farm devastation wrought by insect outbreaks in the decades before widespread pesticide use tended to overwhelm concerns about theoretical public health risks. Although a few physicians and public health professionals worried about increasing evidence of health problems caused by low-grade exposure to lead and arsenic in the pesticides, such concerns were scattered and ineffectively expressed in the face of the economic benefit provided by the poisons. In the 1930s and 1940s, familiar battle lines took shape.

> The two groups in the battle differed in quite fundamental ways. One side— comprised of the farmers, their Congressional allies, economic entomologists, the Public Health Service, and a respectable number of medical scientists— believed that the criteria for safety were those of clinical poisoning; doses that did not produce illness were safe. . . . The other group—the Food and Drug Administration, consumer groups, and some medical scientists—took an entirely different view. Safety, they thought, should not be determined by signs of classical poisoning, but by the evidence of chronic effects, and such data could best be obtained by extrapolating from laboratory tests, preferably conducted on experimental animals over their lifetime.[2]

Next came the chemical revolution. Seeking an effective method of protecting U.S. troops stationed in tropical regions during World War II from lice and malaria-bearing mosquitoes, the U.S. army launched the first massive applications of a newly commercialized compound, dichloro-diphenyl-trichloro-ethane, or DDT. Although DDT was synthesized in Germany in 1874, its insecticidal properties were first recognized in 1939 by Paul Mueller of Switzerland. So effective was the chemical in killing off insect pests during the war that it came home with the troops. DDT had several important advantages over its predecessors. In addition to being highly toxic to many insect species, it was not particularly toxic to mammals, and it was relatively cheap. This opened doors for new uses of pesticides, which had previously been restricted to farms. DDT, it appeared, could be applied to swamps and forests, even in residential areas, to kill off unwanted insects.

In 1948, Mueller was awarded the Nobel Prize in physiology and medicine, but by then studies were already beginning to expose the underbelly of DDT: the heavy or careless use of DDT sprays killed fish and birds.[3] Tests also showed that DDT accumulated in fat tissues and could be passed on in milk.

Any significant reservations these tests may have raised about DDT use were suppressed by the alarming spread of Dutch elm disease in the United States. Fears of a landscape denuded of one of America's favorite trees prompted the widespread use of DDT to kill off the European elm bark beetles, which carry the fungus that destroys a tree's circulatory system. A 1930 shipment of elm logs from the Netherlands introduced the fungus to the United States. By the 1940s, it was attacking elms across the East and Midwest. In 1950, Dutch elm disease reached Michigan, and the state

Department of Agriculture began a program of control with pesticides, including DDT. By the end of the decade, however, over 100 Michigan communities reported the disease.

DDT's use against Dutch elm disease significantly increased amounts of the chemical applied in heavily populated areas. The recommended concentrations of the chemical—2 percent and sometimes higher—and the density of elms in suburban areas led to much greater residues of the chemical than had ever been seen before. It was not long before residents of the treated areas noticed something else: the death of birds.

Although reports of bird mortality were made as early as 1947, they first came to the attention of an important Michigan bird lover in the spring of 1955, the year after the city of East Lansing began its Dutch elm disease control program. A graduate student in zoology at Michigan State University, John Mehner, was performing a study comparing robin populations in unsprayed areas in Pittsburgh with two sprayed areas in East Lansing, including a five-acre plot that had once housed the university's horticultural gardens. Mehner brought the results of his study to Dr. George J. Wallace, a professor of zoology. Wallace would later describe them as "dramatic and disturbing."[4]

By 1958 no study was needed to suggest that something was wrong. Wallace and others observed dead robins in growing numbers. Robins had been virtually eliminated from the main campus and some areas in East Lansing. At first believing the deaths were caused by an affliction of the nervous system, Wallace soon began to suspect DDT, despite assurances from the applicators that the sprays were safe. The robins "invariably exhibited," Wallace said, "the well-known symptoms of loss of balance, followed by tremors, convulsions, and death." He soon traced the birds' exposure to earthworms, which accumulated the chemical in their bodies after feeding from contaminated leaf litter. Consuming the downed leaves in the fall, the earthworms were themselves consumed by robins on their return to the north in the spring, thus causing the increasing seasonal die-offs each year.

In addition to the properties that made it effective in combating insects, DDT had a characteristic not found in natural substances: it failed to break down and in fact accumulated in living tissue in greater and greater concentrations as it passed up the food chain. Concentrations of DDT and others of the so-called persistent bioaccumulative chemicals increased a hundred-, a thousandfold or more as they passed from the lowest level of the food chain to the next level of predators. Hence the MSU robins built up dangerously high levels of the pesticide.

Wallace clanged the alarm. From an estimated 370 adult robins on the north university campus in 1954, the population plummeted to only 15 in 1957, according to Mehner. Wallace himself counted only 3 adults and 1 young bird in a 1958 survey. But in areas of East Lansing treated only for mosquitoes, and not with the much higher dosages used to control Dutch elm disease, robins were still fairly numerous. Wallace acknowledged that the presence of these birds suggested to some that he was an alarmist. "The robin, like the passenger pigeon, would have to be extinct for about ten years before some of these people would admit that it was gone," he complained.

A look at broader numbers underscored the urgency of the problem, Wallace said. Of 77 species that he had counted over 16 summers in East Lansing, 49 had disappeared or measurably decreased in numbers. "Our insectivorous birds are facing the greatest man-made threat they have ever experienced," Wallace warned. Noting that government agencies were now proposing to turn DDT against fire ants, he added, "If this and other pest-eradication programs are carried out as now projected, we shall have been witnesses, within a single decade, to a greater extermination of animal life than in all the previous years of man's history on earth, if not since glaciation profoundly altered the life of the northern hemisphere."

Such a blunt statement was not typical for the quiet Wallace. The 50-year-old ornithologist, born and raised in north central Vermont, was happiest outdoors with his birds. They had been a cherished element of his childhood.

We knew the Barn Swallows that nested in our barns, the phoebes that built or repaired their nest each spring on the ell of the house where it was visible from the sink room window, the crows that supervised spring plowing and planting. . . . [E]ach spring after the long hard winter we anxiously awaited the arrival of the first robins and bluebirds, the latter then common and well-known farm and orchard birds.[5]

Coming to Michigan to study and then teach at Michigan State College, later Michigan State University, Wallace quietly pursued his work but was fierce in defense of his beloved birds. He had equally fierce opponents who did not welcome his message.

Ironically, DDT had begun to plague the grounds of a university whose faculty and agriculture extension agents had enthusiastically promoted the use of it and other chemical pesticides. Convinced of the righteousness of their cause, they deplored Wallace's repeated denunciations of DDT. In 1960, Wallace and graduate students surveyed spring populations of campus robins. The peak was 18 pairs in mid-April; only three remained by the end of May. After chemically analyzing the 22 dead robins collected on campus, Wallace found all "had high, presumably lethal, accumulations of DDT in all of the tissues examined (brain, breast muscle, heart, liver, kidney and gonads). DDT was also present in the developing egg follicles in the ovaries of females, in unlaid but completed eggs, in unhatched eggs in deserted nests, in embryos within the eggs, and in a newly hatched nestling."[6] Wallace had received reports of bird deaths in many communities treating for Dutch elm disease, including Ann Arbor, Battle Creek, Benton Harbor, Birmingham, Bloomfield Hills, Grand Rapids, Jackson, Jonesville, and others. He and his coauthors helpfully suggested several means of reducing bird mortality through more judicious DDT use but concluded, "[W]e are inclined to question the whole program, as currently conducted, on ecological grounds. Any program which destroys 80 or more species of birds and unknown numbers of beneficial predatory and parasitic insects needs further study."

These words angered agriculture officials, who were convinced that DDT was an essential weapon in the war on destructive insects and Dutch elm disease. They set their sights on Wallace. Called to testify in 1960 before a congressional subcommittee chaired by Michigan's own U.S. representative John Dingell, Wallace was the subject of discussion among federal and state agriculture department officials. C. A. Boyer of the state agriculture department, Dingell said, had threatened to bring pressure on the university to discipline or fire Wallace. A U.S. Agriculture Department official, D. R. Sheppard, suggested that Wallace was letting emotions outrun science, telling Dingell that the Wallace campus study was limited to a small area and that "we feel we should not apply the results of the study over a large area." Dingell was furious: "If there's any attempt by the [U.S.] department of agriculture to cause any difficulty, personal or professional, for Dr. Wallace, there'll be some hair and fur flying at the department and the Michigan department of agriculture."[7]

Wallace's message would soon be bigger news. A well-known science writer by the name of Rachel Carson was preparing a book that would bring the issue of pesticides to the attention of millions of Americans. When *Silent Spring* was published in 1962, it aroused an immediate storm of controversy and further publicized Wallace's studies. Carson emphasized Wallace's discovery that DDT appeared to inhibit or prevent the robins' reproduction. Calling the problem "sinister," Carson quoted Wallace's congressional testimony that he had found high concentrations of DDT in the testes and ovaries of breeding birds.[8] In addition to immediate lethality, then, DDT could neuter birds and thus raise the specter of an eventual "silent spring."

The book had a revolutionary effect, although its greatest consequences came years after Carson's death in 1964. It prompted immediate political scurrying, including a request by President John F. Kennedy that his science advisory committee review the issue of pesticide safety.[9] But it had a far more significant impact on the public mind. DDT "had seemed so harmless that it was routinely used around people, and children ran through the sprays from the trucks that fogged small towns and suburbs in the summer. If DDT did spread through the air, if it might cause cancer, if it killed millions of fish and birds what was safe? . . . In developing the case against DDT Carson also made what was the clearest case to that time of the central tenet of the environmental movement: that human action has become the dominant environmental influence on the rest of the planet."[10]

Such a threatening lesson did not go down easily on the MSU campus. John Carew, chairman of the horticulture department, called *Silent Spring* "more poisonous than the pesticides [Carson] condemns." He argued that the risk of DDT to robins and other wildlife was minimal in light of the benefits to man and said critics of the pesticide should be willing "to accept some injury to restricted segments of our wildlife population in return for the irrefutably better standard of living we now enjoy because of agricultural chemicals." The true tragedy of Carson's book, he said, "is that she has destroyed the confidence of the public in the men who produce our food."[11]

The same year, Dr. Alfred G. Etter, assistant professor in the MSU Department of Fisheries and Wildlife, charged that university officials had suppressed 13,000 copies of an agricultural extension service bulletin informing the public about the dangers to wildlife posed by chemical spray programs. Despite being reviewed by 11 MSU staff members, it was withdrawn and never redistributed after objections from three extension agents. Etter complained that most laboratory research on pesticides at the university and elsewhere was biased because it was funded by the producers of the substances, large chemical companies. Dr. Gordon E. Guyer, chairman of the entomology department, replied that the bulletin had overgeneralized about chemical problems and had been pulled to make technical changes.[12]

Guyer, who became the director of the state's Department of Natural Resources in 1986 and of the state Department of Agriculture in the 1990s, was a key figure in the pesticides debate. Although he vigorously defended DDT for a time, he said in 2000 that some uses of DDT could have been salvaged if he and other experts had recognized how quickly the pesticide bred resistance in insects. Overspraying of DDT for Dutch elm disease and mosquito control, not agriculture use, was the prime culprit in environmental contamination, he said. "If only I'd been a little wiser, things might have gone differently," he said.[13]

As public alarm over the dangers to the environment and human health from pesticide use mounted, agriculture officials and chemical industries launched a counterattack on the critics. They used the same arguments and received the same challenges that a later generation of officials would handle in controversies of the 1970s through the 1990s. On one side were the proponents of pesticides, who sought to portray themselves as rationally and scientifically responding to the needs of society for wholesome and abundant food. Their critics, the proponents said, were hysterical alarmists who cared more about bugs and wildlife than people. The opponents cast the issues differently and often dramatically, suggesting that the survival of humankind was at risk. They also questioned the alliance between chemical manufacturers and public officials, particularly those in agriculture agencies, arguing that public servants should care first about protection of health from the chemicals.

At the annual meeting of the Michigan Audubon Society in 1964, George S. McIntyre, director of the state agriculture department, and Roland Clement, a research biologist for National Audubon, clashed publicly on these grounds. Pesticides, McIntyre said, were carefully applied: "Some believe the use of chemicals is upsetting the balance of nature for the entire state. Evidence does not point in this direction." Clement accused officials in public agriculture agencies of being propagandists for chemical use and said that naturalists must "educate those in power" to cut back on pesticides.[14]

The debate simmered through the mid-1960s, but soon events would put Michigan back at center stage of the pesticides controversy. Frustrated by their inability to break the gridlock on pesticides policy held by the government–chemical manufacturer–agriculture alliance, a handful of people on New York's Long Island decided to do something more direct about stopping DDT applications there. Along with Dr. H. Lewis Batts Jr., a biology teacher at Kalamazoo College, they formed a new organization called the Environmental Defense Fund (EDF). Batts had taught one of EDF's founders, Victor J. Yannacone Jr., who had gone on to become an attorney. Described by Batts as "a real scrapper," Yannacone along with the other EDF founders had determined to use the courts as the avenue to force controls on DDT and other dangerous pesticides.[15]

One of their first opportunities came in Michigan. In the fall of 1966, the Michigan Department of Agriculture (MDA) planned to apply 5,000 pounds of dieldrin manufactured by the Shell Chemical Company in southwestern Michigan's Berrien County to kill off Japanese beetles. A close cousin of aldrin, another pesticide also manufactured by Shell Chemical, dieldrin is a persistent and bioaccumulative chlorinated hydrocarbon more toxic than DDT. Batts pledged $10,000 to support court action against dieldrin and DDT in Michigan.

The fledgling environmental group had another significant ally in the state, a man who would become a leading figure in the battle to rid the state of the so-called hard pesticides that did not break down and built up in wildlife and fish. His name was Dr. Ralph A. MacMullan, and he was the director of the state Department of Natural Resources (DNR). Soon the DNR and the MDA, sister agencies in state government, would be openly at war.

Although MacMullan's career to date had followed the typical pattern of conservation professionals in the mid–twentieth century, which often produced individuals concerned primarily with managing fish, wildlife, and forests as resources without particular sensitivity toward issues of environmental pollution, his ecological concerns were not limited to DDT and dieldrin. Early years in the outdoors may have had much to do with that. Born in Detroit in 1917, he moved with his family in boyhood to a western suburb, Garden City, then characterized by remnants of rural land that allowed him to enjoy the outdoors. As DNR director he would write the following reminiscence to a conservationist cleaning up a stretch of the Rouge River: "I caught my first fish (a 3 1/2 inch sunfish) and learned to swim in the Rouge River not far from there." Encouraged by his father, the young MacMullan developed an early love of birds, while the Boy Scouts introduced him to camping and woodcraft.

An intuitive understanding of the outdoors, coupled with scientific training in zoology at Michigan State University—where he was advised by Dr. George Wallace—led to MacMullan's career as a state game biologist, chief of the Department of Conservation's Houghton Lake Wildlife Experiment Station, assistant chief of the Game Division, and finally the directorship of the Department of Conservation in 1964. Within weeks of assuming the job of conservation director (the agency's name was changed to the Department of

Natural Resources in 1968), MacMullan issued a press release saying he was launching an aggressive program that reached beyond the department's typical interests in fish and game matters, including—significantly—"deep analysis of pesticide problems."

Some who worked for MacMullan think that a native intensity was only one of the qualities that sent him into the pesticide fray. Another may have been loyalty to his graduate adviser, the ornithologist Wallace, who would later say that MacMullan "was hardly mine, but I would like to claim him. . . . Like me, he got involved in the pesticide controversy and had many staunch supporters but also a predictable number of severe critics."[16] Outraged about what he increasingly perceived as the threat to fish and wildlife posed by persistent pesticides, MacMullan was also incensed by attacks on and threats against Wallace. He would never relent in his battle to stop the use of the hard pesticides.

One of the reasons MacMullan got the agency director's job, one reporter speculated, was his low profile in the years leading up to his selection, making him a noncontroversial choice. But friends and associates knew a different man—one not afraid to speak out for what he thought was right, even at the risk of offending others or losing his job. A reporter noted in 1964 that while giving the impression of being easygoing, MacMullan "can be plenty tough when he needs to be," according to friends.

While still contemplating its strategy of filing lawsuits to stop DDT use, EDF invited MacMullan to help. He sent an adviser, biologist Dr. C. T. (Ted) Black, to the Kalamazoo Nature Center near Battle Creek to learn what EDF was thinking. EDF attorney Yannacone and Dr. Charles F. Wurster, a marine biologist at the State University of New York, laid out their case. Attending "unofficially," Black returned believing that EDF was on solid ground in its action and recommended that MacMullan support it. Black said, "Mac asked me what the chances were of success in this area, whether it was important enough to do, and when I said it was, he said, 'I've got too many fights going on, but we'll take 'em on.'" From that point on MacMullan was fully committed to the campaign to halt the use of hard pesticides.[17]

With MacMullan's blessing, EDF filed two Michigan lawsuits in the fall of 1967. The first challenged MDA's plans to spray dieldrin in Berrien County, while the other sought an injunction to stop nine local governments in western Michigan from using DDT for Dutch elm control.[18] A lower court judge dismissed the dieldrin lawsuit on the grounds that EDF did not have standing to bring the suit in Michigan, but Yannacone won a temporary injunction and appealed the case to the state court of appeals.[19] By the time the latter court dismissed the dieldrin suit, it was too late to spray the Japanese beetles that year. And EDF's suit against the use of DDT to control Dutch elm disease was successful when, bowing to strong citizen pressure, all the local governments agreed to discontinue its use.

Batts, who had founded and directed the Kalamazoo Nature Center, had supported the antipesticides movement by providing a base for Bob Burnap, an activist from New York and also one of the EDF founders. While at the center, Burnap coordinated the printing of hundreds of copies of Wurster's pesticide-damning affidavit, which included numerous footnotes on studies showing serious damage from the use of hard pesticides. Widely distributed across the state to leaders of citizens groups in communities applying DDT for Dutch elm disease, the copies of Wurster's affidavit galvanized the League of Women Voters and local Audubon clubs to oppose the spraying programs and pressure city councils to stop DDT use.[20]

MacMullan cheered on these developments, saying that he was "dead set against this spraying program." He was deeply troubled by findings of high levels of DDT in coho salmon and their eggs. The state's recent amazing success in bringing sportfishing to Lake Michigan was jeopardized in two ways. High levels of chemicals in the adult fish threatened to make them unsafe for human consumption under federal guidelines. The pesticides might also prevent salmon fry from surviving. In 1968, the death of 700,000 coho salmon fry in a Michigan hatchery, 11 percent of the total, alarmed MacMullan and his agency. The agency concluded that DDT was "the most probable cause" of the fry mortality. MSU's George Wallace would later say, "The salmon have done more to help birds than ornithologists have been able to do in the last 20 years."[21]

It was no accident that the chemical residues were showing up in the Great Lakes ecosystem and particularly in Lake Michigan, which in effect is a backwater isolated from the main flow of the lakes. The Great Lakes, it was turning out, acted as a sink for the pollutants whose persistence and accumulation Rachel Carson had first brought to the attention of a popular audience.

"To add dieldrin to this environment now will only compound this problem because this chemical is about four times as toxic to salmon as DDT is," MacMullan said. "If there is anything that could knock out our salmon program flat, it's the continued use of such death-dealing pesticides."[22] He went even farther in early 1968, using the department's magazine, *Michigan Conservation,* to call for the outlawing of DDT, dieldrin, aldrin, heptachlor, lindane, chlordane, and other persistent chemical compounds. He called the struggle to ban the pesticides possibly

> the most difficult and probably the most important that has ever faced our natural resources. . . . DDT is already found in the Antarctic Ocean, thousands of miles away from any area where it has ever been used. It is found in the fish life of the deep oceans. It is found inside the eggs of eagles and ospreys and falcons—eggs which do not hatch into birds whose numbers are now in decline.[23]

When neither MDA nor MacMullan would back down on the dieldrin issue in 1968, Governor George Romney appointed a three-member advisory panel on the use of hard pesticides. Consisting of MSU entomology professor Gordon Guyer, University of Michigan professor John Bardach, and Eugene Kenaga, an environmental specialist for Dow Chemical Company, the panel was regarded by environmental advocates as tilted toward pesticides. The panel threw a bone to the advocates by acknowledging some risks to the environment from pesticide use but called the chemicals "essential tools" to Michigan agriculture and put no obstacles in the path of MDA's proposed dieldrin application that fall. The agriculture department said the Japanese beetle infestation in southwest Michigan had spread in one year from 2,800 to 5,000 acres and threatened the state's $250 million fruit and nursery belt. Without a controlled application by the state, MDA argued, individual farmers would apply much greater amounts of dieldrin and other chlorinated hydrocarbons.

By now, however, EDF had plenty of Michigan allies besides Batts and MacMullan in the fight against dieldrin. Publicity about declines in populations of bald eagles and peregrine falcons, linked by some researchers to DDT in eggshells, had caught the public imagination. Ann Van Lente, Dale Van Lente, Norman Spring, and Batts founded the Michigan Pesticides Council to help coordinate the citizen fight against hard pesticides. The council quickly encompassed a large cross section of the state's citizen organizations.

Representatives of this increasingly active public movement against pesticides showed up at the September meeting of the state Commission of Agriculture to urge it not to authorize the dieldrin use. "The vast majority of Michigan people are not in agriculture and they are beginning to wonder why their interests are not being considered," said Ann Van Lente of the Federated Garden Clubs of Michigan. "They don't want Lake Michigan poisoned. They are concerned for the fish. They are worried about dwindling bird populations. They fear the unknown consequences of continuing the use of pesticides that remain potent for years and years."

Another Pesticides Council member was Charles Shick, a wildlife biologist for the DNR who had coauthored the bulletin warning of pesticide problems that was suppressed by Michigan State University. Shick later said that the council was critical in the fight because it "exposed and debunked distorted information pumped into the mass communications media by land grant universities, agriculture organizations and state and federal agencies cooperating with agro-business interests."[24] The Pesticides Council unnerved MDA, whose deputy complained to director B. Dale Ball about "the trouble they're aiming to cause."

Aligning itself with MDA was the Michigan Farm Bureau, which said in a telegram to the commission, "Urge favorable action on adequate and immediate control of Japanese beetle infestation. Fully support Commission's efforts to protect Michigan's food and natural resources from this highly destructive pest. Prompt and adequate control now will prevent increased future use of pesticides."[25]

As the meeting approached, the governor temporarily muzzled MacMullan. In a meeting called by the governor four days before the commission meeting and also attended by MDA director Ball, MacMullan agreed to cancel his plans to make a presentation before the commission but declined to support the use of dieldrin. In a confidential note to Ball, he said that MDA should declare it was "thoroughly aware of our thoughts in the matter and that you had taken them into consideration when you made your recommendations." Tensions ran high between the two agency heads. An aide to MacMullan remembered that "sometimes he and the director of agriculture almost came to blows."

The commission voted unanimously on September 13 to authorize the application of 3 tons of dieldrin and 7 1/2 tons of chlordane on 4,800 acres in Chikaming and Lake Townships of Berrien County, noting that "spokesmen for fruit and vegetable interests in that area urged treatment to halt the spread of Japanese beetle before the area is quarantined. This would require inspection and certification of most agricultural products before they could be shipped." The commission's press release stated that "a plea to withhold treatment" in order to protect wildlife came from some speakers, "most of them non-residents of the county." The implication that outsiders were butting into a local issue enraged the advocates of pesticide reduction.

Governor Romney issued a press release saying that he supported the dieldrin application as "the only feasible course of action to deal with the Berrien County situation." MDA officials worked on a public relations offensive to convince the public that dieldrin and other pesticides were important tools, in one memo proposing a television interview "that would be home-gardener oriented, telling how the [Japanese] beetle affects homes, landscaping, and shrubbery; and how important it is to prevent it from becoming established. Of course, a brief discussion of use of pesticides could be integrated with this presentation."[26] In a classic example of agriculture agency cooperation with industry, lobbyists prepared resolutions and press statements supporting the "judicious" use of pesticides as part of the communications strategy.

Still in the fall of 1968, EDF filed another suit to stop MDA's plans—this time, in the state of Wisconsin. It was one of the first modern legal actions premised on the shared nature of the Great Lakes ecosystem. Arguing that persistent pesticides applied in Michigan would build up in Lake Michigan and affect the interests of Wisconsin citizens, EDF ingeniously sought a venue for its lawsuit that might result in a more favorable outcome than its 1967 Michigan legal action. MDA reacted sharply. Director B. Dale Ball said the lawsuit was brought by "New York people" who had forced Michigan to plan a bigger application of pesticides in 1968 by delaying the previous year's proposed treatment. But EDF was in effect making an argument that Michigan DNR director MacMullan had successfully used in developing a "joint statement of agreement" by the natural resource agencies of Illinois, Indiana, Wisconsin, and Michigan that summer. The statement called Lake Michigan "a unique natural asset of vast dimension," valuable for drinking water and as a source of sportfishing and commercial fishing and for other uses. The agency directors added:

> It is the consensus of the four states adopting this policy that irreparable contamination is imminent. Recent findings that DDT was the most probable cause

of death of nearly one million coho salmon fry hatched from Lake-Michigan nurtured eggs has brought the problem into sharp focus. We believe that unless timely steps are taken to control persistent pesticides and other economic poisons, Lake Michigan's usefulness will shrink to a fraction of its potential— indeed to the point of disaster.[27]

The four state agencies said they would strengthen interstate water quality standards to protect against pesticide pollution, urge the revision of laws and rules to control use of the chemicals, and "stimulate understanding [of] the problem by the press, radio and television and by civic and conservation groups."

EDF called MDA director Ball to testify in Milwaukee, challenging him to offer evidence that the presence of beetles in Berrien County amounted to an infestation. But EDF had another, surprise witness—DNR director Ralph MacMullan. MacMullan testified that Lake Michigan was part of a regional ecosystem and dieldrin was a significant pollution problem. His pesticide adviser, Ted Black, told the court that dieldrin applied in southwest Michigan would enter the lake and build up. Governor Romney was not pleased. He "invited MacMullan into his office to 'report' on exactly what happened in the federal district court at Milwaukee," observed the *Ann Arbor News.*[28] In a memo to the governor's office, the chief deputy director of MDA complained that MacMullan's appearance was "like a man committing murder and then his wife testifying that he always did have tendencies this way."[29] Although the attorney general's office said it had known nothing of MacMullan's court appearance before the Milwaukee proceeding, MacMullan said he had received legal advice that he was compelled to respond to an EDF subpoena. The DNR director was willing to risk the governor's wrath in testifying.

While generating headlines and interagency controversy, the EDF lawsuit in Wisconsin was unsuccessful. The judge threw the case out of court again and refused to block the application in Berrien County.[30] But the DNR was undaunted. In a memo distributed to hundreds of households in the area to be treated by pesticides, DNR pesticide adviser Black said the agency was monitoring the chemicals and asked citizens to pick up any dead birds or animals near their homes and deliver them to a nearby state park for chemical analysis. MDA officials were irritated, but the application proceeded.

At the same time, agriculture interests, chemical companies, and MDA attempted to mount another public relations offensive, fearing they would lose authority over pesticides to environmental agencies. At a November 1968 press conference in Detroit, an official of the Michigan Agriculture Conference denounced "public hysteria" leading to unreasonable pesticide restrictions and estimated a 50 percent increase in the retail cost of fruits and vegetables if pesticide and chemical management was further restricted. MDA supplied the conference with unmarked fact sheets about pesticide use to be given to the press.

MDA officials and their colleagues in other state agriculture agencies feared that public sentiment would yank pesticides authority from their control and turn it over to environmental departments. "This Nation is on a great consumer protection, conservation, and anti-pollution spree the likes of which we have never seen," complained Parke C. Brinkley, president of the National Agricultural Chemicals Association, in a letter to all state agriculture agency directors. "Pesticides are primarily production tools for farmers, and in my opinion it is very important for the farmers' welfare for the regulatory control over the use of pesticides to remain in an agriculturally-oriented agency."

MDA director B. Dale Ball wrote the dean of MSU's School of Agriculture and Natural Resources to complain about an October press release from the university in which Dr. Roger Hoopingarner described experiments showing that repeated sprayings of DDT and dieldrin in the laboratory quickly developed insect-resistant "superflies." Hoopingarner recommended a phaseout of DDT, dieldrin, and other hard pesticides, adding, "We cannot keep polluting ourselves and our environment." Ball argued that Hoopingarner's words were "very misleading to the general public and should not be contained in a news release." Bristling at the implied threat to his scientific integrity, Hoopingarner replied with data backing up his claims and retorted to Ball, "I hope you were just unaware of this information and are not trying to mislead the public with false hopes."

The agriculture department also objected strenuously to a CBS News report on the national evening newscast November 13 that blamed the die-off of coho salmon fry on DDT and other pesticides. Writing to CBS anchorman Walter Cronkite, the secretary of the Agriculture Commission said the report "was viewed with considerable shock by many people who have long respected your integrity as a newsman." He added that scientists at MSU had said that "no correlation has been established between DDT and the salmon fry mortality."[31]

Michigan's fight over hard pesticides now intensified. In February 1969 MDA—which had regulatory responsibility over commercial food sales as well as control of pesticides application—tested Lake Michigan salmon captured by a Grand Rapids packing company at weirs on spawning streams. The company had pulled 2 million pounds of fish from the state's waters in the fall of 1968 for dressing, canning, or storage in freezers. To its dismay, MDA found relatively high levels of dieldrin in the salmon and embargoed from sale 500,000 pounds of fish. Soon after, the U.S. Food and Drug Administration examined interstate shipments of coho, found high levels of DDT, and seized 14 tons of fish. Federal agencies moved to set a "tolerance" level—a limit on the amount of DDT residue permitted in fish sold in interstate commerce—of 3.5 parts per million. Only Lake Michigan smelt might pass inspection under that level, said Dr. Wayne Tody, the DNR's fish chief. Now more was at stake than the elusive matter of ecosystem integrity. Two industries, commercial fishing and sportfishing-based tourism, were at risk from the use of pesticides to protect another, agriculture. "End of Sports Fishing Near?" asked a head-line in the April 10, 1969, *Lansing State Journal.*

Significant fear of DDT's effects on human health was relatively recent. Most controversy had concerned its impact on fish and wildlife. DDT caused the livers of birds to produce enzymes that attack hormones governing cal-cium production, thus resulting in eggshells of bald eagles and peregrine fal-cons that were too thin to protect the embryo—and threatening the birds with extinction. But by 1969 studies found an association between high residues of pesticides in human fat and several diseases, including leukemia. The National Cancer Institute had found an elevated incidence of tumors in experimental mice fed DDT. "No reputable scientist will yet condemn DDT as poisonous to humans, but the pesticide has been in use less than three decades. Measurable effects could appear in two or three generations," the *New York Times Magazine* reported. The public was awakening to the possibility that chemicals formerly thought to be harmless might slowly be poisoning the human race.

Stepping up his campaign against the hard pesticides, DNR director MacMullan fought for legislation giving his agency a greater say in—perhaps even final decision-making authority over—pesticide use in Michigan. Trained ecologists who understood the link between pesticides and environmental impacts should have regulatory power over the chemicals, MacMullan argued. He argued for a draft pesticide policy that would have transferred the agriculture department's authority to a four-member state committee includ-ing MacMullan. Agriculture department director Ball strongly objected, and the dispute reached Michigan newspapers. The *Detroit Free Press* observed that the dispute could prove embarrassing to William G. Milliken, who had become governor at the start of the year, and added, "Many farmers are appalled at the thought of MacMullan in a position over pesticides."

But MacMullan's public pressure worked. Facing threats to important industries posed by contaminated fish and also worried about an aroused pub-lic, Michigan's agriculture agency did a quick about-face. Since 1962, the Michigan State University Agricultural Experiment Station had already elim-inated DDT from many of its recommendations for insect control and rec-ommended reduced dosages in the remaining instances. In February 1969, under Dr. Gordon Guyer, the station decided to eliminate DDT from its rec-ommendations altogether. This would have the effect of phasing out, over time, the use of DDT by Michigan farmers. Notified of this decision and wor-ried about losing his pesticide control authority if left alone defending DDT, Michigan Department of Agriculture director Ball chose a more aggressive route: he proposed cancellation of DDT registrations for all but three minor uses, to take effect within 60 days. The Commission of Agriculture agreed with the proposal in April 1969, thus making Michigan the first state to can-cel most uses of DDT.

Although calling the action "a commendable step forward," Guyer denounced "hysteria" about the human health effects of DDT: "I very, very seriously question if there is any significance to findings on DDT build-up in animal and fish tissues."[32] The DNR's Ted Black saw it another way: "If we knew as much about DDT in 1945 as we know now, it probably would not have been registered by the U.S. Department of Agriculture. But it was the miracle chemical of the war. It was in use and people were not dropping dead. We had to learn slowly."[33] He added, "Businessmen may feel they can't afford to develop costly substitutes, but we feel that society can't afford the incalculable costs of the havoc produced in our environment by persistent pesticides." Public opinion was now sharply in favor of a ban on DDT. The *Battle Creek Enquirer and News* observed, "Federal and state agencies have responded to the danger in impressive fashion. It was forthright action in the public's interest." The *Ann Arbor News* discussed the new issue raised by persistent pesticides: "[T]here is an awareness now that Michigan's ecological situation must be preserved in a balanced state. Overload an area or a body of water with contaminants and the effects are wide-ranging."

Michigan's virtual ban on DDT use made national headlines and significantly increased momentum toward a national ban on DDT. After years of legal wrangling initiated by an EDF action and fought vigorously by chemical manufacturers, the federal government finally banned DDT for most domestic uses in 1972. To the end, some farmers and agriculture agencies joined the chemical companies in arguing that DDT's human health risks were overblown, demanding proof of its harms. But MacMullan's point of view prevailed nationally as well as in Michigan. In 1970, George Romney, who had sought to suppress MacMullan's campaign when he was governor, wrote the following comments to the DNR director: "Congratulations on the leadership you have shown in fighting DDT and other pesticides. I can see now that you were on the right side of the issue."[34]

MacMullan had bridged the divide between the old conservation school that concentrated on managing habitats to produce optimum fish and game populations while disregarding chemical pollution and an increasingly vigorous public movement demanding environmental cleanup in order to protect the future of the human race. Indeed, some of his apocalyptic rhetoric would soon rival in fervor that of the most aggressive citizens' organizations. Using his bully pulpit, armed with the credibility earned by scientific training and experience, and unafraid of risking his job and reputation, MacMullan brought decisive clout to the anti-DDT battle. After protecting pesticides for years, Michigan state government had been forced by circumstance, an aroused public, and a courageous public official to become the national leader in outlawing DDT sales. MacMullan had not only given the hard pesticides a knockout blow but had begun raising public awareness of the exquisitely sensitive Great Lakes ecosystem of which Michigan was the heart.

CHAPTER 10

Reclaiming the
Tainted Wonderland

The highly useful crystal clear waters of exceptional quality in Lake Huron become so polluted as they pass through the Detroit metropolitan complex that when they enter Lake Erie they are deprived of much of their usefulness for recreational and water supplies. . . . The City of Detroit and Wayne County sewerage systems are the major source of phosphorus and oxygen-demanding wastes poisoning Lake Erie in addition to causing local defilement. . . . Southeast Michigan, whose wastes affect the entire lake, must bear the major share of responsibility for the pollution of Lake Erie.

—U.S. Department of Interior,
Lake Erie Report, August 1968

*L*ong before Lake Erie was declared dead by *Life* magazine in the 1960s, warning signs of regional environmental decline were hard to miss. But government agencies and industries tried to overlook or deny the importance of these signs. For many years Michigan officials and private tourism bureaus attempted to promote the state to visitors as a "water winter wonderland"—a slogan that ultimately appeared on Michigan vehicle license plates—while the resources on which the booming travel and recreation industry depended steadily deteriorated.

Thus came the second wave of resource consumption and destruction in the state. As concerned public officials and citizens agitated and worked to replenish the exhausted timberlands of the northern two-thirds of the state, government and industry generally cooperated in treating the air, water, and land of the heavily populated southern third of Michigan as a sink for the noxious and increasingly hazardous wastes of the industrial age. Renewal of this region's environment would not come for a full three generations after the forestry movement began to heal the north.

Official boosterism of Michigan's attractiveness to visitors began before the end of the nineteenth century. Increasing leisure time and a growing middle class created a constituency for advertisements promoting the healthful qualities of summer on the state's waters. Prompted by an 1897 resolution of the Michigan legislature,[1] the state Board of Health produced a booklet entitled *Michigan: A Summer and Health Resort State.* Careful to challenge the lingering national reputation of the state as a haven for malaria, the booklet sketched pictures of Michigan's Great Lakes shoreline, "an unfolding panorama as varied as the imagination might paint," and of inland lakes, where visitors could find "quiet and rest and recreation." Among watering spots recommended to tourists was the Detroit River, near Ecorse, where the water "is dotted by numbers of long, low islands, over whose tops the vessels, carriers of the commerce of the Great Lakes, can be seen." Significantly, the booklet did not recommend stepping into the river itself; by 1900 the state Board of Health had recorded cases of typhoid in communities such as Wyandotte, downriver of Detroit's waste discharges.

The explosive development of the Detroit area during the first two decades of the new century created tens of thousands of new jobs, attracted aspiring workers from the rural regions of Michigan as well as from other states, and secured its enduring place as the hub of the automobile industry. It also exacerbated a pollution problem that Dr. Robert C. Kedzie of the state Board of Health had forecast as early as 1878.

Kedzie's concern had been the discharge of raw sewage, which became a more severe problem as the region's population grew, but industrial wastes compounded the danger to the state's waters and to public health. The biennial report of the new Department of Conservation for 1921–22 describes problems with milk plants that dumped their skim milk, buttermilk, and whey directly into streams; sugar companies; a garbage reduction company that compressed Detroit's wastes; paper mills; and a tannery. In the mid- and late 1920s, public disgust about such pollution resulted in cries for state action. The *Kalamazoo Gazette* applauded legal action by the state health and conservation departments against the city of Lansing and action threatened against 20 others in 1927, observing, "The day has long passed when civilized communities can tolerate the antiquated practice of dumping public refuse into public waters." Up-to-date disposal systems, the newspaper noted, were necessary for health and sanitation but also for "common decency."[2] Assuring that all communities had such systems took far longer than most thought; in 1988, the state sued the city of Grand Rapids in the first of a new round of litigation to stop the dumping of raw wastes into rivers by cities with combined sewer systems.

One of the reasons for the long delay in combating gross pollution was the ambivalence of legislators, who largely reflected the duality of public attitudes. Fouling lakes and streams was wrong—but stopping it should be done with care not to interfere unreasonably with business needs and municipal budgets. The result of these sentiments was a series of laws that boldly promised an end to pollution but lacked the enforcement teeth to make it happen. And politicians regularly skimped on funding to implement the laws.

The legislature enacted the first such statute in 1929, establishing the state Stream Pollution Control Commission. Consisting of the directors of the conservation, agriculture, highway, and health departments as well as the attorney general, the commission was charged by Act 245 with policing pollution by both the private sector and municipalities. But both by inclination and legislative limitation, the commission was loath to bring aggressive enforcement action to stop the waste dumping. Its initial staff consisted of four full-time employees and a small, summertime field party; its budget in the early years averaged less than $20,000 annually. It could only pursue enforcement of the law when a public health problem was identified or fish and aquatic life were damaged.

The depression that followed on the heels of the stock market's Black Tuesday in 1929 increased the commission's reluctance to take on polluters. "Under present economic conditions, the Commission is not pressing for the correction of existing unlawful pollution," said the panel's biennial report for 1931–32. "The Commission is attempting to bring all such problems at this time through the 'Preliminary Report' and planning stage, so that construction may promptly proceed as soon as local financial and economic conditions permit."[3]

There was plenty of unlawful pollution. The same report noted "disagreeable odors" adjacent to many heavily polluted streams, suggesting that private parties could bring nuisance lawsuits since the state was limited in its authority unless a demonstrable threat to public health or aquatic life could be identified. An example of more serious pollution was the Clinton River below Mount Clemens, where the commission noted "public health hazards of grave proportions." Angry owners of riparian property along the Clinton River turned out for a September meeting of the commission. The report estimated that across the state, 31 municipalities with an aggregate population of 431,738 had adequate sewage treatment—while 81 municipalities containing 2,502,233 people had no acceptable means of sewage treatment. The economic slump had reduced industrial pollution as well as production, but accidental spills of cyanide from automobile or plating plants killed fish in the Grand River at Lansing, in the Flint River at the city of Flint, in the Fawn River below Sturgis, in the St. Joe River at Buchanan, and at the junction of the Rouge and Detroit Rivers.

The 1935–36 biennial report of the commission described appalling conditions.

Uncontrolled sewage discharges and detrimental industrial wastes overload several public water supplies today, and threaten the development of future ones; many natural bathing places are rendered definitely dangerous, while the quality of water at others is periodically questionable; miles of inland streams, as well as the American side of the Detroit River, are so polluted as to offer no suitable habitat for fish, while other stretches of river become the occasional death bed of fish within those limits. At times pollution so taints the flesh of fish so as to render it inedible. Some shoreline resort properties suffer heavy depreciation in value. Hundreds of agricultural interests sustain health hazards and riparian losses while here and there throughout the state inadequate pollution control is evidenced by objectionable odor nuisance, both public and private.

The commission continued to pursue a policy of encouragement and voluntary compliance—with legal action only as a last resort—throughout the 1930s. When pressed to correct their dumping of raw sewage, municipalities often pleaded poverty. Industries generally promised cooperative research and technology development programs, with dates for the correction of the pollution deferred for years. The advent of World War II diverted the funding and attention of the state to needs considered more urgent. It was only in the postwar boom that public outrage about pollution resumed, keeping pace with an ever-growing economy and the resultant increase in wastes.

The history of the pollution of the Kalamazoo River illustrates the state's generally feeble approach. Already a major source of employment late in the nineteenth century, the local paper industry treated the stream as its refuse dump for years with little effective challenge from the state.

The potential of the river to support commerce was noted in 1847 when the *Kalamazoo Gazette* observed, "Capitalists who would embark on a profitable enterprise would do well to establish a mill in this village. We have the very best facilities." Nineteen years later, businessmen founded the Kalamazoo Paper Company and constructed the first paper mill two miles south of the city of Kalamazoo on a tributary called Portage Creek. The plant specialized in newsprint. Struggling in its first five years, the mill began to prosper after Samuel A. Gibson of Fitchburg, Massachusetts, became general superintendent in 1872. By the time Gibson died as president of the company in 1899, the firm had a strong regional reputation for timely delivery of its book papers. It also had many local competitors and colleagues. The roster included the B. F. Lyon Company of Plainwell, 11 miles north of Kalamazoo; the Michigan Paper Company, also of Plainwell; the Bardeen Paper Company of Otsego, just downstream from Plainwell; and the Bryant Paper Company of Kalamazoo.[4]

The first two decades of the twentieth century accelerated the growth of the local paper industry. Between 1908 and 1917 five new mills located in the city of Kalamazoo, and three new mills opened at Otsego. And a primary reason was the river.

> *It might be wondered why the paper industry located in the Kalamazoo so extensively. In choosing a site for a paper mill the manufacturer must take into consideration several important factors. Chief of these is the necessity of having a large supply of water that should be free from impurities, such as suspended matter and soluble iron. The Kalamazoo River in the Kalamazoo Valley is able to adequately supply water and power such as is desired by the paper industry. For this reason, and undoubtedly for this reason alone, Kalamazoo was chosen for the site of the paper mills which now make it an outstanding contributor to paper manufacturing, not only in the United States, but the entire world.[5]*

The industry was now a formidable force in the community. In 1925, 10 companies with 16 paper mills and 34 paper and board machines employed 5,200 workers and had an annual payroll of $7 million. Related industries provided 2,500 jobs with a payroll of $3.5 million annually.

To pay for the jobs, the community accepted increasing damage to its waterways. The industry noticeably contaminated Portage Creek and the river with noxious wastes, including heavy doses of organic material and sludge that made it an unsuitable habitat for fish and most other aquatic life. In 1930, the *Kalamazoo Gazette* published a nostalgic piece about the days when the local stream was a home for game fish, especially smallmouth bass, which were more abundant there than at any other place in southwestern Michigan. Ironically, it drew that conclusion as it reprinted an 1894 article that told of a massive fish kill in the stream caused by the emptying of a paper mill's bleaching vat. "Those who saw the terrible destruction say that from two to three ton were killed, including almost every kind of carp, weighing nearly 10 pounds, to a million of minnows. Deputy Game Warden O'Byrne was on the scene and saw places where the river bed was white with the dead fish. . . . There was some substance which seemed to eat through the membrane between the gills and the body and caused them to bleed to death." But the *Gazette* was indicating in 1930 that at least there had once been valuable fish to kill in the Kalamazoo River.

Wayne Denniston, who grew up in the Kalamazoo Valley and later joined the state's water pollution control program, remembered that around 1940, when he was eight years old, "A bunch of us kids played all over the river. We used to catch live snapping turtles and sell them to a restaurant. You never ducked your head in the water. I would get a scum line right around my neck. In Allegan, a long ways downstream from Kalamazoo, [the river] used to flow gray from the paper mill waste." Others remembered how, in the 1940s and 1950s, hydrogen sulfide bubbling off decaying sludge deposits from the paper industry turned the white paint on riverside houses black or caused it to peel.

With World War II ending, public attention turned to the conditions of the area's waters. The state Stream Control Commission complained in the summer of 1945 that the river downstream of Kalamazoo completely lacked dissolved oxygen because paper wastes consumed all of it. Commission secretary Milton Adams said the wastes had killed off all fish life and oil was discoloring and coating the shoreline.

Hoping to blunt criticism, the Kalamazoo Valley mills announced in August 1945 a $20,000 annual research program "looking toward the elimination of waste from paper mills into Kalamazoo river," noted the *Gazette*. The focus of the work was the de-inking process, which was now concentrated in the Kalamazoo Valley. In 1948 six local mills, four of them in Kalamazoo, announced plans to build a small demonstration plant to handle the de-inking wastes.

The pollution assault on the river, however, only increased. In 1947 the Battle Creek Plating Works killed several thousand fish when it dumped cyanide waste into the river. In September 1948 the Union Steel Products plant in Albion dumped enough cyanide waste into the stream to kill 200,000 fish. The Stream Control Commission threatened to draft a state rule limiting cyanide discharges. It also turned a critical eye on the city of Kalamazoo and the local paper industry. Speaking at a meeting of the local Jaycees, the executive secretary of the commission urged the city to build a "modern sewage disposal system" costing the average family $1.50 to $2 per month and called on the paper industry to reuse more water. Kalamazoo was the worst offender in the entire river valley, Adams said.

When the state found progress cleaning up the river inadequate, it took another tack. It decided to classify the Kalamazoo as an "industrial river," meaning its most beneficial use was as a treatment mechanism for wastes. The chief engineer for what was now called the state Water Resources Commission said that the Kalamazoo actually had a lot of improving to do even to become an industrial river: "The water is too foul right now to be used for cooling or condensing. I say the river is only suitable to float a boat, and hardly that." He cautioned the public not to look for too much recovery from the stream: "Don't expect the Kalamazoo river will ever become a trout stream again. For the benefits of developing your lake, to attract industry, to be relieved of the foul odors and get a few fish in the river, you must tolerate a continued dumping of wastes."[6] But he proposed cutting the current daily dumping of 180 tons of solids into the river to 80 tons.

Such answers were no longer enough to quell public concern. A conservation community growing in numbers and volume was clamoring for cleanup of the state's fouled waters. In a 1947 edition of its magazine *Michigan Out-of-Doors*, the Michigan United Conservation Clubs called water pollution "an inexcusable waste of a most important resource." Noting that 235 out of 755 municipalities, industries, and institutions covered by the 1929 water pollution law were not complying with it, and that 131 rivers and 43 lakes were seriously polluted, the MUCC derided industry claims that tougher state laws and policies would drive business from the state.[7]

But memories of the Great Depression lingered in the minds of many, and the post–World War II industrial boom was reaping huge economic benefits for Michigan. Between 1939 and 1947, the number of manufacturing establishments in the state rose from 5,961 to 9,889, and the number of production workers jumped from 520,000 to 822,000. Wages and salaries paid the workers shot up 189 percent, from $1.8 to $5.2 billion.[8] The manufacturing lobby exercised considerable influence in state politics.

Agitation by the sportsmen led to the appointment of a special study committee on water pollution by Governor Kim Sigler in 1947. Industry spokespersons turned up at the committee's meetings to argue that some streams should not be reclaimed. Howard Cowles of the Detroit Creamery Company said:

We are of the opinion that in any proposed legislation distinction should be made between the streams in the thickly settled, essentially industrial areas, and those in less settled regions where more opportunity exists for maintaining conditions favorable to native fish and game. In other words, where industry employing considerable numbers of persons exists, and where it would appear

*difficult to again produce native conditions, we doubt if established industries
should be compelled to spend huge sums.*[9]

Another witness was John L. Lovett, general manager of the Michigan
Manufacturers' Association. He suggested that the threat of tougher water
pollution laws had caused General Motors Corporation to decentralize its
operations, moving jobs out of state. Lovett added that the issue of public
health was not related to water pollution, saying, "[I]t is simply an argument
that is dragged into it."

The MUCC sharply opposed the business association's view, calling it
"obstructionist" and "pathetic" and noting that swimming had been forbidden at MUCC's children's summer camp on Lake Allegan the previous summer because of pollution. An angry witness before the study panel was K. J.
Dahlka, chairman of the pollution committee of the Trenton Sportsmen Club
in downriver Detroit: "I have lived in Trenton, Mich., located sixteen miles
down the Detroit River at the head of Lake Erie for thirty six years. I have
watched the Detroit River change from one of the most beautiful rivers in the
State of Mich. to the filthiest river in these United States, with the exception
of the River Rouge," Dahlka said in prepared testimony. "[P]ollution has
increased to the extant [*sic*] that no longer fish are eatable, paint on bottoms
of boats that use these waters is eaten off, aquatic vegetation has diminished
to the extant [*sic*] that it has practically stoped [*sic*] the income from muskrat
trappers, of which hundreds of citizens participate annually. Also swimming
in these waters is a thing of the past."

Public outrage mounted when, in the winter of 1948, pollution killed off
large numbers of waterfowl in a widely publicized incident on the Detroit
River. In its report on the matter, the Department of Conservation called the
incident a "catastrophe" caused by a combination of harsh winter conditions
that left little open water for the ducks—and terrible water pollution: "Miles
of busy factories representing one of the world's most concentrated industrial
areas, making automobiles, steel, chemicals, etc., line the west bank of the
river and its tributaries. Industrial wastes find their way into the river. One of
the worst of these wastes is oil of various types." In mid-January 1948 a thick
flow of oil coiled along the west side of the river, coating several thousand
ducks. Some of them died quickly, the insulation of their feathers broken
down by the oil. Others were "easy prey" for crows, gulls, and eagles, and
"dozens of freshly picked skeletons were mute evidence of the magnitude of
the tragedy." The department pointedly observed, "The control of pollution
evidently offers the best possibility of avoiding future occurrences. . . . So, we
should not regard the loss of several thousand ducks in recent weeks as having been without some gain. The loss has forcibly driven home in the minds
of many persons the evil effects of water pollution; called attention to those
effects in a way that perhaps nothing else could have done outside of the
actual loss of human life."[10]

Spurred by these incidents and by an anti–water pollution crusade by the conservation writer Jack Van Coevering of the *Detroit Free Press* in 1947 and 1948, the legislature abolished the old Stream Control Commission and replaced it with the Water Resources Commission, whose membership included representatives of the public for the first time. In addition to directors of four state agencies, the commission included one member of a conservation group, one member from a municipality, and one from industry. But the commission had less than 30 employees to cover the pollution problems of the entire state. And, said one commission staff member, "Lots of these companies thought they had a right to put their waste in a river."

But public pressure was mounting to force cleanup of the Kalamazoo River. For the first time, a vocal constituency demanded action in the late 1940s and early 1950s. In late 1948 and early 1949, 50 Kalamazoo-area organizations, including sportsmen's clubs and women's clubs, circulated a petition calling for a ban on harmful pollution. The petition was designed to "bring clean water back to Michigan," said local sportsman Guy Kistler. The petition complained of the river's use "as a means of carrying away unwanted wastes, sewage and similar filth which has caused a large portion of the Kalamazoo river to be condemned from a health standpoint" and called on the legislature to enact tougher laws.

Citizens and local officials who received Kalamazoo's wastes downstream in Allegan County were especially unhappy. The Allegan County Conservation League bristled at a resolution passed by the Kalamazoo city commission asking for an industrial stream designation. The Allegan city manager read a resolution of his own city council to the Water Resources Commission that complained, "[O]ur city should not be made to carry the burden of removing a tremendous amount of dead carp." He added that the paper mills "might better spend money trying to take care of their pollution than fighting lawsuits which I am privileged to say are going to be started if this thing isn't cleaned up."

But the city of Kalamazoo was in no hurry to clean up the river. The local manager of the St. Regis Paper mill threatened to close his mill if the state issued a tough order. Although Water Resources Commission secretary Milton Adams brushed the threat aside, pointing out that the company was making a handsome profit and could afford to improve its waste practices, Kalamazoo mayor Paul Todd expressed alarm and appointed a river cleanup study committee at least partly in an attempt to forestall the state order. The committee was then expanded to include downstream representatives. Its final report confirmed the problem.

> *A half mile below [the Kalamazoo Paper Company], Portage Creek was emptying a similar column of gray water into the river. From this point on for two or three miles there was much evidence of septic action. The current of the river was slower. Gas eruptions from the water gave the appearance of splashes from raindrops all about. Chunks of sludge, varying in size up to that of a plat-*

ter, were raised from the bottom of the river by gases formed by bacterial action. When hit with an oar, and the gas knocked out of one, it would sink to the bottom.[11]

The committee conceded that "the condition of the river is not in accord with the best interests of the area" and found the state's plan to abate the problem feasible. But it cautioned that the regulators should adjust the plan to avoid doing unnecessary economic harm to the industry.

By the fall of 1951 the Water Resources Commission had lost patience, adopting orders against the 15 paper mills "to end pollution" of the Kalamazoo River by June 1, 1954. Meetings and draft plans ensued. In September 1953, the river attracted national attention when the oxygen demand caused by the paper wastes killed thousands of carp near Allegan. "Their corpses gorged the valley's streams, as in Dumont Creek, where four acres of carp choked the waters in glistening, smelly death," *Life* magazine reported beside a picture of the casualties. "Back down the Kalamazoo valley the aroused citizens sought injunction to halt the paper mills' pollution of the river. At a meeting one man rose in anger to propose a graphic nonlegal solution: that they each get a dead carp and all together carry them on a tour of the paper mill offices."[12] The commission cracked down on Otsego Falls Paper Mills after the carp killing. The company's wastes were equivalent to those discharged by a city of over 80,000 people, the commission said, pushing ahead even though the company protested that no economical technology existed to control its waste.[13]

The deadline came and went, and pollution continued. Although in 1955 the *Kalamazoo Gazette* reported that "you can almost see the bottom" of the river and that the stream had changed "from a ribbon of rancid waste to something that almost looks like water," initial treatment systems installed by the paper industry were not up to the job. In 1958 the Water Resources Commission said that pollution of the Kalamazoo River had to be cut 62 percent between Kalamazoo and Otsego. A staff report to the commission found that the river's waste load had increased 150 percent between 1930 and 1946, with an additional 12 percent increase between the latter year and 1950. The treatment required of the paper industry had since reduced the oxygen demand made by paper wastes on the river by only 3,500 pounds, or about 5 percent. Rising paper output from the mills was offsetting the benefits of pollution control.

At the same time, a new kind of pollution was about to be introduced to the Kalamazoo River system. Allied Paper Company announced in 1957 plans to build a mill costing up to $7.5 million in Kalamazoo, consuming between 50,000 and 90,000 cords of pulpwood per year. Pollution would not be a problem, the company said. "A process will be used recovering 100 per cent of the waste materials from liquid used in the pulping, so there will be no stream pollution," the *Kalamazoo Gazette* reported. Thirty years later, the state would identify more than 200,000 pounds of toxic polychlorinated biphenyls

(PCBs) in river sediments, with the biggest single source Allied Paper Company's discharges at the same facility that had promised to prevent all stream pollution.[14]

Sparring continued between the paper mills and Kalamazoo officials on one hand and downstream residents and officials on the other for years, with Water Resources Commission staff refereeing the dispute. Allegan city manager P. H. Beauvais complained to the commission that "it will be impossible for the city of Allegan to live with the stench this summer" at the same meeting where Kalamazoo mayor Glenn Allen pointed to a report by the W. E. Upjohn Institute calling papermaking the best economic use of the river and observed that the industry contributed almost half of the factory jobs in the city. The vice president of the Rex Paper Company said that the commission would be "inviting us to go somewhere else" for a planned expansion of its mill if it was too tough on pollution.

Beset by so many conflicting currents, the commission prodded the paper industry and the city to move ahead but continually pushed back deadlines for compliance with its pollution orders. In April 1961 it set a 1964 deadline for secondary treatment of sewage and paper wastes dumped into the river— which several of the paper companies sought to postpone until 1966. A winter 1961 fish kill of more than two tons of carp at Allegan stiffened the commission's resolve. But by December of the same year the commission granted two plants the extension to 1966 that they sought.

In 1963 came a breakthrough. The city of Kalamazoo agreed to build a $3.7 million sewage treatment plant, and four of the mills agreed to join the project, sending their wastes to be managed there. Beginning operation in 1966, the plant made an immediate difference. "Paper mill sludge and scum no longer dominate the look of the river. Gone is the milky cast to the water," reported the *Kalamazoo Gazette*. It added, however, that the river had not been "transformed into a clear, bubbling brook" and that the river's oxygen supply was still too limited to support most fish.

In 1967 the Weyerhauser Paper Company at Plainwell began construction of a $225,000 secondary waste treatment plant. Industry was beginning to talk a new line. The *Kalamazoo Gazette* favorably quoted an official of Mead Paper Company acknowledging that "it would seem surprising if a nation which, in my lifetime, has developed the automobile, the airplane and the atomic bomb couldn't find a relatively inexpensive way to improve its stream pollution situation." Still, the official said, the public should be patient and not unreasonable.

This attempt to hold off an immediate crackdown while appealing to public sentiment for river cleanup was reflective of broader changes sweeping through U.S. society. Increasingly impatient with studies and other delaying tactics, citizens were pressuring public officials to restore lakes and streams. A country working feverishly to land a man on the moon by the end of the 1960s, advocates argued, should be able to handle its own sewage.

One of the most influential voices in this public chorus was that of the labor movement, led by United Automobile Workers (UAW) president Walter P. Reuther. Born to German immigrant parents in 1907, Reuther grew up in West Virginia but came to work as a young man in Michigan's automobile industry. Fired in 1932 for socialist political activity, Reuther traveled to Russia but returned to Detroit to lead union organizing struggles in the auto-motive industry. He and other union activists were attacked and beaten by Ford Motor Company–employed operatives at the famous "Battle of the Overpass" in 1937, leading to the unionization of the company's production workers in 1941. Elected president of the union in 1946, he remained in the post until his 1970 death.

Reuther's wide-ranging interests, which included social justice and inter-national peace as well as improved pay and working conditions for his union members, broadened in the last several decades of his life to include the envi-ronment. A lover of the water, Reuther had taken his family to a cabin on Higgins Lake in the northern Lower Peninsula each summer before moving them to a house on a five-acre plot on Paint Creek, a tributary of the Clinton River in Macomb County, in the 1950s. His daughter remembered him explaining to her when she was 12 years old that man was destroying nature's balance, and years later she said that his "concern for the earth was the ripened fruit of his humanity."[15]

At the same time he was helping organize Boy Scout cleanups of the Paint Creek and seeking money for sewage treatment on the Clinton River, Reuther was establishing a conservation department within the UAW structure and beginning a public campaign for laws to stop water pollution as well as for government acquisition of lands to provide recreation for hard-pressed work-ing families. He appointed Olga Madar to head the new recreation depart-ment, the first woman to hold such a high-level post in the union, and unleashed her and staff to work for progressive federal and state legislation. "It was Walter who started all of our work in this area," said Mildred Jeffries, one of his staff members. "He was always interested in the communities in which UAW members lived, the schools, the parks and the air and water, not just in the members themselves. Olga was a kindred soul with Walter's goals and vision."[16]

By the mid-1960s the deterioration of Lake Erie had concentrated national attention on the problem of water pollution. Fed by enormous amounts of phosphorus and other nutrients from cities and farms, massive algal blooms discouraged swimmers and boaters from using the lake. Conservationists and water users protested the lake's decline. Although the federal government had limited powers under pollution laws in effect at the time, it had responsibility for convening interstate conferences on pollution of shared waters, which it did in August 1965 for Lake Erie.

Detroit's water department director, Gerald Remus, bitterly attacked a report issued by the U.S. Public Health Service before the meeting. The report called the city a major source of the pollution of the Detroit River and Lake Erie, pointing out that the Detroit River contributed 78 percent of the total suspended solids, 70 percent of controllable phosphates, and more than half of the nitrogen compounds entering the lake from tributaries. While not disputing these facts, Remus called the release of the report a "cheap publicity stunt" and said the city should be credited for the $300 million it had spent in recent years to improve the sewage plant. He challenged the federal recommendation that the city install secondary treatment at the sewage plant, saying that it would do nothing to solve the problem of storm water contamination and would actually increase organic chemicals in the river, which he described as a result of the secondary treatment process.[17]

Reuther scolded Remus for brushing aside the U.S. Public Health Service findings. "May I respectfully suggest," he wrote "that it would be the better part of wisdom if you refrain from taking the findings of the report as a personal affront and provide the type of leadership which reflects concern for the health and welfare of the people." He supported the health service recommendation that the city install secondary treatment, saying that it was "not an uncommon request." Mayor Jerome P. Cavanagh wrote a conciliatory reply, agreeing that "none of us can take lightly" the federal report and adding that Remus had differences only with the recommended methods of cleaning up the lake, not the goals.[18]

Reuther sent Madar to Cleveland to represent the UAW at the interstate conference. Noting that the lake basin was inhabited by 500,000 UAW members, she said the UAW was "appalled at the rate of deterioration and the extent of the pollution of Lake Erie" in the federal report. She outlined a six-point plan for addressing the pollution, including secondary treatment of sewage by Detroit and other cities, federal assistance for pollution control projects, and a national policy requiring industry to show it could treat wastes resulting from production of any new products. A federal official wrote Reuther to thank him for the strong UAW statement, saying that it had "stood out prominently in its plea to deal boldly and dramatically with the Detroit area water pollution problem."

Reuther responded to the Lake Erie crisis by planning a conference entitled "United Action for Clear Water Conference" later that year in Detroit, which was attended by 1,000 UAW members and conservationists. His keynote speech revealed the personal roots of his concern about water pollution.

"How bad do things have to get before you do something?" he said.

Things are much worse than we realize. . . . I haven't been around so long, but I can remember the fishing and swimming holes that I enjoyed when I was a kid in West Virginia—Wheeling Creek that emptied into the Ohio River, and the Ohio River where I swam and fished as a kid. They are all open sewers now, and the kid who grows up in the neighborhood that I grew up in can't swim in those swimming holes, and can't catch fish there any more. I think every kid growing up in our kind of free society ought to have access to nature with all of its beauties—the same as I had.

Calling pollution "a national crisis," Reuther said that Lake Erie was dying and the other Great Lakes were troubled. He called for national pollution control standards and a $50 billion, five-year commitment to clean up the environment, the same amount the nation spent every year on the military. "If we don't move aggressively, Michigan will be the wasted wonderland—not the Water Wonderland—and this is true of other states," he added.

Soon after the conference Reuther turned his sights to Michigan's role in combating water pollution. In March 1966 he wrote Governor George Romney and legislators that the state needed $3 billion to achieve clean water by 1980 and urged the governor to call for funding a state share of 30 percent, or almost $1 billion, at a rate of $65 million per year.

The proposal received a cool response initially. Legislative leaders interviewed by the *Detroit News* agreed only that something should be done. "Every one of us wants to do something about water pollution, but $65 million! Just because we have a surplus doesn't mean we can commit the state to a program that will get us into trouble," said state representative Einar Erlandsen, chairperson of the Ways and Means Committee. The federal government or local governments should bear the lion's share of the funding, other legislators said. Romney urged Reuther to support his request for just $1 million for aid to communities to build waste treatment facilities.[19]

But a new federal report issued in 1968 further detailed the problems of Lake Erie. It noted that more than 1.5 billion gallons a day of wastes from cities and industries entered the Detroit River. The report prompted Romney to come to the defense of the state's water pollution efforts, and the Ford Motor Company argued that the Rouge River, feeding the Detroit River, "had never looked so good." Madar, writing to congratulate U.S. interior secretary Stewart Udall on the report, blistered Michigan's program: "These agencies often proceed not with the ardent dedication necessary to clean the waters but instead appear more cognizant of the needs and desires of industry than of the public at large. The usual result of such agencies' work is the concealment of industrial polluters behind a dual smokescreen of focus on municipal pollution and disguising scientific terminology discernible only to the experts."[20]

The state was forced to acknowledge ugly conditions on many of its lakes and streams. In a report prepared for a conference on Lake Michigan pollution convened by the secretary of the interior, the Water Resources Commission admitted that 32 miles of shoreline from south of Muskegon to Benona had "nuisance accumulations" of algae and that 36 of 47 monitoring locations in the Lower Peninsula had bacteriological counts of 1,000 organisms per 100 milliters of water, above recommended standards for swimming. But the state blamed much of this on dead and decaying alewives.[21]

The generally defensive tone of this report and others like it prepared by the state incensed a citizens group in Whitehall called Environment, Inc. In a critique entitled *Rendezvous with Death,* its cover featuring a skull and crossbones occupying the center of Lake Michigan, the group fumed that the state's pollution control program legalized "the continuance of the abhorrent practices of wastewater disposal that have been slowly but surely choking the life from our waters and hastening the eventual death of the Great Lakes." The citizens strongly objected to statements by the commission that it would continue to encourage use of the "waste assimilation capacities of the receiving stream or lake"—in simple terms, dilution of pollution. "The above statement might have been acceptable and logical twenty years ago. Today the entire concept of dilution and assimilation is known to be the wrong approach to wastewater disposal," they wrote.

The drumbeat of negative publicity and increasing concern expressed by the UAW and conservationists helped advance Reuther's proposal for a major state funding program to clean up rivers. Romney supported a $335 million clean water bond proposal that the legislature put on the November 1968 ballot. Approved by a two to one margin, the bond program predated significant federal funding, which would not come until passage of the Clean Water Act in 1972. Reuther's leadership had helped bring Michigan out of the dark ages of water pollution.

Reuther and the UAW would continue pressing business and government to do more. In a 1968 speech to the Water Pollution Control Federation, Reuther said that industry needed to make pollution control "a top office project," not something relegated to junior officials, the way companies had handled labor problems "in the old days." In 1970, just months before the labor leader's death in a plane crash, the UAW organized a demonstration outside a Detroit meeting of the state Water Resources Commission, protesting "kid glove treatment" of polluters, including Ford Motor Company.

It was not always easy for union officials to take a stand against polluting businesses. In 1973, when Madar was being considered by Governor William Milliken as the first female appointee to the state Natural Resources Commission, she advised him to select Joan Wolfe of the West Michigan Environmental Action Council instead, since "I had opposition from within AFL-CIO because of my environmental position."[22] Milliken did appoint Wolfe.

But Reuther's conservation ethic and Madar's stalwart defense of a clean environment never wavered. Reuther had made it possible for workers to challenge their employers to clean up industrial processes—rejecting the choice between jobs and a healthy environment that businesses in the Kalamazoo Valley and elsewhere had offered for years.

From Smoke Abatement to Air Pollution Control

By the end of the nineteenth century, industrialized cities of the United States were sometimes smothered in thick smoke. Although these emissions were welcomed by some as a sign of economic progress, to a growing urban housekeeping movement they were part of a deplorable and unsanitary trend that also included piles of rotting garbage and reeking sewage. In 1887 the Detroit

Board of Aldermen found it necessary to enact an ordinance "for the prevention of smoke nuisances." The city revised the ordinance several times, in 1904 declaring "the emission of black or gray smoke" from any stack or chimney a public nuisance, establishing the office of smoke inspector, and creating a maximum fine of $100 for violations.

Concern about the "nuisance" created by smoke grew across the nation as the twentieth century began. In a 1912 publication, the U.S. Bureau of Mines noted a demand for less smoke from "chambers of commerce and . . . civic associations and leagues, as well as by the passage and enforcement of smoke ordinances by nearly all of the large cities of the country." Brick kilns, furnaces, and locomotive and steamboat boilers were leading culprits, the bureau noted. The bureau said Detroit pursued an educational approach, urging operators to install mechanical stoking equipment.[23]

The emphasis on "smoke" and on the nuisance conditions it caused signaled that the problem was not yet considered one seriously affecting the public health. "To many engineers and businessmen, smoke primarily was waste coal, the result of poorly designed equipment and poorly trained furnace stokers. . . . The solution was innovation and education, not punishment."[24]

But just as rapid industrialization and population growth promoted water pollution, they exacerbated the problem of urban smoke. In 1936 the chief smoke inspector for Detroit estimated that 350 tons of "soot, fly-ash and dirt" fell each year on every square mile of Detroit, up from 56 tons in 1931. "Smoking factory chimneys, long pointed to as symbols of civic prosperity, actually are signs that money is being wasted and health menaced," said Charles J. McCabe. He warned of dangers caused by the release of sulfur dioxide from coal burning, saying it weathered paint, harmed green vegetation, and caused inflammation of the nose and throat. The city's reduction in smoke inspectors from 12 to 2 had crippled the program, he complained. The *Detroit Times* reported that 27,800 tons of soot fell on the city annually, more than 37 pounds for each resident of the city. Pointing the finger at the city's Common Council for its cuts in the smoke abatement staff, the newspaper prompted officials to examine ways to restore some of the inspectors.[25]

Handcuffed by the same paramount concern with economic recovery from the depression that held back water pollution control efforts, smoke abatement programs in the city did little to restrain the problem until after World War II. In the late 1940s disgust with the smoke problem, however, began to mount.

Suburbs downriver from Detroit were especially afflicted by uncontrolled emissions to the air during the postwar period. "South Wyandotte rubbed 69.6 tons of fly-ash from their eyes this week to hear Smoke Abatement Inspector F. W. Classon tell them that things will be better now with installation of a new collector unit at Penn Salt boilers and promise of installation of two more before the year's end," the *Free Press* reported in October 1947. Calling the weekend's smoke and ash emissions "a veritable hurricane," the newspaper reported that harassed homeowners had called Classon for relief.

The 69.6 tons of soot that fell at one spot in a 12-hour period was more than four times what ordinarily landed in a month, he said.

Traffic on the Detroit River was a persistent air pollution problem. Officials from Detroit and Windsor, the Ontario city across the river, monitored passing vessels in the late 1940s and early 1950s, reporting offending ships to the International Joint Commission, the U.S.-Canada boundary panel established by treaty. Photographs in a Windsor newspaper in 1949 showed a passenger steamer leaving its Detroit dock and obscuring the city's skyline with a long plume of thick black smoke.

Public tolerance of the smoke problem, as it was still called, quickly declined. Periodic "blackouts" occurred in which smoke mixed with fog, darkening the city during the daylight hours. A series of articles in the *Detroit News* in early 1947 exposed rats and smoke as serious problems for the city. Both were plagues, the paper observed, and the city needed to find the "gumption" to enact a tough smoke ordinance as well as rat control programs.[26] Citizens responded. Mrs. William McGaughey, who lived in the affluent Indian Village neighborhood, circulated petitions urging the city to strengthen its smoke control program: "I am just one of thousands of women who want cleaner homes," she told a reporter. Mrs. John Neal told the *News* that dirt and smoke buried snow in the winter, making it unhealthy for her two-year-old son to play outdoors: "There is no reason why a clean Detroit should be not as congenial a city to live in as any in the country—if measures are taken to curb smoke."

The resulting 1947 revision of Detroit's smoke ordinance expanded control to pollutants other than smoke. Under its provisions, a city official boasted, a major industrial plant had been successfully compelled to install fly ash collectors on its coal-fired boilers at a cost of $125,000. If it had failed to do so, the official said, the city would have taken the company to court. In 1955, Wayne County, which encompasses Detroit as well as the downriver suburbs, adopted its own air pollution control rules but provided an average of only $13,000 per year in support to the program and the equivalent of one to one and-a-half staff positions. But air pollution was nearing its peak in industrialized southeast Michigan. It was later estimated that Detroit's emissions crested in approximately 1953, with 66 tons per square mile per month of dustfall and record levels of sulfur dioxide and particulates.

The problem was no longer merely smoke. In 1948 the combination of air pollution and an atmospheric inversion (warm air overhead preventing waste from rising and diffusing) killed 20 people at Donora, Pennsylvania. An estimated 4,000 died in a London episode in 1952, and 250 died in five days of air stagnation in New York City in 1953. The public began to worry for its health as a result of the scourge of what was now called "air pollution." Growing national concern led to the November 1958 National Conference on Air Pollution, called by the U.S. surgeon general, and the creation of a Division of Air Pollution in the U.S. Public Health Service in 1960.

By that time air emissions were stirring an outcry in several urban areas of the state. Industries in Grand Rapids and Muskegon created visible problems. A state health department study in 1962 underscored the problem, calculating that 554 tons of pollution filled the skies over Muskegon. The agency said that 73 industrial establishments emitted 106 tons of contaminants and 11 plants dumped 417 tons of coal into the atmosphere, and it warned that this level of pollution could cause health problems. The biggest culprit was the B. C. Cobb coal-burning power plant operated by Consumers Power Company, which emitted 218 tons of sulfur dioxide and 80 tons of fly ash per day. The health department warned that on the two or three days each year when Muskegon faced an atmospheric inversion the situation "could be dangerous, particularly because of the rapid buildup of sulfur dioxide which could take place."[27] The report triggered an immediate response in Muskegon, with the local newspaper calling it "badly needed" and urging action on the department's recommendation that a local board or committee be established to examine how other communities had dealt with air pollution.

Within a few years, Muskegon citizens themselves were clamoring for action. Acting at the urging of Julian Szten, an employee of the Muskegon County health department, a handful of area residents formed Muskegon County Citizens for Clean Air in 1966. Dr. William Schroeder, a chemist and vice president of Burdick and Jackson Laboratories, became the chair.

"This town had gotten a reputation as a dirty town," he said. "The conditions were getting intolerable." Lakey Foundry, located close to downtown Muskegon, was so poorly operated that people parking at the post office and doing business for less than an hour would emerge to find soot and ash blanketing their vehicles. Thomas Spencer, an employee of the local health department, said smoke would "roll out" the doors of the foundry. "You could cut the air when I started working there," Spencer said.[28] Muskegon industry was now emitting 800 tons per day of pollution, the citizens group charged, costing every citizen $300 per year in damage.

Challenging the prevailing view that industry should be permitted to pollute in order to retain jobs was not an easy thing to do. Schroeder said many citizens worried about the deteriorating conditions held back out of fear for their own jobs or reputations. He had the liberty to speak out because many of his customers were not from Muskegon. But when Citizens for Clean Air solicited signatures at a local health fair calling for a county air pollution ordinance and tough state air pollution enforcement, they collected 6,000 names. They used the petitions as evidence of a broad base of community concern and successfully pressured county officials to enact the ordinance. "Our group was comprised of only about 30 dues-paying members at $1 per year. . . . [T]his effort is evidence for how effective a small but vocal and informed group can be in effecting change," Schroeder said.[29] Spencer, the health official, said that the public outcry engineered by Schroeder and allies was critical. "He could get 500 or 600 people to make phone calls or write letters to the [county] commissioners," Spencer said.

The issue was even on the minds of delegates to the state's Constitutional

Convention, which was rewriting the 1908 constitution. Eugene A. Sloane, editor of *Air Engineering* magazine, said Michigan was a "disgraceful" last among the states in air pollution control despite its excellence in general public health protection. "A great many people in the Detroit area are half-sick or below par physically because of the contaminated air they breathe," said Sloane, who added that he sometimes used a gas mask on his commute to work in Detroit from suburban Birmingham. He told the convention's Committee on Emerging Problems that air pollution laws should be written into the constitution to protect public health and reduce damage.[30]

Residents and officials of downriver Detroit suburbs were growing louder in their complaints about air pollution from such sources as the Ford Motor Company's Rouge plant in Dearborn and McLouth Steel's Ecorse mill. In May 1962, the Grosse Ile Township Board voted to sue McLouth for noise, dirt, and smoke nuisances. A 17-page report by a local attorney laid out McLouth's role in producing "gas, noxious odors, dust, continuous and non-continuous loud noises, explosions, sirens and whistles."[31] A woman from Plymouth Township, west of Detroit, showed up at a July 1964 township board meeting holding up a dustrag black with soot, blaming a local company, Evans Products. "How would anyone like to have to wipe this off their furniture?" asked Mrs. Fred Davids.[32] The township promised to keep after the company to correct the problem.

Abetted by expressions of concern from public officials, the demand for state air pollution control grew more intense. John Soet, director of the state health department's Division of Occupational Health, said in March 1964 that pollution was nearing dangerous levels. "Unless a positive program of prevention is undertaken soon, our atmosphere will be clogged with irritating, harmful pollutants. The very air we breathe will be contaminated." He said the new state constitution, which declared protection of public health a state priority, justified a new state air pollution law and listed 36 Michigan communities with serious air pollution problems. He said that it was a partial list.

In 1964, 13 "downriver" communities organized an Air Pollution Committee and received a $130,000 grant to begin air monitoring and enforcing air pollution requirements. This aggressive action drove Wayne County officials to seek coordination with the city of Detroit's better-established program. In late 1965 the county adopted regulations compatible with the city's, and the programs were merged.

By that time the state legislature had acted. Long opposed by industries, legislation to create a statewide air pollution law moved ahead in 1965. Governor George Romney had broken the logjam the previous fall, just before standing for reelection to a second term. On October 22, 1964, he said he would ask for state money to match a federal grant, creating an $80,000 air pollution control program, and called for a state air pollution law. In a letter to the Michigan Tuberculosis and Respiratory Disease Association, Romney said the program would "be a major step toward assuring the people of Michigan that the air we breathe is as free from contamination as modern science and vigorous education and enforcement can make possible." Rep. William Copeland, who represented Wyandotte and other downriver communities upset about poor air quality, introduced the measure in February 1965. "This bill has the backing of every major industrial firm in the state," Copeland said. "They're afraid if they don't cooperate voluntarily with the state, they will face federal intervention." The bill cleared the legislature later that year, becoming Act 348 of 1965. It created an Air Pollution Control Commission to issue air quality permits and authorized the state to make pollution rules and take enforcement actions.

A year later the state health department proposed the first rules to implement the law and faced fierce opposition from industry. The rules addressed open burning in junkyards, emissions from coal-burning power plants, incinerators, steel manufacturing facilities, foundries, cement plants, and asphalt plants and the "opacity," or density, of smokestack emissions.

As they had done for decades about threatened controls on water pollution, spokespersons for industrial associations warned that the rules could drive employers from the state. Calling the rules "superstrict," Frank Cooper of the Michigan Manufacturers Association said the rules were designed to solve problems faced in smoggy California, not Michigan. At a hearing in the state capital, a witness for the American Foundrymen's Society said the proposals would harm his industry, and Saul Bach, president of the Auto Wreckers Association, called for more study before controls on the burning of junk cars took effect.[33]

But the public insisted on cleanup. "Some industries are too lazy to put their mind to this," charged Mrs. Richard Gresla, who was joined by 15 other members of the Citizens for Clean Air of Muskegon County. Added Mrs. Shirley Baker, also of Muskegon, "My rights are being constantly violated by my neighbor—a paper mill." After making some adjustments, the Air Pollution Control Commission adopted the rules in August 1967. A year later, the administrator of the new state program, Bernard D. Bloomfield, reported 223 permit applications, the creation of four air monitoring trailers, fewer uncontrolled asphalt paving plants, a reduction in the number of junkyards burning cars, and a $15 million commitment by Consumers Power Company to upgrade its air pollution control equipment. The gains were heartening, Bloomfield said, "The public has been understanding and probably will continue to tolerate what to many of us if experienced personally would be abhorrent conditions—just so long as progress is being made."[34]

One of the first staff members of the new Air Pollution section of the Department of Public Health in 1967 was Delbert Rector, who would later become deputy director of the Department of Natural Resources. Rector was one of six staff persons, including section chief Bloomfield. By the time he left the program in 1980 as chief of the Air Quality Division of the DNR, Rector was heading a staff of 95.[35]

Initial targets of the state program were coal-fired power plants, foundries, asphalt batch plants, and auto salvage yards. "It was much worse than today. You could find black stacks in every community," Rector said. "It was a fun time to be in the job. We were building a program and making a difference in community after community." Bloomfield emphasized field inspections and challenged industries to develop control programs to meet the new regulations. This included installing new air pollution control equipment for many facilities, while others decided to switch to less polluting fuel or to make other process changes. The technology-forcing provisions of the Federal Clean Air Act for new sources were not yet law, so staff could only encourage use of state-of-the-art air pollution equipment whenever a factory, foundry, or coal burner was constructed.

Starting from such a small base and in a state whose businesses were still leery of air pollution control standards, the program was remarkably effective. In 1970 nearly half of Michigan's population lived in areas where sulfur dioxide pollution exceeded health standards. By the end of the decade, thanks to a limitation on the content of sulfur coal imposed by the Air Pollution Control Commission, the entire state breathed air that complied with the standard. Reductions in regulated pollution at individual facilities were striking. The Fisher Body plant in Lansing emitted 10,000 tons per year of toluene, xylene, and other volatile organic chemicals from approximately 100 stacks when Rector tested them in the late 1960s. By the late 1990s emissions of the same chemicals were less than 2,000 tons.

In a time when the public insisted on environmental cleanup, political interference with the program was rare, according to Rector. State representative Michael Griffin of Jackson County inquired about a complaint from a business in his district, Rector said, but when the health department explained to him that the plant's smoke plume had 100 percent opacity—in other words, it was dark black—he made no complaint about the state's efforts to correct the problem. Although most businesses at least grudgingly tried to work with the state, a handful attempted to evade the law. A coal-fired boiler in southeast Michigan that generated repeated complaints burned cleanly when Rector made an inspection. But after he drove to another facility and returned later the same day, the plant "was just belching smoke." The corporate environmental plant manager then admitted the problem that he had earlier denied.

The commission itself sometimes played a critical role in forcing compliance. After numerous complaints from citizens of Essexville, on the Saginaw Bay, about dust emissions from a cement plant, the commission met in the community to take testimony from both the public and the company. Walking out into the parking lot after the meeting, commissioners found a coating of dust on their vehicles. At the next commission meeting members voted to shut down the plant if it did not come into immediate compliance with the law. The plant stopped producing cement shortly afterward.

But the commission also sometimes retarded clean air progress. The panel received its first complaint about the Hillsdale Foundry Company on September 3, 1965, a little over two months after Governor Romney signed the new air pollution law. Emitting significant amounts of metals, the plant was adjacent to a public school and playground. After several inspections by the air pollution agency staff in 1966 and 1967, the health department urged compliance with the state law by November 1969. Minor improvements in the company's pollution control equipment failed to correct the violations, and in 1970 the company said it was moving to Jonesville, eliminating the need for improvements at the Hillsdale plant. The company canceled the Jonesville move, said it would move to Ohio, then recanted on those plans.

By October 1971 the company had been called before the commission five times, on each visit pledging to comply with the air pollution law. When the foundry's emissions continued to exceed state limits, the commission issued an order giving the company until January 1973 for cleanup. The foundry failed to meet the new deadline and requested another extension. The state estimated that the facility was emitting 127 tons per year of iron oxides; the legal limit was four tons.

State representative John Smeekens appeared before the commission several times, pleading for extensions of the foundry's deadline. His plea on behalf of a constituent business won the sympathy of a majority of the commission. But in early 1974, the *Detroit Free Press* disclosed that Smeekens was on the company's payroll, a possible violation of state law that barred legislators who were also attorneys from appearing before state regulatory commissions. Attorney General Frank Kelley promised an investigation of Smeekens and criticized the commission for not shutting the foundry down as promised, calling it a "reactionary, business-oriented board . . . that is more interested in helping business than cleaning up the air."[36] Stung by the publicity and prodded by Kelley and state health director Maurice Reizen, the commission issued an order to shut the plant down at its April 1974 meeting. A court enforced the order in December 1974, nine years after the first public complaint.

Despite such examples of leniency toward polluting businesses, Michigan's air quality improved dramatically by the mid-1970s. A combination of public disgust with neighborhood nuisances, growing concern about the rapid decline of the state and global environment, and progressive state officials who capitalized on public sentiment helped produce the rapid cleanup.

The Practice of Open Dumping

By the late 1800s, rapidly growing cities across the nation were beginning to cope with the problem of refuse. The use of horsecars for public transit put 100,000 horses and mules to work by the mid-1880s, piling manure and carcasses on city streets. But a far more significant problem, which persisted after automobiles and trucks replaced horses, was the growing volume of trash generated by businesses and homes. Major U.S. cities such as Pittsburgh and Washington, DC, reported refuse increases between 1903 and 1907 of 24 to 31 percent. In 1916, Grand Rapids generated 8,678 tons of garbage and Detroit 72,785 tons, almost 200 pounds per person.[37] Michigan cities experimented with such new technologies as garbage reduction—the process of compacting trash and recovering by-products for sale—and modern incineration. But costs were high, and each approach seemed to generate as many nuisance conditions as solutions.

After World War II, garbage generation increased dramatically as the United States became a throwaway society. Michigan cities struggled to handle mountains of trash. While Detroit relied on incineration to handle most of its garbage, a 1947 survey of garbage management practices by Michigan municipalities revealed that 66 percent of the 168 that responded used hog feeding as a disposal method, some in combination with burial or open dumping. "This is typical procedure," the Michigan Municipal League reported, "especially in northern areas where cooler weather retards deterioration of fresh garbage. . . . [P]resent-day trends indicate a desire to change to other systems for health and sanitary reasons."[38]

The second most common method of managing trash was open dumping, which a quarter of the surveyed municipalities practiced. Many carted the collected municipal garbage to a nearby rural location and dumped it into an unlined pit or depression in the ground. The garbage included liquid wastes and sometimes industrial "refuse." In years to come such dumps would menace drinking water supplies and public health, but in the late 1940s the Municipal League was chiefly concerned that they were unsanitary, breeding flies and attracting other pests. The association reported favorably on the new postwar technology of sanitary landfilling, in which managers applied a daily cover to the dumped waste and covered the site when it reached capacity. But most garbage disposal continued to be managed by the cheapest method—dumping.

In the early 1960s state and local health departments began agitating for a state law to set minimum standards for waste disposal sites. A refuse study committee of the Michigan Public Health Association found that homes and businesses were generating "astronomical" waste amounts—an estimated 14,633 tons daily. There were approximately 833 open dumps in Michigan, 82 percent of all disposal operations, the committee reported, and 456 of them were "undesirable." The state had only 151 sanitary landfills, 69 of them undesirable. Air pollution was a problem at 204 open dumps, rodents at 488, flies at 509, and water pollution at 136 sites. The panel estimated that 182,788 citizens lived within a mile radius of an open dump.[39]

Open dumps in the Upper Peninsula attracted black bears—and tourists with cameras. At a 1961 meeting in Lansing to discuss the problem of waste disposal and litter, a representative of the Department of Conservation "took a mighty dim view" of the problem, pointing out that bears could be dangerous around feeding grounds. "He stated that some bears actually depend on the garbage for their entire food supply." He also reported that his agency had issued 90 permits to cities, villages, and townships to establish open dumps on state land. In the 1980s, the state would spend millions of dollars to close and clean them up.[40]

The partnership of local health agencies and the state health department resulted in passage of the first meaningful state garbage law in 1965. Public Act 87 banned the disposal of liquids in dumps and landfills, set statewide standards for the design of new waste disposal facilities, and gave both state and local agencies limited enforcement powers. Few communities would feed refuse to swine any longer, and the law reduced garbage nuisances. But this measure, like most of the controls on water and air pollution Michigan adopted in the 1960s, was a logical outgrowth of concern about revolting conditions and far from revolutionary. It would take a new wave of laws—promoted by a new wave of concerned citizens—to put Michigan on the map as a national environmental leader.

CHAPTER 11

The Age of Action

Man has so severely despoiled his natural environment that serious concern
exists for his survival. . . . What began as an idea and a desire to do something
about saving our environment by a small study group has now mushroomed
into an officially recognized organization with nearly 200 members.
—ENACT newsletter, November 19–28, 1969

*T*he tradition of activism by Michigan sportsmen was over 80 years old
when the 1960s began. The state's most active and influential conservation organization, the Michigan United Conservation Clubs, was 23 years old.
Three generations of professional wildlife biologists, foresters, and park managers had created an enviable record for the Department of Conservation. But
the movement for a cleaner environment would soon explode beyond this
largely male class, who had forged their connection with environmental concerns chiefly through hunting and fishing.

The new activists also enjoyed the outdoors but were more likely to hike,
backpack, or watch birds with binoculars. Many were educated women raised
in a tradition of community concern and action. Some spent little time relax-
ing or vacationing in rural areas but saw evidence in their own urban backyards of intolerable air and water pollution. A growing number were young
men and women drawn into the fray by a surge of college campus activism.
Some wearing fashionable long hair, others clean cut, some politely organizing river cleanups, others staging mock executions of automobiles, the young
activists added irreverence and energy to conservation and environmental
advocacy—but sometimes annoyed their fishing and hunting allies. In a time
when the nation was convulsed by protests against the Vietnam War and
stirred by social movements for racial and gender equality, the new environmental activists were neither hesitant to speak their minds nor patient with
policies that many saw as excuses for intolerable conditions.

Some historians mark the beginning of the evolution of a narrow conservation movement into more broad-based concern about the environment at the
close of World War II. "Environmental objectives arose out of deep-seated
changes in preferences and values associated with the massive social and economic transformation in the decades after 1945. Conservation had stirred technical and political leaders and then worked its way down from the top of the

political order, but environmental concerns arose later from a broader base and worked their way from the middle levels of society outward, constantly to press upon a reluctant leadership," wrote historian Samuel P. Hays.[1]

The public concern awakened in 1962 by Rachel Carson's *Silent Spring* had deepened with news of the exploding world population and declining wildlife species such as bald eagles, whose numbers plummeted to just 82 pairs in Michigan during the 1960s after DDT exposure thinned their eggshells. As pollution darkened skies and choked rivers, many of the new activists drew a link between environmental problems and threats to the survival of the human race. Sometimes apart from the traditional conservationists, sometimes side by side with them, and sometimes even nose to nose against them, the new movement of environmentalists suddenly became a major force in Michigan during the late 1960s and early 1970s.

Jane Elder, who worked for the Michigan chapter of the Sierra Club in the 1970s, said:

I and many others of the new environmental movement came of political age during the closing scenes of Viet Nam and the crest of civil rights. We knew we could change the world, and saving the environment was part of that agenda. We saw a generation of activists stop a war. Our motivations were driven in part by collective vision and passion, not the inside game.[2]

One of the most effective of the new advocates was not a young college graduate but a bird watcher, mother, and volunteer, Joan Wolfe of Belmont, north of Grand Rapids. Born in Detroit in 1929, Wolfe grew up in Highland Park with parents who contributed considerable time to community affairs. Her mother was president of the local hospital auxiliary and of the Girl Scout Council; her father was president of the Highland Park school board and of the state chapter of the American Institute of Real Estate Appraisers. By contrast, her husband, Willard, had no family tradition of community activism but had become an active fly fisherman. In his childhood living on the Detroit River at Grosse Ile just before World War II, he had seen "tremendous weed growth" and stayed out of the polluted water but had not then made broader observations about the condition of the outdoors. He was delighted to find trout in the Rogue River, which wound through the Rockford area north of Grand Rapids, when the Wolfes moved there in the late 1950s. But the same stream was also fouled by effluent from the Wolverine Tannery and a paper mill. "There was no outcry," Will Wolfe said in 1999. "It was still too close to the Depression. The problem was too close to the bread and butter of the community."[3]

As though talking about an exotic species of bird, the Wolfes recalled neighbor Art Williams, formerly of Wisconsin. "He was the first hands-on conservationist we'd ever met," Will Wolfe said. Soon both of the Wolfes would become activists in their own right. In the early 1960s, Joan Wolfe became president of the Grand Rapids Audubon Club. In that position she tried to call the attention of Audubon members to issues that connected bird conservation to larger trends such as habitat loss and pesticide use.

Her most important work began in 1966. Working with 11 sponsoring organizations, she coordinated an all-day seminar that October at the Fountain Street Church in Grand Rapids to educate the community about problems facing the local, state, and national environments. It was probably the first of its kind in that era, attracting over 500 people, half of them college students. Officials of the state conservation and public health departments spoke on the need for better sewage systems and the dangers of persistent chemicals, but others addressed threats caused by growing population and a social attitude that science could fix any natural resource problem. Dr. Howard Tanner of Michigan State University's Department of Natural Resources said that the predicted U.S. population of 400 million in the year 2000 posed special challenges, adding, "[I]f we don't put a level on our population and give thought to its distribution, we're just stupid. There's no other word for it." Merrill L. Petoskey, assistant manager of the Southern Michigan Region of the Department of Conservation, called humankind "too reckless and too greedy. It's almost past time when we can repair the damage we have caused."[4]

The process of planning the seminar had resulted in general agreement among the sponsoring organizations that the community needed a coordinating organization. Wolfe was too exhausted after the seminar to follow up immediately, but in February 1968 she pulled together a dinner of Grand Rapids community leaders to ask their support for something she was calling the West Michigan Environmental Action Council (WMEAC). The roster of the meeting was extensive and impressive. Paid for by the Dyer-Ives Foundation, the dinner was attended by representatives of the local League of Women Voters, the West Michigan Tourist Association, the Kent County PTA, the Anti-Pollution Committee of the utility workers local union, the Izaak Walton League, the *Grand Rapids Press* and WOOD-TV, the president of Grand Valley State College, and other dignitaries. The group agreed on the need for a council of organizations and individuals who would work together on environmental causes, and they signed up to support it. At the new council's first meeting the following month, Wolfe was named president. The council grew quickly to include 45 organizations and more than 400 individuals. The organization also launched its issues work quickly, speaking at numerous hearings held by government agencies. An official of the state Water Resources Commission exclaimed at a public hearing in 1968, "This is the first time we've heard from the grass roots."

Despite its expanding work and reputation, the council, like most of the new environmental organizations arising across the state, was strictly a volunteer operation for two years. In 1971, WMEAC hired its first part-time staff person, director Shirley Swaney. Wolfe became the first full-time director in 1972. WMEAC was not satisfied with simply organizing the Grand Rapids and west Michigan area. Representatives fanned out across the state, encouraging the formation of other regional councils comprising the League of Women Voters, Jaycees, PTAs, garden clubs, churches, and labor unions.

These councils were crucial in convincing elected and appointed government officials that a large, diverse constituency wanted environmental cleanup and was closely watching their performance.

WMEAC blended the urgency of the increasingly aggressive national environmental movement with a typically civil, even restrained west Michigan character. "WMEAC was born during the Vietnam era of confrontation. We rejected confrontation as counterproductive," Wolfe later wrote. "If we had been confrontational, we would never have attracted the hundred groups—church groups, PTAs, service clubs, Junior Leagues, etc.—that became organizational members in our first five years. We would not have had the financial support of some of Grand Rapids' most respected business leaders. Nor would the TB Society have provided free office space and the use of its equipment."[5]

WMEAC did not need to be strident. Others were clamoring loudly about the condition of the environment—and events themselves were contributing to a general sense of alarm.

Still reeling from the previous year's disclosure of high DDT levels in Lake Michigan fish, Michigan citizens were told in late March and early April 1970 that both the Ontario and Michigan governments had detected high levels of toxic mercury in fish swimming in the St. Clair River, Lake St. Clair, the Detroit River, and Lake Erie. The Canadian government quickly impounded 18,000 pounds of walleye because of the poison. The news was "like a thunder clap," reported the usually prosaic William G. Turney, assistant chief engineer of the Michigan Water Resources Commission, later that year. Mercury poisoning was no casual matter: in 1968, a chemical company in Minamata, Japan, acknowledged that its mercury discharges were responsible for the death or deformity of 111 persons who had consumed fish and shellfish from Minamata Bay between 1953 and 1960. Mercury poisoning was especially frightful because it also attacked the brain and central nervous system, affecting speech, hearing, and motor skills. Like DDT, mercury was persistent and bioaccumulative—that is, even small discharges could cause problems over time, because the metal did not break down.

Mercury had come to the attention of the Canadian authorities because of the work of Norval Fimreite, a doctoral candidate at the University of Western Ontario. Aware of the discovery of mercury in fish from Sweden, and of its tracing by Swedish authorities to chloralkali factories and pulp and paper factories who used it in their processes, Fimreite surveyed Canadian industries and determined that they used approximately 200,000 pounds of mercury per year. The Ontario Water Resources Commission launched a study in 1969, and in early March 1970, Fimreite collected 42 Lake St. Clair fish and sent them to a California laboratory, which revealed they contained mercury.[6] Levels of the toxic compound reached 6 to 8 parts per million in some of the fish. The informal health standard was 0.5 parts per million; the poison fish at Minamata had contained levels from 8 to 12 parts per million. Ontario authorities determined that the Dow Chemical Company chloralkali plant at Sarnia, just across the St. Clair River from Port Huron at the southern tip of Lake Huron, was dumping as much as 200 pounds per day of mercury into the water, with an average of 65 pounds.

The first problem for Michigan was to identify mercury sources within its borders. The state found that only one of its three chloralkali plants, the Wyandotte Chemical Company downriver of Detroit, used mercury in its processes to manufacture chlorine and caustic sodas through a mercury cell process. In the process, saturated mineral brines pumped from underground deposits were passed over the mercury while an electric current was injected through them from a carbon anode to a mercury cathode. The resulting electrolysis released chlorine gas and sodium, with mercury and mercuric chloride resulting as waste products. The company, it turned out, was sending 10 to 20 pounds of mercury daily into the Detroit River. The Water Resources Commission also surveyed 550 industries, commercial establishments, and others discharging pollutants, and while none admitted to discharging mercury, the survey revealed that many were "using significant quantities of toxic metals," a finding that would later galvanize additional state action.

Wyandotte Chemical Company proposed a 16-month program to eliminate mercury losses, but on April 7, the state demanded that the company immediately stop the mercury discharge. The company installed an emergency treatment facility that cost $100,000 but still permitted the release of two pounds of mercury per day. The Water Resources Commission voted on April 15 to take the company to court, and the next day a court shut the mercury cell production process down. The state also moved aggressively against the General Electric Company at Edmore, 25 miles west of Alma, when it found that the company was using a mercury cell in the production of magnetic components. Mercury levels in the bottom sediments below the company's discharge were 1,000 parts per million, far above levels found downstream of Wyandotte Chemical Company. Within a day of the state's receipt of the laboratory data, the Water Resources Commission sent a telegram to General Electric asking it to terminate its mercury discharge immediately—or face legal action. The company complied and later developed a mercury recycling program to stop the losses.

The state's vigor in tracking and attempting to shut down mercury discharges was a far cry from decades of emphasis on working cooperatively with industry over years to correct pollution problems. Fueled by the growing national outrage about pollution and sensitized by the DDT controversy, Michigan citizens and the TV stations and newspapers that served them were making the mercury issue into big news. Even popular music picked up the refrain; in 1971 Motown artist Marvin Gaye issued a record that would become a hit with a song entitled "Mercy Mercy Me (The Ecology)," which deplored humankind's treatment of the environment and lamented "fish full of mercury."

The biggest question posed by reporters to state officials in the spring of 1970 was whether the state would follow the lead of Ontario in banning commercial and sportfishing in Lake St. Clair until mercury levels declined. At first, Michigan balked. On April 8, Governor William Milliken acknowledged that for caution's sake, the public should refrain from eating fish from the St. Clair River, Lake St. Clair, and the Detroit River but said no evidence suggested dangerous levels of mercury in fish likely to be caught by a sport angler. But three days later he reversed his stand after meeting with representatives from Ohio, Ontario, the Canadian federal government, and the U.S. Food and Drug Administration. He issued an executive order closing the Michigan waters of the St. Clair River and Lake St. Clair to fishing.[7]

Critics ridiculed the state's initial response. At an April 17 state legislative hearing on the mercury crisis, Martha Reynolds, a member of the United Automobile Workers' Conservation Department staff, charged that the state had been lax in failing to find out earlier which industries were dumping mercury and other toxic wastes into the state's rivers and lakes. "The qualifications of state authorities entrusted with protecting the health of citizens are certainly open to question when they have to confess they have no information which would indicate 'any mercury poisoning danger in fish from Michigan waters,'" Reynolds testified. "Rather than soft pedaling the dangers of mercury contamination, the governor and the Legislature should take immediate action to identify and stop the flow of all toxic materials into our waterways."

To avoid future embarrassments, Milliken announced his support for legislation requiring users of toxic materials who discharged wastewater to register with the state, calling it a "truth-in-pollution" law. He reiterated his support for the bill in a 30-minute airplane tour over the Detroit River on April 15, accompanied by reporters. Although mercury was on the governor's mind, other pollution problems insisted on the attention of the airplane passengers.

> Downriver, the water was streaked with black industrial pollution, but state officials seemed happy that it didn't look as dirty as it once did. William Turney . . . noted that 15 years ago the Rouge River was a solid mass of oil, that five years ago it was slicks of oil, overlying a base of orange industrial wastes. On Wednesday it was merely streaked with oil, and patches of near blue showed through. However, the governor and the others agreed that there is much yet to do, that even some pollution is a problem.[8]

The media tour came just seven days before an event generally recognized as the birth of the nation's popular environmental movement—Earth Day. Wisconsin U.S. senator Gaylord Nelson had proposed a national environmental "teach-in" on college campuses, urging that it become an opportunity for learning about the nation's and world's grave environmental problems. Fueled by campus activism, the teach-ins evolved into Earth Day and stunned skeptics. An estimated 10,000 schools, 2,000 colleges and universities, and almost every community in the nation participated in events to celebrate and clean up the environment. Cars were banned for two hours on Fifth Avenue in New York City. The U.S. Congress adjourned for Earth Day so that members could attend teach-ins in their districts.

All three major TV networks covered the events around the country. A geology student attending Albion College, Walter Pomeroy, appeared on a CBS-TV prime-time special April 22, "Earth Day: A Question of Survival," hosted by Walter Cronkite. In contrast to protests on other campuses that Cronkite called sometimes "frivolous," the Albion activities Pomeroy organized included the cleanup of a vacant lot to create a small urban park.

Albion called itself "Manufacturing City U.S.A.," CBS reported, and not all its foundries had installed air pollution control equipment. But Pomeroy told reporter Hughes Rudd that he had arranged meetings with the local polluters to promote dialogue. "We were afraid," he said, "that if we picketed the factories, it would actually turn the community against us." The special showed Pomeroy's fellow students jumping up and down on the nonaluminum cans they had collected in the cleanup, making them easier to return to the manufacturer with a message that it should switch to recyclable materials. Michigan television stations also broadcast specials in the season of Earth Day. WOOD-TV in Grand Rapids broadcast a series, *Our Poisoned World*, detailing serious local air, water, and noise pollution and the problem of garbage disposal.

Michigan was one of the hotbeds of Earth Day action. At a five-day teach-in on the University of Michigan campus in Ann Arbor in March, in which an estimated 50,000 persons participated, Victor Yannacone, who in 1967 had filed the Environmental Defense Fund lawsuits to stop the spraying of DDT and dieldrin, spoke on use of the courts to halt pollution. He told students, "This land is your land. It doesn't belong to Ford, General Motors, or Chrysler. . . . it doesn't belong to any soulless corporation. It belongs to you and me."[9] A new student group called ENACT organized the week's events, which included an "Environmental Scream-Out"; a tour of local pollution sites; music by popular singer Gordon Lightfoot; and speeches by entertainer Arthur Godfrey, scientist Barry Commoner, consumer advocate Ralph Nader, and Senators Gaylord Nelson of Wisconsin and Edward Muskie of Maine.

Business Week magazine observed that the Ann Arbor event had attracted the greatest turnout of any teach-in to that date. Noting that President Richard Nixon and college administrators hoped environmental issues would turn students away from Vietnam War protests, the magazine fretted that it appeared "the struggle for clean air and water is producing as many radicals as the war. And if the rhetoric at Michigan is any guide, business will bear the brunt of criticism."[10]

Action took different forms on different campuses. Tom Bailey, a Marquette high school student, worked with students at Northern Michigan University to plan Earth Day activities. One was a "flush-in." Students flushed fluorescent dye tablets down dorm toilets at a synchronized moment in an effort to prove that sewage was directly discharging into Lake Superior. Events like these not only attracted the attention of the press but also gave future environmental professionals their first major public exposure. Bailey later worked for the state Department of Natural Resources, as had his father, and became executive director of the Little Traverse Conservancy. One of ENACT's founders on the University of Michigan campus, John Turner, later became director of the U.S. Fish and Wildlife Service. Doug Scott, a graduate student active in ENACT's teach-in planning, moved on to the national staff of the Wilderness Society and the Sierra Club.

Student concern and action did not stop on Earth Day. Walt Pomeroy of Albion College contacted activists on other campuses who agreed that the next logical step was the formation of a student lobby for the environment. Described as "lobbyists in blue jeans" by one newspaper, the new Michigan Student Environmental Confederation (MSEC) received a surprisingly warm welcome from some in the capital. "Soon we made friends in the legislature on both sides of the aisle," said Pomeroy.

> We learned a day at a time. And since we were in the capital almost every day, our network of friends and supporters expanded from just student groups to a diversity of community, environmental and sportsmen groups. Legislative priorities turned into victories. . . . We started an environmental organization with a good cause, not much financial support, and worked with the sportsmen and other environmental groups. We created the path—the opportunity—for others to also organize environmental groups and hire staff. None had existed solely to focus on state environmental legislative policies prior to the creation of MSEC. Many followed and are now part of the accepted political landscape in Lansing and throughout Michigan.[11]

Another typical student activist of the time was Alex Sagady. Son of a General Motors engineer interested in automobile emissions control, Sagady joined the MSEC in the early 1970s after studying at the University of Michigan. He credited his environmental concern to his father's example and rustic camping with a "significant other." Disdaining automobile ownership and transporting himself on a bicycle, Sagady volunteered for the confederation and then became its head when money ran low in late 1973. An uncompromising, fierce battler, Sagady stirred anger among the legislators he attacked in the MSEC's publication, *Michigan Earth Beat*. His greatest victory came in 1982 when, working for the American Lung Association of Michigan, he mobilized public opinion to enforce the state's sulfur dioxide cleanup rule against the Detroit Edison Company's Monroe plant, cutting emissions by 120,000 tons per year.

The mood of grave concern in 1970 gripped some elders, too. Ralph MacMullan, the director of Michigan's Department of Natural Resources, authored an article in the *Michigan Natural Resources*, his agency's magazine, entitled "Ten Years to Save Mankind." Said MacMullan, "Nature is giving clear signals that it will not continue indefinitely to accept the garbage, the filth, the fumes that are the by-product of this drive to the supersonic life."

At a speech on Earth Day, Governor Milliken talked of making Michigan "a model state" in the fight against pollution.[12] Contrary to the views of a few contemporary skeptics unimpressed with his response to the mercury crisis, Milliken's concern for the environment did not begin with the discovery of mercury pollution or with Earth Day. In fact, he was about to become the first governor in Michigan's history to demonstrate courageous leadership in the fight to protect the environment, fusing with the new public movement to enact landmark reforms.

Born in 1922 to a Traverse City family that had made its fortune in retailing, Milliken later said he "became imbued with the beauty of Michigan" during his childhood.[13] Living in his family's cottage at Acme on the east arm of Traverse Bay in the summer, and never far from the area's woods and waters, Milliken said he spent his boyhood in outdoor pursuits, including fishing, canoeing, and sailing. These habits carried on into later life; at the age of 77 in 1999 he still ran several miles almost daily, his favorite jogging spot in suitable weather a park near the tip of the Old Mission Peninsula, which reaches toward the open waters of Lake Michigan from a base near Traverse City.

"I could see even in my youth the destruction happening," he said, remembering how he had once enjoyed floating down the Boardman River into the west arm of Traverse Bay. That ended when a gas station began disposing of its used oil in the river. "You could see slicks all the way down to the bay," he remembered sadly.

A graduate of Yale, Milliken joined the army and flew numerous combat missions over Europe in World War II, sustaining serious wounds. He returned to work in the Milliken department store business. But political careers ran in the family. His grandfather and father had served in the legislature. In 1960, he was elected to the state Senate and in 1964 won election as the state's lieutenant governor. When George Romney resigned as governor in January 1969 to become secretary of housing and urban development in the administration of President Richard Nixon, Milliken assumed his job.

By Earth Day 1970, Milliken had already sent two "special messages to the legislature" on environmental issues. In February 1969 he detailed how the state should spend the $335 million water cleanup bond approved by voters the previous fall. In January 1970 he called "the preservation of our environment . . . the critical issue of the Seventies. Unless we move without delay to halt the destruction of our land, our water and our air, our own children may see the last traces of earth's beauty crushed beneath the weight of man's waste and ruin." He outlined a 20-point "action agenda for the environment" that called for tougher enforcement of pollution laws, legislation to protect Great Lakes shorelands, improved environmental education, and a review of land use patterns.

As important as his pronouncements was his decision-making style. Trusting the expertise of state agencies, he often met with staff from within environmental agencies, not simply their chiefs. Jack Bails, who briefed Milliken on the mercury issue in 1970, said, "He made you feel immediately at ease, like you were having a conversation with anyone. He listened carefully and asked perceptive questions."[14] He was also impressed with the governor's concentration on the policy implications of proposed actions rather than the political consequences. "I never heard conversations about what would be the political fallout. His concern was what would be the right thing to do in the situation."

The same trust that Milliken placed in his experts could also betray him. Bails said he had the impression that Michigan's initial hesitation in banning fishing on Lake St. Clair when mercury was discovered resulted from advice the governor received from the health department. Because the department's long-standing focus was on communicable diseases, toxic substances were an alien issue in which it had little experience. Later in the 1970s, a different state agency would damage Milliken politically with its slow response to the PBB (polybrominated biphenyl) chemical crisis.

Contemporary observers did not always hail Milliken's environmental performance. The governor lacked style and sometimes substance in the eyes of Hugh McDiarmid, a political columnist for the *Detroit Free Press*. Crediting Milliken's wife, Helen, as "the enforcer" in the governor's environmental work, McDiarmid described the chief executive as "seemingly passionless" in his pursuit of a clean environment. In a column that appeared on the eve of the 1978 gubernatorial election and another in early 1980, he faulted both Milliken and his opponent, William Fitzgerald, for failing to address environmental issues. "You'd have thought, from listening to the campaign for governor this year, that the grand plan for the future of Michigan consisted of wall-to-wall industrial development. . . . Fitzgerald's principal message was simple, even primitive—he meant business for Michigan. Milliken's message was similar but more elaborate, including a few days ago even the boast of an 'unprecedented surge of growth' in northern Michigan, including creation of 103,725 new jobs there in this decade, many of them in manufacturing."[15] In fact, economic issues generally trumped environmental concerns in Michigan elections even during the high-water mark of reform in the 1970s.

But in early 1970 Joan Wolfe and WMEAC, teaming with a statewide coalition of conservationists, unions, legal experts, and citizens passionately aroused by worry about the future of the earth, delivered to Milliken's desk— with his belated blessing—a nationally significant law that would set the tone for the rest of the decade.

WMEAC had begun work on the proposed Natural Resources and Environmental Protection Act early in 1969. Writing to Dr. Joseph L. Sax, an environmental law professor at the University of Michigan Law School, the group asked for "a new tool to protect the environment" but left most of the details to him.[16] Wolfe asked Rep. Peter Kok of the Grand Rapids area, a Republican, to sponsor the bill, but although he was sympathetic, Kok suggested that a member of the majority Democratic Party should introduce it. Thus Rep. Thomas Anderson of Southgate, chairperson of the House Conservation and Recreation Committee, agreed to sponsor the bill. Anderson was a wise choice. A five-year veteran of the House and a former engineer at Ford Motor Company, the 51-year-old Anderson was well liked by his colleagues. An active hunter and angler, he was also sensitive to pollution issues. His outdoor credentials and generous manner prevented colleagues from thinking of him as a revolutionary. He would play an influential role in most Michigan conservation and environmental legislation until 1982, when he retired.

Offered in the spring of 1969, House Bill 3055 was a "bombshell," said Wolfe. It authorized any citizen of the state to bring suit to stop pollution, impairment, or destruction of Michigan's natural resources. Citizens angry with either government or private actions that harmed the environment traditionally had little recourse. Unless they were directly injured by the actions—something difficult to prove in most cases—and could resort to common law remedies such as nuisance or trespass, they had to rely on the attorney general or local prosecutors to file litigation. In many cases these officials had political reasons for failing to sue polluters—or simply lacked interest. House Bill 3055 in effect deputized any citizen willing to go to court to become a defender of the state's environment. Industries soon began to mobilize against the bill.

Anticipating even fiercer opposition, WMEAC chose to make an all-out effort. The group printed 1,000 copies of the bill and a 13-page question-and-answer explanation for members, distributing the materials also to allied organizations and newspapers. The education effort worked. By late 1969 and early 1970, the *Grand Rapids Press* and WOOD-TV, one of the city's two stations, were giving editorial notice to the bill. An influential outdoors publication, the *North Woods Call,* endorsed the bill, calling it perhaps "the most important piece of conservation legislation" the legislature could pass. Representative Anderson scheduled a hearing on the bill for January 21, 1970.

"Since it was obvious that there was powerful opposition to the bill . . . we knew that our first job was to show overwhelming citizen support," Wolfe later wrote. Despite Anderson's sponsorship of the bill and sympathy for its purpose, he had little hope of enacting the bill over the objections of major business associations, which had typically controlled the outcome of such measures. Tireless efforts by Wolfe lined up dozens of organization leaders as witnesses for the hearing. They in turn spread the word. After receiving hundreds of letters from the bill's supporters, Anderson moved the hearing to the floor of the House of Representatives. There Olga Madar from the UAW; Gus Scholle, president of the AFL-CIO; Amer Pederson of the Upper Peninsula citizens group Save Our Air; and Roger Conner, a student at the University of Michigan Law School, testified in support of the bill. The *Lansing State Journal* observed that "one of the most stirring testimonies" came from Conner, who testified: "We must exhaust every effort to see that a citizen has the right—if his life-support system is being destroyed—to go to court rather than into the streets."[17] Depending on which newspaper was doing the estimating, between 300 and 500 supporters of the bill attended the hearing. The extensive press coverage boosted the bill's chances.

Although only a few of the bill's opponents testified at the hearing, strong industry opposition was not hard to find. An analysis by the state Chamber of Commerce declared, "This proposed act would create a serious threat to the operation and growth of business and industry . . . a complete bar to the current method of voluntary and workable cooperation between industry and government."

Another worry was the ambivalence—or in some cases, outright hostility—of state agencies and top officials. Although none of them said so, they appeared to be threatened by the prospect of citizens filing lawsuits when the state failed to act. Attorney General Kelley's staff had issued a bill analysis in his name opposing the legislation in 1969. Prodded by the University of Michigan Environmental Law Society, Kelley announced himself in support of the bill just before a vote on the bill in the full House. The governor's position was equally perplexing for a time. His legal adviser, Joseph Thibodeau, said Milliken supported the bill "in concept" but thought it was too vague. Thibodeau wrote, in a memo to the governor, "[I]t will be politically very difficult for you to oppose this bill. . . . It is entirely too open-ended." He suggested several amendments to preclude "harassing actions" and defining grounds on which courts could adjudicate cases.

Anderson scheduled another hearing. This time it would take place in WMEAC's Grand Rapids backyard on February 26. The group worked furiously again to demonstrate public support for the bill. Despite a severe snowstorm, over 400 citizens showed up for the hearing, and many gave more passionate testimony in favor of House Bill 3055. Significantly, state senator Sander Levin, who was warming up for his campaign for governor, gave a fierce speech in favor of the bill and challenged Milliken "to stand up against the polluters" by supporting it. Mimicking the words of the state Chamber of Commerce, Grand Rapids–area state senator Robert VanderLaan said that the bill should provide for a review by the state attorney general before a complaint could be filed in court. He said the bill was too vague because it did not define "pollution, impairment, or destruction." Retorted Levin: "I think the citizens of this state know what pollution is, and I think the courts do, too."[18]

Anderson set a third hearing in Macomb County for March 6, and again the public turned out in great numbers to support the bill. Only a hearing in Kalamazoo failed to draw citizen multitudes. Anderson was now working closely with the bill's supporters, seeking answers to criticisms of the measure and developing strategy to run it through the House. His House Conservation Committee was ready to take up the bill seriously.

Dr. William Pierce, chairperson of the legal research department at the University of Michigan, acted as the Conservation Committee's legal expert, skillfully rebutting the arguments raised by committee members and lobbyists. He attended one meeting the day his father died to offer "brilliant rebuttal" to the industry arguments, Wolfe said.

But opponents were not easily overcome. Business representatives also deluged Anderson and his committee members with mail. George D. Moffett, chairman of the legislative committee of the Michigan Professional Industrial Development Association, wrote the following comments to Anderson.

As sympathetic as the Association is toward efforts for environmental improvement, those efforts must be carried on without, in turn, destroying the economy of the state. If the bill, as written, ever became law, there'd be no need for anyone, anymore, to feel the slightest concern for further plant development. There wouldn't be any. We believe the machinery already fashioned to control environmental problems has the capabilities of doing it, and doing it well enough without introducing the rights of individuals whose zeal might well surpass their knowledge, or whose motives might not always be quite the purest, to supplement that machinery.[19]

At a hearing on March 18, the governor's legal adviser Thibodeau passed out a substitute bill. Thibodeau was still raising questions about the original bill. Surprising Wolfe, the committee quickly took up the Thibodeau bill, which made what some called a minor change—it authorized lawsuits only against "unreasonable" pollution, impairment, or destruction. Although attorney Peter Steketee, a WMEAC volunteer, and Joseph Sax, the author of the original bill, found the word harmless, Jim Rouman, director of the Michigan United Conservation Clubs, decided it created an unacceptable loophole and threatened to withdraw his support. The MUCC position had some historical foundation: the state's water pollution law penalized "willful" pollution, an adjective that had frustrated many lawsuits.

As the bill reached the House floor, citizen activism reached new heights. In a year of explosive citizen unrest about the declining state of the environment, House Bill 3055 had become a symbol. Its passage, many believed, would signal a new era in which the public itself could enforce environmental laws and end decades of industry coddling by officials unwilling to jeopardize their relationships with employers. Even more, it would mark a historic turning point and create hope for restoration of a polluted environment.

WMEAC sent every member of the House a packet of information countering the opposition's arguments, while a coalition of 13 college groups offered a file folder with a "Give Earth a Chance" button attached to the cover. The House soundly defeated weakening amendments, including one that would have made it impossible to win a lawsuit if a company was operating within existing pollution limits, no matter how weak they were. The amendment to strike the word *unreasonable* from the bill passed with a margin of one vote. A day before Earth Day—April 21—the House sent the bill to the Senate.

By now public opinion was heavily mobilized in favor of the bill. The *Grand Rapids Press* observed that the bill "undoubtedly benefited from the public furor over pollution" and called for quick Senate action. Anderson estimated in May that he had received more than 8,000 letters or petition signatures in favor of House Bill 3055. The governor, whose position had seemed unclear as recently as March, now declared himself strongly in favor of the bill and said he would be glad to "twist a few arms" to get the bill through the Senate. He said it would create "a totally new and bold kind of 'common law' where the public trust in our environment is concerned."

The fight was only beginning. The Sierra Club's Kathy Bjerke met with members of the Senate committee that would hear the bill and found that only Levin, who had spoken in favor of the bill in Grand Rapids, was wholeheartedly in support. When three weeks passed without a hearing, backers of House Bill 3055 worried it would die in committee. WMEAC worked with Grand Rapids organizations, including the Junior League, a normally nonpolitical women's group, to bring Senator VanderLaan around. His position was critical because he was now Senate majority leader. Shortly after a long evening meeting in which league members corrected VanderLaan on his "misconceptions" about the bill, he issued a press statement announcing that he would support the House-passed version of the bill.

The chair of the Senate committee, Gordon Rockwell, had hedged on the bill but suddenly scheduled a hearing for May 12. Despite the lack of notice, the coalition supporting the bill packed the hearing room again. The UAW rounded up members from Detroit; buses brought members of the Downriver Anti-Pollution League.

Wolfe remembered the hearing as a dramatic event. Senator Harvey Lodge accused one witness of threatening the legislature by testifying that measures like House Bill 3055 were needed to give citizens a way to address their grievances without revolution. "A gasp of dismay at the unfair charge brought Senator Lodge's thundering accusation that we were about to start a riot! The audience—shocked beyond belief—and imagining headlines destructive to the bill, sat back almost afraid to breathe," she wrote. But a parade of witnesses, including representatives of the Izaak Walton League, the UAW, the AFL-CIO, the American Association of University Women, and the University of Michigan's Environmental Law Society strongly defended the bill.

At the next day's committee meeting, dozens of industry lobbyists watched as the Michigan Farm Bureau, the Michigan Manufacturers Association (MMA), and the Michigan State Chamber of Commerce called for changes to the bill. Among the most significant was the MMA proposal to change the word *and* to *or* in a section laying out how a defendant could affirmatively defend against an environmental lawsuit. The change would have meant that a defendant could win a lawsuit simply by showing that he or she was doing something useful even if it resulted in pollution, impairment, or destruction of natural resources. Dwight Vincent, an MMA representative, predicted that without the amendment, the bill would provide "a guaranteed annual income for lawyers who will be commencing lawsuits."[20]

When the bill cleared the Senate committee, it indeed bore the word *or* instead of *and* in the clause criticized by the MMA and also seemed to bar new lawsuits that were similar to previous litigation filed under the act. These changes were unacceptable to WMEAC and the environmental coalition, and they swung into action one last time. Mary Swain, a WMEAC volunteer, left preparations for her daughter's graduation and rushed to Lansing with a letter for each senator. An MUCC lobbyist met with as many senators as he could find. WMEAC distributed an emergency letter to its allies, and the groups issued a joint press release, which received statewide attention.

Tempers flared as the bill neared final passage. The head of the state Chamber of Commerce, Harry Hall, wrote an angry letter to Representative Anderson strongly objecting to the latter's characterization of the chamber, in a letter sent to his constituents, as "until now" being a forceful fighter for the environment: "[I]t has not occurred to us that you would be so swayed by the theatrical demonstrations, the orchestrated pressures and the dramatized hysteria created by the neo-politics of latter hour dilettante earth savers who have latched onto the ecological issue with an unending series of demands for unrealistic laws under the false premise that they provide simple legislative solutions to complex technological problems." Anderson turned the other cheek in reply, saying merely, "I study hard, abhor 'latter hour dilettante earth savers' who are less than fully sincere, and will continue to work with the Michigan State Chamber of Commerce to the end of my days trying to improve our lot on this globe, and leave it better for our progeny."[21]

Weeks passed, and the full Senate failed to take up the bill. Worried that the delay might extend past the August primary election—when some legislators might feel safer voting against the measure—the coalition sent a telegram to senators demanding a prompt vote. On June 26, the last day of legislative work before the summer adjournment, the Senate took up the bill. Despite rumors of behind-the-scenes attempts by industry representatives to weaken the bill, the Senate briskly struck the damaging committee amendments and passed the bill with only three dissenting votes. The House approved the Senate version later the same day. The governor signed into law on July 27, 1970, what has been known ever since as the Michigan Environmental Protection Act, or MEPA.

The law turned out to be a less dramatic change than either its supporters or opponents had predicted. It was, instead, a helpful tool for citizens seeking to hold government accountable for potentially harmful environmental plans. In the first three years after its enactment, the bill's author, Joseph Sax, reported, citizens initiated 74 MEPA cases, with 26 resolved in favor of the plaintiffs, 16 in favor of the defendants, and the rest still pending. The most frequent early subjects of litigation were industrial air pollution and land development disputes.[22]

Although many elements combined to prompt the bill's passage, including the tenor of the times, the sheer outpouring of public support for House Bill 3055 was undoubtedly the most important. Stimulated and organized by WMEAC, the public clamor forced many legislators who ordinarily would have opposed the bill to switch sides. In a later era, activists would nostalgically cite the hundreds of citizens who turned out for hearings on the bill and the volunteers who drove back and forth to Lansing at great personal cost to serve as watchdogs on the legislature's actions.

But MEPA was merely a foretaste of the decade's sweeping environmental reforms. Before the legislature finished work in 1970, it passed three more significant environmental measures, including the "truth-in-pollution" law requested by Milliken after the mercury crisis, an act protecting rivers whose shorelines were still largely undeveloped, and a law giving the state power to regulate development along the Great Lakes shoreline.

Early in 1971, Will Wolfe asked the state Department of Natural Resources to do something about destructive damming, dredging, and filling of lakes and streams. Many developers were impounding public waters and choking off river systems. DNR officials replied that they lacked legal authority. Organized by Wolfe, a statewide committee of conservationists, environmentalists, a DNR staff member, and an outdoor writer took six months to draft a bill to give the state control over construction activities affecting lakes and streams. It contained only one, giant loophole: it exempted projects undertaken by elected county drain commissioners, who were empowered by laws originating in the nineteenth century to hasten the flow of water away from farmlands. The bill's sponsor, Rep. Warren Goemaere, said that regulating drain projects would destroy its chances because of the strong drain commissioner and agriculture lobbies.

In 1971, Fred Steketee, a student at the Wharton School of Business, spent his summer vacation producing a report for WMEAC supporting state action to protect inland lakes and streams. The document noted that approximately 50 percent of state waters were open "to abusive and destructive practices such as impounding, filling, channeling, dredging, and diversion. . . . The continued ruination of our small waterways is rapidly bringing about the ruination of our lakes and rivers."[23] The delivery of the report to all members of the state House of Representatives and a press release increased public attention. Minor changes to the bill brought the Michigan Farm Bureau into support, but Consumers Power Company, one of the state's two large electric utilities, and Dow Chemical Company said they were concerned. Consumers Power owned thousands of acres of land on streams, and Dow hoped to build impoundments to store "excess" water for cooling purposes. Both suggested changes to the bill.

The bill seemed to be moving along well until it reached the House floor and weakening amendments prepared by Consumers Power and Dow Chemical suddenly appeared. Senator Basil Brown, an African American legislator crucial in debates on several of the environmental bills of the era, told Joan Wolfe that the amendments were crippling. Rushing back to Grand Rapids, she found her husband home for lunch and asked him to call members of the coalition supporting the bill to urge them to pressure legislators immediately. He delayed appointments with his dental patients to make the calls. By the time Joan Wolfe returned to Lansing, she said, "legislators were acting stunned" by the number of calls they had suddenly received. The bill passed without the amendments.

In late 1972, the legislature was moving toward final adjournment. If the Senate failed to pass the bill before the year's end, House Bill 4948 would die.

The next legislature would have to take it up—and might be less favorable to its purpose. But the Senate committee lacked a quorum: Senator Oscar Bouwsma of Muskegon was out of town and said he could not attend the committee meeting. Governor Milliken stepped in, offering to fly Bouwsma to Lansing and back. Bouwsma showed up to provide the quorum, and the committee was ready to send the bill to the Senate floor.

But Joan Wolfe discovered changes in the committee version of the bill that she feared would gut it—changes that legislative employees said were typographical errors—and successfully persuaded Senator Gordon Rockwell to correct them. Finally, just before Christmas, the night before the Senate adjourned, she roamed the capitol halls awaiting the vote. Because everyone thought that passage was now assured, most of the coalition stayed home. Visiting a Grand Rapids–area senator, Wolfe was handed an amendment that Rockwell had distributed. It would limit the act's authority to two connecting channels, the Detroit and St. Mary's Rivers.

"I rushed out of the senator's office and headed for Senator Rockwell's," Wolfe wrote.[24] Joined by Department of Natural Resources lobbyist Charles Guenther, she invaded Rockwell's lair. At first the senator was unyielding, but Wolfe said, "I think my only persuasive argument was that we would make sure that every one of his constituents in Flint would know what he had done. I said it over and over and he knew we meant it—and thanks to blessed Charlie, I had a witness. [After] what seemed like an unbelievable period of shouting, at last he backed down." He kept his word this time; he withdrew the amendment, and the bill passed without change. Said Wolfe: "Rockwell had made his best effort for whoever had gotten to him, but in the end, the power of the environmental movement had overwhelmed him." The bill passed the House the next day and became Public Act 346 of 1972. Calling the new law "a major victory," outdoor writer Frank Mainville of the *Lansing State Journal* said the environmental coalition "taught the Senate a lesson in eco-politics." The Senate Republican leader, Robert VanderLaan, said the "intense pressure" brought by Joan Wolfe was decisive in winning passage of the bill. "I think we are in a new era of natural resource concern," VanderLaan said.[25]

But some in the capital received Joan Wolfe coolly, unaccustomed to women who spoke out vigorously on public issues. When she became chair of the state Natural Resources Commission in 1977, outgoing chair Harry Whiteley half jokingly said that Wolfe had "come aboard with all the traits of a normal female, not the least of which was a desire to be heard—frequently and with gusto!" He added, "Joan has good looks, personality, charm and all the other attributes we admire—but beyond that, she has the intellect and dedication so necessary in this work."[26] Old-fashioned ways also influenced her treatment by allies. Before naming her to the state panel, Governor Milliken called her husband, Will, to ask for permission.

The legislature was not always willing to tighten environmental protection in the 1970s. In 1974 and 1975, the state plunged into a deep recession. Some business interests and legislators blamed the new environmental laws for part of the dip. When Julia Tibbits of Marquette organized a small coalition to block construction of an iron ore loading dock in her city because it would mar a scenic shoreline, a powerful industry and its allies in legislative leadership in the state capital had a target: the Michigan Environmental Protection Act. Working with young environmental attorney Jim Olson, Tibbits and her group, Superior Public Rights, sued the Cleveland Cliffs Iron Company under MEPA, seeking to force the firm to pursue alternatives to the loading dock. The company said the dock was necessary in the proposed location to help supply electrical power to its nearby mining facilities.

Mining was a formidable force in the Upper Peninsula. Discovered in 1844, the peninsula's iron ore deposits created thousands of jobs for generations of immigrants and fueled the industrialization of the Great Lakes region, particularly in steelmaking. In 2000, Michigan State University experts estimated that Michigan had produced 2.5 billion tons of iron ore, worth nearly $50 billion.[27] The industry and its friends in Lansing, including the colorful state senator Joe Mack, were outraged that a handful of citizens could use MEPA to block the plans of a major mining company. Described by an outdoor writer as "a century behind his time" and author of a "flood of absolutely bad legislation in the field of natural resources," Mack was reviled by environmentalists. But he was hugely popular with his constituents, who generally regarded him as an effective antidote to downstate sentiment that they believed often locked up resources that could have produced jobs. Mack introduced bills designed to gut the 1970 law by essentially exempting from suits mining firms that had received all necessary permits from government agencies.

Under the watchful eye of a vigorous Lansing press corps and the environmentalists, the Mack bills aroused angry protests. The primary author of MEPA, Joseph Sax, called the legislation "a thinly disguised effort basically to repeal" the law. Governor Milliken suggested that the bills would "represent a throwback to the dark ages of environmental responsibility."[28] After considerable maneuvering, a narrow majority in the legislature weakened the Mack legislation so much that it did little to protect the mining industry. But its introduction and initially quick movement signaled continuing strength among Michigan's traditionally powerful industries in retarding or stopping environmental bills.

If elected officials found the persistence of Joan Wolfe and allies impossible to ignore, they were soon about to have an even more difficult time with the new director of the Michigan United Conservation Clubs, the state's largest outdoors organization. Hired in 1974 as the MUCC's executive director, 36-year-old Thomas L. Washington would collect scores of enemies, win fierce loyalty from friends and some employees, and shape most of the key Michigan conservation battles of the next two decades.

Washington was born in 1938 in Detroit but spent most of his childhood in Dearborn, just to the west. The home of Henry Ford and his Ford Motor

Company, the city still had ample open spaces, and Washington remembered fondly "fields to roam through and play in, a creek down the street where we caught frogs and crayfish; it was a young boy's delight."[29] In his teens, Washington took up hunting and fishing, sports that would claim his enthusiasm to the end of his life. It was natural that he should come to work as an advertising salesman for the MUCC magazine, *Michigan-Out-of-Doors,* in 1963. He became advertising director before taking the organization's top job. Inheriting an organizational budget of approximately $50,000, Washington built it to more than $3 million by the 1990s. *Michigan Out-of-Doors* was soon reaching 100,000 households and carrying over 100 pages of copy and advertising.

A complicated man who enraged politicians with his blunt criticisms but could show great sensitivity to friends in trouble, Washington was difficult for many to grasp. A sexist, a fierce defender of gun rights, seemingly eager to brawl but always ready to make a compromise that would benefit his MUCC membership, Washington had a visceral understanding of the outdoors and of the temper of the times. He expected to be acknowledged as the leader he was; several governors courted his approval and endorsement.

He was "a giant of Michigan's conservation movement," said Wayne Schmidt, MUCC's staff ecologist under Washington from 1975 to 1985. "He could be a colossal pain to work for. So what? In the long run we're all dead and what really matters is whether we've made a difference in our passing. Tom made a huge difference and it was an honor to have worked so closely with him."[30]

Staff members often vividly recalled their first meeting and early days working for Washington. Fresh off the Michigan State University campus in 1975, Schmidt eyed the chief appraisingly as he sat in the MUCC head's office interviewing for a job. "I wasn't sure I wanted to work for this crazy fat guy and he wasn't so sure about hiring this hippy with a pony tail," he said. After a trial run with the organization, Schmidt agreed to Washington's demand that he cut his hair, and he started a 10-year career at the organization. Another employee, Kevin Frailey, asked Washington for an organizational chart when he interviewed for an education job in 1984. "He just looked at me and said, 'Why the hell do we need that? I *am* the organizational chart.'"[31] Despite sometimes being maddened by his temper and unpredictability, both Schmidt and Frailey said they appreciated the freedom Washington gave them to do their work. They also supported his approach on most issues.

Washington's biggest impact was in the state capital. His keen understanding of the political process and his use of the right combination of diplomacy and thunder to affect it thwarted anticonservation initiatives and advanced MUCC's ideas.

Many of those ideas were populist ones. Washington thought state government should make natural resources more accessible to hardworking men and women living in urban areas, buying and developing parklands as well as providing boating and fishing access close to home. He was also impatient with industry excuses for delaying cleanup. He began building his legend with one of the simplest of antipollution ideas, a bill to slap a deposit on returnable bottles and cans. The 5¢ and 10¢ deposits, supporters argued, would reduce litter by creating an incentive for the return of the containers and benefit the environment through increased recycling rates and energy savings.

The environmental problems created by throwaway containers were recent. Until the late 1950s, most beverage containers were made from glass and redeemable for deposits under a system voluntarily maintained by bottlers. But the new "no-deposit, no-return" beer bottle quickly displaced the redeemables. In 1962, seeking to thwart a competitor, the Stroh Brewery Company of Detroit briefly succeeded in winning approval of a state rule banning the no-deposit beer bottle, but the glass industry quickly overturned it by promising the siting of a new plant close to Lansing. Stroh's soon brought its own nonreturnable container onto the market.[32] By the mid-1960s nonreturnable bottles and cans smothered roadsides across the state, prompting complaints from residents and tourists alike. MUCC estimated that containers accounted for nearly 80 percent of roadside litter.

Based on legislation already adopted in Oregon, the final Michigan bottle deposit legislation originated with a 15-year-old East Lansing high school student named John Houston. A friend of Alan Fox, who worked as an aide to state representative Lynn Jondahl, Houston had thoroughly researched the bill. In a meeting Jondahl scheduled with environmental attorneys, Houston was able to answer all of their questions about constitutional and other legal issues. In its first version, the bill would have imposed deposits on wine and other alcoholic beverage containers as well as on beer and carbonated beverage cans and bottles, but in 1975 Jondahl trimmed the measure to cover only the latter two classes of containers in order to attract more legislative votes.

Even with the change, the capital swarmed with enemies of the bill. Container manufacturers, beverage wholesalers and retailers, and many labor unions—particularly critical to Democratic legislators like Jondahl—opposed the measure. James W. Deitrich, president of a United Steelworkers local based in Benton Harbor, protested to Jondahl that his bill "would decimate the entire throw-away beverage container industry in Michigan." He said that "many good paying jobs" with wages of $6.03 an hour plus benefits would be permanently displaced at Continental Can Company in St. Joseph.[33] Retailers disliked the measure because it would require them to make space for returned cans and bottles and consume staff time counting and sorting the containers. Wholesalers objected to the burden of collecting and transporting redeemed bottles and cans and said the bill would drive up beer and soda prices. Typical of these arguments was a statement from the executive vice president of the Michigan Beer and Wine Wholesalers Association, Rae Dehncke, who said the cost of a case of beer would rise from $5 to $7.40 if the bill became law, an increase of nearly 50 percent.[34]

Supporters of the deposit had been creative. To dramatize the litter problem, the Michigan Student Environmental Confederation had sent labels to organizations across the state, urging them to stick the labels on cans and send them to the governor's office. Stacks of the cans accumulated in the halls outside the office. Students piled them on the capitol lawn, attracting news photographers and camerapersons.

But the lobby against the bill did a "superb" job, remembered Representative Thomas Anderson, who tried to usher similar legislation through the legislature several times before Jondahl tried. "They beat us at every turn," he said, "once by scheduling a free golf outing for the entire legislature on a day when I had scheduled a committee vote, once by changing votes in my committee I was sure I had, and once by killing the bill on the House floor . . . using local lobbyists and planeloads of visiting industry specialists. They scheduled committee member dinners, took a few of us to their headquarters cities to show us ideas they were working on to 'obviate the need for a bottle bill,' etc."[35]

Killed by the combined opposition in 1974, the bill was reintroduced by Jondahl in 1975. A series of hearings produced amendments to the bill that Jondahl and others thought would yield the necessary committee support. On November 12, the Consumers Committee took up the measure and was expected to send it to the full House. Instead, in a switch that surprised Jondahl and William Rustem, an aide to Governor Milliken who had lobbied for the measure, Republican representative James Smith of Grand Blanc voted to send House Bill 4296 to the Appropriations Committee. The move was considered a death knell for the legislation. It "may never again see the light of day," Jondahl said. Rustem, who speculated that lobbyists for wholesalers or retailers had "gotten to" Smith, said that Washington "blew up."[36] The MUCC head vowed to launch a petition drive to place the measure on the ballot in November 1976. "We would prefer to have this question acted upon by the Legislature," he said, "but since that body has chosen to ignore the issue, we have no alternative but to seek a popular vote on Representative Jondahl's bill."

Washington's move was bold; it would be no easy feat to get the question on the ballot. Under the 1963 Michigan Constitution, citizens could put an issue before the entire electorate only by collecting at least 212,000 signatures of registered voters. The legislature could then either approve the measure or send it to the ballot. Organizing a petition drive was a mammoth undertaking. No conservation measure had ever reached the Michigan ballot this way. But Washington had built the MUCC organization to sufficient strength to run and fund a grassroots campaign and referendum.

The other indispensable ingredient in the campaign was Governor William Milliken, who had first declared his support for a ban on throwaway containers in 1971. Schmidt said Milliken "nearly always knew that line between right and wrong for Michigan's natural resources. Never was there a more unambiguous case—real and symbolic—than the bottle bill." Milliken made his the first petition signature to place the issue on the ballot and instructed his state agencies to do what they could to support the referendum.

Michigan's news media generally supported the measure, adding to the sense that it was a basic reform. "We still believe outlawing the throwaway container will help to solve one of Michigan's worst problems—the miles of litter that clutter our freeway system," editorialized WWJ-TV in Detroit. "So, when you see one of the MUCC petitions, and you're a registered voter, we urge you to sign it. That way, you'll help put the question on the November ballot, and you'll have the chance to 'vote-away' litter."[37] The *Detroit Free Press,* now a consistent champion of environmental quality, pointed out that a state Public Service Commission analysis showed the ban would generate 4,000 new jobs and $28 million in taxable income. The newspaper added that the measure would "cut out a lot of litter and also save on energy required to produce the steady supply of throwaway bottles and cans."

Supporters of the bill were also buoyed by results of a poll conducted in late 1975 for Milliken by a firm called Market Opinion Research, showing that 73.3 percent of those questioned favored the ban on throwaways. Volunteers from the Michigan and Detroit Audubon Societies, Federated Garden Clubs, and other organizations worked daily at MUCC's office distributing information and petitions. Milliken loaned his natural resources adviser, William Rustem, to MUCC to coordinate the collection of signatures. Members of MUCC's local sportsmen's clubs clamored for the petitions, as did eager volunteers from across the state. Despite a late start, the petition drive's gigantic coalition succeeded in placing the question of a throwaway ban on the ballot. In just two months, the MUCC-headed coalition rounded up 400,000 signatures.

But placing the issue before voters was only the first step. Washington and other supporters knew they would face a dizzying campaign of opposition from industry and labor organizations. Joining under the banner of the Committee against Forced Deposits, opponents waged a fierce advertising campaign talking about the job losses that would result from the throwaway ban and promoting alternatives that they said would reduce litter without the burden of deposits. But supporters of the ballot question capitalized on the "fairness doctrine," a Federal Communications Commission regulation that obliged broadcasters to present both sides of a public question, to receive free air time to rebut some of the ads. An attorney representing the deposit coalition wrote to the broadcasters to remind them of the requirement, helping offset the industry advantage.

Jondahl, who toured the state speaking in favor of the proposal, said he feared a defeat as the election approached: "I became frightened that the margin would be seriously eroded and that we could lose it. . . . [T]he level of debate was glib, and not based on the research."[38] But the voters ignored the advertising campaign. On November 2 they approved Proposal A, the beer and soda throwaway container ban, by a margin of 63.8 percent to 36.2 percent, or over 900,000 votes. Two years later, the ban took effect. In 1982, the state Department of Natural Resources found the ban had helped reduce litter 40 percent, saved 15,000 tons of aluminum and 65,000 tons of glass annually, and resulted in only 130 consumer complaints about dirty returned bottles and cans—sanitation being another argument used by opponents.[39] Just as important, surveys showed that lopsided majorities of Michigan residents continued to support the ban two decades after it took effect.

The success of the petition drive and the resulting vote made Washington's reputation and strengthened MUCC as an intimidating force in state conservation and environmental policy. *Detroit Free Press* columnist Hugh McDiarmid later wrote that "when MUCC announced its campaign to circumvent the Legislature and take the issue directly to voters as a ballot initiative . . . well, lots of people snorted and laughed. But they didn't know Tom. . . . Washington applied his ferocious energies to the bitter fall campaign." The result, McDiarmid wrote, was that Michigan became the first industrial state to enact a container deposit.[40]

Although the coalition work on the bottle bill showed that environmentalists and conservationists could work together, it also created jealousies. More than 20 years later, some of the environmental participants still felt slighted that Washington received the lion's share of the credit for the success, while the Sierra Club's Jane Elder remembered Washington as a "bully . . . the last of a breed who thought he could just intimidate people. He did many good things but at a cost."[41] Said another environmentalist: "He absolutely did not understand or agree on the natural values of land. If you couldn't cut it or kill it or cook it, he just found absolutely no benefit in it." The skepticism was mutual. Schmidt remembered accompanying Washington to strategy meetings hosted by the environmentalists in the 1970s. Washington mocked the refreshments as weed tea and seed cakes; he preferred beer and chicken livers. "We would go [to the meetings] because we thought we should and we would sit there agonizing over debates on process and the bragging over minuscule accomplishments," Schmidt said. Washington felt "disdain and genuine bewilderment" toward the environmentalists. These differences exposed a division that often held the two movements at bay and sometimes propelled them into direct collisions.

Leading the Region in Cleaning up Water Pollution

The next target of environmental advocates and the Milliken administration was phosphorus pollution of the state's rivers and the Great Lakes. The "death" of Lake Erie in the 1960s, while prematurely reported by *Life* magazine, signaled a serious pollution problem actually caused by too much life—and phosphates were the prime culprit. Slimy and repulsive mats of algae coated much of Erie's surface in the summertime during the 1960s, turning swimmers away and causing a decline in commercially valuable fish species even while economically less desirable species such as carp and smelt exploded in numbers. Washed off farmland and discharged from sewage treatment plants and industrial discharge pipes, nutrients that included nitrogen, carbon, and phosphorus overenriched Lakes Erie and Michigan particularly, accelerating their natural aging process. Although there were many sources of the nutrients, one stood out: phosphate detergents.

Used to soften water and increase cleaning power, phosphates were introduced to household laundry detergents in the late 1940s. The new products were popular with consumers because they were cheaper than the cleaners they replaced and produced visibly cleaner clothes. They resulted in huge sales for major soap and detergent manufacturers—an estimated $1.7 billion on 6,600 million pounds of product in 1969. And households consumed approximately 90 percent of all detergents by volume.[42]

In 1965, the U.S.-Canada International Joint Commission, which monitored conditions of boundary waters for the two national governments, recommended as one cleanup option for the Great Lakes the removal of phosphorus prior to wastewater discharge. In 1969, the IJC gave stronger advice: it called for the removal of phosphates in laundry detergents used in the lower Great Lakes basin by 1972, estimating that 70 percent of the phosphates in U.S. municipal waste came from laundry detergents.

In 1976, the Milliken administration was ready to move on the issue in Michigan. As it would do on the bottle deposit law, the state was stepping out ahead of most of its neighbors. Indiana, New York, and the city of Chicago were among the few Great Lakes governments that had banned phosphate detergents. Responding to lobbying from the soap and detergent industry, the Michigan legislature had preempted ordinances in the cities of Flint and Detroit. The ordinances would have phased out phosphate detergents, but instead a statewide limit of 8.7 percent phosphorus by weight was substituted, far above the level recommended by experts to control the enrichment of the Great Lakes.

Aware that there would be no better luck in the legislature with a phosphate detergent ban than with the bottle deposit legislation, Governor Milliken and the Department of Natural Resources proposed to go around the lawmakers by writing a rule to ban detergents containing more than 0.5 percent phosphorus by weight. Following administrative hearings, the rule would require only the vote of a small legislative committee before taking effect.

But getting the rule to the committee was not easy. One of the state's largest companies and greatest contributors to candidates of the Republican Party, Amway Corporation of Ada, manufactured phosphate detergents as well as the environmentally preferable low-phosphate alternatives. One of its employees, Cleamon Lay, occupied the industrial representative seat on the state's Water Resources Commission, which had authority over rules governing water quality. Lay was able to keep the commission from proposing a rule to ban high-phosphate detergents. "Never was there a more blatant case of conflict of interest," said Wayne Schmidt, who was MUCC's staff ecologist at the time. Referring to the 1995 elimination of the water commission and others by Governor John Engler, Schmidt said, "Those who get teary-eyed over the demise of Michigan's citizen commissions might recall this history."[43]

The governor himself was hearing from Amway about the issue. Cofounder and top Amway executive Jay Van Andel contacted the governor and urged him to back down.

"I can still remember how incensed he was. He was adamant, but so was I," Milliken later said.[44] "There was always a constant suggestion from industry that anything you wanted to do to solve a chemical pollutant problem would hurt the bottom line. But it was so evident [phosphorus] was harmful that I knew we had to do something."

When the water commission deadlocked on the issue because of Amway's opposition, Milliken used his constitutional powers to transfer the panel's rule making authority to the Natural Resources Commission, which oversaw the entire Department of Natural Resources. In bypassing Lay, Milliken was also dealing now with a commission whose entire membership he had appointed and that was generally in sympathy with his policies. To Hilary Snell, a member of the Natural Resources Commission, Milliken's bold stroke in transferring authority was an example of the governor's willingness to do what was right for the environment regardless of the political consequences. "When we met, we talked about what to do on the issues and I was always concerned about what the political fallout would be. [Milliken] always said, if you think it's good policy, go ahead and do it."[45]

Snell and the other commissioners authorized the DNR to hold public hearings on a rule that would ban the sale of household laundry detergents with more than 0.5 percent elemental phosphorus by weight on July 1, 1977. At three hearings in December 1976 and in written comments, soap and detergent industry representatives and environmental advocates took sharply divergent positions. The detergent manufacturers consistently argued that the best solution to the phosphorus problem was to improve phosphorus removal at sewage plants rather than limit it in their products. An Amway executive, Dr. Bernard Schaafsma, said the ban would cost $5 to $50 per year per Michigan family in double washings to remove dirt, the heating of extra water, and increased additives. Other witnesses argued that substitutes for phosphate detergents would fail to win consumer acceptance because of their inferior cleaning properties.

Witnesses from the League of Women Voters, the West Michigan Environmental Action Council, and the U.S. Environmental Protection Agency called for both the phosphate detergent ban and better phosphorus removal from sewage plants and argued that the science was solid: the detergent limitation would lead to drastic reductions in phosphorus entering Lakes Erie and Michigan and many inland lakes.[46] In his organization's magazine, the MUCC's Schmidt wrote the following comments.

The importance of a phosphorus ban to protect Michigan's water is unchallenged—except by vested industrial interests. . . . The proposed ban will not "solve" eutrophication problems any more than a "throwaway ban" will "solve" litter problems in Michigan. But it is a significant step. It would, for

*example, result in a reduction by six to eight tons per day of phosphorus dis-
charge to the Detroit River and Lake Erie just from Detroit's waste water treatment plant.*[47]

The Natural Resources Commission approved the rule banning high-
phosphate household laundry detergents in February 1977, with an effective
date of August 1. While the soap and detergent industry challenged the rule in
court, the DNR moved ahead to win the legislature's approval of a bill limiting phosphate content in dishwashing soaps and commercial detergents as
well. Because the agency had largely controlled the rules process and was
unmoved by the industry's pleas, the soap and detergent interests had a friend-
lier audience in the state capital. Trotting out home economists who said
homemakers would never accept the low-phosphate detergents, washing
machine parts encrusted with lime from the substitute cleaners, and samples
of "clean" clothes washed in phosphate detergents and other clothes washed
in the substitutes, the industry mounted a successful full-court press to stop
the broader regulation. Mike Stifler, a DNR water quality employee assigned
to support of the bill, remembered a legislator screaming at him about the
arrogance of changing the rule and then seeking the legislature's approval of
the bill. The legislator's district included the headquarters of Whirlpool
Corporation, a manufacturer of washing machines that had consistently
opposed the phosphate limit.

"We decided at the end of 1977 to take our three-quarters of a loaf and go
home," Stifler said.[48] The state supreme court upheld the DNR rule in 1982 in
a case one agency official described as "ring around the collar versus the Great
Lakes."[49] By that time, environmental monitoring confirmed the wisdom of
Milliken's leadership on the issue. Phosphorus entering 14 major sewage
plants declined 30 percent in 1978 and 1979 from the 1976 and 1977 levels, and
phosphorus in their effluent tumbled 25 percent. Phosphorus discharged by
the Detroit sewage plant, a leading source of Lake Erie's overenrichment, fell
40 percent in 1978 and 1979, with most of the decline attributed to the detergent change. Backed by a concerned public, the state had added to its reputation for environmental leadership.

One more major environmental fight loomed in the capital as the decade
neared its end. Thwarted by a narrow margin in the 1978 session of the legislature, environmental and outdoor organizations hoped to make Michigan
one of the first states in the country to pass a strong wetlands protection law
in 1979. The difficulty of this final battle was rooted in the state's long history
of draining and disparaging wetlands.

Almost from the first day of pioneer settlement in the nineteenth century,
public policy and private impulse had demonized Michigan wetlands as
unhealthy wastes that were best filled or drained for productive use. Known
as swamps or "drowned lands," these areas were regarded as ugly and dangerous. In the 1879 report of the state Board of Health, Dr. Henry Lyster said
that one-seventh of the state's surface area lay in "wet marsh or boggy satu-

rated land" below the forty-fifth parallel, where malarial diseases menaced public health. He added, "[A] very large proportion of these lands can be drained and made available and profitable to agriculture, and in the meantime diminish very noticeably the amount of sickness and mortality from disease of a malarial type."[50] Lyster noted with approval the famous Chandler farm 12 miles north and east of Lansing. When Michigan became a state, marsh grass populated what was originally a 5,000-acre lake, but under the ownership of Zachariah Chandler, who represented Michigan in the U.S. Senate, some 2,000 acres were drained by the digging of a ditch, converting his property to "meadow and pasture lands." Lyster added that "since the drainage it has been remarkably healthful on the farm."

"Rather than recognize that excess water in swamps *supplied* bounteous riparian forests, vast flocks of waterfowl, and other natural riches, legislators, along with most citizens, thought that surplus water prevented lands from being even more abundant," environmental historian Ann Vileisis writes of mid–nineteenth century attitudes. "Rather than understand swamps as topographic features inherently wet for reasons of geology, geography and climate, legislators regarded swamps as afflicted and agriculturally barren lands in urgent need of human ingenuity."[51]

Michigan legislators were more than up to the task of curing the wetland blight. Lawmakers passed their first drainage law in 1839 and in 1846 authorized drainage of swamps and marshes if they were determined to be a source of disease. In 1898, the legislature created the elected office of county drain commissioner and granted it extraordinary powers to establish drain districts and assess landowners within the districts the cost of draining wet areas.

Over a century of development, drainage laws and the filling of wetlands for the construction of roads, housing developments, and commercial and industrial projects took an enormous toll on wetlands. The Michigan Department of Agriculture estimates that by 1956, there were 26,261 miles of legally established drains in the state, siphoning water from over 17 million acres of land. A 1996 report prepared by the state Natural Features Inventory estimated that development and drainage had cost 2,391,199 acres of an original total of approximately 8,530,000 acres in the state—a loss of 28 percent. However, the U.S. Fish and Wildlife Service in 1990 put the total at approximately 5.5 million acres of an original 11 million, a 50 percent loss. Monroe and Wayne Counties in southeast Michigan, according to the DNR report, had lost more than 80 percent of their wetlands.[52]

But even as Michigan's legislature was creating county drain commissioners in the 1890s, many Americans were beginning to appreciate the values of wetlands. President Theodore Roosevelt's creation of national wildlife refuges that contained large wetland complexes that provided waterfowl habitat set an important precedent. The signing of the Migratory Bird Treaty by President Woodrow Wilson in 1916 put in motion events that would eventually oblige the federal government to protect prime habitats for the protected species, including wetlands. In the 1930s, President Franklin Roosevelt's chief of the Bureau of Biological Survey, Jay (Ding) Darling, who later founded the National Wildlife Federation, created the federal duck stamp program to help finance the purchase of waterfowl refuges. The voices of poets and scientists added to the growing chorus of concern about the loss of wetland habitats. It was well understood by the 1970s that wetlands, in addition to providing pleasing landscapes, strained pollutants from water; controlled the runoff of sediments; stored floodwaters; and provided habitat for fish, amphibians, and waterfowl.

Passing a state law to protect wetlands was not an easy task because the public values of wetlands collided with the U.S. tradition of private property rights. Restrictions on filling or draining wetlands would limit the ability of property owners to construct homes, commercial developments, and other desired developments. The limitations could also jeopardize the ability of farmers to drain areas for conversion to cropland. Organized interests potentially opposed to wetlands legislation included agricultural organizations, homebuilders, realtors, mining companies (who disposed of tailings in wetlands), pipeline companies, and forest products companies. Commenting on the 1978 wetlands bill, a realtor grumbled, "If this bill goes through as written and the private landowner has a wetlands parcel in excess of five acres, he will not be able to add one shovel full of dirt to that property without an OK from the DNR." The bill was "confiscatory," another complained.

The bill had also died in previous sessions because of the opposition of state senator Mack. Representing the western Upper Peninsula, he argued that "downstaters" had no conception of the conditions of his constituents and that restrictive laws damaged the economic growth of his district: "I believe that the needs of people, in my judgment, shouldn't be superseded by a cattail or a pussywillow. Now, I don't want to see anything destroyed, but I don't want to see wholesale confiscation of property, because the *Detroit Free Press* or somebody else—who own no property, who are not involved—think they have the right in the name of environmental preservation to confiscate through legislation and public hearings individuals' property rights. . . . I think frankly that we're getting into a socialistic government under the disguise of preserving the ecology," Mack told the student publication *Michigan Earth Beat.*[53]

Mack made the comments in 1976 when he chaired the senate Conservation Committee, which controlled all action in that chamber on environmental bills. But early in 1979 Majority Leader William Faust deposed him as chair, replacing him with John Hertel, who was far more sympathetic to environmental legislation.

Two other principal forces combined to help advance the proposed wetland protection act. First, under 1972 amendments to the federal Clean Water Act known as Section 404, the Army Corps of Engineers could authorize state agencies to issue federal "dredge and fill" permits for wetlands developments if the states could demonstrate adequate state laws. This gave development interests a reason not to fight the bill; they could more comfortably work with state Department of Natural Resources staff in field offices around the state than with federal officials housed principally in the Detroit area who were also less subject to political influence.

Second, a 28-year-old graduate of the University of Michigan Law School was on the scene to shepherd the bill through the legislature. John Sobetzer, a native of New York State who had studied under Joseph Sax, the author of the Michigan Environmental Protection Act, devoted himself to passage of the bill on behalf of the organization he directed, the East Michigan Environmental Action Council (EMEAC). Formed in 1970 as a cross-state twin to Joan Wolfe's west Michigan group, EMEAC declared wetlands protection its top priority in 1976 and turned Sobetzer loose. Quiet, patient, and thorough, Sobetzer impressed politicians with the soundness of his reasoning rather than with direct political influence. "I have never in my life seen any citizen do what he did," said Bob Garner, who was an aide to Representative Thomas Anderson, chair of the House Conservation and Recreation Committee. "By just being polite and giving good, thoughtful advice. And he had a little bit of political savvy, too."[54]

Sobetzer was modest about his role.

EMEAC took the wetlands act on as its primary legislative focus and I think that was key to making it the top priority for environmental legislation that session generally. EMEAC provided a lot of good materials on the benefits of wetlands which we supplied other eventual supporters with.[55]

Garner said that when the Michigan Association of Homebuilders proposed a host of weakening amendments to Senate Bill 3, sponsored by Senator Kerry Kammer, Sobetzer talked legislators out of supporting them. "John just shot them down in flames. The committee was in awe of his knowledge." But Sobetzer knew when to compromise, too. To defuse opposition from Upper Peninsula legislators, he and Anderson agreed to an amendment to exempt iron and copper mining companies from the wetlands law. The effect was minor, since the 1972 Inland Lakes and Streams Act already required permits for most uses the mining companies would make of wetlands. Other concessions were made to provide exemptions for most agricultural uses and drain projects initiated before 1973, allowing the powerful Michigan Farm Bureau to endorse the measure. Even with the changes, the bill required a state permit for construction or drainage on millions of acres of private lands.

The bill also moved forward because of a string of editorials from the *Detroit Free Press*. Garner, Sobetzer, and Kammer all remembered the paper's opinions as creating a climate of urgency for the bill. Coming from the Detroit area, Hertel and Kammer were both sensitive to editorial positions of the news media in that metropolitan area. Authored by Barbara Stanton, who had become a bird-watcher and lover of natural landscapes in her adult years, the editorials—on February 8, February 26, March 17, and April 4—helped shore up votes for the bill. Stanton reasoned, threatened, implored, and rhapsodized.

Wetlands—marshes, bogs, ponds, wet meadows, coastal areas—play such a vital role in flood control, maintenance of water quality, preservation of wildlife and recreational opportunities, that we can hardly afford not to save them. They are more efficient than any sewer or storm drain system man has ever devised, and fertile, productive and beautiful besides. We ought to act, at long last, to protect them.[56]

A chorus of other editorial voices joined the *Free Press,* including the *Detroit News,* the *Saginaw News,* and WDIV-TV in Detroit, which complained that "wetlands are being devoured by developers at a rapid rate, causing pollution and flooding. Michigan needs a law to protect this natural resource."[57] Governor Milliken, the UAW, the MUCC, and most environmental organizations were urging passage of the bill. Just as MEPA had come to seem inevitable at the start of the decade, so did the Wetlands Protection Act in 1979.

The final few paces along the road to passage of Senate Bill 3 were difficult ones, however. After a speech from Upper Peninsula state representative Dominic Jacobetti in November that blamed the problems of the nearly bankrupt Chrysler Corporation on environmental laws, the House Conservation Committee weakened the legislation to stall wetlands regulation in counties with populations of less than 100,000 until the state DNR conducted an inventory of their wetlands and provided notice to affected landowners. Swallowing hard, the coalition supporting the bill accepted the change but defeated another that would have enabled landowners whose property values were diminished by the bill to go to court and seek an order to force the state to purchase the property at the previous market price, compensate the landowner for the lost value, or modify the agency decision to preserve the market value. The amendment actually passed 56–42 on its first try but was later stripped from Senate Bill 3.

Final passage of the bill occurred late the final night of the legislative session in 1979. Jane Elder of the Sierra Club watched with friends from the Senate gallery and began to believe that enough senators would flee late at night to kill the bill. "I don't think so," one of her peers said. "Look at the doors down there." UAW representatives stood outside the Senate chambers, sending the message that senators who deserted the vote were spurning the union as well as wetlands protection. The majority favoring the bill held. "It was a glorious moment for coalitions in Michigan," Elder said.[58]

Renamed the Goemaere-Anderson Wetlands Protection Act in honor of its original sponsors, former representative Warren Goemaere and Tom Anderson, the bill became law in 1980. Not long after, Sobetzer quit EMEAC to live in Vermont, where his family had summered in his childhood. "I never liked living in the suburbs, in apartments that reminded me of animal cages, connected by traffic jams, far from friends and family and natural places. I wanted to hike around and live in the mountains," he said.

His work had brought a fitting end to a monumental decade of environmental energy and accomplishment in the capital and the nation. The U.S.

Congress had passed a strong Clean Air Act in 1970, the Clean Water Act in 1972, and dozens of other major environmental laws. At the state capital, Governor Milliken had urged legislators on; Wolfe, Washington, and Sobetzer had fiercely lobbied them; skillful conservation-minded legislators such as Anderson had engineered support from just enough of their colleagues; and editorial writers and common citizens had entreated and scolded lawmakers to do the right thing. In 10 years, the legislature had approved more than 20 major environmental laws—and the people themselves had approved one in the voting booth. On the tenth anniversary of Earth Day in 1980, the *Detroit News* noted, "[D]oomsday never arrived. . . . [T]he protests triggered an avalanche of legislation—federal and local—with dramatic results." The air in southeast Michigan was cleaner than it had been since early in the twentieth century; the amount of public parkland and the number of wildlife refuges in the nation had tripled in a decade; salmon were showing up in the Detroit River; and beaches at formerly polluted sites such as Sterling State Park near Monroe were open again for swimming.[59]

These successes of the conservation and environmental movements, backed by a shift in public opinion, themselves seeded future difficulties. The most atrocious pollution was now cured, leaving invisible problems such as lingering toxic contamination to address. The torrent of laws would require years of patient action and implementation, far less dramatic than the fights to enact them had been. While bursts of widespread public concern had persuaded legislators to pass the new laws in the 1970s, lawmakers regarded environmental activists as politically unsophisticated, purist, and unable to influence critical, complicated implementation issues. In a typical comment, state representative Tom Mathieu observed in 1979 that "environmentalists do not have clout in Michigan. . . . [E]nvironmentalists do not have money or a lobbyist . . . and if and when programs start to be cut . . . environmental programs will be the first to go."[60] *Free Press* columnist Hugh McDiarmid began a 1980 column by commenting, "The environmental lobby in Michigan remains a joke."

As a result, environmental groups that had formerly relied almost exclusively on volunteers were now hiring full-time paid staff. In 1980, six of the groups that had cooperated in fighting for state laws in the previous decade formed the Michigan Environmental Council (MEC) as their Lansing representative and put out an advertisement for a full-time lobbyist at a salary of $18,500 per year. "We can't compete before the Legislature any more without a fulltime lobbyist," said WMEAC executive director Ken Sikkema, who became a legislator himself in the late 1980s.[61] In a prospectus for the new MEC, Sikkema observed:

> The danger signs, as we begin a new decade, are clear and ominous. Policymakers at all levels seem quite willing to postpone increased environmental quality, and even to turn the clock back, as tradeoff for quick fixes in energy and the economy. The effectiveness of a number of Michigan [environmental]

organizations has already been reduced. The media has begun to call our bluff, and others will soon follow.

But some grassroots organizations argued that the new professionalism embodied in organizations such as MEC distanced environmentalists from community problems and the need for radical reform.

As the 1970s closed, Michigan entered its worst economic recession since the Great Depression, threatening to undo the new public environmental consensus. The state's first and only environmental governor would leave office at the end of 1982. Even at the time, conservationists and environmentalists knew that the 1970s had been unprecedented and that they might never see a decade like it again.

CHAPTER 12

Saving Places

Isle Royale which Governor Grosbeck says should be purchased by the state and converted into a park is about twenty miles off the Canadian shore of Lake Superior and something like three times that from the mainland of the Upper Peninsula. . . . It will occur at once to the thoughtful taxpayer that this would make rather a large park to be maintained by the state in such a remote and inaccessible place. . . . Is there nothing that Michigan could do with its money that would be more useful than that?

—*Detroit Free Press,* editorial,
December 29, 1922

Although talk of a park that would preserve a large chunk of the state's primeval forest arose in the 1880s, the powerful, emotional movement to save remnants of wild Michigan did not spring up until early in the twentieth century. As development grasped ever-larger portions of the state's natural heritage, a scattering of outdoor lovers and prominent citizens began to work to save the largest remaining pieces. They would set the precedents of passion and persistence that would guide rescuers of Michigan's last great places for the rest of the century.

Their work began in one of the remotest reaches of the state. A hulk of rock and trees rising majestically out of the world's largest lake, Isle Royale was a territorial anomaly and would ultimately become a singular piece of the national park system. But making a park of it took patient and heroic efforts—and the unflagging support of Michigan's outdoor writers.

Although popular legend has it that Benjamin Franklin insisted the international boundary be adjusted to give the island to the new nation in the 1783 Treaty of Paris, the official park history rejects this proposition. A "major error in map making" made in 1775 is instead responsible, says the accepted chronology.[1] Assigned to Michigan by the 1836 congressional act of statehood, the 130,000-acre, 40-mile-long island and an associated archipelago of hundreds of small islets was far closer to the mainland of Minnesota and Ontario. Frequently isolated in the winter, the island attracted initial interest because of its copper deposits. Exploitation of the island's minerals, in fact, began before recorded history. Visiting the island in mild seasons as early as 4,000 years ago, early peoples mined for more than 1,000 years. Isle Royale and Lake Superior area copper made its way by trade as far as New York, Illinois, and Indiana. These early miners were probably most active on the island from A.D. 800 to 1600. But by the time white miners arrived in the 1840s, the only Native American encampments they encountered were a maple sugaring camp and a seasonal fishing camp.

The new European miners exploited the island's copper for approximately 60 years, disappearing after tapping out the largest commercially valuable deposits. As they departed, resorts and summer residences began to spring up, creating a small but influential constituency of visitors and property owners who cherished the quiet and scenery of Isle Royale. When they learned that the Island Copper Company planned to sell approximately 65,000 acres of its island holdings to the Minnesota Forest Products Company in 1922, they leaped into action, organizing the Citizens Committee of Isle Royale to oppose the new owner's rumored lumbering plans. One of their earliest and most important actions was to propose that the island become a state reserve. Taking up the idea, *Detroit News* outdoor writer Albert Stoll, a member of the state Conservation Commission, began editorializing in favor of state park status for the island. Apparently encouraged by his editor, George Miller, Stoll later pushed to make the island a national park.[2]

In what was apparently his first editorial on the subject, Stoll rhapsodized about the trees that had "never been molested by the lumberman's ax," the moose and caribou that inhabited the island. Warning of threats to the island posed by timber companies, he said, "Preserve Isle Royale. In years to come we shall thank the fates for the foresight of those who planned the acquisition of this property for all of the people."[3] Stoll and the *News* continued championing the island in editorial after editorial. In December 1922 the newspaper again warned several times that the island might be lumbered: "The world would stand aghast if someone suggested the destruction of one of the rare paintings of the great masters of the middle ages. Isle Royale is one of the master pieces of the Great Master; it would be almost a sacrilege to permit its destruction."[4]

After hearing from Stoll, U.S. representative Louis C. Crampton of Michigan sent the *News*'s articles and editorials about Isle Royale to National Park Service director Stephen Mather. Mather endorsed the national park idea in May 1922. Although Michigan governor Alex Groesbeck endorsed creation of a state park on the island in late 1922, Stoll and island residents continued to press for the federal ownership of the island. Stoll's chief tangible success in the early years of the campaign was the decision by both the U.S. Department of Interior and the Michigan Department of Conservation to halt the sale of public lands on the island and to organize a trip to Isle Royale in 1924 by National Parks Service chief Mather and influential Detroit-area businessmen. A major stumbling block to the creation of any park, however, was the stiff price sought by the Minnesota Forest Products Company for turning over its land. The company wanted $2.5 million, and since law required that parklands be turned over at no cost to the national treasury, congressional appropriations could be of no direct help.

Stoll gained another important ally, *Grand Rapids Press* outdoor writer Ben East. "The drive [for national park status] was making slow headway . . . because very few Michigan residents, and almost nobody outside the state, knew where or what it was, and in general the public could not have cared less what happened to it," East reminisced in 1976.[5] "[My] editors shared my belief that a spectacular winter flight to the far-north island would do much to awaken public awareness of its existence and unique importance."

East's memories of his 11-day sojourn on the island in the middle of winter showed the distance Isle Royale had traveled in the minds of Michiganians, who had once seen only the economic wealth it could supply from its abundant copper.

> *I recall a clear cold night, with the thermometer at 20 below, when the full moon climbed above Lake Superior outside the harbor entrance, laying a path of radiance across the restless water and lighting with almost noontime brightness the spruce-crowned ridges behind our cabin. There is a magic quality in winter moonlight on snow, and the magic is even more potent when the moonlight falls on ice-hung cliffs and dark unpeopled forests. . . . There were dawns when the colors in the east beggared description, and windless days when the brooding hush of the northern wilderness lay over everything, a silence that could be felt, when no branch stirred, no bird called, no living thing moved in the white, frozen world.*

East turned out to be an even better promoter than Stoll. The film of his winter trip, made by a Department of Conservation photographer, began to stir public support. His articles in the *Grand Rapids Press,* and a 1932 piece he authored for *National Geographic,* also contributed significantly to public interest in the island. Coupled with scientific investigations of the island by anthropologists from the Milwaukee Public Museum, scholars from the University of Michigan, and Dr. Frank Oastler, a prominent New York naturalist, the writings and photographs of Michigan journalists had helped build momentum for the national park idea.

With home-state support from Representative Louis C. Crampton and Senator Arthur Vandenberg, legislation to authorize a national park cleared Congress and received President Herbert Hoover's signature in March 1931. But that was only one more step forward. The state and federal governments needed to coax the substantial private holdings on the island into public ownership. A five-member Isle Royale National Park Commission struggled for years to accomplish this task. When, in 1934 and 1935, the Minnesota and Ontario Paper Company offered to sell 72,000 island acres and the Consolidated Water and Power Company of Wisconsin Rapids began logging near Siskiwit Bay, the state stepped up its efforts. President Franklin D. Roosevelt's approval of federal funds to establish Civilian Conservation Corps camps on the island and to purchase private lands in 1935 was a significant breakthrough. It helped free $100,000 in state funds for land acquisition. In 1937, agreements with the Island Copper Company and the

Minnesota Forest Products Company delivered over 70 percent of the island into federal hands. But not until April 1940 could the National Park Service declare Isle Royale National Park officially established, deeds to all lands on the island having now come into its possession. And because of World War II, official dedication ceremonies for the island did not occur until August 1946. A quarter century after it had begun, the campaign to make Isle Royale one of the nation's most spectacular wilderness parks had finally succeeded.

Another northern Michigan prize had to be saved not once but three times. Rescued from loggers by Governor Harry Kelly and Department of Conservation director P. J. Hoffmaster in 1944, the Porcupine Mountains State Park faced two subsequent threats. In 1954 the state Conservation Commission dedicated 45,000 acres of the park as a nature reservation, making it off limits to most development. But in 1958 mineral companies took an interest in copper ore believed to lie beneath the park. The Bear Creek Mining Company asked in May of that year for a lease to explore over 900 acres under the park and another 5,200 acres of Lake Superior bottomland.[6] Although the state owned but 30 percent of the mineral rights within park boundaries, it controlled surface access and thus could promote or block the request. The request touched off a bitter debate.

On one side were the company and many residents of the area, which had chronically high unemployment. On the other was a coalition of groups led by the Michigan United Conservation Clubs and guided by its executive director, James Rouman. The coalition united under the banner of the Porcupine Mountains Wilderness Association. Selling 85,000 stamps featuring the Lake of the Clouds, the association marshaled both state and national public opinion against the proposed lease. The possible $6 million income from copper mining, the coalition argued, was far less than the annual $3 to $10 million that would come from tourist businesses for hundreds of years into the future.

Jack Van Coevering, the outdoor editor of the *Detroit Free Press*, credited Conservation Commission member Clarence Messner with helping turn the tide: "Messner took up the cudgels. He alerted conservation groups and other citizens. He built a 'fire' of public indignation which swept first through the Lower Peninsula, then even into the Upper Peninsula where business men and promoters were thirsting for money for the short term."[7]

Ben East, the longtime editor of the *Grand Rapids Press,* captured the reasons for the public outrage: "We in Michigan have grown firm in the belief that once an area is placed in the hands of the Conservation Commission, it is safe. To break that tradition would be the most serious mistake the Commission can make."

But Rouman was the key. He "tackled the job with vigor, criss-crossing the state relentlessly to speak before civic groups, clubs, and whoever would listen. He urged individuals to write to their representatives, senators, Governor, the Michigan Conservation Commission, and anyone who could possibly help."[8] The coalition acquired a critical partner when the United Automobile Workers and the Michigan AFL-CIO announced their opposition to the lease. "If the permit is granted—and the pressure for it is tremendous, inspired by those who would profit—the Porcupine Mountain wilderness will be wilderness no longer," wrote John J. D'Agostino and Olga Madar of the UAW Recreation Department to recreation committee members. Pointing out that copper was in surplus, they added, "It is obvious that leasing of this valuable state land will not provide jobs in the immediate future."[9]

The organizing effort worked. Unwilling to commit to a timetable for exploring and developing whatever copper underlay the park and buffeted by the opposition's wilderness cries, Bear Creek lost its support on the Conservation Commission and withdrew its request for the lease in January 1959.

Protection of the park's wilderness values was still far from guaranteed. In the early 1960s, the Michigan legislature approved funds to extend a state highway west from the park entrance close to the heart of the park at Presque Isle River, but Governor John Swainson vetoed the sum. In 1962, local state senator Joe Mack called for reducing the 30,000 acres of virgin timber in the park to only 10,000 acres to promote economic development. The same coalition that had turned back the copper mining proposal thwarted this proposal as well as Mack's effort to construct a fish ladder on the lower falls of the Presque Isle River.

The climactic battle to save the Porcupines from development occurred in 1971. Prepared in consultation with local officials and environmentalists alike, a proposed state management plan would set aside 35,000 acres of the park as permanent, unspoiled wilderness. In the years since 1958, public sentiment for setting aside untouched lands had only grown stronger. A parade of witnesses at a public hearing in Lansing argued for the wilderness designation. Once again, the UAW's Madar was on hand: "We are proud that the state of Michigan had the foresight to preserve one of the last extensive pieces of unspoiled wilderness in the Midwest for the enjoyment and recreation of all its citizens. We urge that the area continue to be protected for future generations."[10] Margery Fahrenbach, the daughter of the late Department of Conservation director P. J. Hoffmaster, emotionally pleaded with the state: "My father fought long and hard to help acquire this area for the people of Michigan. He loved those mountains with their wild and unspoiled beauty and I believe he envisioned them as a 'preservation,' a bit of country that should and can be preserved as God made it."[11] The only witness speaking in favor of development was Gordon Connor, president of the firm that had raced in 1944 to log what was now the state park. But the Department of Natural Resources rejected his plea, and the park got a new name: Porcupine Mountains Wilderness State Park.

The state was rarely able, as it had done in the Porcupine Mountains, to acquire lands imminently threatened with development or destruction. More frequently, out of ignorance or a bias toward managing lands rather than leaving them alone, the Department of Conservation was itself a threat to lands already in its ownership. That changed in the early 1950s when a volunteer organization called the Michigan Natural Areas Council took root.

Begun as a committee of the Michigan Botanical Club, the council was a collection of public-spirited citizens of diverse scientific backgrounds and outdoors passions who supplied what the Department of Conservation lacked. In an article tracing the history of the council, Paul W. Thompson wrote that department director P. J. Hoffmaster admitted in 1950 that his agency had "neither the funds nor the trained personnel" to inventory state lands with outstanding natural features.[12] The volunteers did the labor for the state, forming reconnaissance committees to survey a worthy site's topography, geology, plant and animal communities, and scenic qualities. A site committee then reviewed the first panel's recommendations and made a report to the council as a whole. It, in turn, submitted its proposals to the state Conservation Commission. The council could recommend that a site be given a maximum of protection as a natural area preserve or a more flexible designation as a nature study area, scenic site, or nature reservation.

The state took the group's recommendations seriously. In April 1951 the Conservation Commission formally protected four sites in Wilderness State Park on the Straits of Mackinac, including the Sturgeon Bay preserves, which included shoreline, dunes, and inland forest and marshland. In 1954 the state designated both a natural area preserve and a nature study area at the Haven Hill site in the Highland Recreation Area in Oakland County. Additional areas were protected in Tahquamenon Falls State Park and at Betsy Lake in the Lake Superior State Forest. More natural areas followed; by the mid-1970s the council's recommendations had led to the protection of more than 100,000 acres, almost all on public lands.

The civil, peaceful efforts of this band of well-trained volunteers contrasted sharply with the increasingly frequent, more urgent, almost desperate bids of coalitions to save vanishing natural areas on private lands. As the 1960s yielded to the 1970s, as a growing number of Americans wondered whether the human race itself was in jeopardy, the pitch of battle rose. One of the fiercest fights was over an astonishing, unlogged trace of Michigan's original landmark, the white pine.

Early in 1970, the Calumet and Hecla Mining Company began logging part of a tract of virgin trees known as the Estivant Pines outside the village of Copper Harbor, not far from the tip of the Keweenaw Peninsula in far northern Michigan. Many of the trees were well over 100 feet tall. Located on land that had accommodated at least two failed copper mining ventures, they had escaped the axe for more than 100 years, first because they were not the resource of primary interest to the owners and later because of either lack of interest or sheer luck. But now the Goodman Lumber Division of the company slated the trees for harvest. A local man, Lauri Leskinen, protested in the *Houghton Mining Gazette,* "Perhaps if the directors of the Goodman Lumber Company were approached in the right spirit they could present this stand of over-mature pine to the state of Michigan. This precious remnant of beauty should be preserved and it would be an act of sacrilege if it was destroyed."[13]

But neither the company nor the state seemed interested in preserving the pines. Instead the Michigan Nature Association (MNA), a private land conservation organization headed by the scrappy Bertha Daubendiek of Avoca, a small town in southeastern Michigan, intervened. After a reconnaissance report by a local member of the association, the MNA urged the Goodman Division to donate a portion of the land. The company declined but said it would entertain an offer to buy a piece. Nearly a year passed with little progress when Leskinen again wrote a letter to the *Mining Gazette*. "Mile upon mile of beautiful white pine from Saginaw to Copper Harbor tumbled to the earth with only a few trees left in one or two isolated spots," he lamented. "And now—the end of the line! The Estivant Pines located south of Copper Harbor are being cut today! The year 1971 when our ears, minds and hearts are being barraged with the words ecology, conservation, pollution and the preservation of natural beauty! I didn't think this could happen in the year 1971 to the last remnant of the beautiful pine forest of Michigan."

Spurred to further action, Daubendiek and the MNA board of directors agreed to try to raise the estimated $40,000 necessary to buy 160 acres of the tract. The new owner of the land, Universal Oil Products, tentatively agreed to halt logging on the 160 acres but refused to commit to selling an option on the land. Collecting funds statewide from sportsmen's groups and civic organizations, at county fairs and a strawberry festival, a local committee established with MNA's cooperation generated considerable publicity and raised $3,654 in 15 months. Further amounts flowed in from around the state, inspired by coverage in major metropolitan newspapers.

Some residents of the area resented the intrusion of "outsiders" and proposed to Universal Oil that they buy a mere 40 acres of the land, leaving the rest on tax rolls. But a bigger obstacle was a report submitted by the company's consultant, Barton and Aschman, which called for selling 80,000 acres including the Estivant Pines to the U.S. Forest Service for $9 million. Convinced that the Forest Service would allow logging of the trees because of its traditions of sustained yield timber management, Daubendiek fired off a letter to the president of Universal Oil in Illinois, John Logan: "We simply cannot believe, Mr. Logan, that the top management of the UOP, after MNA has been instrumental in bringing to its attention the potential of the value of preservation of beauties of the Keweenaw, intends to shut MNA out of further participation in the actual preservation." This letter, dubbed "offensive" by one of Daubendiek's allies, led to a Chicago meeting with the company in which its officials left the door open for private preservation of 200 acres of the pines. Although discussions languished for a time, in August 1973 the MNA turned over a $37,800 check to the company and received a deed to the 200 acres it sought. Included was a 20-acre tract specifically added to assure protection of the great Leaning Giant, a monarch 23 feet in circumference and 110 feet tall that angled out over the Montreal River. Estimated to be between 500 and 600 years old, it was named Michigan's biggest white pine in August 1971 by Paul Thompson of the Michigan Natural Areas Council. Although a storm toppled the Leaning Giant in the 1980s, most of the remaining pines still stand as a monument to a vanished Michigan. Towering far into the sky, the trees dwarf their human admirers, and in the silence that engulfs them on a still day some imagine they can hear echoes of a wild past.

Fighting for the "Big Wild"

Tom Washington, the executive director of the Michigan United Conservation Clubs, made his reputation on the success of the so-called bottle bill, but he made many more enemies and an even more lasting contribution in the fierce fight over oil drilling in the Pigeon River Country State Forest in northern lower Michigan.

The region had its appeal to a young Ernest Hemingway, who excitedly wrote a friend in 1919 about a planned outing there: "It is as wild as the devil and the most wonderful trout fishing you can imagine," Hemingway told Howell Jenkins. "We can fish all we want and loaf around camp and maybe get a crack at a deer or a bear. Scared a bear out of our last camping place."[14]

An enclave of second-growth forest laced with scenic rivers that wind among rolling hills east of Vanderbilt, the Pigeon River Forest was the brainchild of P. S. Lovejoy, described as "Michigan's version, and contemporary of, Aldo Leopold." As an administrator of the Department of Conservation in the 1920s and 1930s, Lovejoy worked to expand the protected area from its original base of approximately 19,500 acres, some tax reverted and others purchased with hunting license revenues. He envisioned it as a "Big Wild," adding, "I'd like to see the Pigeon opened up to insure really good fire protection and damn little more . . . so that it isn't too damn easy for the beerbelly gents and the nice old grandmaws to get to, set on and leave their tin cans at. I figger that a whole lot of the side-road country should be left plenty bumpy and bushy and some so you go in on foot—or don't go at all."[15] Lovejoy's ashes were scattered in the forest after his 1942 death.

In the decades after Lovejoy's passing, the Pigeon River Country State Forest grew in both size and legend. Although its trees were the fruit of natural regeneration and the state's reforestation efforts, the land touched a wild chord in many visitors, who included hunters, anglers, and a growing number of canoeists and hikers longing to escape the stresses of urban life. It seemed to tell of the unspoiled Michigan leveled a century before by the thoughtless logging industry. Inhabited by elk transplanted from the Rocky Mountains in 1918 and 1919, the Pigeon River country also supported black bear, bobcats, and bald eagles, among many other species. It nourished the headwaters of three scenic rivers, the Pigeon, the Sturgeon, and the Black. And thanks to Department of Natural Resources wildlife biologist Ford Kellum, it included a 55-acre pine stump preserve, a place whose soils were too sterile to naturally replenish themselves with trees. The preserve stood as a monument to the mistakes of an earlier generation and the losses Michigan had sustained. But when Shell Oil Company reported in 1970 a major oil find at a site along a two-track path named the Lost Cabin Trail not far from the Pigeon River

Research Station, conservationists and environmentalists wondered if a second round of mistakes was about to occur.

The state had leased the mineral rights underlying extensive reaches of the Pigeon River country during the 1960s, not expecting much to result from the probing of oil companies. But the 1970 discovery by Shell unleashed the oil companies to accelerate their exploration and jacked up lease prices on the private inholdings within the state land. "During the months that followed, Lost Cabin Trail changed from a two-track path to a fifty-foot-wide bulldozed road capable of handling heavy truck traffic at high speeds through the forest."[16]

The fight over oil development in the forest quickly became a bitterly divisive issue. Shell and two other companies were particularly interested in a tract of 16 square miles in the southern end of the Pigeon River country. The Department of Natural Resources ruled that oil interests could drill as much as one well per every 80-acre tract in the forest but also placed a moratorium on lease sales through January 1971. While the agency's field staff scrambled to zone areas of the forest that should be protected from oil and gas development, Governor Milliken instructed the Natural Resources Commission, the department's policy-setting body, to stop the issuance of oil and gas permits within the forest until it completed a reappraisal of leasing and drilling regulations. When the commission did so, the oil industry was livid, threatening legal action.

The DNR's review of its oil development policies resulted in significant changes. In December 1970 it barred drilling within a quarter mile of any lake or major stream; prohibited drilling in state parks, recreation areas, forest campgrounds, and game areas; and conditioned any other development on approval by the area DNR forester of the location of access roads and disposal of cleared timber. But it was unclear whether these policies could legally apply to current leaseholders. Had the department failed to close the barn door in time?

One answer came in an opinion issued by Attorney General Frank Kelley, who ruled in April 1971 that the DNR had not only the authority but the obligation to forbid oil and gas development beneath state-owned lands if the development would compromise the environment. But at the same time, DNR management brushed aside recommendations from field staff on such issues as the placement of gas pipelines in the forest, allowing the clearing of a 50-foot corridor for a gas pipeline through elk and bobcat habitat. Field biologist Ford Kellum and colleagues recommended that the department bar all oil and gas development within the forest because of its sensitivity. After retiring from the department in the fall of 1971 out of dissatisfaction with the agency's policies, Kellum worked to rally public support for a plan to keep a 125-square mile zone of the forest free from development, protecting habitat for 600 elk, 100 bears, and 100 bobcats.

In October 1973, a hearings officer who had taken 20 days of testimony on the issue of oil development within the Pigeon River country recommended that the Natural Resources Commission authorize drilling throughout the area targeted by the industry. At the same meeting, department staff recommended a comprehensive management plan for the forest that would protect a third of it as elk habitat and set in place special management practices to guard the critical elk, bear, and bobcat habitat. The commission adopted the plan in December.

When the commission also denied a drilling permit to Michigan Oil Company within the forest, the firm went to court. In August 1974 it sued for permission to drill at a site the DNR had determined to be too sensitive because of the effect on wildlife populations. Ingham County circuit court judge Thomas Brown ruled in favor of the DNR in June 1975. The agency seemed to hold all of the cards it needed to prevent development in the Pigeon River country.

Less than two months later, however, DNR director Tanner unveiled a hydrocarbon management plan to govern the oil and gas development of the forest. He explained that the agency might lose its authority to manage the forest—perhaps through a bill the oil industry would rush through the legislature—if it continued to oppose most drilling outright. Better to control the drilling under terms acceptable to the DNR, he said, than to risk poorly planned development.

Still inclined to protect the Pigeon River country, Governor Milliken ordered the DNR to prepare an environmental impact statement on the proposed drilling. Tanner gave the assignment to his assistant, Jack Bails. Bails in turn worked with a team of DNR staff, among them Don Inman, a young wildlife ecologist who worked in the Office of Environmental Review. According to Bails, it was Inman who cooked up an idea that would ultimately be incorporated in Michigan's constitution. Since the task force concluded that even the limited drilling the DNR was willing to accept would have unavoidable, harmful effects on the forest, Inman turned his thoughts to the idea of what might mitigate the damage. Inman had been exposed to the relatively recent school of thinking about environmental mitigation during postdoctoral studies at the University of Georgia. He suggested to Bails that the estimated $200 million in state revenue that would be derived from drilling in the forest should be deposited in a separate fund earmarked for the purchase of other recreational lands in the area for public benefit. As Bails put it, the idea was to "take the assets of oil, and turn them into assets of land."

In October 1975, defenders of the forest received a second jolt. MUCC executive director Washington announced his support for drilling in the forest under modifications to the Tanner plan. He, too, cited the risk of losing any control over oil and gas drilling. Washington said the time to win concessions from the oil and gas industry was now, when the state had prevailed in the courts. But the most important argument for the compromise, he reasoned, was the idea of mitigation that Inman had pioneered. Washington seized and expanded upon it, proposing a fund that would receive most revenues from oil and gas drilling on any DNR lands. When Milliken hesitated to endorse the idea of earmarking drilling revenues for land purchases, Washington persuaded state senator Kerry Kammer to introduce the bill. In his January 1976 State of the State message, Milliken endorsed a similar concept, proposing a Heritage Trust Fund to receive all state oil and gas revenues. The Kammer bill quickly became law in the 1976 session.

In 1984, after both Governor Milliken and Governor Blanchard had proposed "borrowing" money from the fund to meet short-term needs in other state programs, Washington succeeded in putting on the election ballot a constitutional amendment walling off the trust fund from such raids in the future. Michigan voters approved it by a margin of nearly two to one. Washington served on the board overseeing the trust fund's recommendations to the legislature for land purchases until his 1995 death.

The *Detroit Free Press,* which crusaded against development of the forest from that point forward, was quick to express its shock at Tanner's position. Outdoor writer Tom Opre said, "Somehow you felt the battle was already won. . . . Somehow you got the idea [the DNR] had decided to stand and fight even though the oil company was sure to appeal the decision—probably all the way to the Michigan Supreme Court, if necessary. It was a case of what was more important: developing the hydrocarbons in the Pigeon Reserve or preserving its natural foliage, wildlife and other values."[17] After canoeing the Pigeon River with Opre, executive editor Joe Stroud observed, "As the hours went by, my conviction grew. This is a treasure, and we have to protect it. . . . It ought to be dealt with now not on the basis of legalisms or expediency, but as it has been for these many years—on the basis of the public interest."[18]

Washington's position may have been based on more than just an assessment of the chances of defeating oil companies in the courts. The state had bought a large chunk of the forest with revenue from hunting licenses. Now environmental groups were clamoring for it to remain—or become—a natural area. "What really was being argued," said MUCC staff ecologist Wayne Schmidt, "was whether the forest should revert to a wilderness-style management that would severely restrict future management for hunting. . . . To Tom and the MUCC, oil and gas development, and the resulting roads and disruption, was consistent with the management and access of the lands for hunting, which required early successional vegetation and not mature forest."[19] Others, however, said Washington's antiwilderness reasoning was a justification after the fact, used to shore up support from sporting organizations angry about his defense of limited oil and gas exploration in the forest.

The environmental impact statement submitted by Bails's team also called for "unitized" drilling limited to the southern one-third of the forest. The term meant that the several companies hoping to exploit the oil and gas deposits would be required to construct roads and drilling pads jointly, minimizing the disruption of the forest.

At a series of public hearings on the DNR's environmental impact statement in late 1975, almost all speakers opposed the idea of drilling in the forest, sometimes in emotional terms. The MUCC's Washington was an exception: "Environmental impacts which would result from competitive exploration and drilling far exceed impacts we can anticipate under a unitized approach," he said at a December 1975 hearing. "We believe the state would lose a legal battle if they tried to prohibit drilling on all sites under application for permit. . . . Now you have found black gold, and it has value. Royalties can and must be the mitigating factor which makes environmental disruption justifiable."[20]

Washington and the MUCC also scoffed at the value of the elk herd that roamed the forest. Pointing out that the elk descended from Colorado animals imported to the state in 1918, Washington said his group was "not enamored with this species and do not feel this will be an irreplaceable loss to the state if, in fact, a total loss will occur."

His view was still that of a distinct minority. When the executive committee of the state chapter of the Sierra Club voted to support drilling in late 1975, members rebelled and reversed the vote the following month. Milliken received thousands of letters and a petition containing more than 30,000 signatures of persons opposed to drilling in the forest. In May 1976, he openly declared his own opposition.

But the Michigan Oil and Gas Association (MOGA) was threatening to take any state ban on drilling in the forest to the highest courts in the land. Seeking to balance competing interests—and forge a political compromise—the Natural Resources Commission voted just days after Milliken's statement to permit "environmentally acceptable" drilling. Although vague, the policy gave agency director Tanner the authorization to negotiate with the oil companies over terms of drilling. In June 1976, the commission approved a more detailed resolution authorizing drilling in 15,000 southern acres of the forest. Milliken responded sadly, lamenting the agency's leasing of the Pigeon River mineral rights in the late 1960s.

When the commission refused to reconsider its decision, a broad coalition of forest defenders led by the West Michigan Environmental Action Council went to court to block the drilling. An Ingham County circuit court judge refused to block the drilling immediately but ruled that the commission had the authority to deny permits if it determined on a case-by-case basis that they would cause severe environmental damage. "This may be an example where you win by losing," said WMEAC executive director Roger Conner, who had pleaded the case in court himself.

In August 1977 DNR director Tanner approved 10 applications from Shell Oil Company to explore for oil beneath the Pigeon River country. Using the Michigan Environmental Protection Act as his legal foundation, Conner went to court again, unsuccessfully seeking a temporary restraining order to block the exploratory drilling. When the case came to trial, an environmental publication described the courthouse scene this way.

A long-haired, blue jeaned environmentalist . . . stood outside the chambers of Ingham County Circuit Court Judge Thomas L. Brown on September 6, holding a small sign which called for "no exploitation" of the Pigeon River

Country State Forest.... The scene in Brown's courtroom was a familiar one to those involved in the ongoing controversy. Seated at one side of a large rectangular table before the white haired judge were Department of Natural Resources and oil industry spokesmen, such as Shell attorney Webb Smith and Assistant Attorney General Stewart Freeman, representing the DNR. Across the table sat Conner, in the beginning confident that Judge Brown would see it his way.[21]

In December, circuit court Judge Brown ruled against the environmental coalition, and Shell moved ahead immediately, drilling one well and clearing four other sites before Conner got an order from the state supreme court halting the work. In an unusual move, the supreme court also agreed to hear the appeal directly, bypassing the appeals court. The court's promising show of interest was a good clue to its intentions. In February 1979, by a 4–3 vote, the court issued what Environmental Action of Michigan called "a stunning victory," saying Brown had erred in deferring to the DNR's judgment on the impact of the Shell drilling. MEPA, the court said, required trial courts to use independent judgment. The court said drilling could result in unacceptable destruction of the forest's herd of 255 elk. Coupled with another supreme court decision the same month on a separate drilling appeal in the forest, the decision effectively barred drilling there.

But the decision did not save the forest. The oil industry decided to undo in the legislature what the environmental groups had accomplished in the courts. With Michigan's economy foundering in a serious recession, Shell and other companies pointed out the riches the state would reap if it allowed drilling in the forest and in other sensitive areas. Early in 1980, industry supporters in the legislature introduced a bill to exempt oil and gas drilling activities from the environmentalists' holy grail, MEPA and other state environmental laws.

The legislative climate frightened environmental groups, who feared they would lose MEPA and other important protective laws if they held out. Conner had left WMEAC, and successor Ken Sikkema, a former state legislative aide, persuaded the coalition to support a compromise on the legislation rather than risk the effective repeal of MEPA.

"In the seeds of a great [supreme court] victory was a great defeat," Sikkema later said.[22] "If the elk increased in population, or if you showed oil drilling didn't impair the herd, the decision could easily be overturned. There was nothing in the ruling about the effect on groundwater, the forest, anything but the elk. I felt there was a way you protect the values of the forest and have limited drilling."

Deciding that compromise was better than defeat, Sikkema led the environmental coalition to negotiate changes to the bill that restricted development in Pigeon River to the southern third of the forest, as the DNR had proposed. Another key concession was phased development. "This was the cornerstone of the deal—holding Shell to the obligation to prove they could and did do it right in phase one before being allowed to proceed," said Grant

Trigger, the director of the Michigan Environmental Council and a participant in the negotiations. "Without it we could not have sold it to the environmental groups."[23] The agreement also prevented exploration and drilling in wetlands and low-lying areas, established an advisory council to oversee the drilling, and barred exploration and construction activity from April 15 to June 30, a critical period for wildlife nesting and rearing of young.

There was one final clash, this time between the environmentalists and Washington. The MUCC head attended the press conference announcing the agreement and enraged Trigger and others by attempting to take credit for it, although he had not participated in the negotiations. But the press ignored Washington. "So in the end Tom's scheme did nothing to get him credit," Trigger said. "To my amazement the press recognized who really did the deal and ignored Tom." Milliken reluctantly signed the bill into law.

The decade-long fight had consumed millions of dollars, made enemies out of former friends, and failed to stop the drilling. The most devout lovers of the Pigeon River country grieved at the clearing of each drilling site and later discoveries of groundwater contamination from disposal of the drilling wastes. But the struggle had resulted in a permanent trust fund to protect important lands for public use and sharply restricted drilling of the forest under terms Bails and Inman later regarded proudly as a model. An important Michigan environmental group later agreed, citing the Pigeon River hydrocarbon management plan as a model for oil development of other sensitive areas.[24] Nobody had won a clear victory—but neither had the forest suffered a clear loss.

Saving the Sand Castles

Michigan's first state geologist, Douglass Houghton, reported an unusual feature of the state's landscape in an 1838 report to the governor and legislature.

> *Nearly the whole western coast of the [lower] peninsula, immediately upon Lake Michigan, is bordered by a succession of sand dunes or hills of loose sand, not unfrequently attaining a considerable altitude. . . . These movable sands, which are now unnoticed, may hereafter become matters of serious inconvenience, more particularly in those portions where the timber may be heedlessly removed. These dunes are not unfrequently composed of sand tolerably well adapted to the manufacture of glass, though its value is frequently much impaired by the presence of particles of dark colored minerals.*[25]

Houghton's description of the nuisance and potential commercial value of the dunes pretty much reflected general opinion of the belt of sand that bound the Lake Michigan shoreline and small reaches of the Upper Peninsula's Lake Superior shore for the next century.

But down in Indiana, at the dawn of the twentieth century, an assortment of Chicago-area outdoor lovers, social welfare activists, and disciples of Thoreau adopted the dune country along Lake Michigan as its special domain. Calling themselves the Saturday Afternoon Walks in recognition of their weekend jaunts to natural areas surrounding the ever-expanding metropolis, the mostly middle-class professionals and wealthy nature enthusiasts found in the Indiana dunes a landscape both wild and close to home. Inspired by the group's explorations, the Chicago landscape architect Jens Jensen, who helped incubate the parks career of Michigan's Genevieve Gillette, became "the first champion of Indiana Dunes preservation." Jensen sought nothing less than a national park in the dunes.[26]

The result of processes unleashed by the last retreat of the glaciers 10,000 years ago, the dunes of Indiana and Michigan were even more youthful geologically—an estimated 1,000 to 4,000 years old—and fragile. Sorted by the wind and piled into heaps as high as 350 feet above the lake, the sands were predominantly quartz, hard and stable, and thus ideal for industrial use. But to twentieth-century eyes they had even more important values. The broad shoulders of the dunes guarded the beaches and waters below, shaping the visitor's perspective of the eternal shore. Dune systems were anything but barren wastes. Sculpted by wave and wind, they resembled the tossing lake in contour. Behind the bald face of the barrier dunes beech-maple forests held older ridges in place, providing a dramatic shaded contrast to the sun-soaked beaches. Small wetlands were often tucked between dunes. Glimpsed through the trees of the climax forest after a long uphill trudge, the sight of a hazy blue line of lake water beyond the barrier dune inspired the visitor.

Half a century would pass before Jensen's dream of an Indiana Dunes national park was realized. In the meantime vast reaches of the Indiana Dunes—and of Michigan's own natural sand castles—were stripped away. Sometimes public officials not only tolerated but promoted dune destruction. The city of Manistee, two-thirds of the way up the Lake Michigan shore, contracted in 1928 with Sand Products Company to remove a large dune within its borders known as "Creeping Joe." According to local lore this dune, perched on the south side of the Manistee River near its mouth, began to move after 1885 Fourth of July celebrants and exuberant Democrats after an 1888 election landslide burned and stripped the dune's vegetation away. The *Manistee News-Advocate* reported, "The dune at present is costing the city a considerable sum each year, for it is alive and winds constantly blow sand over the Fifth Avenue pavement and sidewalk, necessitating much labor to keep this avenue open to traffic."[27] The dune had also begun to cover a few homes. The city would gain 2 1/2¢ per ton for the estimated 40 shiploads of sand per year. Sand Products sold the sand to customers that included Ford Motor Company of Dearborn. The sands of Manistee and much of lower Michigan's west shore were perfect, as Houghton had predicted, in the manufacture of glass. But they were even better in the making of molds to case engine blocks and other components of automobiles, trucks, and heavy machinery. The composition of Lake Michigan sand, the industry said, enabled it when mixed with binders to hold its shape without cracking or warping when molten metal was poured in, yet to break down and pour out of the casting once it cooled. In the 1970s one mining company official estimated it took 350 to 500 pounds of sand to make an automobile and that 40 percent of all the foundry sand used in the United States came from Lake Michigan dunes.[28]

In a 1945 photo spread, Ford chronicled the fate of the Manistee sands in a promotional publication: "Thirty acres of man-made sand dunes, 75 feet high, are now spread out at the Rouge plant of the Ford Motor Company at Dearborn. It's the largest pile of sand in the world heaped up by human effort. . . . All summer long ships carry sand from the dunes of the West Michigan vacation country to the man-made dunes at Dearborn. The last cargo usually arrives around Nov. 15 at which time the dunes of Dearborn are tallest and most spread out."[29] The newspaper estimated that Ford used annually 250,000 tons of Manistee sand.

But a few Michigan voices rose in protest against dune mining even in the early days. The Nugent Sand Company purchased the landmark 300-foot-tall Pigeon Hill in Muskegon in the 1920s and announced plans to mine the hill and build homes on the flatland that would remain. When the Muskegon city commission considered a proposal to authorize a railroad spur to lug away the sands of the dune, which towered over the mouth of the city's harbor, local resident John Bennink is said to have declared, "Pigeon Hill was placed there by God to protect this city. It saves us from storms that sweep in over the lake. If it is removed the wrath of God will be on us."[30] Despite the protests of a citizen coalition that included local artists and a well-known journalist, the company refused to sell the dune to preservationists. "Meetings ended in bitter words, so intense was the feeling at the time," the *Muskegon Chronicle* later reported. By 1938 the dune was gone.

Nearly 30 years passed before the dunes gained important new friends. In the 1960s citizens of Lake and Lincoln Townships in Berrien County organized to fight the mining of dunes in the Grand Mere area. Others fought mining proposals and operations in Bridgman, just south of Grand Mere, and at Ferrysburg, between Grand Haven and Muskegon. Another cluster of angry citizens fought to stop the mining of 160 acres near Silver Lake in Oceana County. The proposal by a developer to remove 18,000 tons per week of sand prompted nearby property owners to seek an injunction until an environmental impact statement could be prepared. But a spokesperson for the sand and gravel industry defended the practice, pointing out that the land would be useful for housing after the dune was removed. "This is just a way to get land in shape for development," said a spokesperson for the Michigan Sand and Gravel Association.[31]

By the early 1970s, as an environmental impulse swept the state, the clamor for protection of the vanishing dunes grew. One environmentalist warned, "The question the citizens of Michigan must ask themselves is whether they will wait until there is no more sand before they see the cold facts before them. Sand mining will continue until the eastern shore of the lake that this state is named for is a blowing wasteland, or until the Michigan people take affirmative action to halt the devastation."[32]

A Republican legislator representing Manistee, Dennis Cawthorne, heard the cries of citizens concerned about dune destruction. But he was also personally indignant about the ruins that Sand Products Company had left behind after leveling the sands of his home city. "They made no effort whatsoever to restore any vegetation. Then they began to mine down beneath the surface. They created a lake. They were in such proximity to Lake Michigan that there was a risk it would break through and change the shoreline with who knows what consequences," Cawthorne said. "The company left behind a barren wasteland and a mess."[33]

It was unusual in the Democrat-controlled state House of Representatives for a member of the minority party to head a special committee, but Conservation Committee chairperson Thomas Anderson was happy to let Cawthorne take the lead on regulatory legislation that was sure to stir fierce opposition from some mining companies. Appointed in the summer of 1974, Cawthorne's five-member committee toured mining sites and held several public meetings on the issue of the "strip mining" of dunes. The panel frequently heard the sentiments expressed by Jerry Lindquist of Grand Haven, chairperson of the Lake Michigan Federation, an advocacy group: "I haven't seen sand dunes anywhere else, anywhere near like the ones on the shore of Lake Michigan. They are simply beautiful and what's left of the dunes should be preserved."[34]

Introduced early in 1975, Cawthorne's bill banned all mining within 2,500 feet of the shoreline, including the most spectacular barrier dunes, and required mining companies to apply to the Department of Natural Resources for permits to work in other dunes within two miles of the shoreline. To address Cawthorne's anger about the poor conditions of the Manistee site after mining, the bill required reclamation plans from any company granted a permit. Response from the mining and auto industries was harshly negative. Richard Robinson of the Michigan Industrial Sand Producers Association said that "the entire auto industry would be out of business" if the bill passed. An unnamed lobbyist for automakers said the bill "could have a serious financial impact on the companies."[35] Cawthorne retorted that foreign auto manufacturers were doing fine without Great Lakes sand. He faced a fierce opponent, however, in Representative Gerrit Hasper of Muskegon, who openly said he was representing an official in a Muskegon sand mining company. Hasper tried repeatedly to kill the bill and to lower the fees it would charge the industry.[36]

Aware of the popularity of dune protection, the industry signaled that it would not oppose the bill if Cawthorne removed the outright ban on mining of the first 2,500 feet of sand. He agreed to the change. The bill would now bar mining only of the barrier dunes, but the Department of Natural Resources could waive even that protection with approval of its managing body, the Natural Resources Commission.

Once again Michigan newspapers weighed in to support an environmental protection measure. The *Muskegon Chronicle, Grand Rapids Press,* and *Detroit Free Press* all published extensive articles in the mid-1970s about the damage to dunes caused by mining. The *Chronicle* editorialized that "the unregulated stripping of our beautiful dunelands must stop—and we won't have to say that twice to those Muskegonites old enough to remember the towering shoreline glory of Pigeon Hill."[37] The *Free Press* observed, "Nature worked 15,000 years to create this unique resource. It took man only 50 years to destroy much of it. Giant sand shovels and bulldozers were the instruments of destruction. . . . Something as urgent as protecting a vanishing resource that belongs to all the people deserves the broadest bipartisan support."[38]

After 10 months Cawthorne's legislation passed the House. It went to the Senate Conservation Committee, chaired by Senator Joe Mack of Ironwood, a notorious foe of environmental regulation. The bill languished in Mack's committee for more than six months, but he extracted a commitment on another issue and released the bill for final approval in the summer of 1976. Governor William Milliken, who had consistently supported the bill, quickly signed it.

Hailed as a "great win for the environment" by the *Muskegon Chronicle,* the new law soon generated sharp conflicts between environmentalists and citizens living near dune mining operations on one hand and the Department of Natural Resources on the other. Like many other statutes whose middle name was "protection," the Sand Dune Protection and Management Act of 1976 was as much about governing dune destruction as it was about preventing it. The permit system established under the law corrected the worst abuses of a few sand mining operations but did little to check the removal of some of the state's most spectacular remaining dunes. And critics of the DNR suspected that the Geological Survey Division, assigned the task of implementing the law, was secretly on the side of the mining industry.

When the Martin Marietta Corporation received tentative approval in 1979 from the DNR to mine 144 acres around a 225-foot-tall dune near Bridgman known as Mount Edwards, Wayne Schmidt of the Michigan United Conservation Clubs exploded: "If Mount Edwards isn't the best of what we have left, then where will the DNR draw the line?" Another conservationist, Mary Alice Kirincic, president of a group formed to save the site called Hope for the Dunes, implored the state to consider the recreational and ecological value of the dunes. "The dollars and cents of big business make it difficult to see both ways, but you can't ignore the value of dunes to people who enjoy them," she said.[39] Dr. Warren (Herb) Wagner, a University of Michigan botanist, called the site part of "the richest dune community of any dune complex in the world." Wagner added in an interview quoted in the *Detroit Free Press,* "I don't think we have the right to destroy areas so rare as this one, especially for a short-term gain. That sand will only last the miners a few years, then they will have to go somewhere else."[40]

The public pressure had an impact. DNR director Howard Tanner told

Martin Marietta in September 1979 that he intended to deny the permit because, under terms of the law, the proposal would have "an irreparable harmful effect on the environment." But this was not a final victory for the dunes. Martin Marietta won an appeal of Tanner's ruling to an administrative law judge. In 1981, this verdict came before the Natural Resources Commission itself. At an emotional public hearing, both sides implored the commissioners. "It took 8,000 years to create these dunes," said Terrence Grady, an assistant attorney general. "It would take only a couple of years to destroy them." The DNR pointed out that foundries did not have to rely on dunes for sand supplies, since a General Motors casting plant in Saginaw used sand dredged from Saginaw Bay.

"You've got to consider the economics of the situation," said John Crow, an attorney representing Martin Marietta. He said the mining of 400,000 tons of sand annually would provide $325,000 each year in payroll to local workers and could last 20 years or more. Pointing out that the state owned nearly 28 miles of Lake Michigan shoreline in parks, he added, "I guess my point is that we're saving enough land already." In the depth of Michigan's worst economic downturn since the Great Depression, the argument carried weight with some members of the commission. "How many places do I need to go to look at beautiful rocks?" asked Charles G. Younglove, a commissioner who was also an official of the United Steelworkers Union.[41] The commission voted 4–3 to approve the mining in November 1981.

Even there the battle did not end. Michigan attorney general Frank Kelley sued the commission to stop the mining, and the operation was stalemated for nearly three years. In 1984, the Michigan chapter of the Nature Conservancy and Thomas Washington of the Michigan United Conservation Clubs, who chaired the board of the Michigan Natural Resources Trust Fund, helped broker a deal in which the state would buy most of the site from the company, protecting Mount Edward while allowing limited mining.

This resolution did not wipe away the bitter taste in the mouths of advocates who had fought to protect the area. Don Wilson, one of the most outspoken organizers and members of Hope for the Dunes, faulted the Department of Natural Resources for failing to exploit what he believed as its mandate to protect the dunes.

> *[The state government] historically steps back as industry steps forward so as to accommodate the industry, which is perceived as having the money and power versus the public groups who are seen by the state agencies as financially weak and not organized. Through the years when I was in Lansing, I was occasionally told by DNR personnel not to get emotionally involved. I explained that if I weren't emotionally involved I wouldn't be there, that unlike government people I wasn't being paid so I could be as unconcerned as they.*

Wilson noted that Martin Marietta wooed Bridgman city officials with food and drink and had access to state officials that a volunteer citizens group could not have.[42] He also argued that the end of mining at the Bridgman site only pushed the miners to other, equally vulnerable areas along the shoreline. Still, the advocacy of Hope for the Dunes had its effect: after the group's formation, no mining took place at Bridgman other than a small five-acre area granted by a local judge.

The conflict over Martin Marietta's mining proposal attracted the attention of Governor James Blanchard, who had taken office in 1983 and was seeking an environmental issue on which to build his record. Coincidentally, Blanchard had spent 11 summers in the dunes at the First Congregational Church Camp, adjacent to the mining site. After celebrating the compromise that protected most of the unmined portion of the site at a press conference in 1984, Blanchard directed the Department of Natural Resources to convene an advisory group to strengthen the law. His target was commercial and residential development of the dunes, unregulated by the 1976 law. Building of expensive homes, particularly along the shore between Holland and Grand Haven, was consuming scenic dunes.

Chairing the advisory group, Natural Resources Commission member Marlene Fluharty produced a report in 1987 that recommended amendments to the law and a new department policy protecting publicly owned dunes. Armed with the committee's report and concern from an East Lansing constituent who owned a summer home in the Lake Michigan dunes, state representative Lynn Jondahl introduced the measure and nearly shepherded it to the governor's desk for signing in late 1988. The bill established a new permit requirement for residential and commercial development of dunes and banned construction on the steepest slopes. In all, the DNR estimated, the bill would govern development on 70,000 acres of dunes, mostly in the Lower Peninsula. Jondahl had strong support from the MUCC, which had collected more than 85,000 citizen signatures in favor of the measure. But, foreshadowing the debates of the 1990s, a reascendant private property rights movement found conservative legislators to kill the bill. A state senator tacked on an amendment requiring automatic compensation to owners for any loss in property value caused by the new regulations.

The bill had enough momentum to survive this setback the following year. MUCC continued its pressure. The defeat of the bill in 1988 "was the greatest disappointment of the session," said MUCC's assistant executive director, Rick Jameson. "It would be unthinkable to allow another construction season to go on without some regulations in place."43 Altered to provide an opportunity for local governments to exercise an option to protect the dunes instead of the state, Jondahl's legislation was split in two and one piece given to state senator Connie Binsfeld. Blanchard signed the bill in July 1989, at the Kitchel-Lundquist sand dune preserve in Grand Haven.

But dune lovers were to be disappointed again. The new law was no more a guarantee of dune protection than had been the original mining statute. As a DNR official pointed out during the debate over the legislation, "We have been hearing that this would prohibit development in the dunes. That is absolutely false. It is designed to protect dunes, not prohibit development.

Development would continue under the guidelines."[44] Given the American tradition of private property rights, only outright purchase of dunes could have stopped development altogether. But environmentalists wondered when, if ever, the state would use the law simply to say no to a development that might compromise the most spectacular dune ecosystems.

The restrictions on residential and commercial development in the new law were effective for a time in shaping the way in which developers and builders put new homes in the Lake Michigan dunes. But in the early 1990s, less than four years after it took effect, the law came under legislative attack. Governor John Engler had clearly signaled his distaste for environmental regulations and his preference for voluntary protection, and the legislature had turned more conservative. The Michigan Association of Homebuilders and the Michigan Association of Realtors, who had contested the bill before its passage, joined with individual property owners aggrieved by restrictions on development of their dune properties to force changes in the law and the appointment of a review committee to study other controversial provisions. Some legislators wanted to go even farther, proposing to override the state's denial of sand dune permits if a private engineer certified the stability of a proposed structure. Typical of the most strident attacks on the law was the comment of Jim Westgate, who turned out at a hearing on this bill to compare the Department of Natural Resources to the Communist Party in the former Soviet Union. "I felt like there was a machine gun at my back," said Westgate, who had sparred with the DNR over his proposed home in the protected dunes. Jim Ribbens, a DNR official, replied mildly that his staff had approved 75 percent of the 2,500 applications to build in critical dunes through mid-1995.[45]

Sure that the DNR had been regulating development in dunes not worthy of protection, in 1994 the legislature amended the law to require that a study team evaluate the maps used to identify areas where permits were required. But the Michigan State University Center for Remote Sensing, hired to conduct the study, surprised lawmakers with a finding that the state should protect an additional 12,162 acres, bringing the total covered by the law to over 83,000 acres.[46] The Department of Environmental Quality (DEQ) and legislators from the affected areas joined in opposing the change.

"My staff feels there are more important things for us to be doing than adding a bunch of dunes" to the law, said DEQ director Russell Harding. Twenty-two legislators wrote to Harding expressing concern about the MSU report, warning that they regarded it "as a document that must be carefully analyzed before the Legislature should consider taking any action." Even legislators considered friendly to environmental protection balked at the recommendation. In a letter to the editor of the *Grand Rapids Press* contesting its support for protection of the extra dunelands, state representative Jon Jellema fretted, "If the new classification results in the addition of some 12,000 acres to the critical dunes list and that further restricts landowners from developing the property, it can be argued that the government has 'taken' some of the value of the land away from the landowners."[47] Three years after the state issued the MSU report, neither the DEQ nor the legislature had taken action to protect the areas the study recommended for protection.

A quarter century after passage of the first state restrictions on dune development, dune lovers questioned how much had been accomplished. A group of property owners near Covert, not far from South Haven on the Lake Michigan shore, was locked in a fight with the DEQ and a mining company, Technisand, over its operations. Uniting under the banner of Preserve the Dunes, they sued the DEQ to stop the expansion of the mining. Meanwhile, the Lake Michigan Federation released a report in 1999 pointing out that the area of sand dunes under active mining had risen from 3,228 acres in the year the law passed, 1976, to 4,848 acres. In the 23 years since passage of the law, the federation pointed out, the state had allowed the mining of 46.5 million tons of sand from the regulated dunes, or a load handled by 2.3 million dump trucks. The report faulted the DEQ's reluctance to apply the tough environmental standards of the law to permits and enforcement.[48]

Other environmental groups had questions about the effectiveness of the restrictions on commercial and residential development. Julie Stoneman, the land programs director of the Michigan Environmental Council, commented in legislative testimony that the standards were "insufficient to protect dune ecology. . . . The reactive, site by site permitting process has left many unhappy with the statute. And we have no means for setting and assessing biological and ecological indicators of sand dune ecosystem health."[49]

A singular setting of apparent desert and water, of drifting sand and stationary, tree-crowned ridges, the Lake Michigan dunes have inspired Americans for a century. Remembering her childhood summers at Lakeside, near Warren Dunes State Park in southwest Michigan, writer Annick Smith said, "There are snakes in the marram grass, and monarch butterflies so fragile we don't dare catch them, and Indian stones from Paleozoic seas. The dunes are moving; the dance is monotonous, shifting . . . one-step, one-step, one-step. It is my heart. I am summer's gray-haired child in love with this blue world."[50] It is impossible to know whether children one hundred years hence will be able to know the same joys. It is impossible to know whether flawed laws of the 1970s and 1980s, compromised in their writing and in their enforcement, will protect the character of the dunelands.

Wrangling over Wilderness

Perhaps no land preservation effort has divided Michigan conservation groups from environmental advocates more than the idea of setting aside wilderness. The West Michigan Environmental Action Council and Michigan United Conservation Clubs sparred over oil and gas development in the Pigeon River country in part because of mutual mistrust about whether the area would revert to a wild state—which the MUCC feared might reduce or eliminate motorized access for hunters and anglers to prime recreation spots.

A battle also broke out in the late 1970s over proposals to set aside areas of Michigan's national forests as protected wilderness areas. Acting under authority granted by the 1964 Wilderness Act, the U.S. Forest Service surveyed roadless areas across the country and announced proposals for 62 million acres of wilderness in January 1979. The Michigan sites recommended by U.S. agriculture secretary Bob Bergland were just a fraction of the state's national forestlands, a mere 56,000 acres. All but one of the areas were in the Upper Peninsula. Included was the Sturgeon River Gorge southwest of L'Anse, a 14,700-acre reserve with "sheer sandstone cliffs, thundering white water, rainbows in the sun," in the words of the Michigan chapter of the Sierra Club, the primary lobbying force for wilderness designations. Another proposed wilderness area was a historic 17,000-acre tract once owned by industrialist Cyrus McCormick, characterized by "rock-rimmed lakes, craggy cliffs, lily-ponds waiting for a moose to stroll by for breakfast, and waterfalls tumbling over black granite," said the Sierra Club.

Even the modest Forest Service recommendations were enough to cause an uproar. Owners of inholdings in some of the proposed wilderness areas, timber and mining companies, and an Upper Peninsula populace suspicious of state and federal environmental restrictions criticized the proposals. They objected not only to the idea of putting areas off limits to motorized transportation and timber harvest but also to the source of the idea—federal land managers and urban environmentalists, whom they accused of being elitists.

"Preservationists and backpack hikers, who represent 1 per cent of the population, are trying to dictate to the other 99 per cent," said Don Tallman, a motel operator in Ontonagon.[51] In a letter to the editor, David Olson, a Marquette man who later served on the state Natural Resources Commission, attacked a *Detroit Free Press* editorial supporting the wilderness designations: "I know there can be no doubt why Upper Peninsula residents are frequently angry and confused by statements coming from Detroit papers and some Lansing legislators. You use the term 'conservationists' loosely. Conservation is usually defined as wise use of resources. Wilderness designation is not use of a resource, nor is it wise in many cases."

The MUCC was also skeptical of Michigan wilderness. In the mid-1980s it officially opposed wilderness on the state's national forestlands after a stormy debate at its annual convention, and through most of the debate on the legislation it was ominously silent. Bill Whippen, a regional director for MUCC, told U.S. senator Carl Levin at a 1980 public hearing that managed forests were more beneficial to wildlife than wilderness areas. "I don't know why anyone would want to go into a wilderness area," Whippen said. "There is nothing to see but tall trees."[52] Fearful of a backlash in his 1982 reelection campaign, the other U.S. senator from Michigan, Donald Riegle, said he would oppose the Levin bill.

Despite the overwhelming opposition of citizens in the Upper Peninsula and of Riegle, the Sierra Club pushed forward unrelentingly. Early in the battle, the club's state chairperson, Virginia Prentice, developed some of the first maps of possible wilderness sites in Michigan. Following the Forest Service's announcement, the club persuaded U.S. representative Bob Carr, a Democrat from the Lansing area, to introduce a bill expanding the designated wilderness to more than 90,000 acres. After Carr was defeated in the 1980 election, Representative Dale Kildee of Flint sponsored a bill similar to Carr's.

Riegle's opposition, and the resistance of President Ronald Reagan's administration to wilderness, stalled the bill until 1985. In most cases, congressional committee chairs were unwilling to take up wilderness bills unless most or all of a state's congressional delegation supported them. But Governor James Blanchard, who had cosponsored the Carr bill while a member of Congress, surprised both foes and supporters of Kildee's legislation when he said that he would support it "unequivocally" at a February 1985 banquet of the Sierra Club in Ann Arbor. The declaration was "most unexpected," wrote *Detroit Free Press* political columnist Hugh McDiarmid, citing previous Blanchard policies that worried the Sierra Club. "Blanchard, of course, is no beau ideal environmentalist," McDiarmid added. "His idea of recreation—aside from dabbling in golf—is to lean back with friends late at night, have a drink or two, puff on one of those preposterous $2 cigars . . . that his pal, former State Rep. Joe Forbes, introduced him to years ago, and talk politics."[53]

While Sierra Club staff member Anne Woiwode said Blanchard's position was "terrific," state senator Joe Mack of Ironwood said it was "like getting stabbed in the back. I was appalled when I heard about it. The last thing we need from him or anyone else is more wilderness. . . . It's like a creeping cancer."

The governor's support broke the five-year logjam on Michigan wilderness legislation. Blanchard's position enabled Levin to position himself as a moderate on the issue, trying to develop a compromise between the 90,000 acres proposed in Kildee's bill and his own slightly smaller version. An Upper Peninsula aide to Levin justified the senator's position by saying, "This issue was not going to go away. Not with environmental groups threatening to take states without federal wilderness legislation to court." He added that the bill would actually remove a cloud from the use of Upper Peninsula forests by prohibiting the Forest Service from studying any more lands for wilderness designation and barring wilderness buffer zones around the designated areas.

Opposition from the MUCC and newspapers persisted, however. The *Detroit News* editorialized that debate on the bill "really comes down to this: What does the state gain by declaring these areas wilderness? The answer is: It gets nothing."[54] The *News* noted that lack of management on the lands would reduce deer herds and hunting opportunities. Upper Peninsula newspapers generally echoed the *News*.

While Mack went to work trying to win a state legislative resolution opposing the proposed Michigan Wilderness Heritage Act, Kildee was able to get a hearing on the measure in the summer of 1985 in a subcommittee of the House Interior Committee. The bill won easy approval from the full committee and the U.S. House but died in the Senate late in 1986, due in part to Riegle's continued opposition.

The Sierra Club refused to quit. Almost single-handedly, the small but aggressive organization continued its pressure on Levin and Riegle, with the friendly Kildee cooperating closely in the group's legislative strategy. Typical of its work was a letter to wilderness supporters observing that the only way opponents of the bill "will win at this point is if they outwait us. The only way they will outwait us is if they think the support is waning." The club's Anne Woiwode urged recipients of the letter to write to the *Detroit News* attacking its position and to again contact Levin and Riegle: " [J]ust like the broken washing machine which does not respond to appropriate actions, or the vending machine which ate your quarter and kept your pop, sometimes it is best to try one more swat, jiggle or shake before calling the plumber or the repair shop. One more letter may do the trick."[55]

Hundreds of letters did. In 1987, with another reelection campaign ahead, Riegle quietly signaled that he would not oppose a compromise bill authored by Kildee and Levin. The Michigan Wilderness Heritage Act cleared Congress and was signed by Reagan—despite a last-minute telegram by the MUCC's president, Tom Washington, urging him to veto the measure. While a significant triumph for the Sierra Club, the effect of the new law was as much symbolic as real. The designated area was less than 3 percent of all national forestlands in Michigan, and most of it was not prime timberland.

Years later, the Sierra Club's Jane Elder, who had helped orchestrate the introduction of the first Michigan wilderness bill in 1980, said she still found "it hard to go visit these places. It is hard to explain. Every place evokes a barrage of memories of debate, conflict, tough choices and things still unresolved. You can't put your heart into something this hard without getting a few scars along the way. I know too much about the Michigan wilderness areas to visit them unaware. We know too much about each other's history."[56]

But putting wilderness into a statute assured that the Forest Service would not tamper with the 11 wilderness areas for the foreseeable future. Perhaps the greatest difference, although hard to measure, was spiritual rather than physical—the knowledge that a small slice of mostly second-growth northern forest could not be unthinkingly logged. Another difference was the possibility of finding silence and solace in a remnant of the wild spirit of the old Michigan.

One sure way of protecting the land since the early twentieth century has been outright purchase. Conservationists and environmentalists at first turned to government to buy outstanding sites menaced by development. But since 1951 a private alternative has rescued millions of acres nationally. Based in the Washington, DC, area, the Nature Conservancy has used donations and private grants to make strategic buys of critical lands. Its first Michigan purchase was of 80 acres on South Manitou Island in 1960. But not until 1974 did the conservancy open a Michigan office, hoping to protect scenic lands along the Au Sable and Manistee Rivers in the northern Lower Peninsula.

In 1980 Tom Woiwode became director of the conservancy's Michigan operations, and soon the organization was a major force in protection of eco-logically unique and sensitive lands. The organization selected lands to be pur-chased on the basis of biology, botany, and other natural sciences and by the 1990s increasingly concentrated on protecting intact ecosystems, rather than scraps of rare habitat. By the end of 1999 the conservancy had directly con-tributed to the protection of 75,000 Michigan acres, including 20,000 in 32 pre-serves it managed. More frequently, however, the conservancy served as an intermediary, moving more quickly than government could to buy the lands and then either donating them or selling them to the state or federal govern-ment, often at a considerable savings to taxpayers. Grand Mere State Park near Stevensville, one of the dunelands threatened with mining for decades, consists largely of land acquired by the conservancy on behalf of the DNR. The conservancy also bought more than five miles of Lake Michigan shoreline and 10,500 total acres west of Naubinway in the Upper Peninsula from Bethlehem Steel, land that is now part of the Lake Superior State Forest.

But state government has not always welcomed the conservancy's assis-tance. For years, some officials of the Department of Natural Resources were cool to the conservancy. Perhaps resenting the visibility of the organization, they also doubted the value of protecting lands simply for their ecological importance. Tom Washington, who chaired the Natural Resources Trust Fund Board, cast the lone dissenting vote on the acquisition of lands for Thompson's Harbor State Park that the conservancy had arranged.

The resistance of Washington and some in the DNR management to pro-tection of sensitive lands reflected the century-old divide between the "sus-tained yield" philosophy of Gifford Pinchot and the belief that wild places had an intrinsic as well as a scientific value, first popularized by John Muir, the founder of the Sierra Club. As Michigan faces the twenty-first century and development captures ever-larger bundles of the state's unspoiled lands, there is little time to continue the debate. The direct action of the Nature Conservancy and more than a dozen local conservancies scattered across the state is critical to the conservation of vanishing wild Michigan.

CHAPTER 13

Chemical Wastelands

Until 3:45 P.M. Wednesday, it was an ordinary workday at Liquid Disposal, Inc., where workers are used to handling lethal liquids and gases. It's their job, disposing of industrial refuse. . . . Then pandemonium. Men in a nearby building were falling over, gasping for air, their lungs seared, no longer functioning.
—*Detroit News*, January 15, 1982

The Michigan public was forced to become familiar with an alphabet soup of pollutants in the late 1960s. First, DDT levels in Lake Michigan salmon forced their seizure in 1969 by the federal government and triggered a ban on most uses of the pesticide in the state. Next, mercury poisoned fish from the St. Clair River downstream to western Lake Erie in 1970, prompting a temporary angling ban and strong state measures to control discharges of the toxic metal. The 1971 discovery of stunningly high levels of PCBs in several Michigan rivers, including the Kalamazoo River, spurred the state to identify and control new releases and put a PCB ban in place by the mid-1970s. At the end of the decade executive branch officials, legislators, and staff in the state capital, whipsawed by the discovery of one exotic pollutant problem after another, would derisively term the latest controversy "chemical of the month."

From 1923 to 1950, chemical production increased nearly fivefold, and the expansion was just beginning.[1] After World War II, in the same revolution that had carried DDT into widespread use, scores of U.S. companies synthesized or introduced into commerce a multitude of new chemicals as pesticides, as fire retardants, and for other uses. The hydrocarbons present in oil and natural gas were key ingredients in a vast number of new products marketed to a growing middle class, as well as feedstocks required by major manufacturing industries. Many of these chemicals were prized, like DDT, for their effectiveness and persistence—and many would pose the same environmental problems and health fears DDT caused.

The front-page newspaper headlines and evening news coverage awakened by the early chemical scares of the 1970s were nothing compared to a chemical crisis that began in 1973. This time the problem compound was PBB, or polybrominated biphenyls, and instead of affecting a limited number of people eating fish from particular lakes or rivers, it would contaminate virtually every citizen of the state. Even so, it was merely a sentinel for a larger army of chemicals that had generated jobs and economic growth for many Michigan communities but would in time cost taxpayers over $1 billion in cleanup costs and pose unknown health risks.

Sometime in May or June 1973, the Michigan Chemical Company accidentally shipped a fire retardant with the brand name of Firemaster to Farm Bureau Services, a supplier for thousands of Michigan farmers, in place of Nutrimaster, a cattle feed containing magnesium oxide. Firemaster was a brand name for PBB, used to reduce the flammability of plastics and electrical circuits. Customers incorporated Firemaster into, among other things, auto dashboards and casings for telephones and hair dryers.[2] The mistake apparently happened at a time when Michigan Chemical ran out of preprinted bags and hand-lettered the trade names of the two products in black. The similarity of product names or even smudging of the letters was all it took to make the first link in a disastrous chain of events.

Farm Bureau Services sold the mislabeled feed to, among others, dairy farmer Fred Halbert of Battle Creek. Halbert purchased 65 tons and after one week of feeding it to his cows in the fall of 1973 noticed that the animals were sick. They lost appetite, lost weight, and produced 25 percent less milk. When Halbert stopped feeding the Firemaster pellets to the cows, they showed signs of recovery. He resumed feeding them with the Farm Bureau product and noticed the symptoms of illness again.

In October 1973, the state Department of Agriculture's head diagnostician inspected the herd and at first suspected lead poisoning. When tests for lead proved negative, the department sought help from Michigan State University and laboratories in Wisconsin, Iowa, and New York to isolate the contaminant in the feed.[3] Not until May 1974 did the department determine, with help from Halbert's son Rick, a chemical engineer, that PBB was the poison. The department then tested feed and farm products across the state. In the first six weeks after the identification of PBB, the state seized 621 tons of feed, quarantined 388,000 chickens, destroyed 13,000 tons of butter and cheese, and imposed a quarantine on 34 dairy herds with 4,100 contaminated animals. By 1975 the state had quarantined more than 500 farms; condemned for slaughter over 17,000 cattle, 3,415 hogs, and 1.5 million chickens; and destroyed 4.8 million eggs.

"Never before in the history of the United States had there been such an incident of extensive contamination of food products by a toxic substance, so there were no precedents to follow in resolving the problem," the Department of Agriculture reported in its final summary of the crisis in 1982. "Because of the complexity of the problem there was widespread public misunderstanding, which greatly increased the difficulty of reaching the goals."[4]

The department's defensive postmortem on PBB contamination reflected the fact that the crisis cost state agencies, elected officials, and the companies responsible enormously. Before the controversy died away, PBB spawned intensive coverage by the national news media, a made-for-TV movie, a special episode of a popular network drama, and bitter charges of government and industrial coverup and incompetence from the affected farmers and families.

PBB contamination was a serious health worry but also a sensation made for the age of electronic news. It was graphic: television reports and newspaper stories displayed sickened and slaughtered herds of cattle and farm families stricken both by their economic loss and by fears of illness. It was upsetting: as Congress moved in the spring and summer of 1974 toward the impeachment of President Nixon for breaking faith with the American people, critics of the Michigan Department of Agriculture said it had misled farmers and the public about the extent of the problem for months, seeking to protect its friends at the Michigan Farm Bureau. And it was exotic: manufactured for only five years, PBB was so new and poorly understood that the U.S. Food and Drug Administration did not even set a safety standard for the chemical in food until *after* it was determined to be the source of Michigan's previously mysterious farm scourge.

PBB was not confined to the small number of farms that bought the specialized feed supplement containing magnesium oxide largely because of the sloppy practices of Michigan Chemical Company of St. Louis, a twin city to Alma some 45 miles north of Lansing in the central Lower Peninsula. Dennis Swanson, an employee of the Department of Natural Resources, inspected the facility not long after its mistake was exposed. A plant executive told him that the company had been monitoring its inventory carefully. But upon entering the building, Swanson spotted what looked like gravel covering the floor, a material that had literally fallen through the cracks from the second floor of the building. "I scooped it up," he said, and took it back for laboratory analysis. It turned out to be pure PBB. Swanson also took three samples of water from the Pine River, which flowed past the plant, and captured some catfish. When analyzed, they all tested positive for PBB. Later, Swanson said, federal authorities collected information from him as part of a criminal prosecution of the company and its plant manager that was dropped when the latter died.[5]

The company's negligence was causing two environmental disasters simultaneously. Locally, PBB—and, it was later discovered, DDT—smothered the bed of the Pine River for miles downstream, and the plant site itself was seriously contaminated. In 1999, the state would still warn anglers not to eat any fish for 20 miles downstream of the old Michigan Chemical facility. In 1982, the state settled environmental claims against the company for cleanup of the plant site and a nearby landfill where it had dumped tons of PBB from 1971 to 1973 for $44 million—but the amount would fall short of the total bill, and the state would have to use public money to clean up the river.

But at the time, the attention of state officials, the national news media, and Michigan citizens was concentrated on the fact that PBB had been introduced into the state's food chain, entering the body of anyone who drank milk or ate chicken or beef from the affected farms. And since many farmers participated in cooperatives that blended products from both contaminated and uncontaminated farms, millions of citizens took PBB into their systems.

The continuous publicity about PBB not only frightened citizens but spurred some to become more active. Elizabeth Harris, a young mother living in southeast Michigan, said that she "learned about the mixing of PBB with cattle feed when my children were under four years old. I was startled that a mistake of that magnitude could be made and that it would not be made known to the public immediately. . . . Feeling very concerned that I might have exposed my children to PBB and might continue to do so, I sought as much information from non-governmental sources as I could find and an activist group also concerned about chemicals in the environment."[6] The impulse changed the direction of her life. Harris later became the executive director of the East Michigan Environmental Action Council in Bloomfield Township.

But what were the health effects of PBB? Scientists knew almost nothing about this angle, since the chemical had entered commerce so recently. It was clear that some dairy herds were severely affected. On farms that received the greatest concentration of PBB in feed, milk production dwindled; there was high calf mortality; and the animals were unstable and listless. Others appeared to be largely unaffected, and one 1975 study by the U.S. Food and Drug Administration concluded that milk production, calf and adult mortality, and even clinical signs such as lameness and wound healing did not appreciably differ between highly exposed herds and uncontaminated herds. The absence of a proof of harm would characterize a steady stream of chemical crises through the decade and in the 1980s, setting up fierce debates between industrial interests and some government officials who dismissed the seriousness of human health concerns, on one hand, and environmental advocates and affected citizens who were outraged that chemicals were presumed innocent until proven guilty, on the other hand. The sparring over what constituted a "safe" level of PBB consumption further depressed public confidence in the competence of officials who, critics argued, had attempted to cover up the contamination from the fall of 1973 until the spring of 1974.

As a precaution, the state ordered the slaughter of the most highly contaminated cattle, hogs, and chickens. Losing trust in the Department of Agriculture, Governor William Milliken directed the Department of Natural Resources to handle the disposal of the farm animals. Burial of the PBB-tainted animals touched off another controversy. Using what it thought was the best technical procedure available, the DNR's Waste Management Division selected two sites on state land. One was in Kalkaska County's Garfield Township, east of Traverse City. The landfill was well sited geologically: the water table was 100 feet below the soil surface, and the nearest important surface water was the Manistee River, over three miles away. No drinking water wells or private dwellings were nearby. The state owned the land. But DNR failed to notify Kalkaska County officials of their plans, and when these became public, the outraged county successfully sought a court injunction. The burial finally went ahead, but only in the teeth of local resistance.

The controversy was even greater at the second PBB-contaminated livestock burial site, near Mio in the northeastern portion of the Lower Peninsula. Again isolated from water bodies and far from private land, the new landfill provoked a massive outcry. When Governor William Milliken visited Mio in 1978 to address local concerns, he found himself the object of a crowd's wrath, and he was hung in effigy for the only time in his career.

"I went to Mio thinking I could reason with people," Milliken said in bewilderment. "But they felt so bitterly. The troopers [Milliken's state police guard] told me I had to leave because the situation was getting out of hand. I still remember a wild-eyed woman trying to break the window of the car down with an umbrella."

Although some of the rage was undoubtedly stirred by the delay in the state's response, agriculture department officials unsympathetic to farmers' complaints about the effects of PBB on their herds, and the state's decision to force burial of the slaughtered animals, the larger part resulted from the lack of clear scientific knowledge of the health effects of the chemical. Farmers and the public at large had been contaminated without being given a choice in the matter. Chemicals that had seemed grave enough when found in fish or bald eagles were doubly alarming when they turned up in the human body.

The Department of Public Health compounded the crisis of public confidence by bungling initial health studies, underfunding and neglecting others, and ultimately trying to portray the results as more positive than they were in fact. An initial 1974 study that compared farmers from quarantined farms and others from unquarantined farms, on the assumption that the latter had no PBB contamination, found there was no appreciable difference in health between the two groups. Bailus Walker, the state health director years later, conceded that the study had been flawed because both groups of farms had some PBB contamination.[7] Still, it and some subsequent studies found no hard evidence of health problems. Worries without answers persisted into the 1980s, when the department confirmed that approximately 95 percent of Michigan's population had residues of PBB in fat tissue. But at the same time a health department official argued that because PBB had been banned from commerce, removed from the food chain, and largely cleaned up or contained in the environment, exposure to the chemical had stopped. "There's no evidence of any harm being caused," said Dr. Harold Humphrey, state director of environmental epidemiology, in 1982. "It looks like people can relax."

In an age when other issues were commanding public attention and chemical manufacturers had spent considerable sums trying to remake the image of their products, these reassuring messages were passed along in the 1980s and 1990s by the same news outlets that had trumpeted PBB as a catastrophe in the 1970s. "Michigan's notorious PBB scare of the 1970s, which predicted alarming spikes in cancer and birth defects by the mid-1990s, turns out to be only that—a scare," reported the *Detroit News* in 1997. " . . . [t]he fears the episode aroused may, in fact, be another example of how allegations of chemical dangers based on incomplete information can escalate into hyped and highly politicized frenzies."[8]

By the 1990s the officials who had borne the brunt of the public's anger after the discovery of PBB, or watched the controversy at close range, were under the impression that PBB had been overblown as a health issue. "As it turned out, the dire results predicted didn't materialize," said Milliken in 1999.

But some of the long-term research suggested that the chemical had harmed Michigan residents. Largely through federal funding from the Centers for Disease Control and Prevention, the state for more than two decades maintained a study group of over 3,500 persons from the most highly exposed farm families in the state. Researchers reported in 1995 that women from the group with higher levels of PBB in their blood had an increased risk of developing breast cancer.[9] A second study published in 1998 revealed higher risks of digestive cancer and lymphoma among members of the group with higher PBB blood levels.[10] "PBB exposure is certainly related to some kinds of cancer," said Dr. David Wade, a state health department official, in 2000.[11] A third study suggested that girls born to women who had the highest levels of the chemical in their blood reached menarche six months earlier than those whose mothers had been less exposed. This raises the question of whether PBB's effects may include damage to reproductive health in the second or later generations of the most exposed families.

The PBB "scare," as the *Detroit News* called it, appeared to be a victim of expectations. The massive outbreak of cancer feared in the mid-1970s did not materialize, permitting some to say that PBB had been largely cleared as a health risk. The subtle, delayed effects that turned up in the 1990s studies failed to generate extensive news coverage. PBB appeared destined to assume its place as one of the many real—but forgotten and overlooked—environmental causes of cancer and other health effects.

PBB was just one of the chemicals, and St. Louis just one of the contaminated communities, that would come to light through the 1970s and early 1980s. It seemed that everywhere they looked, state officials found evidence of contamination. And Michigan was slowly recognizing that industry had ravaged one of its most abundant, sensitive resources—groundwater—in the twentieth century just as the logging industry had ravaged the forests of the north in the second half of the nineteenth century. A critical part of the public trust committed to the care of government had been defiled. It would take over a century to completely clean up the mess.

One of the most sensational examples was the pollution caused by Hooker Chemical Company in Montague, Michigan, about 20 miles north of Muskegon just inland from Lake Michigan on White Lake. Ironically, the Hooker factory was hailed in the 1950s as the foundation of a "chemical empire of the future" that would take the place of the lumber empire that had given the city its first prosperity.[12] Looking for a midwestern site to supply its many regional customers with some of the 100 different chemicals it was already turning out at its Niagara Falls, New York, factory, Hooker Chemical was apparently persuaded in part to build its new plant in Montague by a local plumber.

Arthur Meyer recognized that the deep salt underlying the area would provide the ample supply that the company needed for the making of chlorine and caustic soda, used in pulp and paper and petroleum industries. He pinpointed an excellent plant location on the north shore of White Lake, two miles west of Montague, and urged the company to look it over. In the early 1950s, Hooker built a complex on the site, including eight major buildings, at a cost of $130,000,000. The community looked forward to a new prosperity based on the 120 jobs created at the plant. When Dupont Corporation built an adjacent plant to take anhydrous hydrogen chloride gas from Hooker to help in the manufacture of neoprene, a synthetic rubber, the future seemed bright.

A few voices had been raised against the siting of the plant in the 1950s, but concerns about waste were brushed aside. "Water used in the Hooker plant returns to the lake purer than it was before; there is no air contamination," reported a business magazine in 1954. But there was in fact a darker side to the company's operations that would remain concealed for years. "Hooker had been welcomed into the community because, as individuals, they were well-rounded, well-educated, well-spoken people and nobody had an idea what the attitude of industry was toward our natural environment," said A. Winton Dahlstrom, a local attorney who fought the company. "They said they were dumping nothing but cooling water back in the lake."[13]

Within a few years of the plant's commencement of operations, a consultant pointed out that the highly porous, sandy soils on which Hooker had built the factory posed a potential problem. "Any soluble contaminant placed on the surface," one report warned, "will soon make its way downward and affect the quality of the groundwater." However, the company disposed of many of its wastes in unlined pits, which permitted them to seep into the sand and ultimately into groundwater and White Lake.

The problem was not unique to the Montague area. Michigan is a state rich with groundwater, and major cities such as Lansing and Kalamazoo have relied on it exclusively as a drinking water supply for a century. About 40 percent of the state derived drinking water from groundwater sources in the 1990s. Groundwater does not typically comprise an underground stream or lake but rather percolates through the ground and fills pore spaces very much like water filling a sponge. Water in this saturated zone can flow vertically and horizontally at a rate influenced by the glacial and bedrock geology of the area. Some groundwater flows to the surface to feed lakes and streams. In Michigan, groundwater discharges from aquifers to replenish rivers, lakes, and wetlands. As it becomes visible, so does its contamination.

A critical turning point in the history of Hooker Chemical was its decision in the mid-1950s to manufacture hexachlorocyclopentadiene, or C-56, an important ingredient in pesticides such as kepone, used to kill cockroaches, and mirex, effective against the southern fire ant. C-56 was a chlorinated hydrocarbon like DDT, giving it the same properties of persistence and lethality against the target organisms. But its strength was also its curse: the U.S.

army had reportedly rejected C-56 as a nerve gas in World War II as too dangerous to serve as a defensive weapon.

One newspaper that later examined the Hooker scandal was unable to find evidence that the company responded to a request from the state Water Resources Commission in 1956 for information on the toxicity of chemicals discharged in the C-56 process. Instead, the company got its new water discharge permit without supplying the information, and state officials speculated in the early 1980s that the company may have influenced the state to look the other way.[14] Between 1956 and the mid-1970s, Hooker produced 2 billion pounds of C-56 at the rate of about 25,000 tons per year. No one thought to ask where the residues from the C-56 process were going.

In 1967, the state found a steep decline in the number of bottom-dwelling organisms in White Lake and also noted high concentrations of sodium chlorides near the company's discharge pipes in the lake. In 1968, the Water Resources Commission hauled Hooker Chemical and the Whitehall Leather Company, another company discharging wastes into White Lake, into a conference because of complaints from lake property owners. The problem was not chemical wastes but overenrichment from phosphorus and sulfates. Hooker was also a source of sodium chloride discharges and told the commission it was investigating a deep well disposal method for the chlorides, which had previously proved infeasible. "We have, since the earliest stages of plant design in 1952, considered the possible effect of our operations on the environment and surrounding community, fully recognizing the resort nature of the area," said Duane Colpoys, works manager of the Hooker plant.[15]

The next significant state look at the facility occurred in 1972, after Dow Chemical Company warned that two by-products from the manufacture of C-56, known as C-46 and C-66, could build up in fish and wildlife and cause human health risks as they moved up the food chain. Although Hooker admitted to the state that C-46 and C-66 were present in the plant, company officials said they doubted that the chemicals were being discharged into White Lake. They maintained this position even when the Department of Natural Resources found traces of C-66 in the Hooker discharge pipes. The company argued that the samples had been tainted by a metal container. When a second sampling by the state showed significant levels of C-46 and C-66, the company refused to comply with the state's demand for a plan to clean up its discharge. It also resisted a state request in 1974 for information on potentially hazardous materials stored on its property.

In the mid-1970s, signs of trouble multiplied. Chronic odor problems downwind from the plant worsened. The state's latest biological survey of White Lake showed further steep declines in fingernail clams, worms, and midge larvae in the area of the lake that received Hooker's discharge. A community activist, Marion Dawson, surveyed residents within a two-mile radius of Hooker and organized a meeting to discuss what to do about the problem. She presented the results of the survey at a meeting of the previously unresponsive state Air Pollution Control Commission. Fumes were worst between midnight and 8 A.M.: "People had difficulty breathing; their eyes and noses watered and itched. Children had to be brought in from playing when the fumes were strong. Six people reported dead trees in their yards." There was a smell like laundry bleach in the air.[16]

Assistant attorney general Stewart Freeman, who served as counsel to the commission, heard the presentation and asked staff of the Department of Natural Resources to look into the matter. By now the state was sure that Hooker had been illegally discharging C-56 into White Lake. Freeman's request generated the surprising report from a DNR scientist that C-56 was a component of kepone, which had spilled into and contaminated Virginia's James River the year before and sickened workers at a plant in Hopewell, Virginia. Of C-56 the staff report observed, "This compound is particularly marked by its extremely harsh behavior in air. . . . It has a very pungent odor and is an extreme irritant causing headaches, chest pain, general respiratory problems, kidney damage and liver necrosis." C-56 and two other toxic chemicals in the company's wastewater, the staff said, posed "unresolved problems concerning their potential acute and chronic impacts. At the present time adequate numbers of unresolved questions exist to indicate zero discharge as the only acceptable level."[17]

Events now moved quickly. Federal bans on kepone and mirex virtually wiped out markets for Hooker's C-56. The company shut down its C-56 line at Montague in February 1977. But shortly afterward, the state renewed its water discharge permit for the chlorine and caustic soda process that had been Hooker's initial line of business at Montague. Pollution might have gone on indefinitely had not a Hooker employee, Warren Dobson, come forward with the astonishing information that thousands of drums containing C-56 residues were hidden behind the Hooker plant. Slashed open with an ax, they had drained the poisons into the ground. His bosses had ordered Dobson to drive trucks of the discarded drums behind the plant and dump them there—and after learning that C-56 was in them, Dobson thought that was wrong.

Chuck VanderLaan, a science instructor at Montague High School, had taught Dobson. "He wasn't the shiniest brick in the wall," VanderLaan said, "but he was a good-hearted person. Warren came to visit me at my home. He was concerned about what he should do about the investigation of how C-56 was handled at the Hooker plant. . . . I tried to point out that he might suffer grievous consequences for his actions but he made the choice and did suffer those consequences." Dobson was forced from his Hooker job for blowing the whistle. But after he tipped off community members about the disorganized heaps of approximately 20,000 55-gallon drums, the state stepped in.

The DNR had already strengthened its investigation efforts because contamination in residential drinking water wells near White Lake signaled a significant groundwater contamination source somewhere on Hooker's property. Andrew Hogarth, an employee of the DNR's Water Quality Division, said the agency knew "if we looked hard enough and pressured Hooker hard enough for information, we would find it." He had visited the Hooker plant before and remembered that company managers had restricted the movement of state inspectors around the plant property. "You had to ask to be taken anywhere and have a good reason," he said. Now the DNR decided not to rely on the managers. It sent a plane over the plant site to take photographs clearly displaying huge areas on the property where wastes had been dumped. When Hogarth produced the photographs at an enforcement meeting, the plant manager's "face turned white."[18]

Contamination at the plant turned out to be far worse than even some of the most rabid critics had dreamed. In addition to C-56, the drums were leaking many other by-products of the manufacturing process, including hexachlorobutadiene (C-46), octachlorocyclopentene (C-58), hexachlorobenzene (C-66) and the solvents trichloroethylene and carbon tetrachloride, all serious contaminants. Hogarth described the material flowing out of the drums as a "black, gooey liquid" with a ghastly odor that could cause headaches within minutes.

State government's patience was finally exhausted. When negotiations with the company stalled, Attorney General Frank Kelley sued Hooker Chemical in February 1979. Later that year, the state settled with Hooker in what was at the time the biggest pollution settlement in the history of the state. The company paid $1 million in damages and committed another $14.5 million to clean up massive pollution of groundwater and soils. It agreed to construct a giant vault equivalent in size to 15 football fields to house the tainted soils and to monitor the site for 50 years.

The settlement did not result from sudden pangs of environmental conscience in the offices of Armand Hammer, the chief executive officer of Occidental Petroleum, which now owned Hooker. Early in the negotiations, an Occidental executive returned from a meeting in Montague and told an assistant to Hammer that he had just met with the CEO, telling him that the Hooker plant would have to be cleaned up. But Hammer brushed him off. The assistant, Carl Blumay, went to Hammer, who said, "All chemical plants, not just ours, have to dump their wastes somewhere. It's a fact of life. Anyone who complains about it is purposely making a big thing out of nothing so he can look like a hero and get a raise."[19]

Even the literally monumental settlement did not put the concerns of many in the community to rest. Mary Mahoney lost her father, mother, aunt, and grandmother to cancer. All lived within a mile of the Hooker plant. But the state never completed a health study that was designed to answer questions about the link between Hooker's pollution and health effects. The $1 million Hooker paid in damages went into the state's general fund and did not directly benefit Montague or the cleanup. Air monitoring conducted during the active Hooker cleanup was inadequate to catch what Mahoney called "blasts" of chemicals that sickened neighbors. Mahoney also faults the state for sending wastes from other cleanup sites to the Hooker vault. "They broke their promises to us," she said. "I don't want this to happen to any other community. This settlement looked good in writing, but it didn't turn out to be."[20]

Some of the wastes shipped to the Hooker cleanup vault came from a site that also generated statewide publicity. That site was the Berlin and Farro landfill and incinerator outside Swartz Creek, a small town 15 miles west of Flint. Its story is a compound of greed, carelessness, and ineffective state enforcement.

Verna Courtemanche, a 53-year-old schoolteacher who lived across the road from the facility with her husband, knew the operator of the new waste business that opened its doors for business in 1971, Charles Berlin. She had taught his sister in the local schools and remembered watching him drive by her house in a pickup truck as a teenager. She was unimpressed with his personality then and later with his business ethics. "He knew nothing about the handling of this stuff," Courtemanche said. "He was just in it for the money."[21]

Wayne Schmidt, who became the staff ecologist of the Michigan United Conservation Clubs in 1975, knew Courtemanche because he was dating her daughter. He would later marvel at Berlin's performance. "I always figured that these big toxic waste debacles were driven by Mafia types and big-money firms. Not with Chuck Berlin." Schmidt said he was surprised that Berlin "could get zoned and licensed to operate a hazardous waste incinerator and could get reputable corporations to turn over their scariest poisons for disposal."[22]

First licensed by the state in 1971, the Berlin and Farro waste facility began burning wastes from the nearby plants of General Motors Corporation in October 1972. Although Berlin had assured neighbors that there would be no unpleasant odors or smoke, only "a small amount of steam," by the summer of 1973 neighbors were organizing to complain and fight back against dust, odors, and other nuisance conditions. At times the uncontrolled flames from the incinerator stack shot so high in the sky that locals called the fire department, thinking a blaze had broken out.

The operation of the Berlin and Farro waste company from that point forward was a litany of bungling. The company made a legal agreement with the state in 1974 to upgrade the facility. By 1975 it had violated each of the 11 stipulations in the agreement, including its commitment to install air pollution control equipment to trap hazardous wastes. Raymond Syring, who lived near the dump, said in the summer of 1974, "I complained that the burner was smoking terribly and that soot was found on the snow in my fields. The smoke has a terrible odor and burns your eyes. . . . [N]o corrections were made."

But relying on their traditional philosophy of cooperation with business rather than confrontation, state officials encouraged the company to improve its performance. They insisted that the company would meet the state's terms for continued operation and were skeptical of the neighbors' claims about mysterious shipments of illegal waste. An outspoken woman who could turn suddenly fierce when placated or patronized by state officials, Courtemanche appeared in 1975 with neighbors before the Michigan Environmental Review

Board, an advisory panel. "We have been patient," the group said in a prepared statement. "We have kept our windows shut in the summer. We have often curtailed outdoor picnics, gardening, and other activities. We have watched our windows and cars become covered with industrial wastes. . . . We have depended on the state regulatory agencies to protect the quality of our lives and they have failed us."

Partly as a result of the public pressure, the Department of Natural Resources closed the incinerator down in September 1975. But incredibly, when Berlin and Farro applied for a permit to resume hauling industrial wastes to the site in early 1976, the state issued the license. It later turned out some wastes were pumped into underground tanks while hundreds of drums were simply dumped into the ground and covered. Later the same year, Berlin permitted hazardous chemicals from the lagoons to flow into local drains again. When the DNR ordered a cleanup, the company balked. But now there was a Hooker connection—tipsters alleged that Berlin had accepted 5,000 gallons of C-56 from Montague in March 1976. Although he denied it, the DNR found C-56 in a drain leading from the site.

Attorney General Kelley sued the company in 1978. The litigation resulted in a settlement requiring the removal of the waste lagoons, fencing, a study of the groundwater to pinpoint contamination, and posting of a $500,000 bond. Again Berlin failed to comply.

In the same year, 1978, the issue of toxic waste reached the attention of the U.S. public through news reports about Love Canal, at Niagara Falls, New York. There the same Hooker Chemical Company that was fouling Montague, Michigan, had buried its wastes for approximately 30 years, then sold the site to the city for $1. About 100 homes and a school were built on the site. When corroding industrial drums began to rise to the surface and noxious liquids flowed into basements and backyards, the alarmed residents feared for their health and demanded to be relocated. The resulting relocation awakened the country to the presence of thousands of old industrial dumps that might menace public health. The furor led the U.S. Congress to create the $1.6 billion Superfund to begin hazardous waste cleanup in 1980.

But Michigan's Love Canal was rapidly deteriorating. Berlin sought bankruptcy protection in 1980, and even the state's success in getting a court to declare his company in contempt did nothing to remove an estimated 3 million gallons of wastes. From her vantage point across the street from the dump, Courtemanche had for years noted flatbed trucks passing down the road and through its gates after dark. "It didn't take a genius to figure out they were dumping barrels back there," she said.

A bankruptcy judge, giving priority to creditors, intervened to prevent company funds from being spent to clean up the site. In utter frustration, the angry neighbors went to the state Toxic Substance Control Commission (TSCC), a watchdog agency established in 1978 in the foaming wake of the PBB crisis. After almost a decade of empty assurances from state officials,

Courtemanche and friends had found an agency willing to listen to their concerns. In May 1981, the TSCC asked Governor Milliken to declare the site a "toxic emergency," and he complied.

The declaration failed to resolve the crisis. The law creating the TSCC did not give it power to clean up anything, and the DNR argued that it had no money to clean up Berlin and Farro. Only in November 1981 did the legislature appropriate the first $800,000 of public funds needed to address the site. In December, the state also reached an agreement with Hooker Chemical to remove approximately 15,000 cubic yards of sludge and soil contaminated with C-56 and bury it in the vault at Montague. After Hooker completed its removal of the wastes, the state confirmed the presence of another four tanks containing 26,000 additional gallons of C-56. The DNR asked the legislature for $3.3 million to continue the cleanup, while the U.S. Environmental Protection Agency spent $410,000 to build a fence around the site and begin testing the newly discovered tanks.

When the site's neighbors learned in early 1983 that hydrochloric acid and cyanide might be buried at the site, their outrage and alarm peaked. An accident during removal of the two chemicals might result in a reaction creating toxic fumes that, drifting across the road, could harm or kill the neighbors. Newly installed governor James Blanchard proposed in March to cover the site and postpone cleanup until the fall, when cooler temperatures would minimize the chance of a reaction. A local state representative, Charles Mueller, hired a lawyer who sued to force an immediate cleanup and won. Evacuation of 53 families and a business began on April 21 and continued until May 20.

The return home did not signal an end to the cleanup or to the problems of the nearby residents. Demanding to know what the risks to their health might be, they blocked roads leading to the site in August 1983 after learning by press release that the DNR and Environmental Protection Agency (EPA) were going to remove another 4,000 exposed drums of waste. The agencies hastily scheduled a community meeting and explained the cleanup plans the next day.

By 1984, the state had contributed another $1.4 million and the EPA $9 million, and companies that had sent waste to the site agreed to pay $14 million after being threatened with a lawsuit under the federal Superfund toxic waste cleanup law. The list of waste generators included the state's most prominent companies. General Motors, with its Flint-area automotive assembly plants, topped the waste contributors with an estimated 24.4 million gallons of waste. Other parties included Chrysler Corporation, Ford Motor Company, Dow Corning, Consumers Power Company, and Detroit Edison. After 15 years of cleanup, the EPA and DNR declared the site "clean" in 1998—almost exactly a quarter century after the first complaints about Berlin and Farro.

But the history of the site did not leave Courtemanche feeling clean. It turned out that the company had recklessly handled wastes all along. A former employee told the *Flint Journal* that with Berlin's knowledge, "the incinerator would emit black smoke, liquid wastes would be spilled on the ground, tainted water would be pumped out of open storage lagoons over the ground, and barrels containing liquid wastes would be buried illegally in the landfill."[23] Although Berlin pled no contest and paid a small fine for violating the state's hazardous waste management law in 1981, his company contributed almost no funds to the cleanup, and he tried later to start a second waste disposal business.

Treated "like a complaining housewife who didn't know anything" when she first complained about Berlin's operation in the early 1970s, Courtemanche derived little satisfaction from her ultimate vindication, especially since she believed in 1999 that the site remained contaminated. "I got an education I never really wanted," she said. "I have no faith in anyone. They're doing it again. They're telling people there's no problem."

For the state as a whole, the problem of reckless hazardous waste disposal and resulting contamination was deeper and would linger far longer than expected when Hooker Chemical and Berlin and Farro caused controversy in the 1970s. Particularly since World War II, Michigan's major manufacturing industries had generated mammoth amounts of hazardous wastes—metals such as chromium from plating plants, solvents and paint wastes from the automobile manufacturing process, and by-products such as dioxins from chemical making. Industries had given little thought to their disposal.

Sometimes the wastes were regarded as cheap fill material for low places—often wetlands or other natural habitats. The city of Detroit and industries sent wastes to a 40-acre landfill near the Rouge River in Westland, a Detroit suburb in Wayne County, from the 1920s to the 1950s. In 1962, the Livonia school district built an elementary school atop the old dump. When chemicals began oozing from a school playground in 1991, concerned parents demanded that Cooper School be shut down. Testing that summer showed PCBs more than five times higher than state standards. Although the school was never reopened, parents continued to worry what the effects on their children's health had been—and were angry about the sluggish response of the school district and county and state governments.

"We carry the Cooper legacy with us for the rest of our lives," said Cheryl Graunstadt, who with her husband and neighbors formed the group that shut down the school. "Fearful of any illness that our children might end up with. The testing was limited and the disclosure of the various wastes remains a deadly secret."[24] The *Detroit News* reported that at least nine schools in the Detroit metropolitan area had been built on or near old waste landfills.

At a Macomb County industrial waste site that would require a Superfund cleanup, the G and H Landfill, a railroad spur conveniently brought cars to the dumping site and enabled them to pour their liquid poisons directly into the ground. An accident at another commercial disposal site dramatized the danger posed by the state's industrial wastes—and improper management of them. Liquid Disposal, Inc. (LDI), began operating an incinerator in 1968 near the Macomb County city of Utica, close to major industrial waste generators in metropolitan Detroit. Meeting fierce resistance from neighbors who complained of noxious odors and unsafe conditions at the plant, LDI continued operating despite being sanctioned by state officials twice during the 1970s.

In January 1982, LDI workers were preparing to transfer a tanker load of sodium hydroxide solution shipped from Kalamazoo into the incinerator. The solution came in contact with acids from an unidentified source, releasing deadly hydrogen sulfide gas. "Then pandomonium [*sic*]," the *Detroit News* reported.[25] "Men in a nearby building were falling over, gasping for air, their lungs seared, no longer functioning. . . . A leak of lethal gas had felled two workers who would die. Would-be rescuers were also thrown back, gasping for air from lungs filled by the gas."

In addition to killing the two men, the chemical reaction sent an estimated two dozen workers to the hospital. Randy Lesner, 23 years old, and Paul McKinney, 41, were casualties of a combination of industrial recklessness and a poor understanding of the complex interactions of the many streams of hazardous wastes flowing from Michigan's factories. The state shut LDI down. After the company's bankruptcy, the state Department of Natural Resources and U.S. Environmental Protection Agency spent millions to dispose of chemicals in lagoons, soils, and groundwater at the LDI site.

There were both benign and sinister explanations for the improper management of chemicals and resulting wastes. One state official would later note that until the 1960s, many in industry and government believed that soil was a "magic filter" that would trap or treat wastes. As the precision of technology grew, it became possible to discern chemicals that had previously escaped detection in soils, groundwater, and fish and wildlife. Unthinking local and state governmental land use choices also contributed to the problem. Authorities found several feet of chemical solvents atop groundwater flowing toward the drinking water wells of the city of Battle Creek in 1983. They then surveyed the area and noted that local zoning and state permits had enabled a chemical sales company, a railroad maintenance facility that used chemicals, a landfill, and an oil well to operate within a short distance of drinking water supply wells serving more than 30,000 people. Preventing the poisoning of the supply required emergency action by both the U.S. Environmental Protection Agency and the DNR.

Many businesses simply took no responsibility for the fate of their wastes. Pressed to improve competitiveness by reducing costs, plant managers paid nominal fees to waste haulers and operators with sometimes questionable credentials and disowned any knowledge of where they took the chemicals. In effect, businesses were borrowing from the future, simply getting their wastes out of sight and gambling that they would do no harm. If they did, somebody else would worry about it later.

Paul Parks, a mechanical engineer who oversaw the mechanical operation of the pond treatment system at Whitehall Leather Company from approximately 1968 to 1981, later provided a glimpse into the company's approach to pollution control and stewardship of White Lake, into which the firm discharged its effluent.[26] Employing anywhere from 170 to 200 people during the period Parks worked there, Whitehall Leather provided the tanned hides used in shoe manufacturing by its parent company, Genesco. Genesco manufactured dress shoes, military shoes and boots, and some work boots and casual shoes from the hides handled at Whitehall.

The nation's largest meatpacking companies, located in the Kansas City area, began the process by stripping hides from slaughtered animals and salting them to prevent putrefaction. Receiving the hides by truck or train, Whitehall Leather washed the hides in large baths, approximately 10 by 20 feet wide. Turning wheels in the baths helped remove the salt.

Employees then inserted the washed hides in large, approximately 10-foot-diameter drums. There, the introduction of lime helped soften the hair still attached to the hides. The hides were then placed in a vat where the lime and hair were washed out. The wastewater was then passed through screens, which trapped some of the remaining hair, which could be sold for insulation or other uses.

Parks supervised the next, and final, step in the treatment process. The effluent flowed through a series of six descending ponds to settle out solids before entering White Lake. "It was better than it was before, but that's a relative term," said Parks. Large masses of hair and some solids passed into the lake. Longtime residents had photographs of a "hide island" in the 1960s, built by the accumulation of hides discharged by the company.

But there were other effluent problems. The plant used sulfuric acid, dyes, and oils to soften and tan the leather. Most important, Whitehall Leather used chromium compounds in tanning. The company's chemical engineer struggled to assure proper management of what Parks called a "witch's brew" of chemicals that varied depending on whether the plant was producing hides for dress, casual, or military footwear. More than 20 years after Parks left the company, the state and federal governments would identify a "dead zone" of chromium-contaminated sediments on the bottom of White Lake traceable to the company. The International Joint Commission declared White Lake one of its 42 Great Lakes "areas of concern" in the 1980s, in part because of the tannery wastes as well as residues from Hooker Chemical Company.

However primitive, the treatment done at Whitehall Leather was far beyond what was done at Eagle Ottawa Leather, where Parks worked in the 1950s and 1960s. Eagle Ottawa simply dumped wastes from 21 sewers untreated into the Grand River. When public sentiment began to turn against this method of disposal, the company concentrated the sewers, screened the hairs, and discharged the effluent under water to avoid notice.

Even with the treatment at Whitehall Leather, neighbors just a block away frequently complained of foul odors. Company employees would spray industrial perfume to obliterate the offending aromas. The lilaclike scent was so strong, Parks said, "Sometimes I'd rather smell the hides."

Although the state Water Resources Commission staff inspected the plant frequently during the late 1960s and early 1970s and ordered improvements in the wastewater treatment system, little actual improvement happened until local attorney Winton Dahlstrom organized a citizens group to push the state and Whitehall Leather to act. "The company was not going to spend money on pollution control, something where there was no return on investment, unless it had to," Parks said.

Environmental and community stewardship were not themselves reasons for the company to upgrade, according to Parks. Headquartered in Nashville, Tennessee, Genesco executives were isolated from citizen sentiment in Whitehall and Montague. "Their training was only the bottom line," Park said. "An ecological consideration, even a small consideration, was way down the line. The guys who made the decisions, the guys with the dough, were in Tennessee. They didn't live on White Lake. They didn't swim in White Lake. They weren't affected."

As state and national public outrage about pollution sharpened during the 1970s, and as state government began to tackle pollution aggressively with the support of Governor William Milliken, Dahlstrom's citizens group was successful in pressuring Whitehall Leather and the state Department of Natural Resources to reach an agreement to stop the discharge of wastes into White Lake. The company briefly considered injecting the screened wastewater into geological formations into the ground below the water table but decided against the technology because of the risk of wastes migrating upward through cracks and fissures in local formations. Instead, the company agreed to pretreat the effluent and pipe it to the Muskegon Wastewater Treatment Plant, where it received further treatment and was spray irrigated on agricultural lands.

In-plant practices at other facilities were also inexcusably negligent, even reckless. In one civil action brought by Michigan attorney general Frank Kelley, a former employee of Arco Industries, a medium-sized auto industry supplier in Kalamazoo County, testified to appallingly sloppy management of toxic solvents used to clean equipment and parts. Wesley Tomsheck, who worked for Arco Industries between 1974 and 1982, said that toxic perchloroethylene, trichloroethylene, toluene, oil, vinyls, and other substances were often spilled in the plant. "I have visually seen lift trucks driven into the side of the 55-gallon barrel [of chemicals]," he said. "[A] normal lift truck might stab the side of the barrel and have a barrel rupture." In another case, an employee started filling a 55-gallon tank by pumping a chemical from a larger container, left the no-smoking area to have a cigarette, forgot to shut off the pump, and spilled the substance onto the plant floor. Tomsheck also said that the plant frequently scrubbed the floor with perchloroethylene and some of the chemical may have spilled into the floor drains. Prior to 1980, workers squeegeed spills into the drains to hurry them out of the plant. An exchange between a state assistant attorney general and Tomsheck documents the plant's priorities and the impact of new hazardous waste laws that took effect in the late 1970s. Tomsheck testified that there had always been a plant rule to clean up spills as rapidly as possible.

Q: *But the main—the most important part of the rule was keep the trenches and drains cleaned out otherwise production would back up?*

A: *Right.*

Q: *But more specifically I'm talking about keeping Perchlorethene [sic] out of the trenches and drains. Is it true that that particular managerial rule didn't come into play until the later time that you were there in the 1980s?*

A: *Well, that had always been a significant part of clean-up, keeping things clean. And when the hazardous material laws came into effect, there was more concern from management to make sure that this particular effort in housekeeping—*

Q: *Regardless of management's concern, to your knowledge, these chemicals continued to get into the drains and trenches; is that true?*

A: *On accidental spills, yes.*[27]

Chemicals spilled in the plant would flow through drains to a seepage lagoon behind the facility, where they would slowly discharge into groundwater. The result of the company's practices was extensive pollution of the area's groundwater, an expensive lawsuit, and a cleanup costing several million dollars.

Spurred by nearly continuous discoveries of contamination, the Department of Natural Resources released its first inventory of poisoned sites in late 1979. The tally included 63 sites that were fouling drinking water supplies, 649 sites of known or suspected groundwater contamination, and an estimated 50,000 sites with contamination potential.[28] As the list mushroomed in the 1980s, it was clear that a century of Michigan industrialization had claimed the state's groundwater just as lumber barons had once claimed the state's forests.

In fact, some of the practices threatening Michigan citizens in the last decades of the 1900s had grown out of the same early era of the state's development. The contamination list included a manufactured gas plant in a residential area of Marshall, east of Battle Creek. Gas manufacturing operations began at the plant in 1874. Sloppy practices over 70 years of gas processing left by-products such as benzo(a)pyrene, a hazardous chemical, in the soil around the site. Similar poisons from the late 1800s turned up at Consumers Power Company manufactured gas plants at Manistee, Kalamazoo, Jackson, Charlotte, Plymouth, Royal Oak, Grand Ledge, Hastings, Ionia, St. Johns, Owosso, Flint, Pontiac, Mount Clemens, Saginaw, Alma, Zilwaukee, Bay City, Alpena, and Sault Ste. Marie.

At Cadillac in northwestern Lower Michigan, a sawmill and chemical works that produced wood by-products such as turpentine and charcoal between the 1870s and the 1930s left behind deposits of tarlike waste that oozed up from the ground. In 1999, the state began a $1.4 million publicly funded cleanup to remove 10,500 tons of soil.[29]

At Cheboygan on the coast of Lake Huron just southeast of Mackinaw City, a water-powered sawmill that operated from 1840 to 1930 left 80,000 tons of sawdust behind. It was described as "the world's largest sawdust pile" by a supervisor for the depression-era Federal Writer's Project and as "a monument to the Cheboygan lumbering era" by a local newspaper. In 1917, according to one account, children played on the pile, whose south end was as steep as a cliff. They tied an awning to one of their playmates to use as a parachute and pushed him off the edge of the pile, where he landed unhappy but unhurt. Testing in the 1990s showed that groundwater near the enormous pile contained mercury, copper, nickel, lead, and zinc discharging to the Cheboygan River at unsafe levels. In 1999, the state put a first installment of $1.5 million of public funds into the partial removal of the sawdust, also sinking monitoring wells to determine the exact level of contamination entering the river.[30]

At Kingsford, a town along the Wisconsin border on the Menominee River in the Upper Peninsula, Ford Motor Company produced wooden automobile body parts between 1921 and 1951. Ford built a carbonization and distillation plant to consume the approximately 400 tons of scrap wood produced at the plant every day. The carbonization plant manufactured charcoal and briquettes, while the distillation plant produced methanol, acetates, alcohols, and ketones. Ford and Kingsford Chemical, to whom it sold the property in 1951, discarded the plant wastes into a tar pit and "Riverside Dump." In 1995, more than 30 years after the plant closed, a nearby homeowner removing clothes from his basement dryer generated static electricity and ignited a massive buildup of methane that had seeped into his house from the soil surrounding his basement. Groundwater contamination had generated methane gas, which moved up into the soil at several spots in Kingsford. The man was severely burned, and his house was ruined. He sued Ford and Kingsford Products Company and settled for an undisclosed amount.

After issuing methane detectors to dozens of homes in the neighborhood adjacent to the site, the state Department of Environmental Quality and U.S. Environmental Protection Agency probed the soils and groundwater around the area and found gross contamination by a brew of acetone, arsenic, benzene, copper, lead, phenol, and other compounds. The agencies determined that the chemical poisons were flowing into the Menominee River along a three-quarter-mile stretch. In early 2000, a DEQ official estimated that cleanup of the pollution could cost more than $15 million. The state was negotiating with Ford and the successor owner of the site, Kingsford Products Company, over who would pay for the cleanup and how much it would cost.[31]

Many other contamination sites had more recent origins. A particularly contaminated area was Muskegon County, home not only to Hooker Chemical but dozens of other chemical makers. Mostly locating in the county after the 1930s, the companies contaminated soils and groundwater in the county with dozens of different chemicals. One notorious example was a plant on 20 acres in Dalton Township, five miles north of the city of Muskegon. Operated between 1957 and 1985 by the Ott Chemical Company, the Story Chemical Company, and the Cordova Chemical Company, the facility manufactured veterinary medicines, herbicides, dyestuffs, and agricultural chemicals. The various owners for years disposed of by-products in unlined lagoons or drums. The Ott/Story/Cordova site grossly contaminated soils and groundwater with more than 90 chemicals and poisoned a creek a mile away. After spending hundreds of thousands of dollars to capture the surface wastes and prevent accidents or toxic releases, the U.S. Environmental Protection Agency proposed a $5.6 million plan to excavate the wastes and bury them in a hazardous waste landfill.

What had gone wrong? How had the same state government that began fighting pollution of lakes and streams in the 1920s permitted the despoiling of underground waters? In a state with an abundance of sandy soils and fractured rock formations, which surface contaminants could easily penetrate, why had agencies not acted more vigorously to prevent problems?

One answer was the obvious one: officials and the public could see and sometimes smell the pollution of surface waters. Underground pollution was beyond the senses, a matter for speculation. But by the late 1950s, contaminated drinking water wells became groundwater pollution detectors. The staff of the state Water Resources Commission was sufficiently concerned in 1958 to propose a regulation requiring that "all toxic and offensive wastes . . . be rendered innocuous by adequate treatment or by sufficient dilution before being permitted to enter the ground." To support the proposal, the staff provided a list of 16 groundwater pollution sites. Despite this, the commission tabled the proposed rule.

The state's gradual toughening of controls on surface water polluters may have inadvertently contributed to the worsening groundwater contamination. "OK, we won't dump it in the river, we'll dump it out back," went the reasoning of some companies, according to Karl Zollner, a member of the Water Resources Commission staff beginning in the 1960s. Some companies simply poured wastes onto the ground; others let them trickle down through floor drains.

But it is hard to credit the latter-day defenders of these industrial practices who argued that companies did not know any better, that ecological awareness until the 1960s was so dim that corporate officials believed what they were doing was safe. It was usually cheap, and in some cases it may have been legal—but it was definitely not safe. As assistant attorney general Stewart Freeman said when Hooker Chemical tried to invoke ignorance as a defense for its piles of leaking, rusty drums, "Even Napoleon had enough sense to locate his troop latrines downstream of waters used for coffee and soaping."

The surge of environmental awareness in the 1970s—and horror stories that went far beyond Berlin and Farro and Hooker Chemical—propelled the legislature to act at last. The passage of a solid waste management law in 1978 and a hazardous waste management law in 1979 curbed two of the principal threats to groundwater—landfills and spills of hazardous waste materials. In 1980, the Department of Natural Resources finally promulgated the groundwater discharge rules the Water Resources Commission had set aside in 1958. Regulations affecting petroleum storage in underground storage tanks that took effect in the late 1980s closed another loophole in groundwater protection. But it was too late to prevent many unnecessary health risks and an enormous cleanup bill to taxpayers.

In 1999, after more than 15 years of cleanup, the Department of Environmental Quality's groundwater contamination list still contained 10,047 sites, including 7,164 leaking tanks. Between 1983 and 1999, the state and federal governments spent more than $1.2 billion to control and clean up some of the sites.[32]

To prevent a repetition of the chemical mess, the state Department of Natural Resources created an Environmental Enforcement Division in 1978. The agency's director, Dr. Howard Tanner, said he was hearing "hair-raising stories" about the consequences of years of conciliation and cooperation with polluting industries, including a bankrupt chemical disposal firm in Pontiac that left thousands of pounds of flammable wastes in an unprotected, abandoned building and a bankrupt chemical company in Muskegon that had left thousands of drums at its former production site. A report submitted to Tanner by an internal task force put the problem in bureaucratic terms: "Interviews indicated a [DNR] staff reluctance to pursue formal enforcement action on the premise that such action suggests a 'failure' on the part of the Department to achieve compliance through negotiations and voluntary cooperation."[33]

Under the chief of the new division, Jack Bails, the environmental enforcement staff had a revolutionary new mandate: to bring habitual violators of pollution laws to court to stop the lawbreaking and collect fines and damage payments. In its first two years, the new division referred 170 cases for litigation and was responsible for more than $1.2 million in penalties and damages received by the state.[34] While the new, more aggressive stance undoubtedly deterred new violations with its tone, it also outraged many in the state's business community. Before it even opened its doors for business, legislators friendly to business interests tried virtually to eliminate the division with budget cuts, slashing the governor's proposed budget for enforcement from $357,000 to $28,000.[35] Management consultants also disliked the idea of a separate enforcement division, arguing that the job should be incorporated in the work of the air, water, and waste staff. The division was dissolved in 1986 in one of many internal agency reorganizations.

Who would pay the bill for the huge cost of treating contaminated groundwater, trucking poisoned dirt to hazardous waste landfills, and replacing useless drinking water with clean supplies? For a time the state went after industries that had caused the contamination. Under a 1990 law dubbed "polluter pay" by its original author, state senator Lana Pollack, the attorney general and Department of Natural Resources were given the legal tools of strict joint and several liability to compel private parties to fund the remedies. The law scored some initial successes, resulting in the awarding to the state of more than $51.6 million in cleanup costs and fines in its first four years.[36] Although dwarfed by the $425 million in taxpayer funds that voters had approved for abandoned sites in a 1988 bond proposition, it was a start on putting responsibility for careless and irresponsible corporate behavior where it belonged.

The "polluter pay" law had a short life. Because purchasers of contaminated property could inherit legal liability for cleanup, developers hesitated to buy and return to business use many sites in older cities such as Detroit, Grand Rapids, and Lansing. The state's stringent cleanup standards also meant many sites would require tens of millions of dollars to remedy, even when the contamination was unlikely to reach a drinking water supply or otherwise affect human health.

Beginning with the discovery of widespread groundwater contamination in the late 1970s, the state Departments of Natural Resources and Public Health generally insisted on complete removal of the chemicals. The state policy assumed that all groundwater should be protected for future use as drinking water. While environmental organizations applauded the state's position, it raised increasingly sticky issues in the 1980s. The cleanup program was maturing; state and federal agencies were moving beyond identification of contaminated soils and aquifers to proposed remedies. Now they would have to face tough decisions.

Contamination of groundwater that supplied the city of Charlevoix with drinking water became the test case. In 1981, testing of the city's tap water detected the chemical trichloroethylene (TCE), a suspected human carcinogen used for degreasing equipment, among other things. Later tests also detected perchloroethylene (PCE), a dry cleaning chemical, in the groundwater.

It took very little TCE to exceed desirable levels in drinking water. Most drinking water and cleanup standards measured chemical contaminants in parts per million or billion. In the case of Charlevoix, approximately 16 gallons of TCE—"half a bathtub," in the words of the Michigan Environmental Council—rendered unfit for human consumption an aquifer containing 393 million gallons of groundwater. When the likely source of the TCE was traced back to the Charlevoix Middle School, state officials speculated that a janitor dumping a single drum of waste chemical may have caused the contamination as early as the 1950s.

A bigger question was what to do about getting the TCE out of the groundwater. Pumping and treating the contaminated aquifer would take $4.5 million and still take 30 years to implement, the U.S. EPA estimated. The price tag for a "limited action" alternative in which the agency would prevent use of the aquifer through deed restrictions, monitor the contamination, and let the tainted groundwater discharge to Lake Michigan was a mere $160,000. The federal and state governments would contribute much of the cost of a new $3.2 million drinking water supply for the city, needed already to accommodate the area's growth. The new supply would use Lake Michigan water well away from the discharge point of the contaminated groundwater.

Environmentalists opposed what they called the "writing off" of the Charlevoix aquifer, appealing to Governor James Blanchard and a state advisory panel, the Michigan Environmental Review Board, to demand that the EPA actively address the polluted groundwater. They feared that the decision to abandon the groundwater would set a precedent, permitting companies that contaminated aquifers elsewhere to avoid cleaning up the messes they had created. But state Department of Natural Resources officials pointed out that cleaning up the aquifer would do almost nothing to reduce public health risks, since Charlevoix residents would be drinking water from a different, clean source. "Any decision to require further cleanup at this site inherently involves a decision to do less or no cleanup elsewhere since there is a finite amount of public funds available to conduct cleanups," said Richard Johns, chief of the DNR's Groundwater Division. Despite protests from Blanchard and the review board, EPA held fast on the limited cleanup option.

Spending scarce public funds to address relatively small public health risks raised even more vexing issues in industrial areas. In the mid-1980s, the Chrysler Corporation proposed construction of a new assembly plant employing over 2,500 workers on industrial land on the east side of Detroit. The $1 billion project was massive, relocating 3,500 people and demolishing over 600 homes. But costs escalated dramatically when Detroit city officials, preparing the site for Chrysler, stumbled on dozens of abandoned underground petroleum storage tanks and more than 156,000 cubic yards of contaminated soil from previous operations on a part of the site. The price tag for removing the waste was $28.3 million, stretching the city's budget to the limit.

Critics of a state insistence that most of the contamination should be removed pointed out that no one in Detroit consumed drinking water from the ground; the city's municipal supply was drawn from the Detroit River, Lake St. Clair, and Lake Huron. What were the risks of low levels of industrial contaminants on an industrial site that the public would never enter? Anxious not to impede the badly needed jobs created by the plant, the state DNR reached an agreement with the city and Chrysler to waive its typical cleanup standards and permit some of the contaminants to remain in place. But the issue fueled arguments from Michigan's industrial community that the DNR cleanup program wasted public and private money for little health or environmental benefit.

Mayors of a dozen "core cities" asked the legislature to amend the law in early 1995 to quiet the liability concerns, permitting the renewal of struggling neighborhoods and industrial districts. In a letter to the governor and Representative Ken Sikkema, who sponsored the amendments, the mayors noted, "It is essential that the State and municipalities recognize that today's contamination problems are largely a result of historical practices in the past, many of them legal and 'state of the art' at the time. An assumption of the responsibility for cleanup of this historical contamination must be made by the public at large if we are ever to move forward in the effort to revitalize our urban areas while responsibly addressing the environmental and public health concerns posed by contaminated sites."[37]

They had eager allies in the state's business associations and many major

Michigan corporations, happy to escape the potential for large legal bills and cleanup checks. Governor John Engler made repeal of the "polluter pay" provisions the centerpiece of his environmental policy agenda in 1995.

Debate was fierce. Environmental groups accused the industrial interests of hiding behind mayors' skirts, seeking to shift cleanup costs to the public. "This bill accomplishes only one thing. It exonerates polluters of any liability associated with the contamination they cause," Carol Misseldine, executive director of the Michigan Environmental Council, testified before a House of Representatives committee.[38] Lobbyists for business interests accused the environmentalists of insensitivity to the plight of the cities and their residents, who could use the new jobs that developers would create if they could buy older sites without fear of later huge payouts. A business publication, *Craine's Detroit Business,* summarized the industrial argument: "Under current law, development has been pushed to 'green field' sites—an environmentally undesirable outcome, if you think about it. And current owners of contaminated land are socked with bills for pollution they did not cause."[39]

The contest was an uneven one and quickly settled. Corporate influence was strong in the debate. A sponsor of one of the bills that undid the 1990 law, state representative Thomas Alley, was a close ally of Charles Gelman, whose company was locked in a fierce battle with the DNR over cleanup of thousands of pounds of a chemical called 1,4-dioxane in Ann Arbor. Gelman had belittled the state for years for demanding cleanup of a chemical that the DNR had authorized his company to discharge into the groundwater.

The governor's support, the mayors' pleas, and the dominance of industrial interests in the legislature guaranteed passage of the bill. Just four months after it was introduced in January 1995, a bill to strike the "polluter pay" provisions of the 1990 law cleared the legislature and was signed into law by the governor.

The Michigan Environmental Council estimated that the legislation would cost Michigan taxpayers more than $1 billion over 20 years. The state's Department of Environmental Quality said the changes had quickly reawakened interest in inner city development, with 20 of 33 municipalities it surveyed in 1996 reporting an increase in actual redevelopment of brownfield properties, resulting in $221,573,000 in private investment and creation of 2,379 jobs. On the other hand, collections of cleanup funds and penalties from private parties declined steeply with the changes. The state was awarded only $10.5 million in the first three years after the amendments, a 75 percent decrease from the annual average collected between 1991 and 1995.

The cleanup and the need for public funds to pay for it would continue for years. In 1998, the legislature asked for a second public bond to support cleanup. Voters once again approved the $335 million requested. The best estimate of Department of Environmental Quality officials was that the cleanup would continue through the first half of the twenty-first century.

Under provisions of the 1995 law, many sites might remain contaminated even longer. The amendments permitted companies to "close" the sites by paving them, fencing them, securing deed restrictions, or even seeking local ordinances limiting use of contaminated groundwater to prevent human use—and thus, health risks. Environmental critics said such limited remedies would create hundreds or thousands of contaminated dead zones around the state, off limits to use for generations. Permitting the contaminants to remain where they were also raised risks of ecological harm from seeping groundwater or unconfined wastes. If government maintained constant vigilance over the sites for decades, it might limit such risks. But the track record of Michigan government was not encouraging in that regard. From the 1920s through the 1970s, it had had neither the resources nor the inclination to monitor businesses closely.

As the twenty-first century began, there was little discussion of another matter raised by the changes in state cleanup laws—the simple issue of justice. Few asked whether it was just for state law to permit companies that had fouled public resources, and profited in the process, to prevent their use by the public for decades or even longer as a cost-saving measure.

For over 50 years, parks booster E. Genevieve Gillette crusaded for expansion of the state's park system. Pictured with Governor George Romney, Gillette was an outspoken—and controversial—backer of the creation of Sleeping Bear Dunes National Lakeshore in the 1960s. The U.S. Congress approved legislation creating the park in 1970. (Courtesy of Christopher Graham.)

Visible chemical and sediment discharges from the McLouth Steel Company on the Detroit River were typical of the river's treatment in the 1950s and 1960s. (Courtesy of Wayne Denniston.)

With state fisheries chief Howard Tanner (*left*) looking over his shoulder, Governor George Romney poured a pail of kokanee salmon into Antrim County's Torch Lake in May 1965, part of the Department of Conservation's bold program to stock the Great Lakes system with new game fish. (Courtesy State Archives of Michigan.)

Joan Wolfe, one of the founders of the West Michigan Environmental Action Council, helped coordinate citizen advocacy campaigns that pressured the Michigan legislature to enact the 1970 Michigan Environmental Protection Act and the 1972 Inland Lakes and Streams Act. In 1973, Governor William Milliken appointed her to serve on the state Natural Resources Commission, the first woman to do so since the commission's creation in 1921. (Courtesy of Joan Wolfe.)

Thomas Washington, director of the Michigan United Conservation Clubs for more than 20 years until his death in 1995, awakened both admiration and fierce criticism from industrial interests, elected officials, and environmental advocates. MUCC organized a successful citizen petition campaign for a beverage container deposit law in 1976, a high point of Washington's tenure. (Courtesy of Michigan United Conservation Clubs.)

Governor William G. Milliken, here signing a bill, presided over the enactment of dozens of new environmental and conservation laws during his tenure in office from 1969 to 1982. His personal support for tough controls on phosphorus in laundry detergents contributed to the cleanup of the Great Lakes. (Courtesy State Archives of Michigan.)

Haphazard disposal of industrial wastes created thousands of contamination sites across Michigan and cost several lives, including two workers who were killed in a chemical reaction at the Liquid Disposal, Inc., site near Utica in 1982. Since the late 1970s, Michigan and federal taxpayers have spent nearly $1 billion to clean up such sites, with hundreds of millions more in cleanup costs estimated. (Courtesy of the Michigan Department of Environmental Quality.)

The practice of "strip-mining" Lake Michigan coastal sand dunes stirred increasing citizen protests in the 1970s. One of the bitterest fights was over mining of the Bridgman South site in Berrien County. The citizens group Hope for the Dunes brought a legal action that halted almost all mining at the site. (Photo by Dan Wilson, courtesy of Brad Anderson.)

By the late 1970s, water pollution control had helped produce a rebound in sport fish populations, even along urban waterways. (Photo by David Kenyon, courtesy Michigan Department of Natural Resources.)

CHAPTER 14

The Heart of an Ecosystem

All of us who have reaped the benefits of living in the Great Lakes region share a special affection for the magnificence of our fresh water system. The lakes have met our industrial, agricultural, navigation and recreational needs, while at the same time serving to inspire, to soothe, and to leave us in awe of nature's splendor. . . . While it is true that no stone can crack them, it also is true that our technological advancement has given humankind the potential for altering them in ways which both denigrate the environment and diminish their potential for use.

—William G. Milliken, Great Lakes Water
Resources Conference, June 11, 1982

So large are the Great Lakes that the first French explorers to travel them were persuaded they were the gateway to the Far East, to a fabled land of exotic peoples and abundant riches. When Jean Nicolet landed on the far side of Lake Michigan in 1634 and found that the freshwater seas had not led him to Asia, he may have been disappointed, but he and those who followed still found exotic peoples and riches. In the process, they seem to have forgotten their initial awe at the sheer size and majesty of the lakes that had made possible their travels.

Calculation quickly replaced wonder in the thinking of the early Europeans who explored and settled the Great Lakes region. It was a habit that carried over with the settlers of the territory and then the citizens of the state of Michigan. Plundering first the beaver population, then the forests and the fisheries, and finally the very health of the lakes themselves, the Europeans and later the Michiganians recognized the economic benefits of the world's largest freshwater resources without understanding their fragility and their interrelationship. In time, the exploitation of the Great Lakes forced some hard reckoning on the part of Michigan and other occupants of the region. The unlikely teacher in what would later be recognized as ecosystem health was the city of Chicago.

The city was both the victim of its own wastes and the beneficiary of a quirk in the geography of the Great Lakes basin. Just 10 miles west of the southwestern tip of Lake Michigan is a divide separating the basin from the Mississippi River watershed. Until relatively recent geologic time, the lake actually flowed west and south into the Illinois River and then the Mississippi River. So when the Chicago Drainage and Water Supply Commission recommended in 1888 reversing the flow of the Chicago River and shunting its sewage down the river, through a canal, and ultimately into the Illinois River, it was mimicking natural history. It was also starting a fight over water that would engage Michigan and its Great Lakes neighbors for more than a century.

Chicago won its initial approval from the Illinois legislature to move water from the Chicago River into the Illinois River watershed in 1865, but after an 1880s rainstorm drove sewage into the city's drinking water supply, resulting in thousands of typhoid deaths, there was a new urgency to flushing the city's waste away from Lake Michigan. In January 1900 the sanitary district permanently reversed the flow of the river, sending water that formerly flowed into Lake Michigan down a 28-mile artificial channel to Lockport, Illinois. The U.S. Army Corps of Engineers expressed serious misgivings about the reversal, issuing a permit for the opening of the canal that was conditional on future action of Congress and subject to a shutoff if the current created by the project caused damage to navigation or property. The Corps limited the flow of the reversed river to 200,000 cubic feet per minute, or 3,333 cubic feet per second (cfs). As Chicago grew and its volume of sewage increased, the sanitary district applied for increases of the flow to 300,000 cubic feet per minute in 1901 and 350,000 cubic feet per minute in 1903. The Corps granted both requests, again with conditions. In 1912, the sanitary district asked for an increase to 10,000 cfs, but the corps balked, noting that construction of sewage treatment works would make the increased diversion unnecessary. Early in 1913, the secretary of war denied the application.

In both 1908 and 1913, the United States filed suit against the sanitary district, seeking to limit the diversion to 4,167 cfs. In the latter year, Chicago was taking an average water amount of 7,839 cfs from the Great Lakes basin. After years of delay, the U.S. Supreme Court ruled in favor of the federal government in January 1925. But local congressmen had introduced bills to authorize the increased diversion, and the sanitary district applied again for permission to increase the diversion to 10,000 cfs less than a month after the Supreme Court ruling. Buckling slightly under political pressure, the Corps approved a five-year permit authorizing an increase to 8,500 cfs. But the Corps permit required the sanitary district to complete construction, within the life of the permit, of a sewage treatment plant large enough to handle the wastes of a population of 1.2 million. While accepting the permit, the sanitary district asserted a right to divert 9,900 cfs, using its own calculations.

Now it was time for Michigan and other Great Lakes states to intervene. In its 1926 complaint made directly to the U.S. Supreme Court, Michigan accused the sanitary district of "grossly and willfully" violating each of the permits issued by the federal government. The complaint also charged that the sanitary district had "asserted the right to abstract unlimited quantities of water from the Great Lakes-St. Lawrence System without the consent and in defiance of the government of the United States and of the other states bordering on the waterway."[1]

There it is—the word *system*—applied to the Great Lakes for one of the first times in a legal matter. Knowledge of ecology was not the primary basis for Michigan's case. Rather, the quarter century of reversed flow in the Chicago River had demonstrably lowered water levels in all the Great Lakes but Lake Superior. Michigan alleged that Lakes Michigan and Huron had dropped 6 inches, Lakes Erie and Ontario 5 inches. The 1925 increase was lowering Michigan and Huron by 6 3/4 inches. The drop would be even greater if the sanitary district was successful in its generous interpretation of the most recent Corps permit.

Michigan complained of damage to shipping from reduced drafts on commercial vessels, harm to agriculture from the lowering of the water table along the Lake Michigan shore, injury to drinking water supplies from increased sand and sediment at the mouth of intakes, and costs to the resort industry from reduced value of summer cottages and homes. Almost as an afterthought, the state noted that lowered water levels interfered with "the natural habitat of the wild life indigenous to this territory" and impaired the spawning beds of fish.

The threat from Chicago created the first official Great Lakes coalition, unifying states that might disagree on other issues. In 1922 the *Detroit News* approvingly republished an editorial from the *Milwaukee Journal* accusing Chicago of "supreme insolence" and arguing that the increased diversion was actually a sneak attempt to generate hydropower. Rebutting the argument that the diversion was necessary to dilute sewage, the editorial commented acidly that "no other Great Lakes city has found it necessary to use the lakes so as to safeguard a population. They construct modern sewage disposal systems. These cities, and the smaller disposal ports on the lakes, are justified in expecting as much from Chicago—richest of them all."[2]

The Supreme Court found the law on the side of the complaining states in 1930 but refused to end the diversion for fear of causing too great a hardship for the city and its sanitary district. It gave the defendants a grace period to raise the money for construction of sewage plants and limited the diversion to 1,500 cfs, plus domestic pumpage, after the plants were built. Subsequent rulings in the 1930s and 1960s both sustained the diversion and limited it. The latter decision granted Chicago a diversion of 3,200 cfs, but the Supreme Court retained original jurisdiction to settle future disputes—and does to this day.

In part to keep an eye on the Chicago diversion and in part to form a friendly coalition of all the Great Lakes states, Michigan led in the effort to create the Great Lakes Commission in the mid-1950s. One of the most active lobbyists for the commission was Nicholas V. Olds, an assistant attorney general. Olds traced the idea to a conference on Great Lakes water levels in Lansing held in September 1951. "As we listened to the various and numerous experts that attended that conference," Olds later said, "the thought occurred to some of us that perhaps the Great Lakes states should treat these many problems by cooperative study and consultations, rather than unilateral and single-handed action."[3] Olds got the assignment of drafting a statute that would authorize the state to enter into negotiations on an interstate compact, and the law was quickly enacted. An August 1954 meeting of the eight Great Lakes states, Ontario, and Canada called by Michigan resulted in unanimous support from all the states to write the compact. It also generated home-state support. The *Detroit Times* observed with favor, "Michigan fish die from Ontario pollution and Ontario fish die from Michigan pollution and a ship will ground in a too shallow channel no matter what flag it flies."[4] Although the compact expressly provided that the commission would have no binding authority, Congress balked at approving it. It finally consented to the new interstate body after specifying that the Canadian jurisdictions could not join. The states were barging into international relations, the U.S. State Department asserted.

Just as the threat created by Chicago's water diversion had united all the states except Illinois, so did a new scourge pull the states, Ontario, and the U.S. and Canadian governments together in the mid-1950s. Invading from its saltwater Atlantic home via the Welland Canal bypass around the Niagara Falls, the sea lamprey had nearly extinguished lake trout in Lake Michigan and sharply reduced populations elsewhere. A parasite that attaches itself to fish with a sucking disk and sharp teeth, the lamprey feeds on body fluids, often scarring and killing host fish. Each sea lamprey can kill 40 or more pounds of fish. Sea lampreys are so destructive that under some conditions, only one of seven fish attacked by a sea lamprey will survive.

The Canadian and U.S. governments negotiated a treaty, the Convention on Great Lakes Fisheries, in 1955 and launched joint efforts to control the eel-like lamprey. State and provincial fishery managers became partners in the Great Lakes Fishery Commission's programs.

The alarming declaration of *Life* magazine in the 1960s that Lake Erie was dead became the next lesson in the mechanics of an ecosystem. *U.S. News and World Report* called the Great Lakes "the center of rising fear."[5] Under water quality laws passed by Congress in the 1950s and 1960s, the federal government had a new role that helped bring further public attention to the connection linking the various states to the problems of the lakes. Interstate conferences called by the U.S. Public Health Service in 1965 on Lake Erie and by the U.S. Department of Interior on Lake Michigan in 1968 not only forced the states to report on their water cleanup efforts but pointed fingers at the worst pollution culprits.

The 1965 health service report identified Detroit's sewage plant, constructed in 1948, as one of the major sources of Lake Erie's woes. The plant was already overloaded and "only capable of taking out the big chunks," according to one state official. But there were other sources, including Ford Motor Company and Great Lakes Steel, that dumped oil, acid, and toxic chemicals into the Rouge and Detroit Rivers. It would no longer be possible to flush the toilets and industrial drains of southeast Michigan down the Detroit River into Lake Erie and forget about them. Under federal pressure, Michigan committed to a plan to reduce its effect on the neighboring lake.

A Michigan Water Resources Commission staffer working on the plan,

William Turney, remembered the extraordinary work. Sitting down in a Lansing conference room with the commission's chief engineer, Ralph Purdy, Turney and two others drew up a plan to reduce pollution of the Detroit River. At the time, water quality regulators used the "assimilative capacity" of streams—in essence, their ability to dilute wastes—to determine allowable industrial and municipal discharge levels. The four men decided to leave half the river to Ontario and to set aside another half for future growth. Doing some quick multiplication of the desirable level of dissolved oxygen and the number of pounds of water flowing down the river each day, they decided that they needed to assure 480 million pounds of oxygen. That required an 80 percent reduction in the load of organic wastes entering the river, "which we knew was feasible with well run secondary treatment plants," Turney said.[6]

Still operating unilaterally—without seeking the opinions of either the regulated industries and cities or the public—the commission staffers divided up the reductions among 32 different polluters. When they went public with the plan, Turney said, "There was a huge outcry from all with charges of impracticability, unfairness, not needed and just about every negative reaction one could think of." Threats of litigation from the polluters proved to be bluffs, and when one after another discharger reluctantly agreed to the limits, even the city of Detroit fell into line. The plan cost $750,000 in upgraded treatment and ultimately proved a major factor in the cleanup of Lake Erie.

Lake Michigan had its own interstate problems. *Newsweek* magazine announced a death watch for the lake in 1967, pointing to the washing up of rotting alewives on shore; a five-mile oil slick spreading from East Chicago, Indiana; and malodorous, unsightly algae problems along the urbanized reaches. "Somewhere along the line, we've got to decide how we want to use the lake. If we want a sewer, then we'd better forget about swimming and fishing. You can't have it both ways," said Albert Beeton of the University of Wisconsin's Center for Great Lakes Studies.[7]

At the same time Lake Michigan pollution reached ugly heights, the lake was beginning a remarkable comeback thanks to the planting of coho salmon by Howard Tanner, Wayne Tody, and others in the Fisheries Division of the Michigan Department of Conservation. The lampreys had done their work in the 1950s, turning Lake Michigan into a "desert" as far as deepwater fish were concerned. In 1955, 1,400 miles of nets stretched through the lake had brought up just eight lake and rainbow trout. "Lake Michigan was fishless—except for the coastal waters of its bays and islands. . . . Probably never before had a body of water 300 miles long and 100 wide plummeted so drastically, becoming totally depleted of its chief fish populations in less than a decade," outdoor writer Ben East said in *Outdoor Life*.[8] Denied their recreation, anglers turned away from the lake toward inland fishing.

But the successful introduction of salmon just as suddenly reignited interest in Lake Michigan and in the process created both a sportfishing economy and a large constituency for cleanup and restoration. In 11 counties along the Lake Michigan shore where coho fishing was the big draw, retail sales in 1967 rose \$11.9 million above the 1964–66 average and soared \$26.8 million in 1968.[9] With Department of Natural Resources director Ralph MacMullan demanding cleanup of the pesticides that threatened to make the new sport fish unsafe to eat, outdoors organizations clamored for action. The 1967 Environmental Defense Fund lawsuit in Wisconsin targeting Michigan's use of DDT and dieldrin failed in its short-term objective but helped reinforce MacMullan's point that pollution from one state could affect the entire lake. The discovery of high levels of DDT in the Lake Michigan salmon in early 1969 forced all the states bordering its waters to respond.

But initial cleanup efforts seemed to do little to restore the lakes. Banning or attacking one dangerous chemical at a time was only a stopgap measure. Now, to Michigan residents, the pollution-fouled Great Lakes began to seem more a noose than a necklace. "Michigan stands to lose more than any other state if current efforts to control pollution of the Great Lakes do not succeed and if new efforts are not begun soon," the *Detroit Free Press* warned. "Four of the world's 12 largest lakes lap the shores of Michigan's two peninsulas. No Michigan resident lives more than 80 miles from at least one of the lakes."[10]

The oldest body overseeing the lakes, the International Joint Commission (IJC), provided the impulse that would institutionalize the idea of ecosystem management of the region's water resources. Created by the Boundary Waters Treaty of 1909, the IJC had investigated transboundary pollution in the Great Lakes after a 1912 request from the two federal governments and again after a 1946 request. The latter "reference," as the requests are called, resulted in a 1951 IJC report noting a "serious health menace" from the dumping of untreated and partially treated sewage and growing dangers from chemicals in industrial wastes.[11] When conditions worsened, the United States and Canada handed the IJC another reference in 1964. This time, the IJC was asked to inquire into the extent, causes, and location of pollution in Lake Erie, Lake Ontario, and the international section of the St. Lawrence River.

The time-consuming IJC study produced a final report in 1971. The commission found existing pollution control efforts insufficient and recommended international water quality objectives to drive further cleanup. Speaking of the testimony it received at public hearings around the basin, the commission commented that it "was reminded of the practice common many years ago of keeping a small bird in a cage to give warning of possible imminent danger to man. Today it is a common practice to utilize the fish in our water supplies for a similar purpose. Some of the fish in these waters are dying. It is a warning that must not be ignored."[12]

The IJC report, and the findings of two technical boards the commission had established to examine the pollution of Lake Erie and Lake Ontario, drove the national governments forward. The commission had called upon both the United States and Canada to give it the authority to coordinate and monitor progress toward the water quality objectives it proposed. President Richard Nixon asked the new Council on Environmental Quality, established by an act of Congress he had signed January 1, 1970, to consult with Canada on the recommendation. Between June 1970 and June 1971 officials of both nations and representatives of the states and Ontario worked on the problem, agreeing at the conclusion of their work to pursue a new agreement on Great Lakes water quality.

Governor Milliken endorsed such an agreement, telling a conference of Great Lakes governors and premiers on Mackinac Island in August 1971 that it could provide "an effective framework for a basin-wide approach to our environmental needs. . . . But I think one of the objectives of this conference should be to voice the united stand of our states and provinces that the federal governments not water down this agreement."[13] Milliken supported the agreement on the basis that "no state or province can go it alone," adding that the agreement would complement rather than compete with the programs and objectives of the states and Ontario.

In April 1972, Nixon and Canadian prime minister Pierre Trudeau signed the Great Lakes Water Quality Agreement, not a formal treaty requiring congressional approval in the United States but an executive pact. Establishing basinwide water quality standards and objectives along the lines suggested by the IJC in 1970, the agreement gave the commission responsibility to monitor progress toward clean water with the help of a Great Lakes Water Quality Board. The primary water quality objective of the 1972 agreement was to reduce phosphorus pollution harming the lower lakes. Most important, it formally established the principle that the Great Lakes were no longer to be managed as individual pieces by two federal governments, eight states and a province, and scores of municipalities.

Although heralded as a landmark agreement on its initial signing, the agreement took on added significance in 1978, when renegotiated. This time it targeted toxic pollutants and polluted runoff from farms and cities and called for the virtual elimination of toxic substance discharges. And it defined the Great Lakes basin ecosystem—"the interacting components of air, land, water and living organisms, including man, within the drainage basin of the St. Lawrence River at or upstream from the point at which this river becomes the international boundary between Canada and the United States."

The ecosystem principle took hold. Seeping from government programs into the general consciousness, it became the reference point for policy debates and public discussion about the future of the Great Lakes. Rather than regarding the lakes as bottomless sinks for refuse as had been the case earlier in the twentieth century, governments and the citizens they represented came to see them as an essentially closed system, subject to harmful disruption and as fragile as they were bountiful.

Michigan now became one of the most ardent defenders of the newly recognized ecosystem. A state water quality official said that until the 1960s, the idea of a unifying connection among the lakes "was just kind of ignored. There were so many problems on smaller bodies of water. We were trying to clean up more local problems." By the early 1980s the governor and other politicians were eager to define the future of the lakes as a cornerstone in Michigan's own future.

Two issues helped clinch this understanding. One was a proposal advanced in 1970 by the U.S. Army Corps of Engineers to open the Great Lakes to all-winter commercial shipping. The other was the renewed threat of water diversions—but this time from regions far distant from the Chicago Sanitary District.

Winter navigation, as the year-round shipping proposal came to be called, appeared to offer great benefit to port cities and industries that could expand their use of the "natural" waterway—significantly enhanced since the mid-1800s by locks, canals, and dredging—to ship goods without interruption. Notorious among conservation and environmental groups for its manipulation of natural resources as well as mathematics to benefit commerce, the Corps in 1978 estimated that winter navigation would reap over $5 billion in benefits at a cost of $1.6 billion. But the plan entailed 30 new icebreakers, ice control structures, extensive bubbler and flusher systems, and ice anchoring islands. It also required extensive dredging on both the St. Marys and St. Lawrence Rivers. And the Corps barely took into account the natural resource damage that year-round shipping might cause. Although the Corps had funds to begin a "demonstration" program in the mid-1970s on a limited scale, its ultimate goal was the year-round expansion.

Wayne Schmidt, the staff ecologist of the Michigan United Conservation Clubs, saw the proposal as a "colossal boondoggle that would have retooled the Great Lakes to the interests of shippers at a horrendous environmental cost."[14] Schmidt worried about the effect of churning ship propellers and the waves they generated on spawning and nursery beds for fish, mayflies, muskrats, and other important links in the ecosystem. The risk of oil spills in frigid weather and of disruption of nesting bald eagles along the St. Marys River also concerned environmental groups. Joining U.S. Fish and Wildlife Service biologists aboard the Coast Guard icebreaker *Mackinaw* in January 1978, Schmidt observed the impact of deep-winter operations on the lakes firsthand. Just as important, the trip helped connect Schmidt to opponents of winter navigation in upstate New York, upset about the potential harm to the St. Lawrence River. For the first time, citizens up and down the lakes were beginning to unite in common purpose, breathing life into the ecosystem concept.

Schmidt did much to defeat the proposal. One of his prime weapons, often used by public interest advocates, was to generate nationwide news media attention to the fiscally extravagant program. "Packaging the story for broad public consumption," Schmidt said, was a central part of his job. An even more deft opponent of winter navigation was Barry Freed—an alias for Abbie Hoffman, a nationally known Vietnam War protester, one of the Chicago Seven tried for orchestrating protests at the 1968 Democratic National Convention in Chicago and now a fugitive from the law. Moving to the Thousand Island region of New York State in 1976, Hoffman formed a group called Save the River and organized both a legal and a public relations strategy that tied the corps in knots. The large turnouts Hoffman engineered at public hearings on the year-round navigation demonstration project generated steady coverage from New York news media, and the publicity spilled over into Michigan in the fall and winter of 1978. After the *Detroit Free Press* editorialized against winter navigation, Governor Milliken called for a review of the Corps' economic analysis and asked the Great Lakes Basin Commission to hold a hearing on the proposal. Sensing it was losing the fight, the Corps changed tactics in 1979, saying it was proposing a "season extension" of six to eight weeks, ending January 31, rather than year-round navigation. But its formal studies continued to discuss the full-blown proposal, phased in over 10 to 15 years.[15]

Schmidt, Hoffman, and the state of New York agreed on a strategy with U.S. representative David Bonior of Michigan, who represented a district that included the St. Clair River and Lake St. Clair, both sensitive to the effects of winter navigation. Bonior took on James Oberstar, a fellow Democrat who represented the Duluth area, which stood to benefit economically from the winter transport of taconite, a critical ingredient in steelmaking. Pointing to opposition from the MUCC and the United Automobile Workers, Bonior said the demonstration program was already beginning to suggest harm to the sportfishing industry through the effect of churning and wave action on spawning beds. Bonior succeeded in killing the proposed reauthorization of season extension in 1979. His opposition—made possible by the concerted work of MUCC and its New York allies—made other Michigan elected officials comfortable with the same position. After James Blanchard moved from the state's congressional delegation to become governor of Michigan in 1983, he organized a letter that the other seven Great Lakes states governors signed, urging Congress to kill the proposed $600 million authorization for winter navigation. In April 1984, a U.S. House of Representatives committee scuttled the program. The shipping season on the upper Great Lakes was marginally extended, but it was not expanded on the St. Lawrence River. And the vast public works the Corps had envisioned were never built. It was a triumph for the coalition of Great Lakes citizens.

By the late 1970s the issue of increased Great Lakes water diversion was also stirring public concern. Although the amount of water required would have been relatively slight, a proposal to construct a slurry pipeline from the western end of Lake Superior to coalfields in Wyoming elevated the issue to public attention. Unfavorable economics and opposition from railroads tabled the project. But a 1981 study by the International Joint Commission, conducted at the request of the two federal governments, forecast rising demand for water from arid regions of the United States and Canada and suggested harmful effects to the ecosystem. Although a 1982 U.S. Army Corps of Engineers study found that a diversion of Great Lakes water to restore declining groundwater levels in the Ogallala aquifer underlying the Great Plains was not feasible, the mere discussion of the idea outraged Great Lakes politicians and their constituents, uniting them even more than the original Chicago diversion had done. The region was in the midst of a near depression. The prospect of losing water as well as jobs insulted the region's citizens.

Outgoing governor William Milliken organized a June 1982 meeting of Great Lakes governors and Premier William Davis of Ontario on Mackinac Island to discuss the issue, just as the region's top governmental executives had joined to discuss grave pollution problems on the island in 1970. Attracting considerable press coverage, the conference resulted in no decisions but enabled Milliken to remind the public of the significance of the lakes and to refer to the fast-growing southern and western U.S. as the "Parch Belt" rather than the "Sun Belt." Milliken said that water "can become a major component in our region's economic recovery" but warned of "a growing threat of diversion of Great Lakes waters outside our basin without our mutual consent."[16]

Blanchard, the next governor, had attempted to build a political identification with the lakes by introducing legislation dubbed the "Great Lakes protection act" in his final term in the U.S. House of Representatives. Sensing a virtual consensus of opposition to the idea of sending Great Lakes water out of the region, he declared in his early environmental speeches that he would work to build a barrier against such transfers. Creating an Office of the Great Lakes in the Department of Natural Resources to coordinate the state's lakes policies, Blanchard also named University of Michigan law professor Joseph Sax, the author of the 1970 Michigan Environmental Protection Act, as his negotiator on a proposed interstate agreement to tighten controls on water diversions and major new water uses.

Outright opposition to any water diversions was not something to which all eight Great Lakes states could agree. For one thing, Michigan is the only state lying almost entirely within the Great Lakes basin. The other seven states encompass significant areas outside the basin and wanted to reserve the right to divert water for their own future growth. U.S. Supreme Court rulings on cases involving the Fifth Amendment's interstate commerce clause also complicated the Great Lakes states' work. It was clear that the Court would not look favorably upon a simple diversion ban, on the grounds that it would be a discriminatory interference with commerce not based on protection of the public health, safety, and welfare. Sax took the lead during 1984 in drafting a proposed "Great Lakes charter" that required the states to develop permit programs for all major water uses while developing an information base to monitor uses and a research program to discern the potential harmful effects of lowered water levels that diversions or consumptive uses would cause. This suggested that Michigan might allow water diversions under certain restrictions. The MUCC's executive director, Tom Washington, who had clashed with Sax over the Pigeon River drilling controversy in the 1970s, reacted indignantly to the idea of permitting some diversions. His loud protests, published in newspapers, prompted Blanchard to ask for the removal of the reference to a permitting statute. Sax resigned his post, thinking Michigan's position now legally untenable, but talks on the charter moved forward.

Backed by former governor Milliken, Blanchard chose to go ahead with the signing of the charter despite Washington's continued criticism. Perhaps the nonbinding charter's most important accomplishment was to institutionalize the notion of interstate consultation and cooperation on major water resource decisions. The signing states agreed to notify and consult with each other before approving diversions or major new uses, to develop a water use information base, and to create a collective water management plan. While Michigan made no commitment to enact a permitting law, it would not become a full partner in the charter's processes until it at least enacted laws requiring major water users to report to the state.

Six governors of Great Lakes states and a representative of Quebec signed the charter in Milwaukee in February 1985. Blanchard said it "sent a clear signal to the Sunbelt states—indeed, to any who might covet Great Lakes basin water—that this region stands united and is determined to protect and manage wisely our water resources."[17] Environmentalists and the *Detroit Free Press* were skeptical, with the newspaper pointing out what it regarded as more urgent threats to the lakes, including hazardous pollutants. "But if this business of working together on the Lakes becomes common in the capitals of the Great Lakes states and provinces, the charter will be worth the effort to draft it, and much more important than the cry of defiance against the Sunbelt that it is now."[18]

Despite its limitations, the charter held up in its first 15 years. The states consulted on a proposed Wisconsin diversion in 1989, an Indiana proposal in 1992, and an Ohio project in the late 1990s. The cooperation helped inspire the region's congressional delegation to tack an amendment onto a 1986 federal water projects bill enabling the governor of any Great Lakes state to veto a proposed diversion. The 1989 Wisconsin diversion proceeded when Blanchard did not object. Michigan governor John Engler vetoed the Indiana diversion but approved one in Akron in 1998 on the grounds that the community would return an equal amount of water to the Great Lakes basin. In 2000 Tracy Mehan, appointed by Engler to run the state's Office of the Great Lakes, observed that "the current legal regime, evolving in the context of long-standing, effective interstate and binational cooperation, has worked reasonably well over the last decade and a half." But, he warned, "new challenges arising from globalization, a thirsty world, and a burgeoning science of ecology will, inevitably, require revisiting and reforming this legal system sooner rather than later."[19]

The charter, in fact, was the first of several agreements among the governors and premiers in the next several years. The governors inked a 1986 agreement to control toxic substance discharges into the Great Lakes. They then agreed to create a $100 million Great Lakes Protection Fund to support scientific research on problems vexing the lakes. Michigan voters approved

$25 million, the largest share of any single state, as part of a November 1988 environmental bond. And when the state of Illinois proposed tripling the Chicago diversion during the summer of 1988 to alleviate low flow conditions on the Illinois and Mississippi Rivers during a severe drought, the charter's principle of consultation held. Ontario and most of the Great Lakes states expressed grave reservations about the proposal, and it died.

But governments could only take Great Lakes protection so far. Outside pressure would continue to be necessary to advance the issues. The New York–Michigan link of conservationists and environmentalists that had succeeded in killing year-round Great Lakes navigation evolved in 1982 into a new regional advocacy organization known as Great Lakes United (GLU). The MUCC's Washington and Schmidt, who played instrumental roles in its formation, had what Schmidt called "ugly" clashes with environmentalists over the shape and purpose of GLU. But the organization was an important voice for ecosystem protection and management in most of the Great Lakes debates of the 1980s and early 1990s.

An even more important force in ecosystem protection in the 1980s and 1990s was the Great Lakes Natural Resources Center, a new regional office of the National Wildlife Federation emphasizing litigation to protect the environment. Its first executive director was an articulate, sometimes bombastic young graduate of the University of Michigan Law School who had studied under Joseph Sax. His name was Mark Van Putten.

Within months of the Ann Arbor–based center's opening, Van Putten had determined to make Great Lakes water quality the primary focus. Among his early targets was the discharge of the Dow Chemical Company at Midland into the Tittabawassee River. Among the hazardous pollutants in Dow's discharge was a family of compounds known as dioxins, by-products of various manufacturing and waste incineration processes. Regarded as the most potent toxins known to science, dioxins caused a national controversy in 1983. Members of Congress charged administrators of the U.S. EPA with allowing Dow to doctor a report suggesting that the company was responsible for unsafe levels of dioxins in the soil, water, and fish near its Midland plant.

Founded in 1897 in Midland by Herbert Dow, the company had grown to international prominence by exploiting the abundant underground brine deposits underlying the area. In the early decades of the twentieth century Dow became a major producer of dyes and of magnesium metal, used in World War I aircraft. Dow developed styrene and butadiene, critical ingredients in synthetic rubber, helping the U.S. survive the cutoff of rubber supplies when the Japanese swept the plantations of the Far East during World War II. After World War II, Dow participated in the explosive growth of pesticides manufacture and use and entered the world of consumer products with Saran Wrap. Its success enabled Dow to become a major benefactor of the Midland community, financing or contributing to a hospital, a church, a community center, a library, a center for the arts, an orchestra, a parkway, a golf course, and a residential subdivision.

Dow was no stranger to pollution control controversies. During World War I, Saginaw Bay commercial fishermen received customer complaints about the bad taste and odor of their fish, and Bay City residents noticed a foul taste in their drinking water, drawn from the bay. A scientist at the University of Michigan and Bay City's municipal chemist traced the problem to Dow, 40 miles upstream. They found that "the company was dumping its chemical wastes directly into the river and that the objectionable taste and odor of the fish and water were due to the presence of dichlorobenzol, a heavy, clear, oily liquid."[20] The company explained that an explosion in one of its Midland plants had resulted in a significant loss of paradichlorobenzol. The Bay City chemist, Louis Harrison, found perch unable to live just downstream from Dow's discharge, but farther downstream and in Saginaw Bay, the chemical merely limited the growth of fish. The state won an injunction against the company in 1917, causing Dow to build a settling basin. The installation of this crude pollution control and the cancellation of World War I contracts with Dow a year later helped end the pollution.

Controversy had engulfed Dow at various times over the years since then. In 1969 the state obtained one of the first fines against Dow for violating a pollution "order of determination" issued by the Water Resources Commission. The violation was "an unintentional transgression," the assistant chief engineer for the commission said, "but there had been too many of these unintentional mishaps" to be overlooked again. When a Dow water discharge killed more than 2,000 fish and polluted the Tittabawassee River again, a district judge fined Dow $500, "hitting with all the force of a ballerina playing fullback," the *Detroit Free Press* complained.[21] Angered, Attorney General Frank Kelley called for toughening the state's laws to permit $10,000 fines.[22]

The 1960s and 1970s were decades of increasing public strife for Dow. Its manufacture of a lethal explosive for use in Vietnam, napalm, stimulated protests beginning in 1966. Its manufacture of 2,4,5-T, an herbicide used to defoliate Vietnam and also used to kill weeds on U.S. forestlands, generated anger about potential human health effects including cancer and birth defects. Its partnership with a major Michigan electric utility firm, the Consumers Power Company, in construction of a nuclear power plant plunged it into controversy. A Midland woman, Mary Sinclair, rose to national prominence with her successful battle to stop Dow and the utility from completing the plant, whose vast cost overruns and cracking foundations confirmed the suspicions of its critics that the facility was a public health and environmental risk.

But not even the battle over the nuclear plant compared with the sensational news that Dow was a major source of dioxin pollution. In 1983, an irresponsible waste hauler had poured oil containing dioxins on the roads of Times Beach, Missouri, prompting an evacuation and purchase of the town by the federal government. This focused national attention on Midland, where relatively high levels of dioxins were found in soils and in fish swimming in the Tittabawassee River. The company and its critics sparred over the significance of these findings. While Dow argued that dioxins had killed no one and produced only a skin disease called chloracne, environmental advocates attempted to link the compounds to birth defects, reproductive problems, and soft-tissue sarcoma, a rare form of cancer that affects muscle, nerve, and fat tissue.

Dow's initial reaction to the 1983 controversy over efforts to squelch the EPA dioxin report did not serve the company well. Arguing that common wood-burning fires generated dioxins, Dow issued a "dioxin update" that denied responsibility for contaminating the Great Lakes. "Recent findings that dioxins can be found in over 10 Michigan rivers all of which flow to the Great Lakes show the complexity of the situation. Obviously, Dow plants are not located on all ten rivers or even near most of them, for that matter. These recent findings merely substantiate the fact that combustion of fuels for heat and power produces small levels of dioxins."[23] But local environmental groups were unwilling to let the company off the hook. Andrea Wilson of the Environmental Congress of Mid-Michigan and Larry Fink of the Foresight Society called for a state and federal study of Midland. "We are afraid to live in Midland, and afraid of what we might be exposing our children to," said Wilson. "We need help."[24]

Van Putten of the Great Lakes Natural Resource Center decided to challenge Dow's water pollution permit. Issued in 1979, it had contained no meaningful limits on the amount of dioxin dumped in the Tittabawassee River, despite contamination found in the fish that had resulted in a public health advisory suggesting limited consumption. When the Water Resources Commission issued a new permit in 1982 with a dioxin limit, the company contested it. Complicating things further, the state was proposing a new rule that would set enforceable limits for the first time on several dozen so-called persistent bioaccumulative toxic chemicals that build up in the food chain. Dow and most of Michigan industry were opposing the proposal. Van Putten prepared to file suit against the company and the Water Resources Commission under state law and the federal Clean Water Act, arguing that Dow's discharge of dioxins at a level of 50 parts per quadrillion was 170 times higher than what was needed to protect fish and wildlife in the river and Saginaw Bay.

The litigation promised to be long and nasty. Although a change in Dow management signaled a potential break in its traditional hostility to government regulation, the company feared it would be locked into an unattainable dioxin limit and forced to spend huge sums of money on pollution control. Its counterparts in the chemical industry were watching the fight over the permit closely, wary that national precedents would be set. Van Putten and outdoors organizations wanted not only cleanup of the dioxins but compensation for the lost fishing opportunities it had caused. Sensing an opportunity to break the impasse, Dr. William Cooper, chair of the Michigan Environmental Review Board, convened the parties in a room at Michigan State University early in 1984 and tried to negotiate an agreement.

On the same side of the table with Van Putten was Tom Washington, the executive director of the Michigan United Conservation Clubs. MUCC was the state affiliate of Van Putten's National Wildlife Federation and critical to any settlement. While Van Putten and Wayne Schmidt, Washington's staff ecologist, envisioned a package that would include extensive fish and wildlife monitoring and studies of the health effects of the toxins Dow was discharging, Dow had another idea.

"Apparently, Dow knew, probably from talking with Cooper and the DNR staff, that Tom was interested in new public access sites for fishing and boating," Schmidt later said.

> When Dow proposed that it would build some new launch ramps and picnic tables on these rivers to mitigate the fish contamination it had caused, Tom's eyes lit up and before anyone else could say a thing, his fist came down on the table and he proclaimed, "Deal!" That was the day the Tittabawassee River fishery was sold out for some picnic tables. At least that's the way we always looked back at that moment.[25]

Van Putten, who called Washington one of the "great leaders of the century" in Michigan's environmental movement, admitted to chagrin at the sudden compromise. He suggested to the others in the meeting that "Mr. Washington meant to say" something else, but the MUCC chief pulled him out of the room and said the agreement was final. Van Putten said the boat launch appealed to the "common man's touch" of Washington. It was a tangible benefit he could take to MUCC members.

The agreement contained far more than a boat launch at the mouth of the Saginaw River, however. Dow agreed to an 80 percent reduction in its dioxin discharge to the river within two years. It also agreed to cut the releases of 14 other chemicals, including phenol and chloroform. It was required to boost monitoring of 53 chemicals. And the company also agreed to support the state's proposed new rule limiting the discharge of the persistent bioaccumulative chemicals. The state said the permit was 10 to 100 times tougher than any it had ever issued. "It is the finest we've ever entered for control of toxics," said Paul Zugger, the state's surface water quality chief.[26] The permit became the model for strict limitations on toxic pollution discharges across the Great Lakes, and Michigan's toxic discharge rule became a national precedent. Without the threatened lawsuit from Van Putten's organization, the permit and the rule would not have happened.

The next big step forward in ecosystem protection was a direct result of Van Putten's work. The 1986 agreement of the Great Lakes governors on toxic pollution control had implied that they were trying to address inconsistent treatment of chemical discharges by their states. Although the chief executives had publicly declared that the lakes were the center of a single ecosystem, their water pollution agencies set limits on the dumping of the same toxic compounds that ranged from slightly to significantly different. The distinctions not only made no sense ecologically, since a gram of mercury posed virtually the same hazard no matter what river carried it to a Great Lake, but also created pressures on the agencies to bend or relax strict limits in order to retain a business or to avoid losing a prospective business to a more lenient neighbor.

Invoking the words of the governors in their repeated declarations of ecosystem concern, Van Putten persuaded U.S. senator Carl Levin of Michigan to draft a bill requiring the U.S. Environmental Protection Agency to promulgate a single water quality regime for all eight Great Lakes states. Levin pushed the proposal through Congress in the closing days of the 1990 session as part of the Great Lakes Critical Programs Act. Despite resistance from a new and more conservative batch of Great Lakes governors and delays in the rule making process of the U.S. Environmental Protection Agency, the states ultimately adopted consistent water quality standards for 29 of the most serious bioaccumulative toxic chemicals late in the 1990s. Federal and state law now incorporated an enforceable concept of ecosystem management.

"It had a significance far beyond the Great Lakes," Van Putten said. "It got away from the one-size-fits-all approach to one based on the resource, on ecology."[27]

But the courts were Van Putten's most effective venue in breaking new ground. A lawsuit he filed in 1986 further advanced the mitigation principle that the state Natural Resources Trust Fund had embodied.

In 1982, Ray Denno, the recording secretary of the Saginaw Field and Stream Club, wrote MUCC director Washington a brief letter inquiring about the damage being caused to the Lake Michigan fishery by the Consumers Power Company's pumped storage facility in Ludington. Constructed in the 1970s, the mammoth plant pumped lake water uphill to a storage reservoir during periods of low electric demand, releasing it to generate electricity during daylight hours. A study performed by the Fisheries and Wildlife Department at Michigan State University found that 181 million fish per year, including more than 10 percent of the salmon planted in the lake, were being chewed up in the plant's turbines.[28]

Schmidt went to Van Putten, who was looking for issues that would make a mark for his Ann Arbor–based Natural Resources Center. The two also approached Attorney General Frank Kelley, who enjoyed sparring with utility companies. After several years of unsuccessful pleading with the Department of Natural Resources and Consumers Power Company to stop or compensate for the fish kills, Van Putten sued the company in 1986. He was able to persuade the head of the state Department of Natural Resources, Gordon Guyer, to ask Kelley to file as well to help restore the Lake Michigan fishery.

After years of studies to pinpoint the effect of the plant on fish and to consider technologies to reduce the damage, the parties settled the case in October 1994. The $172 million sum paid by the utility was the largest recovered to that date in the United States for fish mortality. The utility put $5 million into a Great Lakes Fisheries Trust to fund fisheries improvement projects, conveyed 25,800 acres of undeveloped land to the state and the trust, and helped acquire and construct seven new public access facilities to waterfront in southeastern Michigan and four on Lake Michigan. It also agreed to continue operating a barrier net that would exclude approximately 85 percent of all larger fish at the pumped storage facility.[29]

As the century ended, the issue that had first awakened the Great Lakes states to their relationship on the chain of large lakes once again stirred them to action. An Ontario company, the Nova Group, received a permit in the spring of 1998 from the Ontario Ministry of Water Resources to export the equivalent of up to 50 tankers per year of Lake Superior water to anticipated customers in Asia. The news disturbed citizens across the Great Lakes region, and the company voluntarily surrendered its permit to avoid further adverse publicity. What concerned Michigan was that provincial officials had failed even to notify the states of the permit application, a break with the new tradition of consultation. Although the amount the company proposed to withdraw was negligible when compared to the volume of Lake Superior, which is by volume the second largest lake in the world, the permit had the potential to set a precedent that Great Lakes water was a marketable commodity. Hurrying to develop a coherent policy, the U.S. and Canadian governments asked the International Joint Commission to study legal and natural resource issues and make recommendations on ways to conserve water and halt harmful water diversions and other exports in the twenty-first century.

The outrage of the region was reminiscent of the anger seven states had felt at Chicago's original taking of Great Lakes water until the 1930 Supreme Court order. But political leaders did little to harness the public's concern, instead issuing sure-to-please vows never to allow the loss of the resource. "Great Lakes water will never be for sale," thundered Governor John Engler in his 2000 State of the State message. Like Blanchard before him, however, he made no effort to explain to the public that stopping water sales and diversions would require Michigan itself to conserve water as a policy for the first time. The court of national public opinion as well as the Supreme Court would not rule favorably on Michigan's bid to stop water exports if Michiganians were wasting water. Michigan taxpayers had willingly sacrificed between $3.5 and $4 billion since the mid-1960s to upgrade sewage treatment; there was every reason to think they would make the relatively small sacrifice of conservation in order to protect the resource they had come to identify so closely with the future of their own state.

The untapped public will to protect the lakes reflected well on three decades of growing Great Lakes consciousness. Never again would Michigan turn its back on the lakes, as it had done in the 1950s when the lamprey virtually wiped out fishing and beaches began to choke on algae. But sentiment was nothing without action. The work of Van Putten, Schmidt, the National Wildlife Federation, and the MUCC had breathed life into the paper promises of ecosystem management. Governments had been held to their promise of treating the Great Lakes as a fragile, interconnected system whose abuse could no longer be accepted. Pollution would stop—or polluters would pay a price. In the coming decades, the successors to these Great Lakes champions would have equally grave challenges to meet. They would have to stir the people of Michigan to demand from their political leaders the stewardship and sacrifice necessary to protect the quantity and the quality of the lakes.

CHAPTER 15

The Third Wave

It's a Michigan tradition going back 20 or 30 years. Conscientious do-gooders will talk about the need for regional and state land-use planning, especially to combat urban or suburban sprawl and protect farmland and open space. Whereupon, nearly everyone applauds, says, "Yes, yes, a superb idea; let's do it." And then . . . Nothing happens.

—Hugh McDiarmid, *Detroit Free Press*,
December 2, 1999

*P*ublic shame and indignation decisively influenced Michigan's recovery from forest devastation and gross pollution. In the first decade of the twentieth century, a forestry reform movement reversed a state policy that favored the dumping of lands onto the open market, instead retaining forestlands in public ownership and management. The successors of Michigan's pioneer forestry advocates did the patient work of planting trees and continuing the reclamation of denuded lands in the public domain.

Similarly, a storm of public outrage in the 1960s and early 1970s about repulsive rivers such as the Kalamazoo and Rouge Rivers, about slimy algae blooms on the Great Lakes, about black smoke ruling urban skies, about piles of rotting drums containing hazardous waste, and about poisoned drinking water drove state officials to pass laws cleaning up the worst of the mess and establishing national leadership in preventing the contamination from returning. Through the 1980s public officials and advocacy groups, emboldened by the belief that environmental protection was now a fundamental principle in Michigan society, constructed programs to implement and enforce the laws and to supplement them with incentives to encourage businesses to go beyond minimum standards.

But conservation and environmental consensus was an illusion, at least in the capital. In 1990, the same year the legislature enacted the "polluter pay" law that seemed to be the high-water mark of environmental influence on state policy, a new philosophy of environmental management came to power when John Engler won an upset victory over Governor James Blanchard. After less than a year in office, Engler took the first step to remake the state's environmental outlook by reshaping the structure of the Department of Natural Resources.

It was not an unexpected move. It is likely that no other Michigan agency was so frequently studied and reorganized in the twentieth century. The structure of Michigan's conservation programs had stimulated fierce debates as far back as William Mershon's day, when he argued for an "honorary commission" in 1911 to keep politics out of the management of fish and game. James Curwood had made the same issue his rallying cry in the first half of the 1920s, and sportsmen had rallied since the 1930s to stop several governors from retaking the power of the Conservation Commission and then the Natural Resources Commission to hire the director of the agency.

The new layer of pollution commissions spread upon the conservation decision-making system from the 1940s to the 1970s frustrated several governors. The state constitution of 1963 strengthened the traditionally limited powers of Michigan's chief executive, forcing the consolidation of dozens of independent agencies and commissions into no more than 19 principal departments. The practical result was that the new Department of Natural Resources absorbed the Air Pollution and Water Pollution Commissions and a number of other advisory bodies but neither the governor nor the DNR director had direct power over them.

Something about the new conservation and environmental agency also prompted nearly continuous management studies and recommendations for reorganization. The Department of Conservation and then the Department of Natural Resources either commissioned outside studies or were the subject of such studies in 1945, 1953, 1963, and 1970. Each one prompted the shuffling of field and central offices. By far the most sweeping reorganization prior to Engler's was a 1973 order by Governor William Milliken that brought pollution control programs into the DNR from the Department of Public Health and divided the DNR into a natural resources branch and an environmental protection branch.[1] DNR director Howard Tanner launched numerous reorganization initiatives throughout his tenure from 1975 to 1983.

But while Milliken seemed comfortable with the power of the Natural Resources Commission to select Tanner, both Blanchard and Engler chafed at this limitation on their control of state government. When Director Ronald Skoog, whom the commission had selected, floundered in the job and resigned in early 1986, Blanchard observed, "All I can say is Dr. Skoog is a product of a system that has outlived its usefulness."[2] He weighed in heavily when the commission chose Skoog's successor, Gordon Guyer, and then David Hales, who took the job in 1988.

The DNR had not had a long-serving popular director since Ralph A. MacMullan, who served from 1964 until his sudden death in 1972. A trained wildlife biologist from the old school of conservation, MacMullan was one of the few leaders in the natural resources management field who viscerally understood and responded to the new public clamor for pollution cleanup. The champion of a ban on DDT and other hard pesticides in the late 1960s, he welcomed students and environmental activists motivated by the Earth Day events of 1970 into the fray to protect Michigan. But he was as respected as he was loved, largely because he spoke out forthrightly, at risk to his job security.

After MacMullan's death, Glen Sheppard of the *North Woods Call* wrote that environmentalists feared "they will never again have as firm or as daring an ally in such a high position. . . . MacMullan did face these [environmental] issues, with courage and determination. No official of his rank in the nation was as outspoken or effective in taking on the gut environmental issues: population, pesticides, land use reforms, economic growth, water pollution."[3] His commitment even reached to the personal level. One of his aides, Jack Bails, received a note from MacMullan after the birth of a child, congratulating Bails and suggesting that he and his wife should stop at two children for the sake of global environmental quality.

After MacMullan's death, the DNR plunged into almost relentless controversy. His successors, including the cerebral Howard Tanner and phlegmatic Ronald Skoog, had few friends in the legislature. They were also less effective in winning employee respect. "He had the best control of the DNR in this century," said Attorney General Frank Kelley. "When we lost Ralph, we lost a general."[4]

But the agency's responsibilities were a major source of its problems and troubled reputation. The regulations it administered often required the DNR to say "no" to large industries and small property owners alike. The enforcement actions it took had broad popular appeal but sometimes enraged influential corporations. As the DNR implemented the new environmental laws and generated friction with regulated parties, some conservation groups complained that the fish and wildlife programs established prior to 1970 were being harmed by the public battles over environmental cleanup. Shorn of a charismatic leader and forced to address a century's accumulation of industrial pollution, the DNR was a target for legislators throughout the 1970s and 1980s.

Engler moved boldly to establish control of the agency. In November 1991 he issued an executive order abolishing 19 boards and commissions in the DNR, including the decision-making Air Pollution and Water Resources Commissions, and gave himself the authority to name the chair of the Natural Resources Commission. This last, seemingly small reform was in fact quite significant, signaling that the commission would work directly through a chair he selected.

The move was shrewd because the history of independent commissions and their purpose had faded in the public mind. Sweeping them away and consolidating their duties seemed to the press and the public as much a matter of housekeeping as a change in substantive policy. The intricacies of government organization did not interest many outside of Lansing, other than the conservation and environmental groups; in the 1990s the model of the strong executive, able to make changes as he or she saw fit, enjoyed far more support than it had when the legislature created the Conservation Commission in 1921.

Engler's environmental aide, Chad McIntosh, told a reporter that "the existing system was a patchwork and didn't function cohesively."[5] Alerted to the governor's plan in advance, Richard Studley of the Michigan Chamber of Commerce approved the reorganization, saying it would "increase accountability and improve the permitting process."[6]

The MUCC's Tom Washington, who had endorsed Engler for election to the governor's office in 1990, expressed outrage about the changes. "What he's saying is that everything the DNR has done for the last 70 years has failed," Washington said of Engler. Terry Miller, chairman of the Bay City–based environmental group Lone Tree Council, called the plan "anti-democratic, anti-environmental, and anti-people." He said the elimination of the air and water commissions would put permit powers in the hands of staff Engler controlled, giving more influence to developers and industries. Mary Brown, a state representative from Kalamazoo who frequently sponsored environmental legislation, argued that the change would keep technical staff from hearing the public's concerns. "The people they'll be talking to are all on one side of the issue, the industrial side," Brown said. "There's nobody on the other end of the teeter-totter to provide the balance." Brown's name appeared on the lawsuit filed to stop Engler's plan.

Newspaper editorial opinion on the governor's move was divided. "The danger is that Engler is trading a system of too many chiefs for one that is too authoritarian and too distant from public opinion," the *Ann Arbor News* observed.[7] But, while cautious about the overall effect of the plan, the *Grand Rapids Press* noted that the need for government accountability justified parts of Engler's orders: "Ordinarily, especially with first-term governors, the department operates nearly independently of the governor's office. . . . The situation insulates governors from having to answer for what the DNR does, while preventing them from managing a large part of state government. Also, the NRC often seems to be in the grasp of major lobby groups."[8] Although the state House of Representatives, controlled by the opposition Democratic Party, rejected Engler's executive order abolishing the commissions, the Republican-controlled state Senate did not act, which allowed the changes to go into effect. A lawsuit brought by the Democrats and environmental groups challenging Engler's constitutional authority to make the changes wound its way through the court system, resulting in a unanimous state supreme court decision in the governor's favor in 1995.

Engler announced a second and even more stunning reorganization in 1995.[9] With another executive order, he divided the DNR into two parts. Traditional conservation programs such as fisheries, wildlife, and forestry management remained in the DNR, while pollution control and wetlands programs—largely the result of laws passed or strengthened since the 1960s—were administered by the new Department of Environmental Quality (DEQ). It was significant that a governor-appointed director would run the DEQ and no citizen commission would oversee the agency's efforts. The director of the new agency, Russell Harding, said many of the state's environmental problems were controlled and said his job would be to shift the emphasis of the pollution permitting programs away from "command and control" regulation. It was no longer wise, he said, to rely so heavily on laws through which the federal and state governments dictated not only strict environmental standards but specific technologies that businesses must use to achieve the standards. "The point is not to beat up on business," Harding said. "So much environmental protection has been done by environmental crises. We need to do a better job not alarming the public, but getting them involved."[10]

Both this second reorganization and Harding's appointment troubled conservationists and environmentalists. In the 1970s, Governor William Milliken had reasoned that unifying the programs in a single agency would increase coordination and improve protection of resources. Fisheries biologists and water pollution regulators had common interests in the quality of lakes and streams, the argument went, and would achieve better results if they worked in one department. But a spokesperson for Engler had justified the division of the DNR by saying that it would eliminate "the inherent conflict between conservation and environmental protection." The MUCC's Washington retorted:

> There was no conflict between conservation and environmental protection; Engler just invented one. Michigan has a proud history of progressive natural resource management that is the envy of the nation. . . . The most recent chapters of this history are possible only because our last Republican governor, William Milliken, had the prudence and foresight to consolidate natural resource management and environmental protection into a single agency, the DNR, barely two decades ago.

Environmental groups objected specifically to Harding's appointment, arguing that he was too closely aligned with business interests. Earlier the same year, Democratic attorney general Frank Kelley had called a press conference to demand Harding's resignation as the deputy director of the DNR. His opening paragraph: "Ladies and gentlemen of the press, I am here today to inform you of an attempt by various special interest groups, in collusion with certain legislators and certain members of the Department of Natural Resources, to scuttle and emasculate Michigan's most important environmental law—the polluter pay law."[11] He accused Harding of negotiating weakening changes to the law with industry representatives while denying Kelley's staff access to the meetings, threatening a law that he said had resulted in $100 million of cleanups in less than four years. "In a matter of hours," Kelley said, "we could well be on our way from being the best state in the Union for dedication to protecting the environment to the worst state in the Union, if this legislative scullduggery [sic] comes into fruition."

Harding had awakened frequent criticism along these lines. Early in 1994 he had tried to block DNR conservation officers from filing a criminal warrant against an Upper Peninsula company accused of intentionally bypassing its air pollution control equipment to blow 60,000 pounds of dust containing toxic lead into a Menominee neighborhood. The officers ultimately filed the warrant, and the company pleaded no contest to a misdemeanor. Records showed that Harding had met privately with the company's executives several times and had promised to temper the state's enforcement posture toward any violations.[12] In a 1993 episode, 164 employees of the DNR's Environmental Response Division had signed a letter to Director Roland Harmes, opposing amendments to the state's groundwater cleanup law advocated by Harding. They argued that the changes would "remove the obligation to clean up a site and polluters will have less reason to refrain from continuing polluting activities."[13]

But these incidents and the complaints of the conservation and environmental groups did not stop the creation of the new agency. Reelected by a wide margin to a second term the year before he created the DEQ, Engler was at a peak of power in Lansing. By contrast, conservation and environmental groups had lost much of the influence they had enjoyed in the 1970s and 1980s. Legislators no longer perceived them as representing a broad portion of the electorate impatient with delays in environmental improvement. Engler's Republican Party controlled both chambers of the legislature and supported the changes. In October 1995, the DEQ was officially born.

Some saw the changes as long overdue, righting an imbalance that had tilted too far toward environmental protection. The legislature had enacted the 1990 "polluter pay" law not long after the twentieth anniversary of Earth Day, when public opinion in support of further environmental cleanup had peaked. But as Michigan's cyclical economy again slipped into a recession at the end of the year and in 1991, the concerns of the public and its elected representatives once more shifted to economic development. The "polluter pay" law, businesses argued, was a classic example of overreaching by environmental groups. The law required in most cases a complete cleanup of contamination, even in areas where the public had little risk of coming in contact with polluted soils and drinking water. It also snarled innocent parties in fights over liability for cleanup, driving developers away from lands that might be contaminated. A significant proportion of Michigan's press agreed with the business community. These arguments were decisive in the 1995 reversal of the law, putting a difficult burden of proof on the state to demonstrate that a party was liable for cleanup costs.

This change signaled that businesses had adopted sophisticated new strategies on environmental issues, while conservation and environmental groups clung to the righteousness of their position and failed to adapt their approach. Michigan's business associations in Lansing and their large corporate members no longer quarreled with the goals of a healthful environment but instead characterized policy disputes as a difference over methods of attaining the goals. Sometimes they even harnessed environmental goals to support their arguments, noting in the case of the cleanup laws that they contributed to urban sprawl. Meanwhile, the Michigan Environmental Council continued to insist that the changes would dangerously increase health risks. But twenty years after the PBB controversy dominated front pages, chemical contamination was no longer news in Michigan. Having seen no epidemic of cancer or other health effects, many newspaper editorialists and citizens viewed low levels of chemicals as tolerable.

The strategy employed by Engler and Harding did not otherwise require changes in most pollution laws. Instead, through changes in personnel at the top of key divisions, budget policy, and the appointment of administrative law judges generally more favorable to permit applicants than DEQ staff on disputed decisions, they were able to accomplish changes without alarming the public by sacrificing statutory clean air and water protection.

The death of Tom Washington just months after the DEQ opened its doors deprived the conservation movement of its most recognized voice, further weakening the resistance to the new philosophy in Lansing. Despite his support for Engler in two election campaigns, Washington had roared defiance at the governor's 1991 and 1995 executive orders and managed to keep conservation and environmental issues in the headlines on a regular basis. His snarling bear persona was something all politicians had reckoned with.

Like MacMullan, Washington could not be replaced. His talented successor, Rick Jameson, was a striking contrast in demeanor and appearance. Wiry and mild mannered, Jameson had earned his MUCC spurs by working on the successful 1976 bottle deposit petition drive. Washington lured him back to the state from Oklahoma in the late 1980s to become assistant director. After Washington's death, Jameson assumed the top job and faced years of pent-up resentment from an MUCC board that Washington had cowed. This frequently diverted his energies from conservation issues.

Yet Jameson had one triumphant moment. When national animal protective groups and Michigan citizens organized a ballot campaign in 1996 to ban bear hunting with bait and dogs, most Michigan outdoors groups virtually conceded their defeat. An electorate dominated by urban voters who never hunted, they reasoned, would emotionally succumb to television ads showing the tracking down of bear cubs. They saw the inevitable loss as a first step in the erosion of their hunting and fishing rights. Jameson stubbornly refused to surrender. Shrewdly deciding it would be easier to beat the proposal with an alternative rather than with nothing, he persuaded legislators to put an alternative proposal on the ballot placing management of fish and wildlife in the hands of the state Natural Resources Commission. The proposal, Jameson argued, "allows the DNR to manage the game species in Michigan pursuant to sound scientific wildlife management techniques and ensures public input in decisions affecting the taking of our game species."[14] To the shock of many, the bear hunting proposal was soundly defeated, and Jameson's alternative won handily. "It was MUCC's statement to the anti-hunters: not in this state are you going to get rid of bear hunting by going through the back door," said Todd Grischke, who served under Jameson on MUCC's staff.[15] The victory continued, at least for the time being, a tradition of scientific wildlife management dating back to the creation of the Department of Conservation in 1921.

But cancer cut short Jameson's career in 1998. At his death, one of

Jameson's visions was unfulfilled. "He had a real knack for pulling together diverse interests," Grischke said. "He wanted to bring the environmental and fishing and hunting communities together. Fundamentally, they're all working for the same thing. But it's a hard sell."

The deaths of Washington and Jameson in quick succession hobbled MUCC's strength in resisting attacks on conservation launched in the capital. Declining interest among TV stations and newspapers in Lansing-based environmental and conservation stories also enabled the governor and legislature to act without penalty. In the 1970s, the news media watched state agencies and legislators closely. The environment was front-page news. In the 1990s, most of the same media had sharply reduced their Lansing staff, with corresponding reductions in coverage of environmental news. Only Glen Sheppard of the *North Woods Call,* a tabloid circulated among several thousand outdoor enthusiasts and current and former DNR employees, made Engler's reversal of long-established policy a banner headline. "The most radical surgery ever suffered by Michigan conservation has Dept. of Natural Resources personnel and conservationists reeling," Sheppard reported after Engler's executive order splitting DNR in half. "Even those who have advocated separating the DNR into two agencies are in shock at the way it is being done and the motive behind it. They see it as a brazen sellout to polluters and developers, rather than an attempt to strengthen conservation."[16]

Eric Sharp, who joined the *Detroit Free Press* as an environmental reporter in 1975 but in the 1990s was its outdoor editor, reporting chiefly on hunting and fishing, said deteriorating coverage of environmental issues was partly due to a change in the environmental understanding of editors. "I occasionally suggest environmental stories to editors, and they're often puzzled why I think such a story is newsworthy," Sharp said.

> *The first thing they want to know is how it will play with the Perrier and SUV set in Oakland County? And you have to remember that many of the editors are part of that same Perrier set. They are often second- and even third-generation suburbanites who have no real connection to or understanding of environmental issues. To them, environmentalism means the animal rights loonies, or some wacko chaining himself to a tree in an old growth forest. The powerful economic and social forces surrounding environmental issues often seem too complex for these people to understand.*[17]

What was really altered by Engler's changes in the organization of environmental programs? Career employees and members of the Natural Resources Commission saw it as more than just a new organizational chart. Marlene Fluharty, who served as a Republican member of the Natural Resources Commission from 1984 to 1992, deplored the loss of an esprit de corps among the agency's staff that had grown over 70 years of largely nonpolitical resource conservation. Fluharty, who provided leadership training for DNR staff while serving on the commission, said she found that department employees "wanted almost desperately to protect the natural resources of Michigan for quality of life, for the economic welfare of future generations. . . . They felt they had a mission." While serving on the commission, she said, "It was very difficult remembering who was Democrat or Republican. It didn't factor into who was the chair, who served on what committees. It was who had the ability and skill to get the job done." Engler's reforms instituted strict political control and demoralized the employees, Fluharty said.[18]

Others said the trend began under Blanchard. Anne Woiwode, who managed the Michigan chapter of the Sierra Club during a portion of the 1980s, said Blanchard mistrusted the DNR because he lacked the power to appoint the agency director and felt the employees were beyond his control. Worse, she said, he had no feel for environmental protection and valued short-term benefits of economic development too highly. "The Commerce Department was the child Blanchard seemed to like so much better than the DNR—perhaps because of control issues—and so it became his golden child for carrying out policies, sometimes at the expense of the law, the environment and resource protection."[19]

Woiwode added that there were similarities as well as differences between the environmental approaches of Blanchard and Engler. Blanchard, she said, was more sensitive about criticism from environmental groups.

> It did appear to matter in the later years when Blanchard made decisions that weren't sound from an environmental standpoint—he wavered and was concerned about the reaction to those decisions. Engler doesn't care—when he learned to hate us, then the only thing that mattered was keeping us from succeeding, regardless of the consequences in the real world. One thing that united them, unfortunately, was that Blanchard clearly laid the groundwork for taking away public input from DNR and splitting the agency.

Blanchard was fiercely criticized for intervening in a 1986 dispute between the DNR and the city of Detroit. When DNR staff erred in their calculations and underestimated the human health risk caused by air pollution emissions of mercury and dioxins from the city's $470 million new incinerator, they requested that the city agree to a change in its air permit and add control equipment costing at least $17 million. Balking, Detroit officials asked Blanchard to intervene. His staff made clear to members of the Air Pollution Control Commission that it should not revise the permit. After a nine-hour hearing in Detroit in March 1986, the commission voted not to require the additional pollution controls.

Canadians across the Detroit River were particularly outraged by the state's decision, which was later reversed by the U.S. Environmental Protection Agency. "It is inconceivable that in this day and age the otherwise enlightened administration of the City of Detroit plans to build an uncontrolled garbage incinerator about four miles from downtown Windsor," the *Windsor Star* protested. "The abatement equipment . . . is certain to save human lives by reducing the incidence of cancer in the area affected by fallout."[20] Even angrier were environmental groups, who said Blanchard had interfered with the independence of the Air Pollution Commission and sided with the city and against public health. The *Detroit News* characterized the relationship between the governor and the groups as "frayed."[21]

Career DNR employee Chris Shafer agreed that Blanchard intruded on the tradition of conservation independence that had persisted since James Oliver Curwood's day, but Engler, he said, abolished it. He remembered fondly the decision-making style of William Milliken. During the winter navigation fight of the late 1970s Milliken had received calls from several governors of other Great Lakes states asking him to back away from the state's opposition. Along with other DNR staff, Shafer briefed Milliken on the potential harm to fisheries and wildlife that the proposal might cause, and Milliken observed, "We have to watch out for our resources." Milliken accepted the recommendation of the DNR staff to stand firm in opposition to year-round navigation.

In another important battle of the late 1970s, Shafer and DNR colleague Dennis Tierney reviewed the proposed US-2 limited access freeway route reaching west from St. Ignace almost to Escanaba across some of the most sensitive and scenic lands in the Upper Peninsula. Also opposed by Schmidt of the MUCC, the highway would have sacrificed hundreds of acres of wetlands and sand dunes, including the ecologically valuable Pointe Aux Chenes marsh. Envisioning economic development, Upper Peninsula legislators Dominic Jacobetti and Joe Mack strongly supported the highway, as did the DNR's regional director. But Shafer and Tierney persuaded their agency director, Howard Tanner, to publicly oppose the plans of their sister agency, the Michigan Department of Transportation. Jacobetti, Mack, and other politicians sharply criticized Tanner, but the objections raised by the DNR helped kill the highway. Such an open and vigorous dispute between two state agencies would have been unthinkable under succeeding governors Blanchard and Engler.

In the 1980s, Shafer had risen to become a chief of the Great Lakes Shorelands section of the DNR, where he was at center stage in conflicts between the resource protection laws passed in the 1970s and the desire of developers and residential property owners to develop sand dunes, wetlands, and other sensitive areas. The job often brought him to the attention of legislators, who received complaints from constituents that he was inflexible in defense of natural resources. In one case, a prominent Detroit-area businessman sought a permit to fill publicly owned bottomlands of Lake St. Clair in order to build an Olympic-size swimming pool. Because the man owned a lot approximately 1,200 feet deep that could easily have provided room for the pool without intruding on the public's resource, Shafer refused to issue the permit. Shafer said he lost count of the number after having 56 meetings with other DNR officials, legislators, and the man's attorneys who sought to extract the permit from him.

Shafer developed a reputation with Harding and the DEQ management as too zealous in defense of the laws and not sympathetic enough to the interests of property owners. Like other employees below the division chief level, he was forbidden to talk to legislators or their staff without supervisors or front office staff present. "It got so petty you couldn't subscribe to certain publications," he said. His managers refused to approve his subscription renewal to a national land use journal. Frustrated with what he called an "anti-regulatory, anti-enforcement environment," Shafer left the DEQ in 1996 to become a law professor, part of a large exodus of senior professional staff during the decade.[22]

But the continued vigilance of the environmental groups born in the 1960s and later, coupled with the work of the MUCC, assured that the undermining of environmental laws could only go so far. Like a building foundation surviving a flood or hurricane, the system of environmental laws created just before and after Earth Day 1970 weathered the Engler changes. It was impossible for the governor and the legislature to eliminate the laws that sought clean air and clean water, even if their administration and enforcement were compromised.

In fact, during his second reelection campaign in 1998, Engler retreated from strident positions against environmental health protection, wary of being characterized as out of line with Michigan's now "mainstream" values. He had faced fierce criticism for departing from accepted policy in the previous two years. In 1996, under direct orders from the governor's staff and against their professional advice, Department of Public Health officials dropped a human health warning to consumers of large salmon caught in Lake Michigan that had been posted in the 1970s because of PCB and dioxin contamination. "For the first time in 25 years, there is no restriction on eating salmon caught in Michigan's waters of the Great Lakes," read a press release the department issued. "This year's advisory clearly indicates that the overall trend of declining contaminant levels in Great Lakes fish continues."[23]

Michigan, however, was the only state in the Great Lakes region to proclaim the good news. Other states had cautiously continued or even strengthened their advice regarding fish consumption in light of scientific findings that the poisons in sport fish, even at low levels, could harm children. A study conducted by Doctors Joseph L. Jacobson and Sandra W. Jacobson at Wayne State University in the mid-1990s found that "exposure before birth to relatively small amounts of PCB's, a kind of industrial pollutant, can result in long-lasting deficits in a child's intellectual development," the *New York Times* reported. The large salmon posed the greatest risks because of their higher proportions of fat, which accumulated the toxins.

Environmental groups and the Great Lakes Natural Resource Center in Ann Arbor cried foul at the Michigan position. Mark Van Putten of the center complained that Engler's aides were using an "old, outdated methodology which has been rejected by virtually all public health and fisheries managers." Tracey Easthope of the Ecology Center of Ann Arbor pointed out, "Even tiny amounts of these poisons received from the mother's blood at a particularly vulnerable stage can affect fetal growth and development."[24] When Engler refused to reinstate the warning about Lake Michigan salmon in 1997, the U.S.

Environmental Protection Agency mailed its own, more protective advice to more than a million Michigan sportfishing license holders. "I will not be bullied into positions based on politics, instead of science," Engler fumed.[25]

But most Michigan newspapers sided with the EPA and the public health concerns. "Engler's battle with EPA over salmon makes no sense," was the headline of an *Ann Arbor News* editorial. "Despite what the state says, children and young women—until they've delivered and nursed all the babies they plan to have—may want to avoid lake salmon completely," warned the *Detroit Free Press*.[26] Worried about the effect of the controversy on the governor's popularity heading into an election year, the Engler administration changed course and agreed to warn women of childbearing age to limit their consumption of the large salmon. In his 1998 State of the State message, Engler proposed a $500 million environmental bond, which, after tinkering by the legislature, accompanied his name on the November election ballot. Both the bond and the governor enjoyed lopsided margins of approval from the voters.

It was in the courts, generally outside the attention of citizens, that the greatest environmental threats loomed and greatest fights were fought in the 1990s. In one case, the Flint chapter of the National Association for the Advancement of Colored People (NAACP) and a group representing neighborhood residents brought suit against the DEQ for discrimination in the siting of a wood-burning incinerator in Genesee Township, just outside Flint.

The case brought to public attention in Michigan the issue of environmental justice—the need, advocates said, for preventing minority and low-income populations from bearing disproportionate health risks from environmental pollution. For most of the twentieth century, the environmental movement was largely a matter of and for middle-class whites, although on the first Earth Day in 1970, organizers and public officials had pointed out that cleanup would protect the poor. James Farmer, an official of the federal Department of Health, Education, and Welfare, told a rally in Washington that day, "The garbage, the trash, the carbon monoxide, the junk. Who suffers most from it, it if is not the poor? And so the poor, especially the ghettoized poor, the black and the brown and the red, stand to benefit first from any successes in cleaning up the environment."[27] But until the late 1980s, when the NAACP took up the cause of African Americans living near a hazardous waste facility in North Carolina, the law and the press took little note of the effect of pollution on minorities.

Represented by the Guild Law Center of Detroit, the plaintiffs in the Genesee Power Station case charged that the DEQ had subjected them to disproportionate health risks in 1992 by permitting the incinerator, which would emit toxic lead, to operate close to residential areas. The suit invoked both the 1970 Michigan Environmental Protection Act and Title VI of the 1964 federal Civil Rights Act, which prohibited race discrimination by recipients of federal funds such as the DEQ. The population within a one-mile radius of the Genesee Township incinerator was 55 percent African American, compared to only 14 percent for the state as a whole. And the African American population within a one-mile radius of the state's five municipal garbage incinerators and demolition wood waste incinerators was 43 percent.

Both the DEQ and the incinerator owner, CMS Energy, vigorously contested the suit. A CMS Energy spokesperson said only one-quarter of the wood burned in the Genesee Township incinerator would come from demolition projects, where lead was most likely to be found. DEQ director Russell Harding said, "Our whole system of environmental permitting is set up on the premise that we treat everyone the same. . . . I have a hard time understanding the race issue. It is a health issue."[28] Harding and DEQ staff took the position that they did not need to consider the race of populations living close to air pollution sources because the state's regulations were adequate to protect all citizens from unacceptable risk. Outside of court, they and others said incinerators and other pollution sources located in areas with high proportions of minority residents not because of race but because of historic development patterns.

Plaintiffs' attorney Kary Moss argued that the state's rules were inadequate because they did not take into account the cumulative exposure to many air pollution sources. Those living in more industrialized areas, with factories, incinerators, and boilers—who tended to be from disproportionately low-income, minority households—were at greatest risk. A physician testifying for the residents said Flint-area children already suffered a relatively high level of lead exposure—mostly from inhalation of lead dust from paint in older houses—with 17 percent having blood lead levels considered unsafe. "We're people. We're human beings . . . we're not trees. We are people and we need to breathe," said Lillian Robinson, a 69-year-old African American neighbor of the plant.

District judge Archie Hayman's ruling on May 29, 1997, seemed to revolutionize Michigan environmental law. Issuing an injunction against the siting of any new air pollution sources in Genesee County until the state improved its risk assessment and environmental review process, Hayman said the DEQ had failed to protect the health of area residents as required by the state constitution. The agency's "failure to take into consideration the multiple pathways of lead exposure in analyzing the risk to the community" subjected Genesee Township residents near the plant to unacceptable risks, Hayman said.

Engler and the DEQ reacted sharply to the ruling, saying that the injunction would halt vital economic development. The *Flint Journal,* however, noted approvingly that the ruling "asserts that the state's duty is to take the health of all people into account. May the spirit of that ruling be brought fully to fruition."[29] In the end the ruling changed little. Hayman had based his ruling not on the civil rights law cited by the plaintiffs but on a provision in the state constitution that required the state to protect public health. A state appeals court, finding that Hayman had been making law from the bench, overturned his ruling, and its judgment was not appealed. For a brief time the lawsuit had called attention to a gap in the state's environmental laws that would someday have to be closed. But addressing the issue of cumulative risks inevitably meant the state would have to force further reductions in air and water emissions. State officials affirmed again in 2000 that they would await guidance from the U.S. Environmental Protection Agency on how to address cumulative risks, a far different response than Michigan had made when challenged to clean up the environment in the 1970s.[30]

While the Genesee Power Station case failed to prod the state forward, another lawsuit threatened to weaken fatally the system of environmental protection built over a generation. A state appeals court ruled in the mid-1990s that the state's denial of a wetland permit for the construction of a restaurant and bar in Oakland County was a "taking" of private property under the U.S. Constitution that required payment. Alarmed, the DEQ appealed the ruling to the state supreme court. Environmental advocates such as the National Wildlife Federation and the Environmental Policy Institute at Georgetown University submitted friend of the court briefs on the side of the state, as did the U.S. Justice Department, in a rare action. Conservative legal foundations intervened on the side of the property owners, the K and K Construction Company.

The dispute arose over two applications filed by K and K, which had contracted to build a restaurant and sports complex on a 55-acre parcel of land. The owners of the property owned three additional adjacent parcels totaling more than 28 acres, zoned for multifamily residential housing. The state Department of Natural Resources rejected a 1988 wetlands permit application by K and K, finding approximately 27 acres of wetlands on the 55-acre parcel. K and K sued the state, arguing that the permit denial eliminated the economic value of the property and entitled the company to compensation under the Fifth Amendment of the U.S. Constitution. In 1990, the company also submitted a new permit application, avoiding most of the wetlands on the site but still altering 3 acres. The DNR turned down this application as well on the statutory grounds that the company had "feasible and prudent alternatives" to the filling of the wetlands.

The trial court and Michigan Court of Appeals sent shock waves through the nation in, respectively, ruling and affirming that the state had indeed taken the property of the owners through its permit denials. The lower courts ruled that the state owed K and K $3.5 million plus interest for taking the "unusable interior wetlands" on the property and another $500,000 plus interest for a temporary taking of other wetlands that had occurred between the second denial and a subsequent reversal by the DNR.

"The direct import of the lower court decisions was that if government sought to preserve natural resources that were protected by law but existed on private property, government would have to, in effect, condemn and purchase the property at a price that reflected its developed value," said assistant attorney general Stanley Pruss, who argued the state's case in the Supreme Court. "Government couldn't rely on environmental statutes to protect sensitive areas, but would have to become a competitive bidder in the marketplace."[31] The potential costs were staggering. Unable to find the money to buy areas they had once regulated, both the state and local governments would have been required to weaken regulations protecting wetlands, sand dunes, and other important lands.

A Detroit area liberal newsweekly put it more bluntly.

Wanna make a quick million, or a quick hundred million? Buy a piece of swampland and apply for permission to build a casino on it. When authorities tell you you can't, sue them for the cost of the land and the money you might have made. . . . It's just one of many nightmare possibilities being cited by critics of the so-called property rights movement, which says the government shouldn't write laws that interfere with individuals' rights to develop their property.[32]

The significance of the case was clear to both sides. Beginning in the 1980s, associations of home builders and realtors and some individual property owners had launched national tests of environmental and land protection laws in the belief that the statutes overreached, disturbing the nation's tradition of respect for private property rights. The coalition worked with like-minded legislators in many states to introduce and enact "private property rights protection" bills that limited the discretion of environmental agencies to protect lands from development. A Michigan legislator, Ken Sikkema, who had directed the West Michigan Environmental Action Council in the early 1980s, sponsored such a measure. Before its passage, however, Sikkema amended the bill to remove provisions that would have handcuffed the DEQ.

The attorney general's office took the supreme court appeal seriously. Pruss and assistant solicitor Susan Leffler revised the state's brief four times. Pruss and colleagues practiced their arguments in two internal moot courts, one before faculty and students at the Wayne State University Law School. "It was an extraordinary effort because we felt there was so much at stake," Pruss said.

After formal arguments in November 1997, the supreme court ruled 6–0 in favor of the state and the environmental statutes in March 1998. Significantly, the court agreed with the argument Pruss made on behalf of the state that it was incorrect to judge whether a taking had occurred by looking simply at the single 55-acre parcel on which K and K had proposed to build the restaurant and sports complex. Since the same owner controlled at least three of the four contiguous parcels and had proposed a comprehensive development plan for three of them, and because substantial land on which the state would permit development remained when all four were taken into account, the supreme court reversed the lower courts and remanded the case for further consideration. Although decisive, the verdict was not conclusive. The case would again wind through the courts, and changes in the judicial philosophies of state supreme court justices could also change the outcome in similar future cases.

The *Detroit News,* a proponent of the takings argument, stated that environmental groups were wrong to view the ruling as a rebuke to property rights activists and observed that the supreme court had not accepted the entire argument made by the state and environmental groups: "If anything, the Court's narrow ruling acknowledges the right of property owners to be compensated for the loss or 'taking' of their land through government regulations that deprive them of the value of their holdings."[33]

While broad public support for environmental protection halted any formal retrenchment on long-established laws by the legislature, the threat that many regarded as the biggest menace to the state's environmental future went unchecked through the 1990s. The manner in which Michigan managed its private lands noticeably worsened without any meaningful response from Lansing.

Any political leader who wanted to address the issue was chastened by both the United States' tradition of private property rights and by the lesson of Michigan's land use debate in the 1970s. Even the governor regarded as the most sympathetic to conservation in the state's history had failed to improve land use policy significantly. But it was not for lack of trying.

In 1971, William Milliken appointed a special commission on land use to recommend ways to conserve the state's sensitive lands and open spaces. In a February 1972 special message to the legislature, he said, "Before long, it will be too late to bring a rational order to land use in Michigan. In many respects, it is now or never. . . . We can no longer take a parcel-by-parcel approach to land use. We need to develop an overall land use policy."[34] Milliken cited as compelling problems the rapid loss of agricultural land in southern Michigan to commercial and residential development; the scarcity of recreational lands for growing populations in southern lower Michigan; and taxpayer costs for sewage, school, road, and parks programs.

Milliken did what he could administratively, issuing an executive order to give the state Department of Natural Resources land use planning responsibilities. Under chief Karl Hosford, the DNR land use office developed an extensive educational campaign on the need for more land use policy reform. In one of its reports, the DNR predicted that Michigan would need an additional 1.4 million acres of cropland, 40,000 acres for solid waste disposal, and 150,000 acres for local recreation use by the year 2000. But additional automobiles and the highways they required, 600,000 additional dwelling units, and the 40,000 pounds of minerals each person used would place competing demands on the state's land.[35]

The phrasing of such reports—and others that followed in the next quarter century—suggests that the land use issue is difficult for leaders to put into compelling words. More than numbers were involved. In the words of Aldo Leopold, a "land ethic" was required to preserve the spirit of the state. Neither laws nor statistics were likely to instill such an ethic.

Milliken's land use commission held hearings on proposed state land use legislation in the fall of 1972. The chairman of the panel, William Taylor, reported that the largest single group of witnesses testifying at the hearings opposed the legislation either because "they do not believe the government should be involved in the determination of property rights" or because "government involvement is possible, but it should consist only of local government not state and federal."[36] Still, Taylor recommended that Milliken push ahead with an "educational program" to combat public disbelief that land use was even a problem and the idea that, even if it was a problem, state government could not contribute to its solution. It was too early to seek enactment of a bill, Taylor said, noting "a bad situation in view of public relations."

In 1975 Milliken and a considerable number of legislators felt the issue was ripe. Democratic representative Philip Mastin introduced a bill to create a permanent state land use commission in the DNR. The seven-member body was to create a state land use plan "for the protection and proper utilization of the land resources of the state." In classifying lands, the commission was to follow a policy declared by the bill "to encourage the rational use of land resources so as to meet the various needs of present and future generations." The bill called for the interim designation of "critical land areas" to receive special protection, including land suitable for farms and forestry, sensitive areas, undeveloped land containing mineral resources, and historic sites. In these areas, the bill would forbid state agencies from proceeding with development projects until the commission reviewed them. During an interim period the bill barred the platting of subdivisions, development of condominiums and multifamily developments, establishment of mobile home parks, and other conversion of land without approval of the state commission. The state commission would then make permanent rules governing the development of lands.

The Mastin bill provoked great controversy. Hiram Todd, a lobbyist for the Michigan Association of Home Builders, objected that it put "dictatorial power in the hands of the commission." George Graff of the state Chamber of Commerce testified that even a redrafted, weakened version did not "contain adequate guidelines to protect private property rights. In addition . . . the broad scope of the proposed legislation will merely promote and foster a huge bureaucracy during the interim period." In November 1975 the House Urban Affairs Committee sent the bill to the Appropriations Committee, considered a graveyard for environmental bills. At a March 1976 Appropriations Committee hearing on the bill, Senator Gary Byker of Hudsonville condemned it. He said the legislature would be forced into approving the commission's final land use plan. "Because, at that point in time, there will be such a cacophony of a cabal of anti-profit, anti-free enterprise eco-activists, plus the anti-private property earth-beaters, who will all be mobilized with the indispensable aid of the media, so that inevitably the crescendo will produce 56 votes in the House and 20 votes in the Senate to adopt the statewide plan to abolish private property rights," Byker testified.[37]

Arguing the other side was former Oregon governor Tom McCall, who had helped enact his state's landmark land use law. Speaking at a natural resources banquet at Michigan State University that spring, McCall said, "No corporation executive in his right mind would move without a plan—and yet this same executive is likely to say that the public does not have a similar right to plan the use of nonrenewable resources such as land."

But the bill died that year, and a similar bill foundered in 1977 largely on the strength of opposition from powerful legislators from the Upper Peninsula, including Rep. Dominic Jacobetti of Negaunee, chair of the House Appropriations Committee. Opponents of many of the environmental laws enacted in the 1970s, Jacobetti and other northern Michigan representatives were suspicious of further state participation in land use decision making.

Years later, Milliken said the failure of the land use bill was his biggest environmental disappointment as governor: "We knew, we believed that we needed desperately to do something. We were constantly threatened by the real estate interests and others who saw it as a threat to their profits."[38] Even after leaving office, Milliken continued to champion the issue of land use, giving numerous speeches in which he called urban sprawl "a plague upon the land."

Milliken's successor, James Blanchard, gave little attention to land use as a statewide issue. In Lansing the memories of the failed attempt to pass the Mastin bill in the 1970s lingered, forestalling any new legislative initiatives. But the issue once again gained life in the 1990s. A panel appointed by Governor John Engler to rank the state's greatest environmental risks reported in 1992 that "the absence of land use planning that considers resources and the integrity of ecosystems" was at the top of the list.[39] The report recommended that the state develop a land use plan "to demonstrate that good land-use design and management can be both good ecologically and economically."

William Rustem, who had served as Milliken's environmental policy adviser and had played a part in the debate of the 1970s, coordinated the study and pressed the Engler administration to follow up on it. But the issue did not rank high on the administration's action list despite its ranking by the expert panel. In their broadest sense—especially if a state land use plan was involved—the twin issues of urban sprawl and appropriate land use raised ticklish questions with key constituencies of the governor, associations that represented home builders and realtors. Land use was also not yet an issue with tangible public appeal for which a governor could marshal broad support of legislative action.

Urban sprawl entered the Engler lexicon for the first time only when the governor sought to repeal the "polluter pay" law of 1990. The fear instilled in developers and property owners by the law's liability provisions on contaminated sites steered industrial, commercial, and residential projects away from brownfields in older cities and toward greenfields at the urban fringe, Engler argued. Urban mayors and the legislature agreed with him. After passing the changes in the contamination law in 1995, however, both the governor and the legislature did little further on land use for several years.

State associations and the private sector, nevertheless, continued to build awareness of the issue. A September 1995 report by the Michigan Society of

Planning Officials (MSPO) attracted considerable attention.[40] Summarizing an assortment of studies prepared by MSPO and others, the report painted a dire picture of the recent past and the imminent future. The state had lost 7.8 percent of its farmland between 1982 and 1992, or an average of 5 acres per hour during the decade. Among the private and public forestlands of northern Michigan, the rapid division of nonforestlands into both primary homes and cottages was threatening the physical and biological integrity of forests. In one township of Grand Traverse County with extensive state forestland, the number of lots between one and nine acres had increased by more than 1,400 percent between 1964 and 1981.

Between 1990 and 2020, the report projected, the population of Michigan would grow by 11.8 percent, threatening an increase of 63 to 87 percent in land area in urban use. Sprawling development was the reason; large-lot homes in rural areas and large commercial projects in expanding suburbs would alter disproportionately large amounts of land. "This report will have succeeded if it alerts the Michigan public to the immense implications of current land use trends and what is at stake. Sprawl, if it is allowed to continue, will inevitably present society with lost opportunities, a variety of social and environmental problems and immense monetary costs," MSPO concluded.

While the threatened loss of forests, wetlands, and open space moved some, it was finally the disappearance of farmland that began to stir the legislature. Before that could happen, politicians had to be convinced there was a farmland problem. The Michigan Association of Home Builders argued that there was not. The association pointed out that while farmland was shrinking, the amount of land in active crop production had actually increased between 1982 and 1992. The home builders mocked newspapers that deplored "demonic, rapacious home builders [who] are forcing farmers to sell their family farms for hundreds of thousands and sometimes upwards of a million dollars. . . . Thanks to these predatory home builders we are 'losing ten acres of farmland every hour.'"

The concerns of farmers themselves stimulated legislators to consider the issue seriously. In Macomb County, northeast of Detroit, farmland had dwindled from 90,000 acres in 1980 to 60,000 in 2000, with a forecast for 2020 of 28,000. "My family has been farming in Macomb County for 100 years, and I don't know who thinks it's going to make another 100," said Matthew Pruehs.[41] In the year 2000, metropolitan Detroit had swollen to over 1,200 square miles containing more than 5 million people.

"In fringe townships once dominated by farms, roads are being widened and sewer lines expanded in an attempt to meet the needs of thousands of new homes. Meanwhile in Detroit, open spaces are reappearing amid abandoned homes in the heart of a city that has lost half its population in five decades," the Detroit News reported.[42]

Momentum was building for changes in state policy to preserve farmland and to redesign suburban growth to consume less land. But few predicted that the state would move swiftly to check the breathtaking spread of roads, residential developments, stores, factories, and office buildings into areas characterized for most of the twentieth century by cornstalks, cattails, and trees.

Michigan's third wave of heedless resource consumption had struck full force. Just as the loggers had ripped through the northern forests, just as cities and industries had choked air and water with their wastes, now property owners, developers, builders, and local officials were rampaging across the southern farms and open lands. Each was making a rational decision in his or her own interest; few were thinking of the collective interest or the interest of future generations. It was a page from Michigan's past.

Epilogue

I shall never forget the husband of one of our faithful members [of the Michigan Natural Areas Council]. He came to the meetings merely to accompany his wife. Even though he was probably bored, I noticed that he would pay close attention to what was going on. He was truly a "tough businessman," and his profession was law. One night he drew me aside and said: "Herb. I want to tell you something. This business of natural areas and rare species will someday become a big deal. There will be hundreds of thousands of people working on the problems . . . and millions of dollars will go into it." Imagine that! I didn't believe it at the time, but he was dead right. Look at what is going on today.

—Warren "Herb" Wagner, April 25, 1997

*J*f Michigan's environmental history is to mean anything, it must illuminate the way to the future as well as hold a lamp to the past. The business of protecting the state is vitally concerned with tomorrow. Indeed, Michigan's initial conservationists were fixed on the future, desperately hoping to right what they saw as grave wrongs that had been committed against their state.

The chairperson of the Michigan Forestry Commission at the dawn of the twentieth century, Charles Garfield, was excited about the Michigan he envisioned. While most of his public pronouncements about the work of the commission were couched in the safe language of improving economic return from the lands of the north, Garfield became poetic now and then. In perhaps his most personal public statement as commission chair, in the 1900 publication *A Little Talk about Michigan Forestry,* Garfield quoted a Grand Rapids pastor, Dan F. Bradley, who envisioned a dark day in the state's future.

> *Some time, when our State is denuded of its last forest, and the seeds that have been left to renew the face of the State have been burned with careless fires, and the struggling new growth has been ruthlessly slaughtered and slain, then the people of Michigan will begin to appreciate what a wonderful treasure they had in their trees, and how they have pitilessly, foolishly destroyed and damaged their own heritage.*

While Garfield trembled at the thought of a deforested Michigan, he was optimistic that he and others could help prevent the calamity. No one person could turn the tide; the effort would require all citizens to participate. "There is no evading the responsibility upon the shoulders of a public-spirited citizenship," he wrote.

> *Thoughtful, earnest, practical men must be chosen to positions of trust, and chosen because of their ability to take up questions of this character and point out a practical solution. Politicians must be led to do less ranting about things that are not intrinsic, and make a record along the line of State policy in the management of its greatest interest. The pulpit must tackle the question as one of morals, and educate the people that they cannot shirk the responsibility of providing for the future of the State. Educators must not fail to instruct the boys and girls who are to become managers of the affairs of the future in the matter of forestry and its importance in connection with state-craft.*

Quaint as a few of the words seem to a reader 100 years later, their essential truth is undeniable. More important, they did not simply die on the page. Urging, prodding, struggling, sometimes despairing, but always persisting, Garfield and his allies in the great Michigan forestry movement succeeded in remaking the state and providing for a future they could not live to see. Thanks to the revolution they started, in the 1990s Michigan had 18.6 million acres of timberland. Over 3 million acres of that was in state ownership. Timber products industries employed 150,000 people and accounted for $9 billion of economic activity. Another 50,000 jobs grew out of forestry-related tourism and recreation.

Garfield's successors in spirit were the generations that wiped the air clean and stopped the unthinking and reckless discharge of sewage and chemicals into the state's rivers, restocked the Great Lakes with sport fish, and created habitat that provided recreation for hundreds of thousands of hunters. Their work had demonstrable results.

Numbers tell a startling story, starting with reductions in air pollution. In 1972 the state enacted a tough rule to control sulfur dioxide emissions because of their threat to human respiratory health. Although not all of Michigan exceeded health standards for sulfur dioxide in air, the DNR, with Governor William Milliken's support, chose to limit sulfur content in coal burned in any large boiler or power plant within the state's borders. At the time some argued this was overkill. Not until the late 1970s did national policymakers begin seriously to study whether sulfur dioxide also sterilized lakes and killed aquatic life through the phenomenon known as acid rain—but Michigan's strong statewide policy was already addressing that problem. The sulfur content rule slashed Michigan's sulfur dioxide emissions from 1.56 million tons in 1974 to 508,000 tons in 1997 at a time when the state experienced substantial economic growth. Other air pollutants also declined significantly. Emissions of soot—the ashy wastes that buried Detroit and other major Michigan cities in the 1930s—declined from 331,000 tons in 1974 to 55,000 tons in 1997.

Water pollution dwindled, too. Thanks in part to the rule championed by Governor William Milliken in 1977 against fierce resistance from the soap and detergent industry, phosphorus levels dropped nearly 80 percent at most river mouths entering the Great Lakes between the early 1970s and the mid-1980s.

Comparing the turn of the twenty-first century to the chemical contamination era of the early 1970s, levels of DDT and PCBs in Great Lakes fish were down more than 70 percent.

A new attitude toward threatened wildlife had produced remarkable results. After plummeting to a low of a half dozen in the 1960s, Michigan's population of wolves rebounded to 216 in 1999, above the official "recovery" level of 200. Changing public attitudes toward the animals, who had once been hunted down at every turn, contributed significantly to the turnaround. Another sentinel species, the bald eagle, had more than tripled in numbers since the ban on DDT.

The state's continuing conservation commitment yielded enormous recreational and economic benefits. In 1999 hunters took a near-record 550,000 deer. Two million anglers spent approximately $1 billion in pursuit of their sport. Hundreds of thousands of hikers, backpackers, and other lovers of wild things roamed among state and federal forestlands and Michigan's three national parks. And 27.7 million visitors entered Michigan's state parks and recreation areas.

None of this was accomplished accidentally or without sacrifice. Conservationists, environmentalists, and public officials—some obscure, some prominent—turned their faces to the future. A vigilant and outspoken press, led by writers Albert Stoll, Ben East, Jack Van Coevering, Tom Opre, Barbara Stanton, and Glen Sheppard, persuaded and shamed politicians into acting for long-term rather than immediate benefit. Seeding the earth of conservation with their ideas and energies, all of these Michiganians tended the soil carefully and passed the job of stewardship to another generation that would begin to realize the harvest. The question at the dawn of the twenty-first century was whether fate would supply another batch like Garfield, Munger, Lovejoy, Gillette, MacMullan, Wolfe, Milliken, and Washington. For surely they would be in demand once again.

When they emerge, they will find that meeting the twenty-first century's challenges requires conservation and environmental leaders to adapt their strategies. Former workers in the movement questioned the methods—and the effectiveness—of the Michigan environmental community in the year 2000.

Ken Sikkema directed the West Michigan Environmental Action Council from 1979 to 1982 and was harshly criticized by his former peers when, as a state representative in 1995, he sponsored a law revising Michigan's environmental contamination liability and cleanup standards. Like other lawmakers, he questioned the political and policy judgment of environmental groups, generally perceived in the capital during the 1990s as ineffective in influencing policy. Sikkema declared in 2000 that environmentalists were "too far off on the edge somewhere."[1]

Sikkema observed:

You should never compromise your principles, but you have to be willing to compromise nonessentials. I think the environmental community doesn't understand that, or has no nonessentials on its list. They let a philosophical position get in the way of good environmental policy. In the environment of Lansing, nobody can get everything they want.

Some questioned whether the emphasis on regulating all businesses alike had gone too far. Jeff Dauphin, a staff member of WMEAC from 1974 to 1980 who helped draft the state's modern solid and hazardous waste laws in 1978 and 1979, was critical of the environmental movement's treatment of small businesses. Dauphin observed that small businesses are rooted in communities, unlike larger businesses that may have headquarters in distant cities, states, or countries and are therefore less likely to show concern for local opinion and the local environment. "Environmentalists have been insensitive to the small business factor and have instead seemed to argue that all businesses are bad and are willfully destructive of the natural environment," Dauphin said. "Future laws should be much more sensitive to this factor, and if the environmental movement gained a new appreciation of it an alliance of small business and environmental groups could emerge. However, a lot of damage has already been done and many small business operators will be suspect of any such efforts."[2] Tom Bailey, the executive director of the Little Traverse Conservancy, criticized an "excessive orthodoxy" among environmentalists, saying that the movement should be permitted to evolve and should better incorporate economic reasoning into its case.

Environmental problems are also more complicated than they seemed in the 1970s. If anything, the challenges of the next century seem more daunting than those of the last. While a formidable problem, the renewal of millions of acres of Michigan lands through reforestation was at least largely within the state's control. Even the cleanup of air and water in the 1960s and 1970s, while partially dependent on the work of states and provinces upwind and upstream, was a mission within Michigan's grasp. The twenty-first century poses some risks to the state that begin and end far beyond its borders. Most dangerous is the unknown effect of global climate change. It could dramatically lower the Great Lakes, drive native flora and fauna northward, dry up marginal wetlands and cropland, increase destructive flooding, and kill aged citizens and other vulnerable people with summer heat.

Similarly, the threat of exotic organisms to the state and the Great Lakes system seems to become more overwhelming each year. The state's Office of the Great Lakes estimated in 1998 that at least 139 nonindigenous aquatic species had already become established in the Great Lakes ecosystem, and experts agreed that future introductions from ballast water of oceangoing vessels, aquaculture operations, and other sources were still highly probable. Despite publicity generated by the arrival of the zebra mussel, ruffe, goby, spiny water flea, Eurasian water milfoil, and others in the late 1980s and 1990s, controls on new invasions were largely ineffective. They would require policies and laws from national as well as state governments—including bodies far removed from the Great Lakes, where the vessels originated. More than ever before, the lesson of ecology—the lesson of unfathomable interconnections among natural systems, now under humankind's sway—foreshadows the state's future.

But the people of Michigan are not helpless in the face of prospective change. If aroused, their indignation and shame could once again serve a decisive purpose.

More than 30 years after the unflinching advocacy of DNR director Ralph MacMullan and the discovery of tainted coho salmon forced Michigan to be first in the nation to cancel most uses of DDT, businesses and industries are still freely making use of other persistent toxic chemicals. Michigan businesses covered by a federal law emitted to the environment or shipped away for disposal 307 million pounds of toxic chemicals in 1997. Many of these chemicals have the same dangerous characteristics—persistence and bioaccumulation—as the "hard pesticides" MacMullan fought so fiercely. But there is little public outrage, and there is plenty of private sector self-congratulation for the incomplete job of making industrial processes clean rather than a menace to public health.

Perhaps a greater scandal is the continued use by thousands of Michigan businesses of chemicals increasingly suspected of interfering with the development of children. Research on wildlife in the 1980s and 1990s showed that a variety of chemicals had profound effects on the hormonal systems of animals and their young. Scientists linked abnormalities of the neurologic, immune, and reproductive systems in wildlife with exposure to these chemicals. Often it was not the exposed animals who exhibited these malfunctioning systems but their offspring. What did this mean for children? Two studies on the effect of prenatal exposure on child behavior documented developmental injury. Doctors Sandra W. Jacobson and Joseph L. Jacobson, Wayne State University researchers, conducted one of the studies (also discussed in chap. 15), linking exposure to PCBs in the womb with perceptible developmental delays in children.[3] While the findings and suspicions spurred research, they did not immediately drive chemical manufacturers and users to safer alternatives. In fact, defenders of the chemical industry dug in their heels, implying that, as they saw it, a slight risk of transgenerational effects was worth taking in return for short-term economic convenience. While the state Department of Environmental Quality agreed with the industry position, environmental advocates said enough research showing harmful effects was available already.

"What will we do with this understanding?" asked Mary Beth Doyle, coordinator of the Environmental Health Project of Ann Arbor's Ecology Center.

Every student of public health learns the story of John Snow, who identified a community well as the source of an epidemic, and stopped the epidemic by taking the handle off the pump. He didn't know that cholera caused the disease, but he traced it to its origin and took action. Will we be remembered as modern John Snows? Or will this time be remembered as one when insistence on proof and "sound science" overruled common sense and sound judgment?[4]

The permissive position of state government on these chemicals was the norm, rather than a departure from the norm. At almost every difficult turn during the 1980s and 1990s, state officials and industries agreed on an unalterable conflict between environmental protection and development and chose the latter over the former. In 1990, the International Joint Commission, the U.S.-Canada treaty body overseeing the boundary waters, had concluded "that there is a threat to the health of our children emanating from our exposure to persistent toxic substances, even at very low levels."[5] The IJC also made the dramatic proposition that the United States and Canada, working with the states and Ontario, should designate the relatively clean watershed of Lake Superior as a "demonstration area where no point source discharge of any persistent toxic substance will be permitted." This so-called zero discharge demonstration zone proposal awakened enormous controversy but the zone itself did not materialize in the next decade.

At the time the IJC made its report, in fact, the Michigan Department of Commerce was actively seeking to site a new pulp and paper mill, a potential source of dioxin discharges, on Keweenaw Bay. Fearful of recriminations about lost job opportunities, neither Governor James Blanchard nor the Department of Commerce seriously acknowledged the zero discharge demonstration idea. They also made no effort to adapt their economic development strategy to lure to the Upper Peninsula either large- or small-scale enterprises that had no need of persistent toxic chemicals. Blanchard's successor Engler similarly shied away from the IJC idea, launching voluntary pollution prevention projects that could at best reduce a fraction of the toxic chemical load entering Lake Superior. Michigan's governmental leadership was clearly unable to rise to the majesty of the world's largest lake.[6] A future administration would be required to develop a strategy for clean economic growth in the Lake Superior watershed but would do so only if public impatience or a toxic chemical crisis forced it to.

How far had the state or the nation traveled since the turning points of the 1960s—especially the nationally trumpeted declaration of Lake Erie's death—if business associations continued to resist cleanup of their processes? Individual corporations might be awakening to their responsibilities to the future, but too much of the rhetoric from trade lobbyists in the state capital sounded like the invective of the 1970s, when the editor of the Michigan State Chamber of Commerce magazine observed:

> Contrary to so much of the pap being spewed these days by the current batch of environmental saviors/entrepreneurs, Michigan citizens have it good . . . environmentally speaking! If the funds and energy expended by sincere, well-meaning Michiganians—those who are being duped by silver-tongued devils more adept at self-preservation than resource conservation—were redirected toward key issues like unemployment compensation reform, workers' compensation reform, welfare reform, tax limitation and enforcement of existing laws, many more Michigan people would benefit.[7]

The author of the chamber's editorial then went on to quote, approvingly, the president of his organization opposing the restriction on phosphate content in laundry detergents. Ultimately adopted over the chamber's objections, the phosphate limit was instrumental in helping restore Lake Erie and Lake Michigan.

Now the same pollution controls that the business associations had opposed in the 1970s, and which had worked so well, were their justification for inaction. The dramatic declines in contamination brought about by Michigan's nationally significant cleanup programs were a reason for complacency, despite evidence that even low levels of some chemicals threatened human and ecological health. The state Department of Environmental Quality's 1998 fish contaminant monitoring report, for example, acknowledged that PCB levels in fish at 78 percent of its collection sites exceeded levels considered safe for women and children, that dioxin concentrations topped health standards in 50 percent of its sites, and that mercury was found at levels of concern at 54 percent of the sites.[8] Industries, municipal waste incinerators, and hospitals were still releasing significant amounts of dioxins and mercury, but in a sharp contrast to the state's clean-it-up ethic of the 1970s, the DEQ was not requiring further reductions in emissions.

Individual businesses were beginning, however, to suggest the possibility of hopeful change. Challenged by the Natural Resources Defense Council (NRDC), a Washington, DC–based environmental organization, the Dow Chemical Company agreed in 1996 to permit local environmentalists as well as NRDC staff to examine its Midland processes to evaluate opportunities for pollution prevention. Despite mistrust on both sides, the unprecedented opening of Dow's doors to its critics resulted in surprising and measurable improvements. By 1999, the project resulted in an estimated reduction of 43 percent in air and water releases of a list of toxic chemicals that included styrene, toluene, and chloroethane. The changes saved the company an estimated $5.4 million per year on an initial investment of $3.1 million. But the project proved another point—that without a legal mandate even to examine such pollution prevention opportunities, many businesses were probably overlooking them.[9] "No one knows what a sustainable company looks like, but pollution prevention has to be a first step," said Dow's Jeffrey Feerer, the environment, health, and safety manager for the Midland plant.

Other Michigan firms were beginning to rethink their environmental strategies, moving away from a defensive position of trying to avoid costly liabilities or governmental enforcement actions. "As the true costs of toxic emissions become more apparent, environmental health and safety staff will become more of an offensive asset to the company to help lead them down a path that allows the company to meet its customer's needs in the most benign way possible," said William Stough, a staff member of the West Michigan Environmental Action Council from 1980 to 1983 who had become vice president of environmental performance services for BLDI Environmental and Safety Management of Grand Rapids.

Herman Miller of Zeeland, one of the nation's largest office furniture manufacturers, institutionalized environmental values. The company quadrupled recycling of wood wastes between 1994 and 1998 and reduced the landfilling of the wastes by almost 40 percent in the same period. Herman Miller reduced solvent emissions to the air by 96 percent through installation of systems to capture and incinerate the materials in 1990. But its most ambitious goals were ahead of it in the year 2000: the firm proposed to become a "sustainable business," which it defined as "manufacturing products without reducing the capacity of the environment to provide for future generations."[10] Its Equa 2 work chair was one of the most advanced in the industry, containing 77 percent recycled content by weight, including steel, polypropylene, aluminum, plastic, and fabric. The company's environmental manager, Paul Murray, credited Herman Miller founder D. J. DePree with these achievements. DePree included environmental stewardship in the firm's corporate mandate in the 1950s. He also required that half the company's land should be left green and that no employees should be farther than 75 feet from a window. "These ideas . . . set the stage for the environmental program we have today," said Murray.[11]

While companies were beginning to show signs of alertness to the environmental challenge of reducing pollution and resource consumption, ravenous water use by Michigan industries and institutions threatened the future of the Great Lakes. Again, the International Joint Commission was the conscience of the Great Lakes basin. Asked to study the problem of water exports by the Canadian and U.S. governments in 1999, the commission submitted a report urging Michigan and other basin governments to collect the data necessary to understand existing water uses and implement a research program to understand the ecological effects of lowered water levels. The commission said a water conservation program in the center of a water-wealthy ecosystem might also be necessary to defend against water exports, requests—or raids. "Global population growth or climate changes could result in requests for shipments of Great Lakes water to meet short-term humanitarian needs," the commission said. But the IJC suggested that an even greater threat might be the nibbling effect of dozens of new small diversions or consumptive uses by the Great Lakes states themselves.[12] In June 2000, Engler proposed an amendment to the 1985 Great Lakes Charter that would, for the first time, set a legal standard for determining which, if any, major new water uses could be permitted. But it was unclear whether he or the legislature would be willing to enact a necessary new state law requiring government approval of such major new uses by Michigan industries and agriculture.

Michigan was also madly embarked on a course toward increasing, rather than weaning itself from, a diet of fossil fuels redolent of the early twentieth century. In 1996, Michigan's coal-burning power plants dumped more than 170,000 tons of nitrogen oxides, over 336,000 tons of sulfur dioxide, and nearly 67.5 million tons of carbon dioxide into the environment.[13] By 1999, the state was generating 80 percent of its electricity from burning coal and had shut off its mandates that utilities provide energy efficiency programs that reduced emissions while lowering the bills electric customers paid. Coal burning contributed to acid deposition, summertime smog, potentially lethal soot, and climate change. Decision makers turned a blind eye to the connection between coal burning, the largest source of mercury emissions, and a statewide public health advisory that cautioned consumers of sport fish because of mercury in the fish. Rather than seeking to outdo federal requirements for air pollution cleanup, in early 2000 the state was engaged in 10 different lawsuits to block the U.S. Environmental Protection Agency's rules. It was not likely that future generations of Michiganians would bless this policy, especially when proven and cost-effective efficiency programs, cleaner-burning natural gas, and emerging wind and solar technologies were all at hand.

While most of the environmental and conservation problems of the 1990s were old sores that simply festered, one emerged anew. The near abandonment of environmental law enforcement was a foolish turn away from a 20-year consensus that had begun to make pollution socially unacceptable as well as injurious to the public health, safety, and welfare. Under 34-year attorney general Frank Kelley, Michigan had been one of the first states in the nation to establish a unit to prosecute civil and criminal environmental offenses, and Kelley had made national headlines with some of his precedent-setting settlements. Department of Natural Resources director Howard Tanner had, in the 1970s, made Michigan the first state to put commissioned officers on the street to investigate and deter environmental crimes. Now a governor and state environmental agency director were saying that Michigan could dispense with most enforcement and instead cooperate with socially minded businesses. But veterans of environmental enforcement saw this as simply a new label for an old wine. Michigan had encouraged and implored businesses to clean up from the turn of the twentieth century until the 1960s, with steadily worsening pollution—and cleanup bills costing taxpayers hundreds of millions of dollars—the result.

"The temptation to maximize profits by cutting corners will always be present. Some laws by their nature are very difficult to violate. Environmental laws are easier to violate, because it can be done without the workers in general or the local community being immediately aware of what's occurring," said William Murphy, the former head of the state's Environmental Investigations section, who retired in 1996.

"The whole issue of loyalty to a local community also enters into it," Murphy said. "As a society, we're choosing to place more of our well-being in the laps of business people than on the shoulders of government officials. In an increasingly competitive world, the temptation to save money wherever possible will become a central theme of corporate life."[14] Lana Pollack, the president of the Michigan Environmental Council, said Michigan would need to revive an enforcement program to do to pollution what public education and enforcement had done to drunk driving and spousal abuse in the 1980s and 1990s.

Michigan's tragic forest history haunted environmental advocates as the new century began, but the forest products industry discounted the applicability of its lessons to the present. In the late 1990s, responding to complaints from the industry about the failure of the state to make enough timber from state forests available for commercial harvest, members of the legislature from northern Michigan successfully proposed setting timber marking quotas for the Department of Natural Resources. The Sierra Club's Mackinac chapter objected to the new policy. "The timber industry seems to be asserting an entitlement to the woods all of us own," said the club's Anne Woiwode.[15] "It's an ironic and troubling posture, particularly because the industry has aggressively pursued this agenda through the hiring of many more lobbyists and more campaign contributions in recent years to push this message, along with cultivating their new, improved public image as stewards of the forests."

The industry was in fact working to improve its reputation, still colored by residual public memories of the slash-and-burn tactics of the late nineteenth century. In an article authored by *Detroit Free Press* editorial page editor Ron Dzwonkowski in late 1999, logger Earl St. John acknowledged, "Loggers have had a bad image." A contract logger in the vast Michigan forests owned by the Mead Paper Company, St. John added, "But we have gotten a lot smarter about what we do. Times have changed, people have changed, markets and equipment have changed." Dzwonkowski stressed Mead's sustainable forestry initiative, which replanted 3 million seedlings in 1999, as well as the high-technology cutting equipment used in the industry and the fact that better roads enabled loggers to commute to and from their workplace, rather than being "rowdies who live in isolated camps."[16] Brad Homeier, Mead's Upper Peninsula land manager, summarized the firm's forest philosophy: "Our object is to manage the forest so it's healthy and productive, just as much for future generations as for ours . . . but also to utilize the wood products we all need."[17]

Woiwode and the Sierra Club said the state forests should be managed primarily for ecosystem health and biodiversity, rather than as a resource for the timber industry. Sierra Club member Tim Flynn argued angrily against a proposed state forest timber sales mandate in 2000 of at least 855,000 cords, or 69,000 acres. He calculated that when lands off limits to logging were set aside, the mandate would result in a logged-over forest in 36 years. "This rate of cut exceeds the devastating overcutting at the turn of the century," Flynn said. "It's time for all of us to stand up and let our representatives know that the owners of these forests say, 'Never again.' We will not let our forest be devastated by overcutting a second time."[18] Professional forester Mike Moore, who served briefly as the director of the Department of Natural Resources in the 1990s, testified against the timber sales mandate at a legislative committee meeting in 2000. "I'm a timber-harvest guy," he told a reporter. "It makes me very uncomfortable to be on the same side as the Sierra Club on this. They're usually suing me instead of sitting with me. But you can't manage with a 50- or 100-year vision on the basis of two- or four year election cycles."[19] The unusual coalition of environmentalists and advocates for science-based management of state forests suggested a route toward a sensible state forest policy, one that would better balance timber harvest with conservation of forest ecosystems similar to the state's original forests. Such a policy would also reflect the public bias toward recreational and natural forest values.

But if future residents of the state shake their heads at the timidity and shortsightedness that characterized state policies in the year 2000 on toxic substances and forest management, they are sure to be simply outraged at the consumption of valuable lands in the 1970s and 1980s, which became gluttonous in the 1990s. As much the responsibility of millions of individuals as of their governments, the problem of land use was deeply rooted in the American attitudes that had shaped responses to Michigan's landscape since just before statehood. The speculators who profited from the purchase, division, and development of land did not scout their future investments on horseback like the speculators of the 1830s, but they reaped similarly huge dividends. Their market was an affluent class of land buyers, many of them seeking a retreat from the stresses of urban living to attain a personal version of the pastoral ideal. But their individual actions were accumulating in an altered landscape nobody could love.

For one thing, the state laws designed to protect critical and sensitive lands were failing to do the job. Responding to the clamor of local officials and neighborhoods for economic development, state natural resource regulators frequently permitted the nibbling to death of key ecosystems despite the laws. John Trimberger, a Department of Natural Resources fisheries biologist from 1969 to late 1997, remembered one illustrative case. A businessman applied to expand a small marina accommodating approximately 20 to 100 slips in a 100-acre marsh along the Grand River at Grand Haven. Several other small marinas already dotted the area and lower Spring Lake.

> We had substantial data from fish and wildlife surveys documenting the importance of this marsh. . . . [But] the decision was made by a deputy director in concurrence with the regional manager and assistant fisheries chief to issue a permit. We knew there was some politics involved but never did understand all of it—we weren't supposed to. Whatever the politics were they were big enough to get the feds to back off on any objections also. Now look at what you have. No marsh in that area of the river, more marinas in the lower Grand River and Spring Lake. . . . This is a prime example of what is good for the economics of a few—the communities, property owners, boat owners—is a total permanent loss for the environment. Fish don't spawn well on sheet piling, critters like frogs and turtles cannot access high ground, productive shallow water for zooplankton is lost, muskrats are gone.

Even more significant losses of habitats and open spaces resulted from both the absence of good land use planning and an insatiable appetite for development. "This used to all be farmland, from here to town there were not more than 20 houses," said Bud Wynings, who lived in South Lyon, 40 miles northwest of Detroit. He pointed to a row of homes, a new fire station, and a convenience store just beyond his farm. "But today, they can't build fast enough. And we can't handle it. We don't have the roads. We don't have the schools. They just keep coming out here."[20]

A planner who has observed the state's consumptive land use patterns since the 1970s, Mark Wyckoff, says:

> If we let these trends continue we will pass on to our children a state with fewer assets, higher public service costs, and more uncertainty than we inherited from our parents. It will have less open space and less natural appeal than the landscape of today. It will not be sustainable from an environmental or economic perspective. But if we embrace land stewardship as an ethic and sustainability as a principle around which to organize public policy, we will give our children and theirs a gift of immeasurable significance.[21]

"How *could* they have done that?" is the question many modern Michiganians ask about the devastation of the great Michigan forests in the second half of the 1800s. Future Michiganians may have the same thing to say about the conversion of land needed to grow food crops; of wetlands needed to filter pollutants and abate floods; of open spaces needed for recreation; of places needed to refresh aching souls; of healthy, functioning ecosystems.

The logging of the north woods did not advance without protests and warnings. Careful observers saw Michigan's future even before the peak of the logging boom. A new resident of Oceana County in the early 1870s, Charles W. Jay, recorded his impressions of the countryside in his generally whimsical book *My New Home in Northern Michigan*. But he turned off the humor as he looked about the west coast of Michigan.

> The founders of these embryo cities seem to contemplate the no distant day when their now villages will rival New York and Philadelphia in population and wealth. Muskegon takes in many square miles, and the lots in its only business street are held at $175 per foot. And yet, in less than ten years from now, the valuable timber of this region will have all disappeared, and the decay of the town will be as swift as its incidental prosperity.[22]

Predictions like Jay's attracted sneers from logging's boosters. How much different was their scoffing from the refrain of the Michigan Association of Home Builders in the 1990s? Calling land use the "non-crisis crisis," the association observed, "Much of the 'farmland' that is being converted to homes is land which may be growing weeds but precious little else. . . .[A]t the same time that we have more cropland in production we also have more land dedicated to open space through rural parks and wildlife areas." The association was correct in the narrowest sense, while ignoring the dangerous future consequences of the rapid conversion of open spaces. Timber volumes reached their peak in the same decades of the late 1800s in which a grim future was locked into place through the absence of replanting and careful harvest. Michigan's economy surged in the late 1900s as the *potential* of the land to support food production and to provide ecosystem services such as flood control and clean water was fast eroding. In both cases, the state was snatching prosperity from the future. As historian Bruce Catton said:

> [Michigan] is a state that grew up in the belief that abundance is forever. Men gabbled about inexhaustible forests and unlimited ores, right up to the moment when further self-deception became impossible. They adjusted their whole social structure to a force whose life span was similarly limited and kept from worrying unduly by increasing reliance on the faith that sustains the modern world—a faith not in the goodness of God, but in the endless ingenuity of man.[23]

Jay was wrong only in his estimate of the time it would take to reap the forest bonanza before decline began. Muskegon's lumber production peaked 13 years after the publication of Jay's book, and in 1895, 21 years after its publication, the city "was a mere fraction of its peak," lamented the *Muskegon Chronicle*. "The game was over and Muskegon paid the penalty of a wasted heritage."[24]

It is not possible to predict when the land development game in southern Michigan and in urban areas of the north will be over. But just like the whitefish in the Great Lakes and the white pine in the great forests, the supply of land is finite, not inexhaustible. Michigan has spent more than $1 billion since the 1980s to clean up groundwater and soils that private interests took from the public during decades of industrialization. The state may spend many more billions in the twenty-first century to create a "superfund" to peel commercial strip malls and mammoth homes off prime farmland, to unpave cement channels and replenish wetlands starved of water.

The long shadow of Henry Ford falls over any discussion of Michigan's environmental history. The automobile whose mass production Ford perfected powered the state to industrial greatness through most of the twentieth century. But he is an important study in another way. He reflects the colossally ambivalent attitude of Michiganians toward their place.

Ford was more than a shrewd, visionary industrial tycoon. He "was a conservationist who railed against the waste of wood as well as bird life."[25] To check the waste of wood, he promoted the production of Kingsford charcoal, turning scrap into a useful product. But the thoughtless disposal practices at the company's Upper Peninsula production site generated a waste far more dangerous than scrap wood—a toxic stew that was threatening neighbors of that site in the year 2000.

To check the waste of bird life, Ford allowed lands he owned in Dearborn to be managed as a bird sanctuary for a time, and 50 years after his death, the Ford estate was regarded as one of the prime birding spots in southeast Michigan. The estate itself became a model of ecological architecture for its time. Designed by the same Jens Jensen who encouraged Michigan parks pioneer Genevieve Gillette in her conservation work, Fair Lane contained appealing lawns and ponds, trees, and flowers. Its pulsing ecological heart was the Rouge River, dammed to supply hydropower to power Ford's home.

It was a lovely scene, indicative of a tender concern for at least a manicured nature. It was also no doubt for Ford a refreshing retreat from the quite different scene just a few miles downriver at his famous Rouge complex. There, by the time of his death in the late 1940s, more than 2.5 million tons of coal, 1.5 million tons of iron ore, 600,000 tons of sand—most of this from Michigan's scenic dunes—and 450,000 tons of limestone arrived annually. Enough gas to supply a city of 1.5 million population was used each day. Ninety acres of parking space made room for over 20,000 employee-owned cars. And the river that made it an ideal site for auto production was horribly abused.

A state water quality engineer who visited the Rouge 15 years later described a boat trip up the Detroit River: "When we turned into the Rouge River I was absolutely shocked by the sight of the water. About half of the Rouge was covered with a heavy black layer of oil. Where it wasn't covered with oil, the river water showed as a bright orange color that was caused by pickle liquor discharges." Turning to his companion, the man commented on how much work was to be done. The companion agreed but noted proudly that the orange color was actually an improvement. Fifteen years before, oil discharges had been so abundant that at one point the orange had been impossible to see under the black.[26]

The same Henry Ford who said one of his first memories was of a bird and its song and who built a bucolic retreat on a picturesque stream overlooked the ruin of the same river by his own Ford Motor Company. His ambivalence is ours. Caught between a profound pride in the land we inhabit and a conviction that it is ours to do with as we please, we lurch into the twenty-first century. Ruin or recovery is within our collective grasp.

Perhaps a people cannot be said to truly cherish a place until they have a central myth that links them to it. For this purpose, "myth" means the way in which we interpret and comprehend our common place in human society. What are the myths on which Michigan children are fed?

You can find one at the Hartwick Pines, that nearly last-of-its-kind scrap of virgin white pine northeast of Grayling. Park interpreters dress as lumberjacks and attempt to recreate an ancient day when brawny men heroically chopped giant trees in a primeval forest. An official state historical brochure declares:

> Here, visitors return to the state's nineteenth-century logging era, when thousands of men cut millions of board feet of lumber and Michigan led the nation in sawed lumber production. Within the forest visitor center and logging camp buildings, exhibits and period rooms tell the story of the loggers, rivermen and entrepreneurs who powered Michigan's white pine industry.

The color and drama of the lumberjack era deserve recognition as essential elements of Michigan's past. But what the brochure does not tell—and what the park scarcely mentions—is the stirring story of the state's forestry pioneers. While there are exhibits displaying the forest products made from

Michigan wood in the 1800s and today, there is scarcely a mention of the men and women who healed the damage caused by a 40-year spree of timber slaughter. W. J. Beal and Filibert Roth flank Gifford Pinchot, the first director of the U.S. Forest Service, in one exhibit celebrating Pinchot's doctrine of "wise use of natural resources."

But no brochure or exhibit celebrates conservation fighters Charles Garfield or W. B. Mershon; no park interpreter dresses as the flamboyant bear hunter turned preservationist James Oliver Curwood, out to avenge the theft of the state's riches of wildlife, fish, and north woods. Yet whose courage was greater? The destroyers of the woods were pursuing an accepted self-interest, while the forest healers were challenging the prevailing view that private benefit equaled—or trumped—public interest. One might object that the story of conservation is far too tame to turn into an object of historical curiosity and amusement, but the argument says more about the objector than it does about conservation. The work of conservation and environmental protection is inherently unpopular, at least at the start of each wave of action, and usually a matter of long odds.

Even a glassed display just outside the entrance to the Forest Visitor Center at the park falls short of capturing the passions that animated the early Michigan conservationists. It tells the sweet story of Karen Hartwick's purchase and donation of the remnant pines as a monument to her deceased husband, and it recognizes the contribution of Genevieve Gillette to the state park system. But it shears both Hartwick's and Gillette's actions of their context. Their work is explained as a gentle effort to preserve pieces of nature, rather than a blow against the prevailing ethic of resource consumption. The areas they worked and paid to protect are, pure and simple, off limits to development. The thought may be too daring even for the official Michigan view of the new century.

Hartwick Pines is a museum of a vanished landscape. By the time of its acquisition in 1927, Michigan was already sufficiently ashamed about the excesses of the logging era to set aside a small piece of what was. But the Michigan of 2000 is ignorantly destroying the last of some other native lands. The largest Michigan remnant of a "globally imperiled" natural community known as lake plain prairie, a tallgrass landscape in Brownstown Township of Wayne County, was in danger of becoming a golf course in 2000.[27] In 1999, a state legislator threatened to eliminate funding for the Michigan Natural Features Inventory, a scientific program housed in the Department of Natural Resources, because the inventory staff identified important plants on the site that might have stopped its development. The political ax has replaced the woodsman's.

Perhaps it is wrong to turn to state parks for the myths that will challenge a culture, just as it is clearly wrong to turn to elected officials for conservation leadership. State institutions can only express what is acceptable to the majority, and elected officials can only do what the powerful or numerous compel them to do. Big lumber owned the state capital in the 1880s; big manufacturing owned it in the 1940s and 1950s; big realty and home building in the 1990s. Lumber and manufacturing loosened their grip on the guardians of the public trust only when the conditions that had propelled them to power suffered wrenching change—and when conservation's peaceful citizen-soldiers rolled up their sleeves and went to work on the politicians.

But from where will the next set of peaceful soldiers come if there is not a myth to stir the public to send them into action?

There is abundant raw material out of which to fashion a myth of place that will bond the people to Michigan in a way that will assure our state's character endures. Before the arrival of the Europeans, a people lived on this same land in a way that enabled them, and it, to thrive. These natives occupied this ecosystem for approximately 12,000 years; the Europeans have been here but 350 years. Sentimentalism about a perfect past does not do the Native Americans justice. Flawed and frail just as all humans are, they still fashioned a way of being that generally lived within the bounds of what nature could bear. This was in part the result of a myth, or myths, that placed them securely in their home. The Ojibwa people, for example, had a legend of a bird created by the Great Spirit who flew high over the earth westward from the Atlantic until landing on a hill overlooking Sault Ste. Marie and finding a pleasing prospect and abundant whitefish in the foaming rapids. The legend's loving description of this new place and the creatures and spirits who inhabited it was an allegory of the Ojibwa migration and of their satisfaction in the place they had found.[28] Neither a tale of conquest nor a legend of a pristine, uninhabited wilderness, it serves the purpose of ratifying and supporting a wholesome and sustaining relationship between a people and their home. Ejecting this people and occupying their land, the Europeans sought to dominate both.

Still, the descendants of those Europeans possess the makings of our own Michigan legend. It cannot begin in innocence; our ancestors' first vision of this land was as greedy as admiring, founded in part on a dream of limitless material wealth. But the very ashes of the first wave of Michigan destruction provided the setting for one of the most famous stories in American letters, Ernest Hemingway's "Big Two-Hearted River." Stepping off a train in the fire-ravaged town of Seney in the Upper Peninsula, World War I veteran Nick Adams finds a landscape that reflects his own desolation. Only the stone foundation of the Mansion House hotel remains from the scorched town. But the river endures, running through the ruins, a stream populated by gorgeous trout.

Nick tramps away from Seney into a landscape of stumps and remnant trees, finding his stopping place along the Two-Hearted River and performing the comforting rituals of setting up camp. The next day, after landing a big trout using grasshoppers as lures, he sits down to a contented lunch. He observes the scene while smoking a cigarette.

Ahead the river narrowed and went into a swamp. The river became smooth and deep and the swamp looked solid with cedar trees, their trunks close

*together, their branches solid. It would not be possible to walk through a swamp
like that. The branches grew so low. You would have to keep almost level with
the ground to move at all. You could not crash through the branches. That must
be why the animals that lived in swamps were built the way they were.*

During Nick's time in the "wild" Michigan—much of it horribly altered
by logging and fire, yet somehow unspoiled—he begins to furnish his barren
interior landscape, as if he is taking pieces of the river and swamp and stump
lands and woods into himself. Nick feels at home in the place he has chosen
to re-create himself.

Nick Adams must recover from a war. So must we, and so must the land
with which we have warred for two centuries.

It is not too late to provide for our future, as the conservationists and environmentalists provided for the future we now inhabit. The increasing success
of Michigan's local land conservancies in securing biologically significant
lands and open spaces is the start of an endowment.[29] The slowly building
public concern about land consumption adds to its principal. But the people,
working through government, must support bolder steps.

The state must take action before it is too late to protect the last remaining intact ecosystems and the species that depend on them. Former DNR
director Gordon Guyer calls resort and summer home development "the
breaking up of the north." It will be far more difficult to piece together frag-
mented landscapes than to preserve undivided land. A proposal in the 1980s
to create a national river park protecting the entire watershed of the Two-
Hearted River foundered because a few Upper Peninsula development advocates opposed the intrusion on marginal logging operations in the area. They
convinced local U.S. representative Robert Davis to express anger about the
idea. Conceived by National Park Service director William Penn Mott, the
plan would have protected over 120,000 acres in the first ecosystem-based
park in the United States.[30] Although Hemingway's Two-Hearted River story
actually describes the Fox River to the south, park proponents believed the
name of the watershed alone would attract tourists and recreationists. The
land is still available, if the will exists to secure it for posterity. Other large
northern preserves protecting the Keweenaw Peninsula and northern Lake
Huron shores are possible. With proper care, individuals and communities
surrounding these preserves can derive economic return from tourism, carefully managed timber harvest, and other resource-based development.

Even more critical is the protection of the last remaining scraps of some
of Michigan's native ecosystems, now under intense pressure in the southern
half of the Lower Peninsula.[31] It was long ago too late to protect the extinct
oak savannas of southwest lower Michigan. The state should immediately create the landscape equivalent of Noah's ark, acquiring and protecting at least
two additional viable examples of such vanishing native ecosystems as the
lake plain prairie, salt marsh, and Great Lakes marsh. The public steward of
this irreplaceable ark should be a new division of nature reserves in the state

Department of Natural Resources—a division whose mission is the conservation and protection of sensitive lands. The establishment of such a division would mark Michigan's maturity, signaling that public lands have values besides logging, wildlife production, and recreation.

Further, because short-term political concerns often thwart preservation efforts by the legislature, the governor of Michigan, like the president of the United States, should possess a new statutory authority to proclaim areas of public land monuments permanently off limits to development because of their scientific or historic significance. These Michigan monuments will serve the people of the state down through time. Like the Hartwick Pines and Porcupine Mountains, they will furnish future generations important examples of what Michigan once was and prevent a repetition of thoughtless destruction.

Restoring degraded lands is the vital work of the generation to come, but providing the necessary tools is today's task. In the late 1980s, Department of Natural Resources director David Hales called for "creating" 500,000 acres of wetlands, a goal possible only through restoration of drained or converted farms. Robert Grese, an associate professor of landscape architecture at the University of Michigan, says:

> Not all lands are equally restorable and in many parts of the state—particularly in the rapidly growing areas in southeast Michigan—we may be the last generation with the option of restoring many lands. We need to make sure we maintain the raw materials for restoring lands and aquatic systems in the future, and this means saving many of the small remnants where vestiges of our native vegetation and at least some of the fauna remain.[32]

Citizens should support efforts of the Department of Natural Resources to knock down some of Michigan's hundreds of dams, freeing more and more of our rivers to run again untrammeled as they have through most of their existence.

Even these public efforts will not be enough. A private change of heart will be necessary.

For one thing, Michigan's conservationists and environmentalists, weakened by their divisions since the 1970s, will need to reconcile if they are to restore the state's national leadership. The diversity of the movement, once a strength, had become a liability by the end of the twentieth century. Politicians were often able to ignore both conservationists and environmentalists as the latter groups fought among themselves or focused on local issues at the expense of the systematic statewide abuse and neglect of the environment. Said Eric Sharp, outdoor editor for the *Detroit Free Press:* "All hunters should be strong environmentalists and recognize that the woods and waters aren't a giant game farm or aquarium where they can kill things. And all environmentalists, whether they hunt or not, must recognize that in these days of hugely expanded human populations and loss of natural habitat, many wildlife populations must be managed."

A change of heart must also occur in the daily thinking and acting of millions of Michigan citizens. This will not happen easily. So much of modern American life conspires against it. Tanya Cabala, director of the Muskegon office of the Lake Michigan Federation, observed:

Our lifestyle is simply too fast and more than that, too complicated. We've engineered a lifestyle that truly stops us from gaining a deeper knowledge and appreciation of the connections we have to our natural environment. We have the latest technology. We're outside very little. Always in cars or in our comfortable offices or homes, with heat, hot water, and such luxury compared to the rest of the world. The effects of abuse are unseen, unknown or easy to dismiss.

Ecological education that begins early in life is the answer most likely to succeed, said Cabala, who remained optimistic that Michigan citizens would rise to the challenge.[33]

The strategy to rally them can take its cue from the recent past, according to Joan Wolfe, the founder of the West Michigan Environmental Action Council. Arguing that environmental problems gravely threatened future generations, Wolfe said in 2000:

Environmentalists must lead the way. It is not enough to scholarly educate; we must also grab people with the facts and tell them what they can do. We need to enlist the aid of scientists and physicians. We must spend much more time communicating with all kinds of groups—professional, educational, religious, recreational, racial and ethnic. We must include students, especially college and university students with all their energy. As in the 70's, we need to enlist all of them to work for their own destiny, for without that army of truly concerned citizens, we wield little power.[34]

Further evidence to support the optimism of Cabala and Wolfe is displayed in numerous battles waged by Michigan citizens to protect special local places that awaken their fierce loyalty. A grassroots organization called Friends of the Crystal River organized in 1986 to protect the sensitive stream and adjacent lands near Sleeping Bear Dunes National Lakeshore from a proposed golf course and housing development; in 2000, the organization had successfully blocked government approvals for development of the scenic watershed and was still fighting the developer. Far away in Trenton and Gibraltar in southeast Michigan, a group calling itself Friends of Humbug Marsh was battling a developer to protect the last major stretch of undeveloped U.S. shoreline along the Detroit River. Federal officials had denied permission for a golf course and housing project near the marsh and on Humbug Island, but the developer continued to challenge the ruling. In these and dozens of other struggles across the state, dentists, lawyers, businessmen and businesswomen, educators, and others were volunteering their time to guard a place they loved.

For many Michiganians and Michigan visitors, such a personal identification with the land dawns in the benign days of a childhood imagination. It began that way for a man named Aldo Leopold, the thoughtful teacher of a new American land ethic in the first half of the twentieth century. Like later children of the automobile era, he left urban comforts to taste the summer wonders of Michigan's north. In the 1890s, he accompanied his Iowa family on August trips to Marquette Island, in Les Cheneaux Islands at the northern end of Lake Huron. "The train ride from Chicago to Mackinaw City took all night," writes Leopold's biographer, Curt Meine.[35]

> When the family awoke and looked out the windows, they found themselves in the recently cutover northwoods. Young scrub forests of jack pine, aspen, and paper birch grew up in the lands where the slash fires had burned. On the farmsteads that dotted the gaunt landscape, farmers fenced their fields not with barbed wire, but with the massive, upturned stumps of the old white pines.

On Marquette Island, the destination of the Leopolds, there were tennis courts, a golf course, and a clubhouse, but there was also good fishing for smallmouth bass, pike, and brook trout. There were a rugged shoreline, stark rock, and a view to the Upper Peninsula mainland and the north country beyond. Leopold sometimes rode with his father to the mainland to hunt ruffed grouse and to fish for trout. He dreamed of finding a river beyond the northern horizon and paddling a canoe to the faraway, mysterious sub-Arctic north. The young Leopold felt summer yield to fall on the island. He no doubt felt there the stinging, exhilarating raw wind of the first autumn storm, low clouds scudding out of the northwest streaming cold rain as geese rose making their wild cry.

Something about Leopold's experience of Michigan is expressed in his famous *Sand County Almanac*. The sand counties of Wisconsin, like the sand lands of northern Michigan, had suffered the exploitation of their virgin timber and the privations that followed. With quiet bitterness, Leopold wrote of a lethal blow to some of the last wildness that remained, the Flambeau River, dammed to create power for agriculture. "Perhaps our grandsons, having never seen a wild river, will never miss the chance to set a canoe in singing waters," he lamented.

But he also prescribed a cure for what ailed the Wisconsin of his time and the Michigan of 2000: "It is inconceivable to me that an ethical relation to land can exist without love, respect and admiration for land, and a high regard for its value. By value, I mean of course something far broader than mere economic value; I mean value in the philosophical sense."

The state called Michigan is a construct of humankind, not something natural. It embraces dozens of small ecosystems and is divided not only by the Straits of Mackinac but also by a boundary almost as sharp as any drawn by governments. The "tension zone" that slices across the center of the Lower Peninsula marks the transition between what was once a northern forest of hardwoods and conifers and a southern landscape of oak forest, savanna, and prairie. Today that line is familiar to Michiganians as a boundary between productive agriculture lands and the great northern forests. Despite over 150 years of settlement and development, this division is still indelible. Attitudes of citizens above and below the line toward the proper role of government in protecting land and the best use of that land also differ. Yet all profess a loyalty to Michigan. No one who has exulted in the touch of south winds in a Michigan spring or north winds in fall, heard the deafening chorus of spring peepers bursting from wetlands, or glimpsed a vista of endless blue waters can ever extinguish that loyalty from the heart.

Emerging from a century in which economic values triumphed over all others, the people of Michigan have a difficult mission in trying to form an allegiance to their place that is based on more than money. Yet they possess all the tools they need to accomplish the task. They have the cautionary lessons of a rapacious past. They have the inspiration of our conservation and environmental pioneers, who were stirred by an anger and a passion born of love for the place they inhabited. They have a connection deepening with time. And they are surrounded by a ravishingly beautiful land. They have demonstrated for the 100 years a growing affection for it.

The Michiganians of the new century live in exciting times. The business of protecting an entire land, like the business of protecting natural areas and rare species in the 1950s, is about to become a "big deal." It is a work worthy of the place that compels it.

Notes

Chapter 1

1. Henry R. Schoolcraft, *Narrative Journal of Travels Through the Northwestern Regions of the United States Extending from Detroit through the Great Chain of American Lakes to the Sources of the Mississippi River in the Year 1820*, ed. Mentor L. Williams (East Lansing: Michigan State College Press, 1953).

2. Schoolcraft had visited the Arkansas Ozarks in 1818–19.

3. Sylvestor W. Higgins, deputy surveyor, from land surveyor's notes quoted in frontispiece to Michigan Department of Natural Resources, Michigan Natural Features Inventory, *Michigan's Native Landscape, as Interpreted from the General Land Office Surveys 1816–1856*, Patrick J. Comer, Dennis A. Albert, H. A. Wells, B. L. Hart, Jodi B. Raab, D. L. Price, D. M. Kashian, Richard A. Corner, and D. W. Schuen (Lansing, 1995).

4. George Clark, "Recollections," *Pioneer Collections*, Report of the Pioneer Society of the State of Michigan (1876), 501.

5. John Nowlin, *The Bark Covered House*, ed. Milo M. Quaife (reprint, Chicago: Lakeside Press, 1937).

6. John M. Gordon, "Michigan Journal, 1836," ed. Douglas H. Gordon and George S. May, *Michigan History* (September 1959): 277.

7. Robert C. Kedzie, "Pioneer and Professional Life in Michigan," Historical Collections, Michigan Pioneer and Historical Society (1901), 528.

8. Dennis A. Albert, Michigan Natural Features Inventory, personal communication, August 26, 1999.

9. Gordon, "Michigan Journal, 1836," 266, 287.

10. Bela Hubbard, *Memorials of a Half-Century in Michigan and the Lake Region* (New York, 1888), 231.

11. Michigan Department of Natural Resources, Michigan Natural Features Inventory, *Michigan's Native Landscape as Interpreted from the General Land Office Surveys 1816–1856* (1995), 13.

12. Rollin H. Baker, *Michigan Mammals* (East Lansing: Michigan State University Press, 1983), 622.

13. Helen Hornbeck Tanner, ed., *Atlas of Great Lakes Indian History* (Oklahoma City: University of Oklahoma Press, 1987), 96.

14. The Michigan Natural Features Inventory, housed in the state Department of Natural Resources in 1999, is a scientific canvass of the state's animal and plant species, communities, and landscapes.

15. Willis F. Dunbar, *Michigan: A History of the Wolverine State,* 3d rev. ed. by George S. May (Grand Rapids, MI: William B. Eerdmans, 1995), 157.

16. Madison Kuhn, "Tiffin, Morse, and the Reluctant Pioneer," *Michigan History* (June 1966): 113.

17. Michigan Employment Security Commission, *Michigan Statistical Abstract 1996* (Ann Arbor: University of Michigan Press, 1996).

18. The following description is chiefly drawn from information compiled by the Michigan Natural Features Inventory, Michigan Department of Natural Resources.

19. De La Mothe, "Description of the River of Detroit by M. De La Mothe, the Commandant There," October 5, 1701, Historical Collections, vol. 33, Michigan Pioneer and Historical Society (1904), 111.

20. Hubbard, *Memorials,* 5–6.

21. John Harris Forster, "Early Settlement of the Copper Regions of Lake Superior," Pioneer Society of Michigan (1884), 181–82.

22. Alexis de Tocqueville, "A Fortnight in the Wilderness," in *The Making of Michigan, 1820–1860,* ed. Justin L. Kestenbaum (Detroit: Wayne State University Press, 1990), 41–42.

Chapter 2

1. Nowlin, *Bark Covered House,* 7.

2. Gordon, "Michigan Journal, 1836," 284.

3. Michigan House of Representatives, *Report of the State Geologist, January 26, 1838,* H. Doc. 24.

4. Michigan State Board of Fish Commissioners, *First Report of the State Commissioners and Superintendent on State Fisheries for 1873–74, Ending December 1, 1874* (1875), appendix.

5. Dunbar, *Michigan: A History of the Wolverine State,* 263.

6. Michigan Department of Natural Resources, Fisheries Division, *Michigan Fisheries Centennial Report, 1873–1973,* Fisheries Management Report 6 (1973), 49.

7. Michigan Department of Natural Resources, Fisheries Division, *Michigan Fisheries Centennial Report, 1873–1973* (1973), 51.

8. Michigan State Board of Fish Commissioners, *Ninth Report of State Fish Commissioners* (1888).

9. Michigan State Board of Fish Commissioners, *Thirteenth Biennial Report of State Fish Commissioners* (1898).

10. James W. Milner, "Fisheries of the Great Lakes," in *Report of U.S. Commissioner of Fish and Fisheries, 1872–1873* (1874), 19.

11. Michigan Department of Natural Resources, Fisheries Division, *Michigan Fisheries Centennial Report,* 59.

12. "Will Fight! Gov. Pingree Has Taken up the Fishery Squabble," *Detroit Free Press,* January 17, 1897.

13. William B. Mershon, *Recollections of My Fifty Years Hunting and Fishing* (Boston: Stratford, 1923): 168–69.

14. L. D. Norris, cited in Mershon, *Recollections,* 178.

15. Mershon, *Recollections,* 172.

16. De La Mothe, "Description of the River," 111.

17. Eugene T. Petersen, "The Michigan Sportsmen's Association: A Pioneer in Game Conservation," *Michigan History* (December 1953).

18. Reginald Sharkey, *The Blue Meteor: The Tragic Story of the Passenger Pigeon* (Petoskey, MI: Little Traverse Historical Society, 1997), 5.

19. Henry B. Roney, in *The Passenger Pigeon,* ed. William B. Mershon (New York: Outing Publishing, 1907), 89. First published in *American Field,* January 11, 1879.

20. Eugene T. Petersen, "Passenger Pigeons and Stool Pigeons," *Michigan Alumnus Quarterly Review,* May 26, 1956, 265.

21. Barbara E. Benson, *Logs and Lumber: The Development of the Lumber Industry in Michigan's Lower Peninsula, 1837–1870* (Mount Pleasant: Clarke Historical Library, Central Michigan University, 1989), 160.

22. *Michigan Lumberman* 1, no. 1 (February 1873): 7.

23. David Ward, *The Autobiography of David Ward* (privately printed, 1912). Kedzie letter, dated August 16, 1900, printed as illustration after p. 62.

24. Ward, *Autobiography,* 77.

25. Dunbar, *Michigan: A History of the Wolverine State,* 340.

26. Rolland H. Maybee, "Michigan's White Pine Era, 1840–1900," *Michigan History* (December 1959): 403.

27. C. A. Harper, quoted in Forest B. Meek, *Michigan's Timber Battleground: A History of Clare County 1674–1900* (published in conjunction with the Clare County Bicentennial Historical Committee, 1976), 105.

28. *Northwestern Lumberman,* March 18, 1882, 5.

29. Maybee, "Michigan's White Pine Era," 418.

30. Irene M. Hargreaves and Harold M. Foehl, *The Story of Logging the White Pine in the Saginaw Valley* (Bay City, MI: Red Keg Press, 1964), 43.

31. William Cronon, *Nature's Metropolis: Chicago and the Great West* (New York: W. W. Norton, 1990), 180.

32. "The Lumber Region of Michigan," *North American Review* (July 1868): 94.

33. "Lumber Region of Michigan," 95.

34. Michigan Department of Natural Resources, Fisheries Division, *Manistee River Assessment,* by Thomas J. Rozich, Special Report 21 (June 1998), 34.

35. "Lumber Region of Michigan," 77–103.

36. "Depleted Forests," *Northwest Lumberman,* February 7, 1880, 5.

37. "Very Big Timber Cut Is Expected," *Sunday Mining Gazette,* October 7, 1906.

38. U.S. Department of Agriculture, *Lumber Cut of the United States, 1870–1920,* by R. V. Reynolds and Albert H. Pierson (1923), 30–33.

39. " 'Roarin' Jimmie' Gleason, One of Old School of 'Jacks, Gone," *Marquette Daily Mining Journal,* April 21, 1927.

40. "Wellington R. Burt: His Story Continues Long after His Death," *Saginaw News,* April 18, 1948.

41. James Cooke Mills, *History of Saginaw County, Michigan,* rev. ed. (Saginaw: Seeman and Peters, 1918), 748.

42. U.S. Department of Agriculture, *The Economic Aspects of Forest Destruction in Northern Michigan,* by William N. Sparhawk and Warren D. Brush, Technical Bulletin 92 (January 1929), 9–10.

43. U.S. Department of Agriculture, *Economic Aspects of Forest Destruction,* 7.

44. Harold Titus, *Timber* (New York: Small, Maynard, 1922), 27–28.

Chapter 3

1. Michigan Senate, 1859, S. Doc. 4, 5–6.

2. Michigan Senate, *Journal of the Senate,* January 20, 1859, 133.

3. Stephen Fox, *John Muir and His Legacy: The American Conservation Movement* (Boston: Little, Brown), 60.

4. *Transactions of the Michigan Sportsmen's Association for the Protection of Fish, Game, and Birds,* fourth annual session, January 21–23, 1879.

5. Eugene T. Petersen, "The History of Wildlife Conservation in Michigan, 1859–1921" (Ph.D. diss., University of Michigan, 1952), 25. Petersen's thesis is an invaluable source of information on the work of the association and early fish and game conservation efforts in Michigan.

6. Petersen, "Michigan Sportsmen's Association," 365.

7. William B. Mershon Collection, Michigan Historical Collections, University of Michigan, reported in Eugene Petersen, "The Michigan Sportsmen's Association: A Pioneer in Game Conservation," *Michigan History* (December 1953): 368.

8. William Alden Smith to Honorable Cyrus G. Luce, March 26, 1887, State Archives of Michigan.

9. William Alden Smith to Honorable Cyrus G. Luce, April 2, 1887, State Archives of Michigan.

10. *Kalamazoo Gazette,* January 13, 1888.

11. William Alden Smith, *First Biennial Report of the State Game and Fish Warden* (Lansing, 1889), 6.

12. William B. Mershon to Honorable John T. Rich, April 21, 1894, State Archives of Michigan.

13. Charles S. Hampton to Honorable John T. Rich, November 2, 1893, State Archives of Michigan.

14. Charles S. Hampton to Major A. P. Loomis, Executive Office, October 26, 1894, State Archives of Michigan.

15. Petersen, "History of Wildlife Conservation in Michigan," 102.

16. Robert M. Warner, *Chase Salmon Osborn, 1860–1949* (Ann Arbor: University of Michigan Press, 1960), 8.

17. Warner, *Chase Salmon Osborn,* 8.

18. *Detroit Journal,* July 4, 1895.

19. Chase Osborn, *Fifth Biennial Report, State Game and Fish Warden* (Lansing, 1897), 12.

20. Grand Rapids Gun Club to His Excellency Cyrus G. Luce, March 22, 1889, State Archives of Michigan.

21. Honorable L. W. Watkins, state senator, remarks, Minutes of the Fourth Annual Meeting of the Michigan Association for the Protection and Propagation of Fish and Game, September 14, 1910, 35.

Chapter 4

1. Frederick Starr Jr., "American Forests: Their Destruction and Preservation," *Report of the Commissioner of Agriculture for the Year 1865* (1866), cited in Donald J. Pisani, "Forests and Conservation, 1865–1890," *Journal of American History* 72 (September 1985): 343.

2. Michigan House of Representatives, *Documents Accompanying the Journal*

of the House of Representatives of the State of Michigan at the Regular Session of 1867, H. Doc. 6, 13.

3. Robert C. Kedzie, *Address to Livingston County Agricultural Society, October 11, 1867,* Michigan State University Archives.

4. "Timber Waste a National Suicide," *Scientific American* (February 12, 1876), quoted in Donald J. Pisani, "Forests and Conservation, 1865–1890," *Journal of American History* 72 (September 1985): 351.

5. Mary Emily Schroeder, *The Charles W. Garfield Story* (Grand Rapids: Serfling, 1977), 7.

6. Michigan, Public Act 259 (1887).

7. *The Great Fires: Selections for Portrait and Biographical Album of Huron County, 1884* (Port Austin Township Library, 1969), 4.

8. Professor Emeritus Leigh J. Young, "Pioneering in Forestry in Michigan" (paper presented to the Washtenaw County Historical Society, February 1960).

9. Michigan State Forestry Commission, *First Report of the Directors of the State Forestry Commission of Michigan for the Years 1887 and 1888* (1888), 21.

10. Michigan State Forestry Commission, *First Report of the Directors for the Years 1887 and 1888,* 31.

11. *Grand Rapids Daily Democrat,* January 28, 1888.

12. Michigan Bureau of Labor and Industrial Statistics, *Arbor Day at the Michigan Agricultural College,* Fourteenth Annual Report (1897), 334–43.

13. Garfield may have been the designer of the commission's stationery, which included statements that the panel "stands for a rational solution of the most important economic problem before the people of Michigan" and that among other things, the "unparalleled beauty of our state" was at stake. Much of the destruction of the original forest of Michigan, among the finest in the world, was "inexcusable waste," according to another statement printed on the stationery.

14. Michigan House of Representatives, *Journal of the House of Representatives,* May 28, 1901, 2378.

15. Michigan State College Agricultural Experiment Station, *The Land Nobody Wanted,* by Harold Titus (1945), Special Bulletin 132, 17.

16. Michigan Forestry Commission, *First Annual Report of the Michigan Forestry Commission for the Year 1900* (1901), 13–14, 17.

17. Michigan Forestry Commission, *A Little Talk about Michigan Forestry* (1900), 9–10.

18. Stanley Fontana, "History of the Department of Conservation," manuscript, State Archives of Michigan, 94.

19. *Roscommon News,* May 21, 1902.

20. Michigan Forestry Commission, *Report of the Michigan Forestry Commission for the Years 1903–4* (1905), 17.

21. Michigan Forestry Commission, *Report of the Michigan Forestry Commission for the Year 1902* (1903), 103.

22. Samuel T. Dana, "Filibert Roth: Master Teacher," *Michigan Alumnus Quarterly Review,* February 26, 1955.

23. "Yearly Report of the Warden of Forest Reserves," in *Report of the Michigan Forestry Commission for the Years 1903–4,* Michigan Forestry Commission (1905), 23.

24. Professor Filibert Roth, "What the State Should Do and Why It Should Do

It Now," in *Report of the Michigan Forestry Commission for the Years 1903–4,* Michigan Forestry Commission (1905), 80–96.

25. *Proceedings of a Conference of Governors in the White House, Washington, D.C., May 13–15, 1908* (Washington, DC: Government Printing Office, 1909), 331.

26. Samuel P. Hays, *Conservation and the Gospel of Efficiency: The Progressive Conservation Movement, 1890–1920* (Cambridge, MA: Harvard University Press, 1959), 132.

27. Michigan Commission of Inquiry, *Report of Commission of Inquiry, Tax Lands and Forestry* (1908), 13.

28. "Michigan Has Lost $5,753,578 on the Tax Lands," *Detroit News,* May 12, 1909.

29. Michigan Commission of Inquiry, quoted in Michigan House of Representatives, *Report of the Special Committee on State Tax Lands* (1909), 24.

30. U.S. Department of Agriculture, *Economic Aspects of Forest Destruction,* 14.

31. Frederick W. Newton to Governor Fred M. Warner, April 15, 1909, State Archives of Michigan.

32. Michigan Senate, *Journal of the Senate,* April 22, 1909, 788.

33. Frederick W. Newton to Governor Fred M. Warner, May 14, 1909, State Archives of Michigan.

34. Charles Garfield to William B. Mershon, October 30, 1908, Mershon Collection.

35. William B. Mershon to J. H. Bissell, May 3, 1909, Mershon Collection.

36. Pierce had, in his biennial report for 1908, suggested that the benefits of the 1908 fire in clearing lands might actually have exceeded the damage done (although he did not calculate the value of lives lost.) He said exaggerated death counts and damage estimates had been issued "for political effect." His calculations were challenged by the U.S. Forest Service, which pegged the total damage at more than $28 million.

37. *Detroit News,* May 13, 1909.

38. Charles Garfield to William B. Mershon, May 7, 1909, Mershon Collection.

39. Michigan Senate, *Journal of the Senate,* May 22, 1909, 1343.

40. This would largely have been of symbolic value, since the Public Domain Commission also absorbed the Forestry Commission under the new law.

41. Draft letter on Michigan Forestry Commission stationery dated May 18, 1909, Mershon Collection.

42. "The state tax lands crowd in the State House and in the legislative halls surrendered this morning," the *Detroit News* reported on May 19, pointing out that the new commission could expand the forest reserve without limit and that patronage was under its control, not the governor's.

Chapter 5

1. Earl E. Kleinschmidt, "Pioneer Sanitarians in Michigan," *Journal of the Michigan State Medical Society* (August 1939).

2. Ibid.

3. Robert C. Kedzie, "The Use of Poisons in Agriculture," in *State Board of*

Health, Report of Secretary for 1875–1876, Michigan State Board of Health (1877), 13–25.

4. Michigan State Board of Health, *Report of the State Board of Health for Fiscal 1874* (1875), 136.

5. Report of the Committee on the Pollution of Water Supplies, Appointed by the American Public Health Association (presented at the annual meeting, Milwaukee, WI, November 20–23, 1888), 1.

6. "Death in the Water: Is the Element We Drink Decimating the People?" *Detroit Free Press*, March 11, 1887.

7. Michigan State Board of Health, *Sixth Annual Report of the State Board of Health of the State of Michigan* (1878), 10.

8. *Attorney General, ex. Rel. Township of Wyoming, v. City of Grand Rapids*, 175 Michigan Reports 513–14 (May 1913).

9. *Attorney General v. City of Grand Rapids*, 534–35.

10. "The Sewage Muddle," *Grand Rapids News*, May 29, 1913.

11. O'Ryan Rickard, *A Just Verdict: The Life of Caroline Bartlett Crane* (Kalamazoo: New Issues Press, Western Michigan University, 1994).

12. Caroline Bartlett Crane, "Municipal Housekeeping," in *Proceedings of Baltimore City-Wide Congress, March 8–10, 1911*.

13. Opinion of sanitary experts cited in International Joint Commission, *Final Report of the International Joint Commission on the Pollution of Boundary Waters, Reference,* 21 (1918).

14. Mary Durfee and Susan T. Bagley, "Bacteriology and Diplomacy in the Great Lakes, 1912–1920" (paper presented at the 1997 biennial meeting of the American Society for Environmental History, Michigan Technological University, Houghton), 10.

15. Michigan State Board of Health, *Forty-Fourth and Forty-Fifth Annual Report of the Secretary of the State Board of Health of the State of Michigan for the Fiscal Years Ending June 30, 1916 and June 30, 1917* (1917), 38–39.

16. Michigan Bureau of Engineering, quoted in Michigan State Board of Health, *Forty-Ninth and Fiftieth Annual Report of the Commissioner of the Michigan Department of Health for the Fiscal Years Ending June 30, 1921 and June 30, 1922* (1922), 19–21.

17. *Traverse City Record Eagle*, March 31, 1927.

Chapter 6

1. Samuel P. Hays, *Conservation and the Gospel of Efficiency: The Progressive Conservation Movement, 1890–1920* (Cambridge, MA: Harvard University Press, 1959), 141.

2. Sierra Club, written statement for the White House conservation conference, 1908, quoted in Stephen Fox, *John Muir and His Legacy: The American Conservation Movement* (Boston: Little, Brown), 130.

3. "George Shiras, III, Father of Wildlife Photography," *Naturalist* (spring 1960).

4. Jefferson Butler, *The History, Work, and Aims of the Michigan Audubon Society* (Detroit: Michigan Audubon Society, 1907), 7.

5. Ibid, 8.

6. Edith C. Munger, "The Michigan Audubon Society," *Michigan History* 2 (1918): 330–40.

7. Butler, *History of the Michigan Audubon Society*, 48.

8. "A Brief Sketch of Conservation Activities of Edith C. Munger, President of Michigan Audubon Society," Edith Munger Papers, Michigan Historical Collections, University of Michigan.

9. Munger estimated that in 1914 she spoke in 36 locations to 86 groups and reached 11,359 people. In 1926 she estimated that she spoke to Michigan audiences containing more than 84,000 people.

10. Helen Augur Gilliland, interview by author, January 28, 2000.

11. Kathleen Longcore, *Chadwick-Munger: The Story of a House* (Oceana County Historical Society, 1986), 19.

12. *Detroit News*, January 2, 1929.

13. Charles Hoyt to Edith Munger, January 15, 1918, Edith Munger Papers.

14. Edith Munger, "Story of the State Bird Contest," *Michigan History* (April 1930): 268–75.

15. Lena L. Mautner, "Conservation," *Club Woman*, Detroit Federation of Women's Clubs (November 1913).

16. James Oliver Curwood, "Thou Shalt Not Kill—," *American Magazine* (December 1927).

17. Michigan, Public Act 17 (1921). The statute also called upon the department "to prevent the destruction of timber by fire or otherwise; to promote the reforesting of nonagricultural lands belonging to the state; to guard against the pollution of lakes and streams within the state; and to foster and encourage the protecting and propagating of game and fish."

18. James Oliver Curwood to Albert Stoll Jr., September 8, 1921, James Oliver Curwood Papers, Michigan Historical Collections, University of Michigan.

19. *Flint Daily Journal*, December 11, 1921.

20. James Oliver Curwood to John Baird, December 24, 1921, Curwood Papers.

21. Edward G. Weeks, "Game Conservation in Michigan," *Michigan Sportsman* (February 1922): 20–21.

22. Filibert Roth to James Oliver Curwood, December 17, 1921, Curwood Papers.

23. "Political Bunglers Rule State's Conservation Work, Says Curwood," *Grand Rapids Herald*, November 26, 1922; "Urges Ouster of Baird, Stoll," *Detroit Free Press*, December 27, 1922.

24. *Escanaba Daily Press*, December 4, 1926.

25. James Oliver Curwood to Matheson, January 20, 1927, Curwood Papers.

26. Kenneth S. Lowe, "Curwood," *Michigan Out-of-Doors* (August–September 1977).

27. James Oliver Curwood to Lee Smits, quoted in Judith A. Eldredge, *James Oliver Curwood: God's Country and the Man* (Bowling Green: Bowling Green State University Popular Press, 1993), 222.

28. Although virtually all of the surrounding lands were logged over by the end of the nineteenth century, the small virgin white pine tract that would become the core of the preserved area escaped the ax and saw because of an 1893 depression, the relative youth of the trees in the stand when compared to those on surrounding

acres, and mounting public sentiment for a park including the pines, according to the state park historian, Wil Shapton.

29. *Bay City Sunday Times,* April 23, 1933.

Chapter 7

1. Genevieve Gillette, handwritten autobiography, Genevieve Gillette Papers, Michigan Historical Collections, University of Michigan.

2. Genevieve Gillette, oral history interview with Patricia M. Frank, November 9, 1971 through March 30, 1972, Gillette Papers.

3. Christopher Graham, interview with author, October 1, 1999. Graham served as Gillette's guardian late in her life.

4. Christopher Graham, personal communication, September 23, 1999.

5. Mackinac Island had been established as a national park in 1875, only three years after the creation of the first such park, Yellowstone. The federal government transferred the island to state control as a park in 1895, and Fort Michilimackinac on the Lower Peninsula mainland was added to the park in 1904.

6. Claire V. Korn, *Yesterday through Tomorrow: Michigan State Parks* (East Lansing: Michigan State University Press, 1989), 14.

7. "Michigan: The Ideal Summers Resort for Tourists," *Michigan Sportsman* (July 1921): 30. First published in the *Detroit News.*

8. Korn, *Yesterday through Tomorrow,* 96–97.

9. Michigan Department of Conservation, Division of State Parks, *First Biennial Report of the Michigan Department of Conservation, 1921–22* (1922), 217–19.

10. P. J. Hoffmaster, "Education, Resources, and Citizenship" (paper presented at the regional meeting of American Association of School Administrators, March 1, 1949).

11. Christopher Graham, manuscript, December 1999, 3.

12. *Detroit News,* April 12, 1936.

13. Michigan Department of Conservation, *A Program for the Purchase of a Recreation Area in the Porcupine Mountains* (December 1943).

14. "Porcupine Park Project Advocated 19 Years Ago by State Conservation Chief," *Marquette Daily Mining Journal,* March 7, 1944.

15. "Logging Crews Slash Deep into Timber of Porcupines," *Marquette Daily Mining Journal,* July 18, 1942.

16. Raymond Dick, "Going, Going: The Forest of the Porcupines," *National Parks Magazine* (July–September 1943).

17. "A Report to Governor Harry Kelly in Answer to Donald M. Nelson's Letter of May 1 Relative to the Lands of the Connor Lumber and Land Company within the Porcupine Mountains Area Submitted by Department of Conservation, May 18, 1944," State Archives of Michigan.

18. Harry H. Whiteley, chair, Conservation Commission, to Governor Harry F. Kelly, May 16, 1944.

19. Automobile Club of Michigan, *The State of Our Parks: A Report Prepared by the Automobile Club of Michigan* (Detroit, November 1936).

20. Gillette, oral history interview.

21. Herbert Wagner, letter in commemoration of the fiftieth anniversary of the Michigan Natural Areas Council, April 25, 1997.

22. Gillette, oral history interview.

23. U.S. Department of the Interior, National Park Service, *A Proposal: Sleeping Bear National Seashore* (1961).

24. Citizens' Council of the Sleeping Bear Dunes Area, Platte Lakes Area Association, *The Bear Is Asleep—but the People Are Awake! The Sleeping Bear Dunes National Recreation Area Proposal* (January 15, 1962).

25. *Traverse City Record Eagle,* November 14, 1961.

26. *U.S. News and World Report,* June 10, 1963.

27. Senate Subcommittee on Public Lands, Committee on Interior and Insular Affairs, *Hearings on S. 792,* 88th Cong., 1st sess., 1963, p. 383.

28. Senate Subcommittee, *S. 792,* 411.

29. *Leelanau Enterprise Tribune,* July 11, 1963.

30. *Traverse City Record Eagle,* July 8, 1963.

31. Virginia Prentice, "Sleeping Bear Dunes . . . a National Lakeshore for Michigan," *Sierra Club Bulletin* (June 1969).

32. Graham, interview.

Chapter 8

1. Michigan Public Domain Commission, *Report of the Public Domain Commission, January 1, 1911, to June 30, 1913* (1913), 16.

2. Augustus C. Carton, "What the Press Can Do to Assist in the Development of Michigan" (address presented at the annual banquet of the Press Associations of Michigan, February 21, 1914).

3. Parrish Storrs Lovejoy, quoted in Norman J. Schmaltz, "Academic Gets Involved in Michigan Forest Conservation," *Michigan Academician* (summer 1979).

4. Norman John Schmaltz, "Cutover Land Crusade: The Michigan Forest Conservation Movement, 1899–1931" (Ph.D. diss., University of Michigan, 1972).

5. R. A. Smith, "The Land-Economic Survey in Michigan," *Roosevelt Wild Life Bulletin* (October 1926).

6. "Agricultural Engineering—When Par Is Datum," *Agricultural Engineering* (September 1924).

7. "Citizens Will Plant Pines as Memorials," *Detroit News,* September 22, 1929.

8. Michigan Department of Conservation, *What Are We Going to Do . . . with 2,208,975 Added Acres?* by Arthur W. Stace (1941).

9. "Today's Forests: He Helped Them Grow," *Michigan Conservation* (May–June 1949).

10. Michigan Historical Center, Michigan Department of State, "Civilian Conservation Corps Museum." November 9, 2000. <http://www.sos.state.mi.us/history/museum/museccc/index.html> (December 15, 2000).

11. "Harry Gaines Founder, First President," *Michigan Out-of-Doors* (July 1987): 104.

12. Fred Brown, interview by author, November 4, 1999.

13. Eugene T. Petersen, *Hunters' Heritage: A History of Hunting in Michigan* (Michigan United Conservation Clubs, n.d.).

14. Aldo Leopold, *Report of Game Survey of Michigan, Submitted to the Game Restoration Committee, Sporting Arms and Ammunition Manufacturers' Institute* (July 20, 1928).

15. "A Big Man!" *Michigan Conservation* (March–April 1967).

16. Merrill L. Petoskey, interview by author, October 14, 1999.

17. Merrill L. Petoskey, "Man Is Dependent on the Land," *Michigan Natural Resources* (September 1969).

18. Michigan Department of Conservation, Fish Division, *Coho Salmon for the Great Lakes: Fish Management Report No. 1,* by Wayne H. Tody and Howard A. Tanner (1966).

19. Howard A. Tanner, interview by author, October 6, 1999.

20. "The Risen Giant?" *Outdoor Life* (June 1969).

21. Al Spiers, "Miracle of the Fishes," *Saturday Evening Post* (fall 1972).

22. "Fishstory," *Michigan Conservation* (November–December 1967).

23. Spiers, "Miracle of the Fishes.

Chapter 9

1. James Whorton, *Before Silent Spring: Pesticides and Public Health in Pre-DDT America* (Princeton, NJ: Princeton University Press, 1974).

2. Thomas R. Dunlap, *DDT: Scientists, Citizens, and Public Policy* (Princeton, NJ: Princeton University Press, 1981), 54.

3. Ibid, 77.

4. George J. Wallace, "Insecticides and Birds," *Audubon Magazine* (January–February 1959). Originally presented at fifty-fourth annual convention of the National Audubon Society.

5. George J. Wallace, *My World of Birds: Memoirs of an Ornithologist* (Philadelphia: Dorrance, 1979), 1.

6. George J. Wallace, Walter P. Nickell, and Richard F. Bernard, *Bird Mortality in the Dutch Elm Disease Program in Michigan,* Cranbrook Institute of Science Bulletin 41 (Bloomfield Hills, MI, 1961).

7. "M.S.U. Man Protected by Dingell," *Lansing State Journal,* May 5, 1960.

8. Rachel L. Carson, *Silent Spring* (New York: Houghton Mifflin, 1962), 109.

9. Kennedy's panel, while pointing out the "great merits" of pesticides, called for "more judicious use of pesticides or alternate methods of pest control," while recommending additional research to understand the impact of pesticides on human health and the environment.

10. Dunlap, *DDT,* 101.

11. John Carew, "As It Looks to Me," *American Vegetable Grower* (November 1963).

12. "Pesticide Research Draws Fire," *Lansing State Journal,* April 5, 1963.

13. Gordon E. Guyer, interview by author, March 14, 2000.

14. "MSU Worm Study Shows DDT Content Fatal to Birds," *North Woods Call,* April 1, 1964.

15. In a 1986 article in Kalamazoo's *Encore Magazine*, Batts said Yannacone phoned him about the Long Island DDT applications because "as far as [Yannacone] was concerned, I was the only one who ever used the term ecology or talked about it in my classroom," ("A Wise Old Owl," February 1986, 10).

16. Wallace, *My World of Birds,* 92.

17. Ted Black, conversation with author, September 29, 1999.

18. Cities involved were East Grand Rapids, East Lansing, Fremont, Greenville, Holland, Lansing, Muskegon, Rockford, and Spring Lake.

19. *Environmental Defense Fund, Inc. vs. Director of Agriculture Dept.* 11 Mich. App 693 (1968).

20. Joan Wolfe, a citizen actively engaged in the fight against DDT, provided this account.

21. *Lansing State Journal,* April 20, 1969.

22. "Temporary Halt OK'd in Pesticide Case," *Lansing State Journal,* November 4, 1967.

23. "The Case against Hard Pesticides," *Michigan Conservation* (January–February 1968).

24. Charles Shick, "The 'Fall' of DDT in Michigan—1969: A Report to the Michigan Pesticides Council," February 20, 1970, in author's possession.

25. Robert E. Smith, legislative counsel, Michigan Farm Bureau, telegram, September 12, 1968, State Archives of Michigan.

26. John Calkins, chief deputy director, MDA, to Margaret McCall, information specialist, memorandum, September 27, 1968, Michigan State Archives.

27. *Joint Statement of Agreement by Lake Michigan Basin States: Policy on Protection of the Lake Michigan Environment from Uncontrolled Use of Persistent Pesticides and Similar Economic Poisons* (1968).

28. " 'Star' Witness Disturbs Romney," *Ann Arbor News,* October 17, 1968.

29. John Calkins, chief deputy director, MDA, to James Kellogg, executive assistant, memorandum, October 11, 1968, State Archives of Michigan.

30. A separate action EDF brought against use of DDT to control Dutch elm disease in Wisconsin was more successful, putting the chemical "on trial" in late 1968 and early 1969 and generating considerable publicity about the chemical's hazards. Dr. George Wallace of Michigan State University was one of the key witnesses called by EDF to testify about DDT's impacts.

31. H. Thomas Dewhirst, secretary, Michigan Agriculture Commission, to Walter Cronkite, December 2, 1968.

32. "State Moves to Ban Sale of DDT," *Detroit Free Press,* April 17, 1969.

33. "Obituary for DDT (in Michigan)," *New York Times Magazine,* July 6, 1969.

34. George Romney, secretary, Department of Housing and Urban Development, to Ralph A. MacMullan, March 9, 1970, State Archives of Michigan.

Chapter 10

1. The resolution requested that the railroad commissioner and the state Board of Health facilitate "the attendance of representative excursionists from other States, and [place] before those who may visit Michigan on that occasion, the beauties of the numerous delightful summer resorts around the shores of the Great Lakes, and at the numerous inland lakes and other sanitaria, the general healthfulness of the State, and the unparalleled advantages of Michigan as a summer resort state."

2. "Halting Stream Pollution," *Kalamazoo Gazette,* July 10, 1927.

3. Michigan Stream Control Commission, *Biennial Report of the Michigan Stream Control Commission, 1931–1932* (1932).

4. Wilbert Hosler, "Development of the Paper Industry in Michigan" (term paper prepared for Michigan history class, Western State Teachers College, Kalamazoo, 1935).

5. Department of Research and Guidance, Kalamazoo Public Schools,

Information about Job Opportunities in the Paper Industry for Kalamazoo and Vicinity, Bulletin C-137 (May 1940).

6. *Kalamazoo Gazette,* August 18, 1951.

7. "Michigan's Shame: Pollution," *Michigan Out-of-Doors,* 1947, month unknown.

8. "Michigan Industry Registers Tremendous Growth in Eight Years: Holds Fifth Ranking," *Michigan Manufacturer and Financial Record* (June 1949).

9. Howard E. Cowles, *Statement to Committee at Hearing Considering Pollution Control Law,* Detroit Creamery Company, March 26, 1947, State Archives of Michigan.

10. *Michigan Conservation* (April 1948): 11.

11. Citizens Study Committee on Kalamazoo River Waste, *Report of Findings of the Citizens Study Committee on Kalamazoo River Waste* (September 1951).

12. "Four Acres of Carp Corpses on the Kalamazoo," *Life,* October 5, 1953.

13. "Water Board Votes to Crack down on Otsego Falls Mill," *Kalamazoo Gazette,* September 30, 1953.

14. NUS Corporation, *Feasibility Study of Alternatives,* vol. 1, *Kalamazoo River PCB Project, Kalamazoo and Allegan Counties, Michigan* (March 1986).

15. Elisabeth Reuther Dickmeyer, *Reuther: A Daughter Strikes* (Southfield, MI: Spelman, 1989).

16. Mildred Jeffries, interview by author, November 5, 1999.

17. "Remus Defends City Program," *Detroit Free Press,* May 25, 1965.

18. Walter P. Reuther to Gerald Remus, June 2, 1965; Jerome P. Cavanagh to Walter P. Reuther, June 9, 1965, Walter Reuther Collection, Walter P. Reuther Library, Archives of Labor and Urban Affairs, Wayne State University.

19. "Lawmakers Cool to Reuther Pollution Program," *Detroit News,* March 20, 1966.

20. Olga Madar to Stewart L. Udall, October 28, 1968, Olga Madar Collection, Walter P. Reuther Library, Archives of Labor and Urban Affairs, Wayne State University.

21. Michigan Water Resources Commission, *Report on Water Pollution Control in the Michigan Portion of the Lake Michigan Basin and Its Tributaries, Prepared for Presentation on Behalf of the Michigan Water Resources Commission of the Department of Conservation and Michigan Department of Public Health at the Conference Called by the Secretary of the Interior on Pollution of the Waters of Lake Michigan and Its Tributary Basin* (January 31, 1968).

22. Madar made this notation at the bottom of a letter from Wolfe urging Madar to pursue the seat on the Natural Resources Commission. Letter dated July 24, 1973, Madar Collection.

23. U.S. Department of Interior, Bureau of Mines, *City Smoke Ordinances and Smoke Abatement,* by Samuel P. Flagg (1912).

24. Adam W. Rome, "Coming to Terms with Pollution: The Language of Environmental Reform, 1865–1915," *Environmental History* 1 (July 1996): 6–28.

25. "Smoke Evil Costs City Millions Yearly as Council Fails to Pass Inspection Funds," *Detroit Times,* February 1936.

26. "Time for Action on These Plagues," *Detroit Free Press,* January 28, 1947.

27. "List Sources of Air Pollution," *Muskegon Chronicle,* March 14, 1962.

28. Thomas Spencer, interview by author, March 9, 2000.

29. William Schroeder, personal communication, March 28, 2000.

30. "Con-Con Committee Told to Stop State Air Pollution," *Detroit News,* February 22, 1962; "Dirty Air Perils Life," *Detroit Free Press,* February 22, 1962.

31. "Township Asks End to Noise, Dirt, Smoke," *Wyandotte News-Herald,* May 4, 1962.

32. "Smoke Problem Flares up Again," *Plymouth Mail,* July 24, 1964.

33. "Industry Warns Air Controls Too Rigid," *Lansing State Journal,* October 14, 1966.

34. Bernard D. Bloomfield, *Air Pollution Control in Michigan: 1967–68* (paper presented at House of Representatives Air Pollution Meeting, Port Huron, Michigan, September 10, 1968), State Archives of Michigan.

35. Delbert Rector, interview by author, December 20, 1999.

36. "Legislator's Tie to Polluter Probed," *Detroit Free Press,* April 9, 1974. Smeekens resigned from the legislature later that year to prevent an expulsion vote by the Michigan House of Representatives.

37. Martin V. Melosi, *Garbage in the Cities: Refuse, Reform, and the Environment 1880–1890* (College Station: Texas A & M University Press, 1981).

38. Michigan Municipal League, *Garbage Collection Practices in Michigan Municipalities,* Information Bulletin 52 (July 1947).

39. Michigan Public Health Association, Environmental Health Section, William F. Hohloch, chairman, *Final Committee Report, Refuse Disposal Committee* (May 9, 1962), in author's possession.

40. Michigan Department of Conservation, *Summary Report of an Exploratory Meeting on Problems Related to Garbage and Refuse Disposal* (February 24, 1961), in author's possession.

Chapter 11

1. Samuel P. Hays, in collaboration with Barbara D. Hays, *Beauty, Health, and Permanence: Environmental Politics in the United States, 1955–1985* (New York: Cambridge University Press, 1987).

2. Jane Elder, personal communication, April 17, 2000.

3. Joan Wolfe and Will Wolfe, interview by author, October 14, 1999.

4. "Dwindling Natural Resources Peril U.S.," *Grand Rapids Press,* October 14, 1966.

5. "WMEAC History and Our Unsung Heroes," *Action Issue* (newsletter of WMEAC) (July 1994).

6. Michigan Water Resources Commission, *The Mercury Pollution Problem in Michigan and the Lower Great Lakes Area: A Summary of Information and Action Programs,* by William G. Turney, assistant chief engineer (September 1, 1970).

7. Executive Office press release, April 14, 1970.

8. "Milliken Urges 'Truth in Pollution,'" *Detroit Free Press,* April 16, 1970.

9. "Anti-Pollution Heroes Emerge: Students Find New Battleground," *Detroit Free Press,* March 11, 1970.

10. *Business Week,* March 21, 1970.

11. Walt Pomeroy, personal communication, May 10, 2000.

12. "The Nation Leaps to the Earth's Rescue," *Detroit Free Press,* April 23, 1970.

13. William G. Milliken, interview by author, October 15, 1999.

14. Jack Bails, interview by author, October 11, 1999.

15. From columns in the *Detroit Free Press* dated, respectively, January 8, 1980, and November 7, 1978.

16. Joan Wolfe, "History of the Michigan Environmental Protection Act," manuscript, August 1970.

17. "Pollution Hearing Draws Nearly 500," *Lansing State Journal,* January 22, 1970.

18. "Public Overwhelmingly Supports Antipollution Bill at Hearing Here," *Grand Rapids Press,* February 27, 1970.

19. George D. Moffett to Thomas J. Anderson, March 6, 1970, State Archives of Michigan.

20. "Ecology Bill Called Lawyer's Bonanza," *Lansing State Journal,* May 14, 1970.

21. Harry Hall to Representative Thomas Anderson, dated June 1, 1970; Representative Thomas Anderson letter to Harry Hall, June 3, 1970, State Archives of Michigan.

22. "Environmental Citizen Suits: Three Years' Experience under the Michigan Environmental Protection Act," *Ecology Law Quarterly* 4, no. 1 (winter 1974): 7–8.

23. West Michigan Environmental Action Council and others, *Will Our Legislators Help Save Michigan Lakes and Streams? A Report on the Inland Lakes and Streams Bill, H.B. 4948* (1971).

24. Joan Wolfe, "History of the Inland Lakes and Streams Act 346 of 1972," manuscript, October 1999.

25. "Streams Bill a Major Victory," *Lansing State Journal,* December 1972.

26. Transcript of Natural Resources Commission meeting, January 1977.

27. Peter Kakela and Howard Haas, "Michigan's Mineral Wealth," manuscript.

28. "Saga of Iron Mining Bill in Lansing," *Detroit Free Press,* August 18, 1975.

29. "Michigan's MUCC-raker," *Michigan: The Magazine of the Detroit News,* March 10, 1985.

30. Wayne Schmidt, "Observations on Michigan's Environmental History," January 3, 2000, in author's possession.

31. Wayne Schmidt, interview by author, October 27, 1999.

32. "Stroh's Switched Stand on Returnables," *Michigan Earth Beat,* September 16, 1976; "Beer Bottle Ban Still On," *Michigan Out-of-Doors* (January 1962).

33. James W. Deitrich to Representative H. Lynn Jondahl, May 22, 1975, State Archives of Michigan.

34. "Price of Beer May Increase 50% If Nonreturnable Bottle Plan Ok'd," *State News,* Michigan State University, January 1976.

35. Thomas Anderson, personal communication, May 6, 1992.

36. William Rustem, interview by author, August 17, 1999.

'37. Editorial aired April 9, 1976, WWJ-TV, Detroit, H. Lynn Jondahl Papers, State Archives of Michigan.

38. Lynn Jondahl, quoted in "Goodbye Throwaways," *Michigan Earth Beat,* November 17, 1976.

39. Bill Rustem to Governor William G. Milliken, October 4, 1982, William G. Milliken Papers, Michigan Historical Collections, Bentley Historical Collection, University of Michigan.

40. Hugh McDiarmid, "Washington Assured More Attractive State," *Detroit Free Press,* December 7, 1995.

41. Jane Elder, interview by author, March 21, 2000.

42. Terence Kehoe, "Merchants of Pollution? The Soap and Detergent Industry and the Fight to Restore Great Lakes Water Quality," *Environmental History Review* (fall 1992): 26.

43. Schmidt, "Observations on Michigan's Environmental History."

44. Milliken, interview.

45. Hilary Snell, interview by author, October 29, 1999.

46. Michigan Department of Natural Resources, *Report on Proposed Changes to the Administrative Rules for Act 226, Public Acts 1971,* State Archives of Michigan.

47. "Michigan Soap Opera," *Michigan Out-of-Doors* (March 1977).

48. Mike Stifler, interview by author, December 16, 1999.

49. "State Soap Opera: As the Lakes Turn," *Detroit News,* June 10, 1982.

50. Henry F. Lyster, "The Reclaiming of Drowned Lands," *Seventh Annual Report of the Secretary of the State Board of Health for the Fiscal Year Ending Sept. 30, 1879* (1880).

51. Ann Vileisis, *Discovering the Unknown Landscape: A History of America's Wetlands* (Washington, DC: Island Press, 1997), 76.

52. Michigan Department of Natural Resources, Michigan Natural Features Inventory, *Wetland Trends in Michigan since 1800: A Preliminary Assessment,* by Patrick Comer (June 1996).

53. "Wetlands Bill Dies in Senate Conservation Committee," *Michigan Earth Beat,* December 17, 1976.

54. Bob Garner, interview by author, October 1999.

55. John Sobetzer, personal communication, October 17, 1999.

56. Barbara Stanton, "Wetlands: Murky Dealings in the Senate Threaten Needed Protection," *Detroit Free Press,* February 26, 1979.

57. Editorial broadcast February 28, 1979, and March 1, 1979, WDIV-TV, Detroit.

58. Joan Elder, personal communication, April 17, 2000.

59. "Earth Day Spurred Decade of Progress," *Detroit News,* April 20, 1980.

60. Tom Mathieu, quoted in a prospectus prepared for the Michigan Environmental Council by the West Michigan Environmental Action Council, 1980.

61. "Environmental Lobbyist Sought," *Ann Arbor News,* February 26, 1980.

Chapter 12

1. Isle Royale National Park, *Isle Royale Chronology,* by Joyce Seward (summer 1993).

2. Theodore J. Karamanski and Richard Zeitlin with Joseph Derose, *Narrative History of Isle Royale National Park* (Chicago: Mid-American Research Center, Loyola University of Chicago, 1988).

3. "Isle Royale," *Detroit News,* December 3, 1921.

4. "Preserve Isle Royale," *Detroit News,* December 17, 1922.

5. Ben East, "Fifty Years Ago: My Visits to Isle Royale," *Michigan Out-of-Doors* (January/February 1981).

6. Korn, *Yesterday through Tomorrow,* 104.

7. Jack Van Coevering to Howard Tanner, director, Department of Natural Resources, September 8, 1975.

8. "Saving the Porkies Wilderness," *Michigan Out-of-Doors* (July 1987): 78.

9. John J. D'Agostino and Olga Madar to recreation chairmen and committee members, Regions I and IA, Madar Collection.

10. "Retain Porcupine Mountains as Wilderness, UAW Urges," press release, October 1, 1971, Madar Collection.

11. "Witnesses Urge 'Save the Porkies,'" *Lansing State Journal,* October 2, 1971.

12. Paul W. Thompson, "The Michigan Natural Areas Council Program and Its Early History," *Michigan Botanist* 15 (1976).

13. Lauri Leskinen, quoted in Charles Esbach, *Sawmill to Sanctuary: The Estivant Pines Story* (Houghton, MI: North Forty Publishing, 1976).

14. *Ernest Hemingway: Selected Letters, 1917–1961,* ed. Carlos Baker (New York: Charles Scribner's Sons, 1981), 26.

15. Quoted from P. S. Lovejoy papers in Gordon Charles, *Pigeon River Country: The Big Wild* (Grand Rapids, MI: William B. Eerdmans, 1985).

16. Charles, *Pigeon River Country,* 17.

17. "Pigeon River Country: For Nature or Oil?" *Detroit Free Press,* August 17, 1975.

18. "The Value of the Pigeon River Forest Goes Far beyond Its Oil," *Detroit Free Press,* August 31, 1975.

19. Schmidt, "Observations on Michigan's Environmental History."

20. "Pigeon River EIS Opens a Can of Worms," *Michigan Earth Beat,* January 21, 1976.

21. "Pigeon River Drilling: Is There an Alternative?" *Michigan Earth Beat,* September 16, 1977.

22. Ken Sikkema, interview by author, May 4, 2000.

23. Grant Trigger, personal communication, March 12, 2000.

24. Michigan Land Use Institute, *Rivers at Risk: The Case for Reviving Hydrocarbon Development Planning in Michigan* (November 1997).

25. *Report of the State Geologist,* H. Doc. 24.

26. Kay Franklin and Norma Schaeffer, *Duel for the Dunes: Land Use Conflict on the Shores of Lake Michigan* (Urbana and Chicago: University of Illinois Press, 1983), 26.

27. "Hubbell Concern Gets Contract to Take Sand Here," *Manistee News-Advocate,* April 18, 1928.

28. Harry G. Flynn (of Manley Brothers), "Mining Industry's Side of Story," letter to the editor, *Benton Harbor Herald-Palladium,* March 1, 1975.

29. *Dunes of Dearborn Tallest in November,* Ford Motor Company (1945).

30. "Protective Role of Dunes Recalls Pigeon Hill Controversy in 1920's," *Muskegon Chronicle,* May 22, 1956.

31. "Resorters Ask State to Control Sand Mining," *Muskegon Chronicle,* December 21, 1974.

32. "Sand Mining in Michigan," *Michigan Earth Beat,* June 25, 1972.

33. Dennis Cawthorne, interview by author, February 3, 2000.

34. "What's Left of the Dunes Should Be Preserved," *Grand Rapids Press,* December 22, 1974.

35. "Sand Miners Say Cawthorne Bill Would Rack Auto Industry," *Muskegon Chronicle,* January 17, 1975.

36. "Mining Bill Shifts Like Sand," *Muskegon Chronicle,* August 2, 1975.

37. "Stop Sand-Mining; Halt Ravishment of Dunes!" *Muskegon Chronicle,* January 13, 1975.

38. "Saving Michigan's Dunes," undated editorial, *Detroit Free Press,* 1976.

39. "Dune Mine Law Faces Challenges," *Muskegon Chronicle,* June 18, 1979.

40. "Botanist Blasts Sand Mining," *Detroit Free Press,* September 6, 1979.

41. "DNR Faces Sand Dune Ruling," *Muskegon Chronicle,* October 10, 1981.

42. Don Wilson, personal communication, March 22, 2000.

43. "Compromise Sought on Sand Dune Bill," *Muskegon Chronicle,* May 25, 1989.

44. "Muskegon Area Focus of 'Save Dunes' Drive," *Muskegon Chronicle,* March 7, 1989.

45. "Lawmakers Propose More Construction in Area's Sand Dunes," *Muskegon Chronicle,* August 31, 1995.

46. Michigan State University, Center for Remote Sensing, *Final Report: Evaluation of Critical Dune Areas Designated under Part 353, Sand Dune Protection and Management, of the Natural Resources and Environmental Protection Act, 1994 PA 451,* by David P. Lusch et al. (June 1996).

47. "Big Questions about Dunes Strategy," *Grand Rapids Press,* October 23, 1997.

48. Lake Michigan Federation, *Vanishing Lake Michigan Sand Dunes: Threats from Mining* (Chicago and Muskegon, 1999).

49. Testimony of the Michigan Environmental Council on S.B. 646 and H.B. 4295 before the House Conservation, Environment, and Great Lakes Committee, November 28, 1995.

50. Annick Smith, "The Importance of Dunes," *Outside* (July 1991).

51. "Wilderness Plan Angers Residents," *Detroit News,* January 21, 1979.

52. "UP Residents Tell Levin of Fears about U.S. Wilderness Areas Plan," *Detroit Free Press,* June 9, 1980.

53. "Cry of Wilderness Comforts Sierras," *Detroit Free Press,* February 3, 1985.

54. "Public Lands, 'Private' Uses," *Detroit News,* January 13, 1986.

55. Sierra Club, Mackinac Chapter, to wilderness supporters, January 13, 1986.

56. Jane Elder, personal communication, April 27, 2000.

Chapter 13

1. Cathy Trost, *Elements of Risk: The Chemical Industry and Its Threat to America* (New York: Times Books, 1984), 20.

2. Joyce Egginton, *The Poisoning of Michigan* (New York and London: W. W. Norton, 1980), 26.

3. Michigan Senate, Special Senate Investigating Committee, *The Contamination Crisis in Michigan: Polybrominated Biphenyls, A Report from the Special Senate Investigating Committee,* by Senator John A. Welborn, chairperson (July 1975).

4. Michigan Department of Agriculture, *Final PBB Report from the Michigan Department of Agriculture* (November 9, 1982).

5. Dennis Swanson, interview by author, August 27, 1999.

6. Elizabeth Harris, personal communication, November 3, 1999.

7. "PBB: A Curse without a Cure," part 2, *Detroit News Magazine,* September 19, 1982.

8. "PBB Fears Unwarranted, Study Shows," *Detroit News*, August 19, 1997.

9. Alden K. Henderson et al., "Breast Cancer among Women Exposed to Polybrominated Biphenyls," *Epidemiology* (September 1995).

10. Ashraful Hoque, "Cancer among a Michigan Cohort Exposed to Polybrominated Biphenyls in 1973," *Epidemiology* (July 1998).

11. David Wade, interview by author, February 1, 2000.

12. "Montague: Michigan's $30,000,000 Chemical Empire of the Future," *Business Topics* (June 1954).

13. "The Poisoning of Montague, Michigan," *Detroit Free Press Magazine*, July 19, 1981.

14. "Poisoning of Montague."

15. Transcript of Conference, White Lake, Muskegon County, City of Whitehall, Whitehall Leather Company, Hooker Chemical Company; Water Resources Commission meeting, East Lansing, Michigan, July 24, 1968.

16. "Poisoning of Montague."

17. Michigan Department of Natural Resources, *Discharges from Hooker Chemical Company*, by Dennis Swanson, Staff Report (July 1976).

18. Andrew Hogarth, interview by author, October 7, 1999.

19. Carl Blumay with Henry Edwards, *The Dark Side of Power: The Real Armand Hammer* (New York: Simon and Schuster, 1992).

20. Mary Mahoney, interview by author, January 28, 2000.

21. Verna Courtemanche, interview by author, October 26, 1999.

22. Schmidt, "Observations on Michigan's Environmental History."

23. "Berlin and Farro: Continuing Story of Failures, Fears," *Flint Journal*, April 10, 1983.

24. Cheryl Graunstadt, personal communication, June 29, 2000.

25. "Fatal Fumes: Workers See Victims Gasp and Crumple as Gas Spreads," *Detroit News*, January 15, 1982.

26. Paul Parks, interview by author, June 14, 2000.

27. Deposition of Wesley Tomsheck, files of Michigan Department of Attorney General, *Kelley v. Arco Industries*.

28. "DNR Reveals Contamination Sites," *Michigan Earth Beat*, December 15, 1979.

29. "Cadillac Cleanup Could Cause a Stink," *Traverse City Record Eagle*, December 6, 1999.

30. Michigan Department of Environmental Quality, *Site Summary, Cheboygan City Park* (1999).

31. Michigan Department of Environmental Quality, *Information Bulletin, Kingsford/Breitung Township Site, Kingsford, Dickinson County* (January 1999). Cleanup cost figure estimated by Andrew Hogarth, assistant chief, Environmental Response Division, January 11, 2000.

32. Estimates supplied by Andrew Hogarth, assistant chief, Environmental Response Division, Department of Environmental Quality, October and November 1999.

33. "Tanner to Begin Shakeup of DNR to fight pollution," *Flint Journal*, January 8, 1978.

34. Michigan Department of Natural Resources, *Thirtieth Biennial Report of the Department of Natural Resources, 1979–1980* (1980), 22.

35. "DNR Money Bill a 'Mixed Bag,'" *Michigan Earth Beat*, July 22, 1978.

36. Michigan Department of Environmental Quality, *Enforcement Statistics, 7/1/91 through 1/31/98* (February 3, 1998).

37. Dennis W. Archer, mayor of Detroit, and John H. Logie, mayor of Grand Rapids, to Governor John Engler and Representative Ken Sikkema, March 9, 1995.

38. House Conservation, Environment, and Recreation Committee, *Michigan Environmental Council Statement on H.B. 4596*, March 28, 1995.

39. *Craine's Detroit Business*, April 3, 1995. *Greenfield* is a term describing undeveloped lands, usually on the suburban fringe. *Brownfield* refers to abandoned industrial or commercial sites, usually in older cities.

Chapter 14

1. *State of Michigan v. State of Illinois and the Sanitary District of Chicago*, complaint in the Supreme Court of the United States, October term, 1926, William W. Potter, attorney general.

2. "Stealing Lake Michigan," editorial, *Detroit News*, December 24, 1922. First published in *Milwaukee Journal*, 1922.

3. *Proposed Compact of the Great Lakes States: A Statement Presented by Nicholas V. Olds, Assistant Attorney General, State of Michigan, to the Third Annual Meeting of the Great Lakes States Industrial Development Council, January 6, 1955*, Michigan Law Library, Department of Attorney General.

4. "Great Lakes Interests," *Detroit Times*, December 27, 1954.

5. "A 50-Billion-Dollar Job: Cleaning up the Nation's Waters," *U.S. News and World Report*, October 4, 1965.

6. William G. Turney, "Recollections about the Allocation of Detroit River Resources," letter to author, February 3, 2000.

7. "Dying Lake Michigan," *Newsweek*, November 13, 1967.

8. Ben East, "The Risen Giant?" *Outdoor Life* (June 1969).

9. Spiers, "Miracle of the Fishes."

10. "Michigan Holds Biggest Stakes in Clean Lakes," *Detroit Free Press*, March 8, 1970.

11. International Joint Commission, *Report of the International Joint Commission, United States and Canada, on the Pollution of the Boundary Waters* (1951).

12. International Joint Commission, *Pollution of Lake Erie, Lake Ontario, and the International Section of the St. Lawrence River* (1970).

13. Governor William G. Milliken, remarks presented at Conference of Great Lakes Governors and Premiers, Mackinac Island, Michigan, August 16, 1971.

14. Schmidt, "Observations on Michigan's Environmental History."

15. Richard Spencer, "Winter Navigation on the Great Lakes and St. Lawrence Seaway: A Study in Congressional Decision Making" (master's thesis, Cornell University, 1992).

16. Governor William G. Milliken, remarks presented at Great Lakes Water Resources Conference, June 11, 1982, Mackinac Island, Michigan.

17. "Provinces, States Agree to Protect Great Lakes," *Detroit Free Press*, February 12, 1985.

18. "Great Lakes: Maybe Now Leaders Can Join Hands against the Real Enemy," *Detroit Free Press*, February 12, 1985.

19. G. Tracy Mehan III, "The States' Experience Managing the Waters of the

Great Lakes" (paper presented at Great Lakes Water Law Conference, February 25, 2000).

20. U.S. Bureau of Fisheries, *Life History of the Lake Herring of Lake Huron as Revealed by Its Scales,* by John Van Oosten, Bulletin 44 (1928).

21. "Judges' Laxity Necessitates Tougher Antipollution Law," *Detroit Free Press,* August 6, 1971.

22. "Kelley Asks $10,000 Fines in Fish Kills," *Detroit News,* August 5, 1971. The article notes that Dow had been fined $500 in 1969 for the previous fish kill and promised "it would never happen again."

23. "Dioxin Update No. 2: Commentary," *Dow Today,* March 22, 1983.

24. "Two Groups Call for Midland Dioxin Study," *Midland Daily News,* March 14, 1983.

25. Schmidt, "Observations on Michigan's Environmental History."

26. "Pollution Pact Is Reached by State and Dow," *Detroit Free Press,* April 13, 1984.

27. Mark Van Putten, interview by author, December 27, 1999.

28. "Power Plant Kills Fish, but Some Say It Doesn't Matter," *Detroit News,* undated clipping.

29. Assistant Attorney General Stanley F. Pruss to Edith C. Harsh, Department of Attorney General, memorandum, February 16, 1995, author's possession.

Chapter 15

1. Michigan Legislature, Science and Technology Division, Legislative Service Bureau, *Managing Michigan's Natural Resources: A Historical Overview of the Department of Natural Resources* (April 1991).

2. "Blanchard Sidesteps Chance to Back Embattled DNR Chief," *Detroit Free Press,* March 29, 1986.

3. "Mac: No Man Can, or Ever Will Do More," *North Woods Call,* September 27, 1972.

4. Frank Kelley, interview by author, January 18, 2000.

5. "Governor Turns DNR Inside Out," *Detroit Free Press,* November 9, 1991.

6. "Environmentalists: Engler Trying to Take over DNR," *Lansing State Journal,* November 9, 1991.

7. "DNR Plan: Reorganization Could Insulate Bureaucracy from Public Scrutiny," *Ann Arbor News,* November 15, 1991.

8. "A Public Voice in New DNR?" *Grand Rapids Press,* November 17, 1991.

9. According to Jerry Bartnik, a member of the Natural Resources Commission, neither DNR director Roland Harmes nor most members of the commission were made aware of the governor's order in advance of its public announcement.

10. "Harding Says DEQ Change in Focus Improves Environment," *Michigan Report,* Gongwer News Service, April 9, 1996.

11. Attorney General Frank J. Kelley, press conference, Lansing, Michigan, March 27, 1995.

12. Documents obtained by environmental groups through a Freedom of Information Act request showed that Harding had met with the company's executives February 11, 1994. The environmental groups also unearthed a February 8 letter from the firm, Giddings and Lewis, complaining about a search warrant that had

been issued by the DNR to inspect company files in 1993 and requesting a "dialogue" with Harding "that will lead to a mutually satisfactory solution . . . and to a normalization of the relationship between the company and MDNR."

13. 164 employees of the DNR's Environmental Response Division to Roland Harmes, director, Department of Natural Resources, June 18, 1993.

14. Rick Jameson, executive director, MUCC, to MUCC Executive Committee et al., memorandum, June 7, 1996.

15. Todd Grischke, interview by author, April 28, 2000.

16. "Conservation Whiplashed as Engler Performs DNR Surgery," *North Woods Call*, August 2, 1995.

17. Eric Sharp, personal communication, June 20, 2000.

18. Marlene Fluharty, interview by author, January 11, 2000.

19. Anne Woiwode, personal communication, December 22, 1999.

20. "Detroit Waste: The High-Risk Solution," *Windsor Star*, March 8, 1986.

21. "Environmentalists, Governor Feud over Detroit Incinerator," *Detroit News*, July 14, 1986.

22. Chris Shafer, interview by author, January 26, 2000.

23. Michigan Department of Public Health, "Salmon Restrictions Lifted in 1996 Fish Consumption Advisory," press release, February 2, 1996.

24. National Wildlife Federation and Michigan Environmental Health Coalition, "Michigan Health Department Gives Bad Advice on Safety of Eating Great Lakes Fish," media advisory, March 18, 1996.

25. "Michigan Balks at Tainted-Salmon Warning," *New York Times*, February 8, 1997.

26. "Salmon Warnings: The State Wrongly Chooses to Ignore Health Risks," *Detroit Free Press*, February 10, 1997.

27. "A Question of Survival," CBS News Special broadcast April 22, 1970.

28. "Flint Pollution-Permit Case Could Result in Landmark Decision," *Flint Journal*, May 28, 1997.

29. "Hayman's Ruling Protects Public," *Flint Journal*, June 4, 1997.

30. Michigan Environmental Science Board, *Analysis of the Michigan Department of Environmental Quality's Administered Environmental Standards to Protect Children's Health,* by J. A. Gracki, M. DeVito, R. A. Etzel, M. A. Kamrin, W. B. Weil, G. T. Wolff, and K. G. Harrison (Lansing, February 2000).

31. Stanley Pruss, personal communication, February 25, 2000.

32. "Takings to Extremes," *Detroit Metro Times*, August 14–20, 1996.

33. "Property Rights Live," *Detroit News*, March 31, 1998.

34. Governor William G. Milliken, *Special Message to the Legislature on Land Use and the Environment,* February 10, 1972.

35. Michigan Department of Natural Resources, *Michigan's Future Was Today* (1974).

36. William C. Taylor, Executive Office, to Governor William G. Milliken, memorandum, December 8, 1972.

37. "Appropriations Committee Land Use Vote Approaches," *Michigan Earth Beat*, March 31, 1976.

38. Milliken, interview.

39. Public Sector Consultants, Inc., *Michigan's Environment and Relative Risk: Michigan Relative Risk Analysis Project,* study conducted by William R. Rustem et al. (1992).

40. Michigan Society of Planning Officials, *Patterns on the Land: Our Choices—Our Future,* final report of the Michigan Society of Planning Officials Trend Future Project (September 1995).

41. "State's Farmers Try to Save Space from Hungry Developers," *Detroit Free Press,* February 26, 2000.

42. "Unchecked Sprawl Throws Region into Uncertain Future," *Detroit News,* January 2, 2000.

Epilogue

1. Ken Sikkema, interview, May 4, 2000.

2. Jeff Dauphin, personal communication, March 2, 2000.

3. Joseph L. Jacobson and Sandra W. Jacobson, "Intellectual Impairment in Children Exposed to Polychlorinated Biphenyls in Utero," *New England Journal of Medicine* 335, no. 11 (September 12, 1996): 783–89. See also "Report Links PCB Exposure with Children's Development," *New York Times,* May 23, 1997. The study correlated " 'low normal' IQ scores, poor reading comprehension, memory problems and difficulty paying attention in 11-year-old children prenatally exposed to polychlorinated biphenyls, or PCB's, in concentrations only slightly higher than those found in the general population."

4. Mary Beth Doyle, personal communication, March 8, 2000.

5. International Joint Commission, *Fifth Biennial Report under the Great Lakes Water Quality Agreement of 1978* (1990).

6. Lake Superior is the world's largest lake in surface area, while Russia's Lake Baikal is largest in water volume.

7. "Viewpoint," *Michigan Challenge* (October 1976).

8. Michigan Department of Environmental Quality, *Michigan Fish Contaminant Monitoring Program: 1998 Annual Report* (December 1998).

9. The Michigan environmental groups participating in the project were the Lone Tree Council, represented by Terry Miller; the Ecology Center of Ann Arbor, represented by Tracy Easthope; and Diane Hebert, representing Environmental Health Watch. The *New York Times* reported on the project in its Sunday, July 18, 1999, edition in an article headlined "Chemistry Cleans up a Factory."

10. Herman Miller, Inc., *Journey to Sustainability: An Environmental Report,* Internet document, April 2000.

11. Paul Murray, personal communication, April 20, 2000.

12. International Joint Commission, *Protection of the Waters of the Great Lakes: Interim Report to the Governments of Canada and the United States* (August 10, 1999).

13. The figure is drawn from emissions data supplied by the Air Quality Division, Michigan Department of Environmental Quality.

14. William Murphy, personal communication, February 12, 2000.

15. Anne Woiwode, personal communication, March 9, 2000.

16. "A New Breed of Loggers Cuts and Plants Michigan's Woods," *Detroit Free Press,* October 24, 1999.

17. "Loggers Proud of Efforts to Replenish State Forests," *Detroit News,* December 16, 1999.

18. "Why Cut So Many Trees?" *Detroit Free Press,* April 8, 2000.

19. "Let DNR Choose How Lumber Should Be Cut in State Forests," *Grand Rapids Press*, April 22, 2000.

20. "Unchecked Sprawl Throws Region into Uncertain Future," *Detroit News*, January 2, 2000.

21. Mark Wyckoff, personal communication, March 31, 2000.

22. Charles W. Jay, *My New Home in Northern Michigan and Other Tales* (1874).

23. Bruce Catton, *Michigan: A History* (New York and London: W. W. Norton, 1976), 191.

24. "Lumbering: Story of Vast Wealth, Wasted Heritage," *Muskegon Chronicle*, July 10, 1937.

25. "Henry Ford, Conservationist," *Michigan Out-of-Doors* (March 1988).

26. Willliam Turney, personal communication, February 25, 2000.

27. According to a report prepared for the Coastal Management Program of the Michigan Department of Natural Resources in 1995, only 1,068 of 158,000 acres of lakeplain prairie found in Michigan in the early 1800s, or 0.7 percent, remained "with some integrity."

28. For a retelling of this legend, and many other valuable insights into the Native American history of Michigan, see Charles E. Cleland, *Rites of Conquest: The History and Culture of Michigan's Native Americans* (Ann Arbor: University of Michigan Press, 1992).

29. Between 1994 and 1998, the number of Michigan land trusts rose from 28 to 38. The number of permanently protected acres attributable to their work rose from nearly 71,000 to 105,000.

30. Between 1986 and 1997, the National Park Service and Nature Conservancy worked with U.S. representative Dale Kildee on legislation to establish the river park, but it was never introduced because of Upper Peninsula opposition. Governors Blanchard and Engler both expressed opposition to the proposal. Records of discussion of the park proposal are maintained at the Pictured Rocks National Lakeshore office in Munising.

31. In a report entitled *Precious Heritage* released in March 2000, the Nature Conservancy pointed out that a third of Michigan's and the nation's native species were in danger of extinction, in large part from habitat destruction and competition from nonnative species. Michigan's list contained 342 threatened and endangered species, including 260 plant species, and hundreds more species on a watch list.

32. Robert Grese, personal communication, March 19, 2000.

33. Tanya Cabala, personal communication, December 22, 1999.

34. Joan Wolfe, personal communication, June 10, 2000.

35. Curt Meine, *Aldo Leopold: His Life and Work* (Madison: University of Wisconsin Press, 1988), 22.

Index

Air pollution
   control of by state, 157–59, 284
   in downriver Detroit, 153–54, 156,
      157
   in Muskegon, 155
   as smoke pollution, 70, 152–53
   after World War II, 153–54
Air Pollution Control Commission, 156,
   157, 227, 264, 265, 271
Albion, 2, 143, 168
Alexander, George, 24
Allegan, 3
Allegan County, 40, 146
Allegan Lake, 1, 145
Amway Corporation, 185–86
Anderson, Thomas, 171–72, 173, 176,
   182, 190, 210
Ann Arbor, 53, 104, 127, 168
Arco Industries, 236–37
Au Sable River, 24, 28, 39, 46, 218
Automobile Club of Michigan, 99

Bailey, Tom, 168–69, 286
Bails, Jack, 120, 121, 170, 203, 204, 240,
   265
Baird, John, 83–87, 95, 97
Ball, B. Dale, 133, 134, 136, 137
Battle Creek, 3, 8, 16, 40, 127, 131, 143,
   221, 234
Batts, H. Lewis, Jr., 130–31
Bay City, 17, 32, 257
Beal, W. J., 35, 53–54, 297
Bedford, James, 2
Benton Harbor, 181
Berlin and Farro landfill and incinera-
   tor, 230–33

Berrien County, 131, 134, 135
Black, Dr. C. T. (Ted), 131, 135, 138
Blanchard, Governor James, 116, 213,
   217, 232, 241, 253, 254, 263, 270–72,
   288
Bloomfield, Bernard, 157–58
Bonior, U.S. Representative David, 253
Bridgman, 211
Brown, Senator Basil, 177
Brown, Fred, 115–17
Brown, Mary, 266
Burnap, Bob, 131–32
Burt, Wellington, 35

Cabala, Tanya, 301
Cadillac, 237
Calhoun County, 12
Carson, Rachel, and *Silent Spring*, 128,
   163
Cass River, 52
Catton, Bruce, 295
Cawthorne, Dennis, 210, 211
Chandler, Zachariah, 188
Charlevoix, 241
Cheboygan, 237–38
Chemical contamination, 220–44
Children's environmental health,
   287–88
Chrysler Corporation, 232
Civilian Conservation Corps, 114, 196
Clare County, 30, 44
Clark, George, 12, 20–21
Clean Water Act, 189, 258
Clinton River, 141, 149
Coho salmon, 119–23
Conner, Roger, 172, 205, 206

Conservation
  clash of conservationists and envi-
    ronmentalists, 184, 207, 300
  early Michigan sentiment in favor of,
    39–40
  early twentieth century movement in
    Michigan, 74, 85
  see also Michigan Commission of
    Conservation; Michigan
    Department of Conservation
Consumers Power Company, 92, 157,
  177, 232, 237, 260
Cooper, William, 258–59
Copper Harbor, 199
Courtemanche, Verna, 230, 231,
  232–33
Covert, 215
Crampton, Rep. Louis, 196, 197
Crane, Caroline Bartlett, 70–71
Crawford County, 59, 87
Curwood, James Oliver, 81–90, 91, 117,
  264, 272, 297

Dahlstrom, A. Winton, 226, 236
Daubendiek, Bertha, 200
Dauphin, Jeff, 286
DDT
  effects on wildlife, 125–30
  in Great Lakes fish, 4, 132, 136, 137,
    285
  on Michigan State University cam-
    pus, 126–29
  use of, in Michigan, 126–28, 287
Denniston, Wayne, 143
Detroit, 14, 15, 16, 29, 93, 130, 149, 150,
  153, 156, 160, 233, 242, 248
Detroit Edison Company, 169, 232
Detroit Free Press, 2, 67, 122, 137, 159,
  190–91, 194, 204, 250, 263, 270, 292,
  300
Detroit incinerator, 271–72
Detroit News, 6–8, 61, 63, 94, 110, 111,
  192, 195, 217, 220, 224, 234, 272,
  274, 276, 281
Detroit River, 12, 13, 16, 20, 24, 41, 65,
  71, 141, 145, 151, 154, 163, 165,
  167, 178, 222, 248, 249, 296, 301
Dick, Raymond, 97–98
Dieldrin, 130–36

Dingell, U.S. Representative John, 102,
  128
Dioxins, 257–58
Dobson, Warren, 228
Dow Chemical Company, 116, 132,
  165–66, 177, 227, 256–58, 289
Doyle, Mary Beth, 287

Earth Day 1970, 167–69
East, Ben, 89, 97–98, 196, 197, 285
Easthope, Tracey, 273
East Lansing, 55, 101, 126, 127, 181,
  213
East Michigan Environmental Action
  Council (EMEAC), 190
Ecology Center (of Ann Arbor), 273,
  287
Elder, Jane, 163, 184, 191, 218
Energy policies, 290–91
Engler, Governor John, 185, 214, 261,
  263, 265, 266, 273, 274, 275, 280,
  288, 290
Environmental Defense Fund, 130–35,
  250
Environmental movement
  growth of, in 1960s, 162–63
  political effectiveness of, 192–93
  presaged in words of James Oliver
    Curwood, 89
Environmental Protection Agency, U.S.,
  232, 234, 238, 241, 256, 260, 273–74,
  276, 291
Estivant Pines, 199–200

Fish Commissioners, State Board of,
  22–23, 39
Fish contaminant advisories, 273–74
Fisheries
  effects of Atlantic sea lamprey on,
    119–20, 248
  exploitation of, in nineteenth
    century, 20–24
  first state regulation of, 22, 38, 39
  influence of commercial industry on
    take, 22–23, 41
Flint, 84, 86, 274
Fluharty, Marlene, 213, 270
Flynn, Tim, 292
Ford, Henry, 78, 96, 295–96

Ford Motor Company, 151, 171, 208, 209, 232, 238, 248, 296
Forestry Commission, 55–56, 283
Forests
 backlash against preservation of, 54, 57–58
 creation of state forest reserves, 55–56
 early sentiment for preservation of, 49–50, 52
 expansion of state forest system, 113–14
 exploitation of, in nineteenth century, 27–36
 fires in nineteenth century, 5–9, 52
 production figures in nineteenth century, 27, 32, 34, 36
 protection of old growth in, 292–93
 rise of Michigan forestry movement, 54–64
Frailey, Kevin, 180
Freeman, Stewart, 228, 239
Fur trade, 14–15

Gaines, Harry, 114–15
Game and fish warden, state office of, 42–46
Garbage. See solid waste
Garfield, Charles
 as director of Independent Forestry Commission, 53
 early life of, 51
 legislation offered by, 52
 as president of state Forestry Commission, 48, 55–57, 59, 62–64, 283, 284, 297
Garner, Bob, 190
General Motors Corporation, 230, 232
Genesee Power Station, 275, 276
Genesee Township, 275
Gillette, E. Genevieve, 91–97, 99–107, 297
Goemaere, State Representative Warren, 177, 191
Graham, Christopher, 106
Grand Haven, 213, 293
Grand Rapids, 14, 43, 51, 54, 67, 68–69, 114, 127, 136, 155, 163, 164, 165, 171, 173, 175

Granger, Dale, 3
Graunstadt, Cheryl, 233
Grayling, depletion of, 23–24
Great Lakes
 charter, 254–55
 diversion of, 246–47, 253–55, 261
 ecosystem, 246–47, 251
 exotic species in, 286
 fishery commission, 248
 future threats to, 286–87
 International Joint Commission and, 250, 288–89, 290
 Natural Resources Center, 256
 winter navigation on, 252–53
Great Lakes Commission, 247–48
Great Lakes United, 256
Green, Governor Fred, 81, 87, 112
Grese, Robert, 300
Grischke, Todd, 269
Groundwater contamination, 239, 240, 241
Guyer, Gordon E., 129, 132, 137–38, 260, 299

Hales, David, 264, 300
Hammer, Armand, 229
Hampton, Charles (state game warden), 44–45
Harding, Russell, 214, 266, 267, 272, 275
Harmes, Roland, 268
Harris, Elizabeth, 223
Hart, 78, 79
Hart, Senator Philip, 102–3, 105–6
Hartwick Pines State Park, 88, 296–97, 300
Health, State Board of,
 establishment of, 66
 promotion of tourism by, 139–40
 reports of, 65, 67
 and wetlands, 187–88
Hemingway, Ernest, 201, 298–99
Herbert, Paul, 115
Herman Miller Corporation, 290
Hesse, John, 1–2
Higgins Lake, 53, 113
Hillsdale, 158, 159
Hoffman, Abbie, 252–53
Hoffmaster, P. J., 94–100, 107, 198, 199

Hogarth, Andrew, 2, 228–29
Holland, 213
Hooker Chemical Company, 225–29, 239
Hope for the Dunes, 210–11
Houghton, Douglass, 20, 207
Houghton Lake, 29, 53
Houston, John, 181
Hubbard, Bela, 14–15, 17
Hunting, 39, 41, 42, 46, 87, 88, 117, 118, 119

Inman, Don, 203
Isle Royale National Park, 114, 194–97

Jackson, 72, 127
Jackson County, 3, 15
Jackson Prison, 67–68
Jacobetti, Representative Dominic, 191, 272, 280
Jacobson, Drs. Sandra W. and Joseph L., 273, 287
Jameson, Rick, 213, 269, 270
Jensen, Jens, 92–93, 95, 102, 208, 295
Jondahl, Lynn, 181–83, 213

K and K Construction Company, litigation involving, 276–77
Kalamazoo, 16, 52, 66, 70, 147, 148, 226, 234
Kalamazoo County, 236
Kalamazoo Nature Center, 131
Kalamazoo River, pollution of, 1–5, 142–44, 146–48, 263
Kammer, State Senator Kerry, 190, 204
Kedzie, Robert C.
    childhood in pioneer Michigan, 13
    as classmate of David Ward, 28
    as forestry advocate, 50–51, 55
    as member of State Board of Health, 65–68, 140
Kelley, Attorney General Frank, 159, 173, 202, 229, 236, 260, 265, 267, 291
Kelly, Governor Harry, 97–98
Kildee, U.S. Representative Dale, 217, 218
Kingsford, 238

Lake Erie, 23, 71, 120, 139, 149–51, 165, 184, 220, 248
Lake Huron, 7, 20, 21, 22, 107, 119, 122, 237, 302
Lake Michigan, 4, 20, 22, 106, 119, 120, 121, 122, 132, 134, 184, 207, 208, 214, 219, 220, 241, 245, 246, 247, 248, 249–50, 273
Lake Michigan Federation, 210, 215, 301
Lake St. Clair, 4, 41, 165, 166, 167, 171, 253, 272
Lake Superior, 21, 22, 97, 288
Land economic survey of Michigan, 110
Land speculation in pioneer Michigan, 12
Land use, 278–82
Lansing, 17, 56, 91, 92, 118, 140, 141, 158, 198, 226, 268, 269
League of Women Voters, 186
Leffler, Susan, 277
Leopold, Aldo, 97, 98, 111, 117, 302
Levin, U.S. Senator Carl, 216, 217, 218, 260
Liquid Disposal, Inc., 220, 233, 234
Livingston County, 50
Lovejoy, P. S., 108–11, 201
Ludington pumped storage facility, 260
Ludington State Park, 93, 94
Lumber industry
    early predictions of decline, 33–34, 51
    life in lumber camps, 30–32
    logging methods in nineteenth century, 31–33
    skepticism of forestry efforts, 54, 58

Mack, Senator Joe, 179, 189, 211, 217, 272
MacMullan, Ralph A., 117–19, 124, 130–35, 137–38, 169, 250, 264–65, 287
Macomb County, 149, 173, 233, 281
Madar, Olga, 149, 150, 152, 172, 198
Mahoney, Mary, 229–30
Manistee, 52, 58, 94, 208, 210
Manistee River, 28, 33, 55, 121, 122, 218
Marquette, 34, 73, 75, 179, 216
Marsh, George P., 37–38, 50

Mason County, 89
McDiarmid, Hugh, 171, 184, 192, 217, 263
Mehan, Tracy, 255
Menominee, 267
Mercury contamination of fish in Lake St. Clair and Detroit River, 4, 165–67, 170
Mershon, William B., 23–24, 26, 42, 44, 46–48, 62–64, 76, 91, 264, 297
Metz, fire of 1908, 5–9, 61–62
Michigan AFL-CIO, 197
Michigan Agricultural College, 92, 124
Michigan Association of Homebuilders, 190, 214, 279, 281, 294
Michigan Association of Realtors, 214
Michigan Audubon Society, 76–81, 183
Michigan Beer and Wine Wholesalers Association, 181
Michigan Chemical Company, 221, 222
Michigan Commission of Conservation, 83, 84, 86, 89–90, 265
Michigan Department of Agriculture, 128, 129, 130, 133, 134, 188, 221, 223
Michigan Department of Conservation, 73, 83–90, 110, 117, 130, 145, 160, 264
Michigan Department of Environmental Quality, 116, 214, 215, 238, 240, 243, 266, 268, 269, 272, 273, 274, 275, 289
Michigan Department of Natural Resources, 183, 185, 202–6, 210, 223, 231, 237, 242, 260, 264, 267, 278, 292, 300
Michigan Department of Public Health, 3, 73, 224, 264, 273
Michigan Environmental Council, 192–93, 215, 243, 268, 291
Michigan Environmental Protection Act
  and mining, 179
  passage of, 172–76
  role of in controversy over oil drilling in Pigeon River Country State Forest, 205, 206
  role of in Genesee Power Station case, 274–75
Michigan Farm Bureau, 133, 175, 221
Michigan Forestry Association, 8–9
Michigan Manufacturers Association, 145, 175
Michigan Natural Areas Council, 100, 198–99, 200, 283
Michigan Natural Features Inventory, 15, 188, 297
Michigan Natural Resources Trust Fund, 203, 204, 212
Michigan Nature Association, 200
Michigan Oil and Gas Association, 205
Michigan Parks Association, 100–101, 104
Michigan Pesticides Council, 133
Michigan Society of Planning Officials, 281–82
Michigan Sportsmen's Association
  advocacy of state park in 1888, 53
  decline of, 46
  origins of, 40–43
  role in creation of office of state game warden, 42–43
Michigan State Chamber of Commerce, 172–73, 176, 266, 279, 288
Michigan State University, 101, 115, 126–30, 133, 136, 137, 180, 214, 260
Michigan United Conservation Clubs
  and bottle deposit law, 181–84
  establishment of, 90, 114–15
  and oil drilling in Pigeon River Country State Forest, 203, 204, 205
  and protection of Porcupine Mountains State Park, 197–98
  role of in combating water pollution, 144, 145
  role of in enacting sand dune protection law, 213
  role of in supporting state parks, 100
  support for Sleeping Bear Dunes National Lakeshore, 105
  and wilderness protection, 216–17
  and winter navigation on Great Lakes, 252–53

Midland, 256, 257
Midland nuclear power plant, 257

Miller, Terry, 266
Milliken, Governor William G., 4, 167, 169, 170–71, 173, 178, 179, 182, 183, 185, 186, 191, 192, 202, 207, 223, 224, 225, 236, 242, 250, 264, 267, 272, 278, 284
Milliken, Helen, 171
Mining, 17–18, 179
Mio, 224
Misseldine, Carol, 243
Monroe, 169
Montague, 225, 226, 231, 232, 236
Moore, Michael, 292
Mt. Clemens, 141
Mt. Pleasant, 28
Muir, John, 74, 219
Munger, Edith, 78–81
Murphy, William, 291
Murray, Paul, 290
Muskegon, 22, 155, 209, 211, 295
Muskegon County
    air pollution in, 155, 157
    chemical contamination of, 238–39
Muskegon River, 32

National Association for the Advancement of Colored People (NAACP), 274
National Wildlife Federation, 115, 259, 261, 276
Native Americans
    evidence of prior settlement in Michigan, 13–14
    relationship of, to land, 298
    use of fire as management tool in pre-European Michigan, 14
Native landscapes of Michigan before European settlement, 16–18
Natural Resources Commission, 178, 186, 187, 202, 210, 211, 269, 270
Natural Resources Defense Council, 289
Nature Conservancy, The, 212, 218–19
Nixon, Richard, 250–51
North Woods Call, 172, 265, 270

Olson, Jim, 179
Onaway, 6
Osborn, Chase S., 45–46, 76, 98

Otsego, 3, 142, 147
Owosso, 81, 87, 90

Parks
    creation and early development of state park system, 93–96
    early sentiment for Michigan state park, 53
    funding for state park system, 99, 101
Parks, Paul, 234–36
Passenger pigeon, 25–27, 47
Pentwater, 80
Pesticides
    concerns about, in nineteenth century, 66, 124
    controversies about, in 1950s and 1960s, 126–39
Petoskey, 25, 26
Petoskey, Merrill L. "Pete," 118–19, 164
Phosphorus detergents, control of, 185–87, 284, 289
Pictured Rocks shoreline, 17
Pigeon River Country State Forest, oil drilling in, 201–7
Pinchot, Gifford, 60, 74, 219, 297
Pine River, 222
Pingree, Governor Hazen, 23
Plainwell, 3, 142
Pollack, Lana, 240, 291
Politics
    calls for separation of, from conservation policy, 42–43, 47–48, 61, 83–90
    role in office of state game warden, 45–46
"Polluter pay" law, 240, 241, 242–43, 268, 280
Polybrominated biphenyls (PBBs), 221–25, 268
Polychlorinated biphenyls (PCBs), 4, 5, 148, 273, 285, 287, 289
Pomeroy, Walter, 168, 169
Porcupine Mountains State Park, 97–99, 197–98, 300
Prentice, Virginia, 105, 216
Presque Isle River, 98
Pruss, Stanley, 276–77
Public Domain Commission, 9, 61, 93, 108–9

Public health and early environmental pollution, 65, 67

Raisin River, 13, 73
Rector, Delbert, 157–59
Reuther, Walter P., 149–52
Rich, Governor George, 44, 45, 55
Riegle, U.S. Senator Donald, 216, 218
Romney, Governor George, 101, 132, 134, 135, 138, 151, 152, 156, 158, 170
Roney, Henry B., 25–26, 41
Roosevelt, Franklin, 188, 196
Roosevelt, Theodore, 9, 60, 74, 80, 188
Roscommon, 57
Roscommon County, 25, 87, 119
Roth, Professor Filibert, 8–9, 58–60, 83, 85–86, 108, 297
Rouge River, 13, 141, 151, 223, 248, 263, 296
Rouman, Jim, 115, 174, 197
Ruhl, Harry, 117–18
Rustem, William, 182, 183, 280

Sagady, Alex, 169, 183
Saginaw, 16, 55
Saginaw Bay, 16, 158, 257, 258
Saginaw County, 35
Saginaw River, 32
Saginaw Valley, 30, 35, 47
Sand dunes, mining, development, and protection of, 207–15
Sault Ste. Marie, 14, 45, 76
Sax, Joseph, 171, 174, 176, 179, 190, 256
Schaaf, Marcus, 113–14
Schmidt, Wayne, 180, 182, 185, 186–87, 204, 211, 230, 252, 253, 256, 259, 272
Schoolcraft, Henry Rowe, 11
Sewage, 65, 67–68, 71
Shafer, Chris, 272–73
Sharp, Eric, 270, 300
Sheppard, Glen, 265, 270, 285
Shiawassee River, 30, 73, 81, 82, 88
Shick, Charles, 133
Shiras, George III, 75
Sierra Club, 74, 105, 205, 216–19, 271, 292

Sigler, Governor Kim, 144
Sikkema, Ken, 192–93, 206, 242, 277, 285
Sinclair, Mary, 257
Skoog, Ronald, 264
Sleeper, Governor Albert, 110
Sleeping Bear Dunes National Lakeshore, 101–6, 301
Smith, William Alden, 43–44
Snell, Hilary, 186
Sobetzer, John, 190–91
Solid waste, 159–61
South Haven, 17
Stanton, Barbara, 190, 285
St. Clair River, 4, 11, 71, 165, 166, 220, 253
St. Joseph, 181
St. Louis, 222
St. Marys River, 252
Stifler, Mike, 187
Stoll, Albert, Jr., 79–80, 83, 195, 196, 285
Stoneman, Julie, 215
Stough, William, 289
Stream Pollution Control Commission, 2–3, 140–42, 143
Sturgeon, 21, 22
Swanson, Dennis, 222

Tanner, Howard, 119–22, 164, 203, 205, 211–12, 249, 272, 291
Tax-reverted lands, 55–56, 59–60, 112–13
Thompson, Paul, 199, 200
Thompson's Harbor State Park, 107
Tittabawassee River, 29, 30, 34, 256, 257, 258, 259
Titus, Harold, 86, 111–12
Tocqueville, Alexis de, 18
Tody, Wayne, 120–22, 136, 249
Toxic Substance Control Commission, 231–32
Traverse City, 73, 94, 103, 111, 170
Trenton, 145, 301
Trigger, Grant, 206–7
Trimberger, John, 293
Turney, William, 165, 248–49
Two-Hearted River, 299

United Automobile Workers (UAW), 100, 105, 149, 150, 152, 167, 175, 191, 197, 198, 253

University of Michigan, 59, 76, 81, 86, 87, 171, 173, 175

Van Coevering, Jack, 2–3, 146, 197, 285

Van Putten, Mark, 256, 258, 259, 260, 261, 273

Wade, David, 225

Wagner, Warren (Herb), 100, 211, 283

Wallace, George J., 126–28, 130–32

Ward, David, 28–30

Warner, Governor Fred, 8, 60, 61, 62, 63, 64

Warren Dunes State Park, 215

Washington, Thomas L., 179–84, 201, 203, 204, 205, 218, 256, 259, 266, 267, 269, 270

Water pollution
  by industrial wastes, 2–4, 140, 143–48
  in the 1870s, 22, 65, 67–68
  in the early 1900s, 68–69
  international Joint Commission investigation of (1912–18), 71–72
  and typhoid, 72

Water Resources Commission, 3, 144, 146, 147, 151, 166, 185, 227, 235, 239, 248, 257, 258, 264, 265

Wayne County, 154, 156, 188, 297

Wayne State University, 273

West Michigan Environmental Action Council (WMEAC), 164–65, 171–77, 186, 205, 277, 285, 286, 289, 301

Wetlands
  development of, 188
  effect of, in retarding European settlement, 15

passage of Wetlands Protection Act, 189–91

Whitefish, nineteenth century decline of, 22

Whitehall, 78, 151, 236

Whitehall Leather Company, 227, 234–36

White Lake, 225, 226, 227, 228

Whiteley, Harry, 98–99

White pine, 17, 20, 27, 29, 30, 32, 34, 35, 36, 54, 55, 59, 296, 297

White River, 28

Wilderness, protection of, 215–19

Wildlife
  descriptions of, in early Michigan, 24–25
  effects of early European settlement on, 15
  effect of market hunting on, 25–26, 41
  first state game laws, 39, 41–42

Wilson, Don, 212–13

Woiwode, Anne, 217, 271, 292

Woiwode, Tom, 218–19

Wolfe, Joan, 163–65, 171, 177–78, 301

Wolfe, Will, 163, 177

Women, role of, in early twentieth century conservation, 80–81, 89

Wurster, Charles F., 131–32

Wyandotte, 134, 153, 157

Wyandotte Chemical Company, 166

Wyckoff, Mark, 294

Yannacone, Victor J., Jr., 130–31, 168

Young, Leigh, 53, 87

Zeeland, 290

Zugger, Paul, 259